REGIME CHANGES

REGIME CHANGES

Macroeconomic Policy and Financial Regulation in Europe from the 1930s to the 1990s

Edited by

Douglas J. Forsyth

and

Ton Notermans

Berghahn Books

NEW YORK OXFORD

Published in 1997 by

Berghahn Books
Editorial offices:
165 Taber Avenue, Providence, RI 02906, USA
Bush House, Merewood Avenue, Oxford, OX3 8EF, UK

Library of Congress Cataloging-in-Publication Data
Regime changes : macroeconomic policy and financial regulation in Europe from the 1930s to the 1990s / edited by Douglas J. Forsyth and Ton Notermans.
p. cm.
Includes bibliographical references and index.
ISBN 1-57181-043-9 (alk. paper)
1. Monetary policy--Europe--History--20th century. 2. Finance--Europe--History--20th century. 3. Europe--Economic policy. I. Forsyth, Douglas J. II. Notermans, Ton. III. Title: Macroeconomic policy and financial regulation in Europe from the 1930s to the 1990s
HG924.R43 1996
332.4'94--dc20 96-26895
CIP

British Library Cataloguing in Publication Data
A CIP catalogue record for this book is available from
the British Library.

Printed in the United States on acid-free paper.

CONTENTS

CONTRIBUTORS

Douglas J. Forsyth is Assistant Professor of History at Bowling Green State University in Ohio. His publications include: *The Crisis of Liberal Italy: Monetary and Financial Policy, 1914–1922* (1993).

Hansjörg Herr is Professor of Economics at the Fachhochschule für Wirtschaft, Berlin, and Privatdozent at the Freie Universität, Berlin. His publications include: *Geld, Währungswettbewerb und Währungssysteme. Theoretische und historische Analyse der internationalen Geldwirtschaft* (1992); *Geld, Kredit und Ökonomische Dynamik in Marktvermittelten Ökonomien—die Vision einer Geldwirtschaft* (1986); and "On Post-Keynesian Crisis Theory: The Meaning of Financial Instability," in Werner Väth, ed., *Political Regulation in the Great Crisis* (1989).

Jan A. Kregel is Professor of Economics at the University of Bologna. He is currently writing a history of capital markets. His past publications include: *The Rate of Profit, Distribtuion, and Growth: Two Views* (1971); with Paul Davidson he is editor and contributor to *Economic Problems of the 1990s: Europe, the Developing Countries, and the United States* (1991); and *Macroeconomic Problems and Policies of Income Distribution: Functional, Personal, International* (1989).

Ton Notermans is a Research Fellow with the ARENA (Advanced Research on the Europeanization of the Nation-State) Project, organized by The Research Council of Norway. He is affiliated with the Department of Social Sciences, University of Tromsø. His publications include: "The Abdication from National Policy Autonomy: Why the Macroeconomic Policy Regime Has Become So Unfavorable to Labor," *Politics and Society*, 21 (1993), no. 2, pp. 133–167.

Sofía A. Pérez is Assistant Professor of Political Science at Boston University. Her book, *Banking on Privilege: The Politics of Spanish Financial Reform*, will be published by Cornell University Press in late spring or early summer 1997.

Sigurt Vitols is Research Fellow at the Wissenschaftszentrum, Berlin. His publications include: "Deindustrialisierung und Strukturpolitik in den West Midlands: Neue Wege der Strukturpolitik?", in H. Kilper and D. Rehfeld, eds., *Modernisierungsstrategien von Grossunternehmen zwischen endogener und exogener Orientierung: "Alte" Industrieregionen im Vergleich* (forthcoming); and (with Wolfgang Streeck) "European Works Councils: Between Statutory Enactment and Voluntary Adoption," in J. Rogers and W. Streeck, eds., *Works Councils: Consultation, Representation and Cooperation* (forthcoming).

INTRODUCTION

Douglas J. Forsyth and Ton Notermans

This volume explores two "periods of movement," from approximately 1931 to 1948, and from 1973 to 1990, during which most European nations, indeed most industrial nations, undertook major changes in economic policy. Policy innovation in both of these periods of movement was set in motion by economic crises. These periods of movement bracket the *trente glorieuses*, as they are referred to in France —thirty, or nearly thirty, years of unprecedented economic growth and relative stability in the institutional setting and basic orientation of economic policy. The focus of our volume is on monetary policy and the regulation of financial markets. We suggest that in both periods of movement changes in monetary policy came first, forcing or permitting a series of second-order changes in financial regulation. Changes in monetary policy and financial regulation, in turn, had significant implications for other areas of policymaking, including labor-market policy, industrial policy, even social policy. We refer to these broad shifts as "macroeconomic policy regime changes."

In Chapter 1, Forsyth and Notermans seek to develop more fully the concept of macroeconomic-policy regimes and regime changes. They argue that both of the regime changes at issue here were set in motion by accelerating instability in the nominal price level. In the early 1930s, a cumulative *deflationary* movement in the price level led to a shift in macroeconomic policy, from defense of fixed exchange parities to stabilization of prices and promotion of economic recovery—the "gold standard regime" was replaced by a "high growth and employment regime." In the 1970s and 1980s a cumulative *inflationary* dynamic led to a shift from growth and employment-oriented macropolicies to an emphasis on fighting inflation—the "high growth and employment regime" gave way to a "disinflationary regime." The core issue differentiating these regimes involves the policy assignments of central banks. Under both the interwar gold standard and the contemporary disinflationary regime, the priorities of monetary policy were and are holding inflation in check and maintaining external balance, and the main instrument at the disposal of central bankers was and is interest rate policy. Under the intervening growth regime, however, fighting inflation was often the task of incomes policy and/or credit rationing. In other words, the assignment of micro- and macroeconomic policy instruments is reversed. The growth regime relied on monetary and fiscal policy (macropolicies) to stimulate demand, and thereby promote growth and employment, while it used labor-market policies and regulation of financial markets (micropolicies) to curb inflation; the interwar gold standard and the disinflationary regimes relied and rely primarily on monetary policy (macropolicy) to fight inflation and maintain external balance, and on supply-side policies, including selective tax cuts and other investment incentives (micropolicies), to promote growth and employment.

Forsyth and Notermans suggest that their concept of macropolicy regime changes, driven by the imperative of forestalling cumulative deflationary or inflationary movements in the nominal price level, provides a more satisfactory explanation for broad economic policy convergence across industrial nations during the two periods of movement in question than the coalition-centered, historical-institutional, and political power of ideas approaches, which currently dominate the field of comparative political economy. Coalition-centered approaches, they point out, fail to explain why in both eras governments of the left and right alike carried out broadly similar shifts in the basic orientation of their economic policies. Historical-institutional approaches, they suggest, are useful in exploring how institutions constrain policy choices during periods of relative stability, but they fail to specify the conditions under which the wholesale reordering of economic institutions and basic policy orientation occurs. Both approaches are more effective at exploring differences in performance between nations during periods of stability than policy convergence across nations during periods of movement, they conclude. Forsyth and Notermans also insist that changes in economic ideas, such as the spread of Keynesianism in the 1930s and 1940s and the growing popularity of monetarism in the 1970s and 1980s cannot account adequately for policy regime changes. Neither the "high growth and employment regime" nor the "disinflationary regime" are fully consistent with the policy prescriptions of Keynesianism or monetarism, they point out, nor have policymakers consistently justified their choices with reference to economic doctrine.

Forsyth and Notermans reject the widely held view that the shift to more restrictive macroeconomic policies and to deregulation of the financial sector since the mid-1970s has been driven primarily by the globalization of business and financial markets. International financial integration, they note, has been a discontinuous process during the twentieth century, and its rhythms have been determined more by changes in the macroeconomic policy goals of the authorities than by technological change or the multinationalization of business. They note that during the 1980s many European nations, inside and outside the European Monetary System, dismantled restrictions on international financial transactions and tied their currencies to the German mark in order to bolster the credibility of domestic anti-inflationary policies. The authors do allow, however, that the monetary policies of international reserve centers may constrain the policy choices of other nations—a theme discussed in greater detail in Hansjörg Herr's essay in this volume (see below).

Forsyth and Notermans also briefly discuss the consequences of macropolicy regime changes in three other areas of economic policy-making: administered credit policies, the relationship of the state to organized interests (corporatism), and social policy. Administered credit systems were among the most significant of the regulatory innovations adopted in many European countries in the wake of the Great Depression. Through the use of credit controls, policymakers could channel loans to economic sectors or single firms at below market interest rates. France and Spain adopted selective credit controls as an instrument of industrial policy; Norway and Sweden used them to subsidize the construction of low-cost housing. Forsyth and Notermans argue that the collapse of the gold standard was a necessary precondition for this type of regulatory innovation. Under the interwar gold standard, interest-rate policy was the principal instrument the authorities deployed to fight inflation and maintain fixed exchange parities. The effectiveness of monetary policy, therefore, depended on the absence of barriers to interest-rate signals within the financial sector. Once microeconomic instruments, including price controls, incomes policies, and credit rationing were assigned the task of fighting inflation, states were free to deploy an array of credit controls as instruments of selective micropolicies. The shift to the disinflationary macropolicy regime in the 1970s and 1980s, in turn, apparently has led universally to the dismantling of administered credit systems—on this see the discussion of Sofía Pérez's essay below.

Forsyth and Notermans argue that macropolicy regime changes have had significant consequences for the relationship between the state and organized interest groups. Under the logic of the interwar gold standard, downward flexibility in nominal prices and wages was necessary to bring about adjustment to international payments imbalances. Since producers' associations and trade unions made prices and wages sticky, their existence was in conflict with the imperatives of the macropolicy regime. However, once policymakers abandoned their efforts to defend fixed exchange parities and reoriented their macroeconomic policies to break the fall in nominal prices, agricultural marketing boards, manufacturers' cartels, and trade unions could become allies, rather than adversaries. Meanwhile, the shift to a disinflationary macropolicy regime in the 1970s and 1980s has once again placed organized interests in conflict with the imperatives of macroeconomic policy, and it is therefore not surprising that these decades have seen a weakening of trade unions, the disintegration of neo-corporatist centralized collective bargaining arrangements, and growing criticism of the system of agricultural price and income supports initially set up in the 1930s.

With regard to the impact of macropolicy regime changes on social policy, Forsyth and Notermans recall Esping-Andersen's argument that a generous, universalist welfare system presupposes full or near full employment. Generous provision of welfare requires that most people work and that the smallest number possible live off social transfers. Moreover, Forsyth and Notermans argue that even a relatively poor society may support a social welfare structure that gives citizens the opportunity to withdraw from the labor market under certain conditions, and that sustains demand during economic downturns, if it is locked in a deflationary spiral or if past experience suggests deflation is a serious danger. Even a relatively wealthy society, in contrast, may seek to roll back social-welfare programs that ratchet labor costs upward, and that sustain demand during economic downturns, if fighting inflation becomes the primary goal of macroeconomic policy.

In Chapter 2, Forsyth expands upon the macropolicy regimes concept developed in Chapter 1 through examination of the goals, instruments, and institutional setting of monetary policymaking and financial regulation in Britain, France, Germany/West Germany, and Italy between 1931 and 1948 (1957 in the case of West Germany). In a search for common ground in the transformation of policymaking across nations during these years, Forsyth assigns logical and temporal primacy to the reordering of the goals of monetary policymaking and of the instruments assigned to achieve them. In his view, the collapse of the gold standard was the crucial event that set in motion the transformation of the state's role in the economy. Delinking from gold allowed policymakers to reorder the priorities of macroeconomic policy, permitting economic recovery. This process began in September 1931 when Britain abandoned its gold parity. By the spring of 1932, the British authorities took advantage of the relaxation of the external constraint to lower interest rates in order to stimulate a revival of investment and economic activity. All three of the other countries discussed in the essay followed Britain in *de facto* or *de jure* abandonment of gold, and in the reordering of macroeconomic priorities to the promotion of recovery within six years. Thereafter, policymakers sought to combine high levels of output, employment, and growth with price stability and external balance. Under the "high growth and employment regime," the impact of monetary policy on growth and employment was never ignored. Despite the many twists and turns in monetary policy formation within individual nations after the collapse of gold, Forsyth makes a case for underlying continuity in monetary policy formation. Considerable differences in fiscal policy orientation, in contrast, are identifiable across nations, and no common denominator can be established. Forsyth argues that, while a "fiscal policy revolution" may have taken place in some nations after World War II, the monetary policy revolution that took place between 1931 and 1936 was more generalized, taking place throughout Europe.

In Forsyth's view, changes in monetary policymaking also created opportunities for, although they did not necessarily require, a set of second-order microeconomic changes in regulation of the financial sector. He argues that the process of micro re-regulation of national financial systems took much longer than the basic shift in monetary policy orientation. Moreover, it was driven by several different motives. First, in Germany and Italy the Depression had produced major bank failures, and it was necessary to clear away the wreckage and reconstruct national financial systems. In all four countries the difficulties of banks during the Depression induced the authorities to extend banking supervision, and to expand the lender-of-last resort responsibilities of central banks. Second, since the primary or sole mission of monetary policy was no longer achievement of external balance, foreign-exchange controls were adopted to isolate national financial markets from international influences, which limited national policy autonomy under the gold standard. On the domestic front, European nations also created new regulatory instruments to control the creation of commercial bank credit as alternatives to the use of interest-rate policy to fight inflation. Third, postwar planners utilized financial controls as key instruments of economic modernization programs and regional development policies.

Thus the lengthier process of financial re-regulation was the product of policy objectives that arose during and after World War II, as well as directly out of the Depression. It was the result of complex legislation, often preceded by lengthy study and debate. The objectives of financial re-regulation varied more widely across nations than the goals of monetary policy. National financial systems retained or acquired distinctive characteristics.

Hansjörg Herr's essay (Chapter 3) discusses the evolution of international monetary relations since the collapse of the Bretton Woods system of fixed exchange rates in 1973. Like Forsyth and Notermans, Herr identifies the core dilemma facing economic policymakers as being the reconciliation of price level stability with full employment. In the long run, he argues, microeconomic policies such as incomes policies will be ineffective in checking inflation, and the only consistently reliable instrument for combating inflation at the disposal of the authorities will be restrictive macroeconomic polices. The constraints acting upon policymakers within individual countries may be exacerbated by relations of dominance in the international monetary system. Differences in rates of inflation across nations, Herr suggests, will create a hierarchy of currencies, as investors seek to transfer their liquid assets into currencies with higher store-of-value quality. Currencies with high store-of-value quality, therefore, will become reserve currencies; a currency's status as a reserve currency may be further enhanced by the political and military power of the issuing nation.

Herr proceeds by arguing that international monetary systems can be classified according to two criteria: the degree to which a single currency exercises dominance, and the trade and monetary policies of the reserve currency nations. In a hegemonic monetary system, a single currency exists uncontested as key currency; in a multicurrency system several reserve currencies hold the potential to dominate monetary policy within the international monetary system. Herr argues that a hegemonic system is potentially most stable, with the outcome depending on upon whether the hegemonic power pursues monetary policies that are functional on the international level. A multicurrency system, in Herr's view, is least stable, especially if several nations vie for monetary dominance, each using the store-of-value quality of its currency as its principal weapon in the competition.

In Herr's view, the Bretton Woods system established after World War II was a hegemonic system with the dollar as the uncontested key currency, due to the United States' economic, political, and military dominance. It was inevitable, Herr observes, that European and Japanese recovery and economic growth would erode the United States' hegemonic position in due course. However, Herr argues that, in addition, U.S. monetary and trade polices changed over time from being functional to being increasingly dysfunctional for the international monetary system. In the early postwar years, the United States ran current-account deficits, allowing other countries to accumulate dollar reserves, but pursued sufficiently restrictive macroeconomic policies to maintain a high store-of-value quality for the dollar, and hence its uncontested role as reserve currency. As U.S. fiscal and monetary policy became more inflationary in the course of the late 1960s and early 1970s, however, other currencies, notably the German mark and the Japanese yen, became important reserve currencies alongside the dollar. Whereas Herr faults the United States for pursuing an excessively inflationary policy to ensure international monetary stability, he faults Germany and Japan for pursuing "stability-oriented mercantilism." In other words, these two nations strove to run perennial current-account surpluses, while at the same time keeping their inflation rates lower than those of most other nations. The high store-of-value quality of the mark and yen increased demand for these currencies internationally, even as German and Japanese current-account surpluses limited their supply. The flight out of other currencies increased pressures on monetary authorities in third countries to adopt restrictive policies. Moreover, German and Japanese policies produced a restructuring of international reserve portfolios away from the dollar and into marks and yen, contributing to the collapse of fixed exchange rates in 1973.

Herr therefore argues that the conflict between high employment and price-level stability experienced by all industrial nations since the early 1970s was exacerbated by the instability of the international monetary system. Since the early 1970s the hegemonic position of the U.S. dollar has weakened, and with the growing importance of the mark and yen as reserve currencies, elements of a multicurrency system have emerged, imposing a restrictive bias on the international monetary system.

Herr's forecasts for the evolution of monetary policy in Europe are not optimistic. He suggests that the United States will continue to put domestic concerns ahead of international concerns in the formulation of monetary and fiscal policy and that the dollar's role as reserve currency will continue to erode. Germany will, in his view, continue to pursue "stability-oriented mercantilism" in its monetary and trade policies, forcing monetary authorities in other European countries to follow the Bundesbank in pursuing restrictive policies. European monetary integration, he concludes, will lead to the marginalization of regions with lower-than-average rates of productivity growth.

The final three essays in the volume (Chapters 4, 5 and 6) deal with regulatory change. They address three key questions: (1) How have changes in macroeconomic policy affected the regulation of the financial sector? (2) To what extent will the broad trend toward deregulation of the financial sector apparent since the mid-1970s produce convergence between national financial systems? And (3) how has social-security legislation since the 1930s affected contractual savings, and by extension the supply side of national capital markets and the regulatory framework?

In Chapter 4, Sofía Pérez discusses the creation of administered credit systems in France and Spain in the late 1940s and late 1950s respectively, and the subsequent disintegration of these systems in the course of the 1970s and 1980s. In both nations, extensive controls on bank credit and supplementary measures, such as guaranteed rediscounts of certain types of medium- and long-term loans by the central banks and interest subsidies, were utilized as the principal instruments of industrial policy. Pérez argues that both nations established administered-credit systems because policymakers were convinced that their financial systems previously had provided insufficient investment capital to industry. Moreover, in both countries policymakers feared that more intrusive forms of state intervention in the economy would give radical politicians, including minority groups within governing coalitions, the levers with which to attempt undesirable socioeconomic experiments.

The difficulty with administered-credit systems, in Pérez's view, was that they subordinated monetary policy to industrial policy. Credit rationing was never tight enough to secure price stability, and during much of the postwar era France and Spain accepted higher rates of inflation than other industrialized nations, where industrial policy either was not practiced extensively or where it was divorced from monetary policy. According to Pérez, when inflation rates accelerated throughout the industrialized world in the 1970s, France and Spain, like other nations, were compelled to use monetary policy to fight inflation. At first they tried to do so within the framework of administered credit, but within a few years policymakers in both countries elected to abolish their extensive regulatory apparatuses and use high interest rates to break inflationary expectations.

She notes that official explanations for this policy change in both countries were largely technical in nature. The authorities noted that credit ceilings were evaded by the proliferation of black and gray financial markets. They also argued that credit rationing had proved too blunt an instrument to use effectively to modulate the rate of monetary growth. But in Pérez's view, the primary reason for deregulation in both countries was that imposing disinflation through an administered-credit system exacted too high a political price. Changing inflationary expectations required imposing costs on borrowers, including bankruptcies. In a market-based financial system, these costs were allocated impersonally; in an administered-credit system, the authorities essentially had to decide which firms would go bankrupt and which would not. Politicians and functionaries naturally were reluctant to assume such responsibility.

Pérez concludes by arguing that the dismantling of administered-credit systems in France and Spain does not imply convergence among national regulatory systems, and even less among national financial systems. As was noted, in her view, regulatory change in France and Spain was driven by the unacceptably high political costs of administering disinflation, and not by the internationalization of finance or the erosion of states' ability to regulate their banking systems *tout court*. In Spain, she points out, the divorce of industrial policy from monetary policy did not really liberalize the financial sector. The government still requires banks to hold public debt in their portfolios in fixed quotas. An effective banking cartel remains in existence. The result has been that real interest rates paid by nongovernmental borrowers have risen sharply, while the banks and the state have protected their own interests. Pérez notes that in France the authorities hoped that regulatory reform would produce a banking system similar to Germany's, where banks maintain close, long-term relationships with industrial clients. However, French banks lack the monitoring capacity of their German counterparts, and they have tended to stay clear of long- and medium-term finance to industry. Instead, liberalization has forced French industry to rely more heavily on the capital markets for finance, causing the French financial system to move more in the direction of the British, rather than the German, model.

In Chapter 5, Sigurt Vitols also asks whether the international trend toward deregulation of the financial sector will lead to a convergence in national regulatory and banking systems. Like Pérez, he doubts that this will be the case. Vitols concedes that there is some evidence that the differences between the three ideal-types of national financial systems identified by John Zysman in his classic study of 1983—(securities) market-based systems, such as in Britain and the United States; bank-based systems, such as in Germany; and state-based, administered-credit systems, such as those studied by Pérez in France and Spain—appear to be diminishing.[1] Consistent with Pérez, he observes that administered-credit systems evidently are unraveling everywhere. Even market- and bank-based systems, he notes, appear to be taking on similar features. In Germany, the close relationship between firms and their banks (Hausbanken) has been weakened by the ability and willingness of large corporations to avail themselves of the services of competing banks, especially in foreign markets; in the United States and Britain, competitive pressures and deregulation have eliminated the traditional market segmentation between investment and commercial banking. It has been argued, he notes, that everywhere a new type of financial institution is emerging, to wit, the

1. John Zysman, *Governments, Markets and Growth: Financial Systems and the Politics of Industrial Change* (Berkeley: University of California, 1983).

internationally active financial supermarket, which competes with similar institutions on the basis of short-term price orientation for a pool of price-discriminating customers.

However, through a comparison of Britain and Germany, Vitols concludes that the convergence hypothesis ignores areas where states maintain significant regulatory discretion. One important area is corporate governance. Vitols points out that German law and administrative practice tend to enhance the influence of banks in corporate governance, for example by allowing them to vote proxy shares, and by limiting the rights of minority shareholders to challenge management. The British regulatory framework, in contrast, places greater importance on maximization of shareholder value. Another area in which regulatory discretion persists is household savings. German companies, Vitols points out, are allowed to retain pension funds and invest them internally, a practice expressly prohibited in Britain. Moreover, the public-banking sector continues to be much larger in Germany than in Britain. The network of savings banks, owned by municipalities and the Länder, holds a significant proportion (35 percent) of the total assets of the German banking sector. As Vitols points out, the savings banks have shown a strong inclination to invest in the regions and towns where they are located, while Britain's clearing banks, with their extensive branch networks, have less regional loyalty. Special-purpose public-credit institutions, Vitols notes, exist in both countries; however, in Germany they hold a much larger share of the banking system's total assets than in Britain and are hence far more important.

Vitols also suggests that convergence between national financial systems will be inhibited by the "embeddedness" of industrial finance within a larger national institutional framework, which includes the production regime of individual countries. He notes there is evidence that industrialized countries have diverged in their productive profiles since the 1970s. British and American firms have emphasized flexibility in hiring and firing workers in order to reduce the costs of standardized goods. German and Japanese firms, in contrast, have developed long-term attachments to workers, and hence tend to specialize in higher-quality, non-price-competitive production. Different types of production regimes may produce demands for different types of capital, he suggests, and this may also promote or sustain differentiation in the structure of financial institutions. Moreover, evaluating risk in lending requires specialized knowledge, which cannot be reduced to quantifiable criteria. Acquiring this specialized knowledge has proved to be not only time-consuming but also place-oriented; hence competitors in unregulated markets have proven less successful in encroaching on the territory of established banks than was once supposed. The internationalization of finance, Vitols suggests, has remained confined to interbank lending and finance for the largest blue-chip companies. Among small and medium-size firms, the Hausbank relationship appears to be alive and well in Germany.

Vitols is cautious in drawing global conclusions about the strengths and weaknesses of the German and British financial systems. The German system, he suggests, may be more effective in meeting the needs of declining industries. These industries' fortunes can be reversed or ameliorated if they can reduce capacity through coordination or develop new products or specializations through additional investment. However, raising additional funds may be difficult if their current performance makes them appear to be poor credit risks. In Germany, where commercial banks traditionally maintain close, long-term relationships to firms and where the savings banks have an interest in preserving the industrial infrastructure of their regions, financial institutions may have an interest in, and the capacity for, solving coordination problems. In Britain, in contrast, where equity ownership is highly fragmented and the stakes of banks in individual firms is limited, financial institutions may be more inclined to abandon declining sectors. However, Vitols also notes that Britain has been highly successful in developing a venture-capital market that supports emerging industries. Germany's universal banks, in contrast, appear to have lost the capacity ascribed to them at the end of the last century to identify promising growth fields and pick winners.

In Chapter 6, Jan Kregel examines changes in the regulation of the financial sector since the 1930s in Britain, Germany, and the United States. He argues that the wave of financial regulation that began in the 1930s was in response to two concerns: (1) limiting the impact of price volatility on the payments system and on the financing of production; and (2) making money and financial markets more effective instruments of macroeconomic policy. In other words, the authorities strove both to enhance the capacity of financial systems to withstand future deflationary shocks and at the same time, to harness financial institutions as instruments of macroeconomic policy so as to make such shocks less likely. These innovations in the regulation of the financial sector, he suggests, were accompanied by the rise of the welfare state, which changed patterns of consumption and savings formation, and in turn had feedback effects on the supply side of capital markets. The nature of the choices made in all three of these areas, he suggests, would influence the dynamics of financial deregulation in the 1970s and 1980s.

Kregel argues that regulatory reform in Germany and the United States was more far-reaching than in Britain, because the former countries experienced significant bank failures in the early 1930s. The problems facing German and American authorities were in many respects similar. In both countries regulators sought to bolster the stability of banks by eliminating fraud and maturity mismatches between bank assets and liabilities. However, they took very different paths to secure these ends.

In the United States, the authorities sought to reverse a trend toward financial market integration that had become apparent in the decade prior to the Wall Street crash in 1929. They imposed extensive market segmentation, devising separate regulatory regimes and supervisory authorities for savings and loan institutions (active in the home mortgage sector) and commercial banks, while also separating commercial and investment banking. Kregel suggests that U.S. regulators could have taken a very different approach to strengthening the banking system. By relaxing branching restrictions, they could have allowed banks to acquire more diversified loan portfolios, making them less vulnerable to crises in a single economic sector (e.g., agriculture or urban real estate) or a single state. The Banking Act of June 1933 also introduced Regulation Q, allowing the government to set maximum rates on time and savings deposits in order to limit competition for deposits. Interest payments on demand deposits were prohibited. Although he notes that the architects of the U.S. regulatory system do not appear to have fully appreciated it, Kregel argues that the edifice of banking segmentation rested on the control of maximum interest rates by sector.

In Kregel's view, the U.S. regulatory system was undone by the transformation of the macroeconomic environment. The growth of inflationary pressures beginning in the 1950s, and accelerating in the 1970s, and the increasing reliance of the Federal Reserve on interest-rate policy to combat inflation put the regulators in growing conflict with market incentives, leading to evasion and the proliferation of new financial instruments. In the 1950s large firms were already moving their deposits out of the commercial banks, where they earned little interest, and into treasury bills and savings and loan accounts, which were not yet subject to Regulation Q. The commercial banks responded by offering certificates of deposit, the first break in the system of interest rate controls. By the 1960s, the commercial banks had discovered the Eurocurrency markets as a source of capital outside the purview of U.S. regulators. When Regulation Q was extended to savings and loan institutions, the latter responded by introducing new financial instruments, including the "negotiable order of withdrawal." By 1980 market segmentation was collapsing, leading to calls for deregulation, and the creation of a level playing field. As the regulatory system set up in the 1930s was dismantled piece by piece, the old problems of maturity mismatches and fraud returned. The commercial banks took a beating in real estate markets in the 1970s, before being even more seriously weakened by the Third World debt crisis in the early 1980s. Savings and loan institutions were caught in a classic moral-hazard problem in the 1980s, when restrictions on their investment activity were eliminated even though federal deposit insurance remained in place.

Meanwhile, Kregel notes, investment banking firms underwent a transformation from relatively small partnerships, which underwrote share issues by firms but held very modest positions in the securities markets themselves, into very substantial institutions with large capital bases. He argues that this transformation was brought about by changes in both the demand side and the supply side of capital markets. On the demand side, firms looked largely to the securities markets to raise capital, since commercial banks were prohibited, by legislation in the 1930s, from engaging in investment banking activities. The supply side of the market was transformed by the rise of institutional investors. The Social Security Act of 1935 stimulated the creation of private pension plans. As pension funds, insurance companies, and other institutional investors grew in size, they increasingly dominated the supply side of capital markets. Investment banking houses were forced to expand as well, since the size of the positions they took on the market when they bought or sold shares for their institutional clients grew with the volume of trading. As U.S. authorities contemplate eliminating the remaining regulations that still separate commercial and investment banking, Kregel notes, the investment banking houses may be better placed than their commercial rivals to take advantage of new opportunities.

Kregel argues that Germany solved the maturity mismatches problem that led to the collapse of its universal banks in 1931 not by separating investment from commercial banking but by insisting that universal banks match long-term liabilities with long-term assets—a sort of segmentation within institutions. This regulatory solution, Kregel notes, required a strong, centralized authority, an option that was not available in the United States, with its tradition of decentralized banking. Although Germany made no effort to use its regulatory and supervisory authority to transform radically the structure of its banking system, Kregel notes that the role of the universal banks as intermediaries between investors and firms nonetheless changed fundamentally as a result of the currency reform of 1948 and subsequent tax legislation. Prior to 1931, Germany's universal banks had financed investment through loans to firms. Subsequently, they underwrote equity issues. Firms used the proceeds of new share issues to repay bank loans. However, the German stock market never recovered after World War II. The currency reform of 1948 left German firms undervalued, and hence reluctant to issue shares. The Capital Market Law of 1952 encouraged the issue of long-term, fixed-interest rate bonds, but not of shares. Since the war, the share capital of German firms has remained tightly held. Households, therefore, have held their assets in bank deposits, while banks have purchased long-term bonds. In Germany, the expansion of the social-security system did not transform the supply side of capital markets as it did in the United States. Kregel points out that German companies are free to plough pension funds back into their own operations. Although the past two and a half decades have witnessed a steady growth in the resources managed by supplementary pension funds and insurance companies, they have been invested mainly in bonds, not in shares.

Thus the regulatory reforms introduced in Germany during the 1930s and 1940s have generated few pressures for change. Kregel argues that, insofar as Germany deregulates its financial markets, it will do so more because of pressure from foreign banks, and interest in making Frankfurt a competitive international financial market, rather than because of internal contradictions in its regulatory system or conflicts between financial regulation and macroeconomic policy regime.

With regard to Britain, Kregel notes that investment and commercial banking had been carried out by separate classes of institutions long before the Depression, and in the absence of regulatory intervention. Few British banks failed during the 1930s, and there was little incentive to expand dramatically the informal supervisory role that the Bank of England had long exercised over the clearing banks. However, Kregel notes, after World War II the British authorities used financial regulation as an instrument for imposing monetary restraint. Until 1958 the Bank of England used moral suasion to restrain lending by the clearing banks. In that year, moral suasion was supplemented by "special deposits," later called "supplementary deposits," or more colloquially "the corset," that is, reserves deposited with the Bank of England that did not count as part of the normal ratio of liquid assets to total deposits. Restrictions on the lending capacity of clearing banks had the predictable effect of fostering the growth of secondary credit markets. As the rate of inflation accelerated in the late 1970s, Mrs. Thatcher's government decided to abandon its microeconomic instruments of monetary restraint and rely on high interest rates instead. Foreign exchange controls were removed in 1979. The clearing banks could now borrow on the Eurocurrency markets, rendering the "corset" completely ineffective. It was abolished the following year.

Capital markets in Britain developed in a manner broadly comparable with those in the United States. British investment banking houses, which had long focused on foreign issues, turned their attentions to domestic companies during the Depression years. The expansion of contractual savings beginning in the early postwar years brought about a steady expansion of the supply side of the market, as the resources controlled by company pension funds and insurance companies steadily increased. The secondary securities market in Britain traditionally had been segmented between brokers, who bought and sold stocks on behalf of third parties, and jobbers, who took positions on the market themselves and were required to sell through brokers. All of this was swept away by the "Big Bang" in 1986. Although the main force driving the Big Bang was the government's desire to fund its own debt more cheaply and to keep London competitive with New York as a financial center, Kregel argues, a wave of consolidations has since overtaken the securities industry, and, as in New York, a few large, multipurpose firms now dominate the market.

To summarize, Pérez, Vitols, and Kregel identify a multitude of regulatory changes in national financial systems that have been permitted or forced by macropolicy regime changes. The shift to a growth regime during the early 1930s opened up the possibility for much more extensive regulation on the micro level than had been the case under the interwar gold standard. Not all European nations chose to regulate extensively, however. Among the nations that did develop extensive state controls over the financial sector, the timing and goals of intervention varied considerably. France and Spain developed credit-rationing systems in the late 1940s and late 1950s, respectively, in order to promote industrial modernization; Norway and Sweden developed similar credit controls during the 1950s to divert financial resources into housing construction. Other variables must be examined in order to explain differences in the use of selective micropolicies across nations; the essays of Pérez, Vitols, and Kregel explore these differences and their causes. Meanwhile, the shift to a disinflationary macropolicy regime in the 1970s and 1980s appears to have forced the dismantling of credit-rationing systems across Europe. Restrictive monetary policy conducted in isolation by the central bank proved a more effective means of achieving disinflation than administered- and negotiated-credit ceilings. Despite the basic trend toward policy and regulatory convergence, the contributors to this volume have found that significant cross-national differences remain. Moreover, the liberalization of financial regulation has not led to convergence in national financial systems. The structure of corporate ownership, and the structure of the supply side of capital markets, particularly the role of institutional investors, account for persistent differences across nations.

In the course of bringing this volume to press, we have incurred many debts. Our greatest debt is to the Program for the Study of Germany and Europe at the Center for European Studies at Harvard University, from which we have received generous financial support. We also have received financial support from the Robert-Bosch-Stiftung in Stuttgart, the Stifterverband für die deutschen Wissenschaft in Essen, and the Center for International Studies at MIT. Prof. David Soskice, of the Wissenschaftszentrum, Berlin, put his institution at our disposal for a working conference in July 1992. We would also like to thank Abby Collins, the Associate Director of the Center for European Studies at Harvard, and her staff for their help in hosting a second working conference at CES in January 1993. Our thanks also go to the many individuals who participated in these two conferences as discussants: Christopher S. Allen, Robert Boyer, Benjamin Cohen, Richard Deeg, J. Bradford DeLong, Josef Esser, Carl-Ludwig Holtfrerich, Harold James, Charles S. Maier, Giangiacomo Nardozzi, Jonas Pontusson, David Soskice, Heinz-Peter Spahn, Nobert Walter, and John Zysman. At Berghahn Books, our thanks go to publisher Marion Berghahn and copyeditors Jeff Howard and Shawn Kendrick. Yuliya Korshunova, at Bowling Green State University, assisted Forsyth in preparing the index. All errors and omissions are, of course, our own.

Chapter 1

MACROECONOMIC POLICY REGIMES AND FINANCIAL REGULATION IN EUROPE, 1931–1994

Douglas J. Forsyth and Ton Notermans

Policy Convergence Across Nations During Two Periods of Movement

Since 1973 European states have engineered a sea change in their economic policies. As late as the mid-1970s, achieving full employment and high rates of economic growth were generally considered to be among the most important goals of macroeconomic policy; a decade and a half later, the fight against inflation had been embraced almost universally as the first priority of monetary policy, even at the expense of unemployment and sluggish growth. The shift in government priorities has proceeded *pari passu* with a decline in economic growth rates to the lowest levels since World War II and the expansion of the number of unemployed to levels not seen since the Great Depression.

This reorientation in the goals of macroeconomic policy has been accompanied in many countries by changes in the institutional setting of macroeconomic policymaking, most notably initiatives to give central banks more policy autonomy from legislative and executive bodies. In Italy, for example, in 1981 the central bank was no longer required to be the residual purchaser of treasury securities tendered at auction, "divorcing" the conduct of monetary policy from fiscal policy. In Sweden and France the statutes of the central bank have been rewritten to make it more independent. The terms of the Maastricht Treaty require participants in the European Monetary Union to create independent central banks as a first step toward the creation of an independent European central bank. At the time this volume goes to press, it appears that only a handful of EU members are likely to participate in the EMU from its inception, but proponents of central bank independence remain influential in other European countries as well. Champions of central bank reform throughout Europe tend to look to Germany's independent Bundesbank as a model.

Accompanying these transformations in the goals, and more tentatively in the institutional setting, of macroeconomic policymaking has been a pervasive trend toward the deregulation of financial markets. Controls designed to insulate domestic capital and money markets from international financial flows have been steadily reduced. This development has been accompanied by the wholesale dismantling of selective credit mechanisms, which had been the principal instrument of industrial policy in France and Spain and a means of promoting construction of affordable housing in Norway and Sweden. Many restrictions on the activities of commercial and investment banks have been removed. Several countries where a large share of the commercial banking sector was in state hands, such as France and Italy, have embarked on reprivatization programs. The privatization of the banks and the elimination of selective financial controls has been symptomatic of a broad effort across Europe to reduce the role of the state in economic development and planning. In addition to downgrading or junking state indicative-planning agencies, abolishing credit controls, and divesting themselves of commercial banking functions, states across Europe have been engaged in an extensive program of privatizing manufacturing and service enterprises. In many countries, including once again France and Italy, these initiatives have coincided with efforts to breathe new life into stock markets, as an alternative source of (private) investment capital.

In labor relations, changes have been no less significant or broadly based. There has been a generalized weakening of the trade union movement, in large measure as a consequence of rising continentwide unemployment rates since the mid-1970s. In countries where centralized collective bargaining once was common and where incomes policies negotiated in tripartite agreements between trade unions, employers' federations, and the state were once important instruments of macroeconomic policymaking, such as Austria, the Low Countries, and Scandinavia, the neo-corporatist system has broken down, wage agreements have become less centralized and more fragmented, and the role of trade unions in macroeconomic policy formation has been reduced.

These developments in macroeconomic policy formation and in financial and labor market regulation have been accompanied by retrenchment in social programs and a rollback of welfare benefits. Conservative governments in the United States and Britain may have launched the opening attacks on the welfare state, but growing budget deficits, the change in macroeconomic policy stance, and a general disenchantment with the costs and results of social policy have led more recently to retrenchment and reform throughout Europe, even in the Nordic countries, where the welfare state achieved its fullest development and long enjoyed extensive popular support.

Such broad changes in the state's role in the economy, within a wide array of countries with quite different governing coalitions and ideological orientations, have not taken place in Europe since the 1930s and 1940s, in the aftermath of the Great Depression and World War II. As we will make clearer below, we do not believe it would be accurate to characterize the recent wave of changes as a consistent reversal of the reforms ushered in during those years, and a return to the *status quo ante*; but there can be little doubt that the current wave of policy and institutional innovation differs markedly from the process of state-building that began in the 1930s. Using a metaphor from mathematics, one could characterize the processes of change in these two eras as having reversed signs.

Consider the key features of the reforms of the 1930s and 1940s. After the collapse of the gold standard in 1931, a major transformation in the goals of macroeconomic policymaking, comparable to recent changes, occurred. Under the interwar gold standard, monetary and fiscal policymaking had been subordinated to the exigencies of maintaining external balance. Fixed gold parities had been considered sacrosanct, and restrictive monetary and fiscal policies had been considered the only acceptable remedies for closing balance-of-payments deficits and restoring the confidence of financial markets in exchange rates. But soon after the collapse of the gold standard, policymakers in one nation after another put domestic recovery ahead of exchange-rate stability and financial openness as the priority of macroeconomic policy. After 1945, European nations were just as insistent that a variety of domestic policy goals which can be summarized under the two rubrics full or high employment and/or rapid economic growth must have weight in macroeconomic policymaking at least equal to that of maintenance of external balance and price stability.

Because of the new tasks assigned to macroeconomic policymaking, there was a broad movement to bring central banks under the closer control of executives and legislatures. Beginning in the mid-1930s the private or semi-public banks, which were the ancestors of today's central banks, were nationalized. Earning dividends for private shareholders would no longer be among their priorities. New directors would henceforth be appointed by the government or by parliament, instead of being co-opted by the existing directors, who had been largely or completely insulated from the democratic process.

Financial markets also emerged from depression and war more tightly regulated. Continental countries with mixed or universal banking systems prior to 1931 had experienced a wave of bank failures during the 1920s and early 1930s. Now the activities of banks were subjected to much closer supervision. In some countries, notably Belgium, Italy, and Sweden, segmentation was introduced into financial markets by legislation. In order to accomplish important national goals that the authorities felt had been neglected in the less-regulated environment existing before 1931, selective credit mechanisms were introduced: as was noted above, they were set up in France in the 1940s and in Spain in the 1950s to promote growth and modernization, and in the Nordic countries during the 1950s to promote construction of affordable housing. In many nations, the authorities also utilized the extensive financial controls they had acquired as an instrument of macroeconomic policy. Central banks now could influence the volume of credit in national financial systems not only by varying the discount rate but also by credit rationing.

In many European countries stock markets never recovered the role they had played, prior to 1931, as a source of investment capital for firms. Investors would have been shy of the markets anyway, after the crashes of share values during the Great Depression; but tax laws in Germany and the creation of new circuits for industrial finance in Italy and France contributed to the decline of continental stock markets. Bank finance, which was often more closely controlled by the state due to regulatory innovations, became a more important source of long-term capital in France and Germany. In many countries, publicly owned institutions now played a larger or even predominant role in the banking system, even as the public sector in manufacturing and other services expanded. In Italy the large publicly owned manufacturing sector raised capital by issuing long-term debentures guaranteed by the state.

Unions everywhere emerged strengthened from depression and war. In France, the Low Countries, and Scandinavia, labor legislation adopted in the 1930s tended to strengthen the trade unions. In Scandinavia during the 1930s, and in the Low Countries after World War II, the political influence of organized labor was institutionalized through agreements between the social partners, which undergirded political alliances struck between parties representing workers, farmers, and sometimes business interests. In Nazi-occupied Europe, organized labor achieved prestige and power through its active involvement in the struggle against fascism.

The resounding victory of the Labour Party at the polls in Britain in the summer of 1945 contributed to the institutionalization of the trade unions' role in economic policymaking there as well. In Scandinavia, the Low countries, and Austria, collective bargaining tended to emerge from the war more centralized than before, with the state playing a more active role in mediating labor agreements. In these countries a high degree of coordination between monetary and fiscal policy, on the one hand, and incomes policy, on the other, was achieved.

These changes were accompanied by the most sustained expansion of social and welfare commitments during the twentieth century. National health care systems were created. Unemployment- and disability-insurance schemes were expanded and made more generous. Pension funds were overhauled and encompassed more individuals. Contractual-savings schemes were greatly expanded and for the first time came to make up a significant share of total national savings.

Policy Convergence and Comparative Political Economy

The two periods of institution-building and reorientation of the goals of state economic and social policy described above each lasted about fifteen years, from about 1931 to 1947 and from about 1973 to 1990. They bracketed the era described in France as the *trente glorieuses*, thirty, or nearly thirty, years of unprecedented economic growth, as well as of much greater continuity in the institutional framework and the orientation of social and economic policymaking. From today's perspective, what is most striking about both "periods of movement" is the high degree of institutional and policy convergence across national boundaries.

This was not nearly so clear to observers who sought to make sense of these events with less temporal perspective. During the 1930s, for example, contrasts between the economic and social programs of the continental dictatorships—fascist Italy, Nazi Germany, clerico-fascist Austria, and later Francist Spain and Vichy France—and the policies pursued in Europe's remaining democracies were evident enough. Most importantly, the dictatorships crushed independent trade unions, whereas in Scandinavia and France labor negotiated more explicit and far-reaching social and economic pacts with employers and governments than ever before, while in Britain the unions at least held their own. In their foreign economic policies, the dictatorships pursued autarky, using bilateral clearing agreements to organize the minimal levels of requisite trade. International financial flows were severely restricted and closely monitored. The democratic nations also erected tariffs and other barriers to trade, but they remained more committed to multilateralism. Foreign-exchange markets remained sufficiently broad and unrestricted to convey important information about the balance-of-payments position and about macroeconomic and political stability.

It was not until after World War II, and the defeat of the Axis, that the trend toward economic and social policy convergence across European nations self-evidently prevailed over the trend toward divergence. Independent trade unions were now restored in the ex-dictatorships. Autarky was repudiated, and the defeated nations participated in the Bretton Woods system, GATT negotiations, and the European Community alongside the victors. In 1965 Andrew Shonfield argued in an influential study that, since the Great Depression, the political economies of all of Europe's leading industrialized nations had undergone comparable processes of profound change, with the state assuming greater responsibility than ever before for smoothing out business cycles and promoting development. Other scholars produced similar formulations describing social, political, and economic convergence among advanced industrial societies, placing the emphasis on the growing role of managers in increasingly bureaucratized societies; on the waning of ideological conflict and its replacement with interest conflict; on the tendency of similar socioeconomic systems to produce similar political parties and interest groups; or on the broad expansion of the welfare state.[1]

In retrospect, the degree of policy convergence even during the 1930s appears clearer than it did at the time. For example, despite its hostility to the trade unions, even Nazi Germany adopted full employment as the first priority of macropolicy and introduced a minimum wage. Vichy's banking legislation, along with elements of its social-welfare policy, including family allowances, were embraced by the Resistance parties after World War II. In Italy, the bank reforms enacted in 1934–36, and IRI, the state holding company set up at that time to manage the nationalized manufacturing sector, were accepted as the institutional basis for recovery and growth by postwar governments. Peter Temin recently has characterized the recovery programs enacted by industrial nations beginning in 1931 as "socialism in many countries." Leaving aside the issue of whether all of

1. Andrew Shonfield, *Modern Capitalism: The Changing Balance of Public and Private Power* (New York: Oxford University, 1965); John Kenneth Galbraith, *The New Industrial State* (Boston: Houghton Mifflin, 1967); Daniel Bell, *The End of Ideology: On the Exhaustion of Political Ideas in the Fifties* (Glencoe, Ill.: Free Press, 1960). Suzanne Berger provides an excellent discussion of the dominant paradigm in interpreting political party and interest group cleavages in advanced industrial societies in the late 1950s in her Introduction to Berger, ed., *Organizing Interests in Western Europe* (New York: Cambridge University, 1981), pp. 1–23.

these policies should be characterized as socialist, we agree with Temin that the common imperative of breaking the deflationary dynamic of the Great Depression led to convergence in economic and social policymaking across nations, a convergence which was accelerated by the ideological and political convergence created by the Allied victory in World War II and by postwar U.S. hegemony in Western Europe.[2]

The more turbulent economic environment after 1973 tended to revive interest among comparative political economists in policy differences across nations. Rates of growth, inflation, and unemployment fluctuated wildly across nations during the 1970s and early 1980s, and it took time before the broad lines of convergence in economic policymaking and institutional reform emerged.

From the present vantage point, however, it appears essential to explain why, in the long run, not just Thatcherite Britain but also social-democratic Sweden have declared price stability to be the primary goal of macropolicy; why central bankers in Oslo and Stockholm have come to agree with their counterparts in London and Frankfurt that the purpose of monetary policy is to achieve price-level stability, and not full employment; and why not just America and Britain but also the Netherlands and Sweden have tolerated growing inequality in wealth and income distribution. Being unemployed may well continue to be less unpleasant in the German Federal Republic or in Sweden than it is in Britain; and welfare benefits in the Nordic countries, even in the current climate of austerity, remain comparatively high. Nevertheless, it is clear that over the last fifteen years, as far as policy orientation is concerned, the *direction* of change has been similar across Europe; and if we keep our focus on policy goals, it is convergence, not differences, that need to be explained.

Given scholars' predominate concern with explaining differences in national policy outcomes, it is not surprising that the theoretical models which now dominate the comparative political economy literature are of little utility in explaining broad processes of policy convergence. This is true, for example, of both the coalition-centered and institutional approaches, which have enjoyed widespread currency in recent years. Coalition-centered approaches explain policy as the product of group

2. Peter Temin, *Lessons from the Great Depression* (Cambridge, Mass.: MIT, 1989), pp. 89–90 and *passim*. On Nazi Germany's adoption of a minimum wage, see Arthur Schweitzer, *Big Business in the Third Reich* (Bloomington: Indiana University, 1964), p. 401; Tilla Siegel, "Lohnpolitik im nationalsozialistischen Deutschland," in Carola Sachse, Tilla Siegel, Hasso Spoda, and Wolfgang Spohn, eds., *Angst, Belohnung, Zucht und Ordnung* (Opladen: Westdeutscher Verlag, 1982); Tilla Siegel, "Wage policy in Nazi Germany," *Politics and Society* 14 (1985), no. 1, pp. 1–51. On the continuity between Vichy's social and economic reforms and postwar policy, see Richard F. Kuisel, *Capitalism and the State in Modern France: Renovation and Economic Management in the Twentieth Century* (New York:

conflict and compromise. Scholars using this framework argue that the range of policy alternatives will be constrained by the relative balance of power among social actors, notably social classes and interest groups. In a well-received study, Peter Gourevitch, a leading practitioner of this approach, has in fact applied this argument to explain institutional change across the two periods of movement we examine here. His explanations for short-term policy variations during both the 1930s and the 1970s and early 1980s as a function of contrasting political and interest group coalitions across nations appear to have a certain plausibility. In his comparative analysis of politics in the 1930s, Gourevitch is most concerned to explain the political preconditions for a break with the prevailing orthodoxy in economic policy of deflation. He defines the alternative to this policy as a combination of protectionism and demand stimulus. In Gourevitch's view, the strongest coalition that could be marshalled in support of such policies consisted of an alliance of workers, farmers, and some business leaders. He believes that this reflationary bloc was exemplified by the New Deal coalition in the United States, by the political alliance struck in Sweden between Social Democrats and Agrarians in the "cow trade" in 1932, and by the neo-corporatist agreements between business, labor, farmer, and government representatives negotiated in the Saltsjöbaden Accords of 1938. Gourevitch seeks to explain deviations from this pattern in terms of differences in the relative strength and organizational coherency of interest groups. Thus he argues that Weimar Germany was unable to forge a similar coalition after the onset of the Great Depression due to the inability of workers and farmers to reconcile their differences. He argues that Britain failed to embrace demand stimulus during the 1930s because the agricultural sector was too small and the political influence of the City of London too great to make a worker-farmer coalition a politically viable option.[3]

This argument is subject to criticism on a number of grounds. A glance at public deficit to GDP ratios indicates that the fiscal-stimulus programs adopted during the 1930s in Sweden and the United States were far too moderate to have played a significant role in promoting

---

Cambridge University, 1981); Henry Russo, "Les paradoxes de Vichy et de l'Occupation. Contraintes, archaïsmes et modernités," in Patrick Fridenson and André Straus, eds., *Le capitalisme français XiXe-XXe siècle. Blocages et dynamismes d'úne croissance* (Paris: Fayard, 1987), pp. 67–82; Robert Paxton, *Vichy France: Old Guard and New Order, 1940–1944*, 2nd rev. ed. (New York: Columbia University, 1982). On institutional continuity in Italy from the reforms of the 1930s through the postwar era, see Sabino Cassese, "The long life of the financial institutions set up in the thirties," *Journal of European Economic History* 13 (1984), no. 2, special issue on banks and industry in the interwar period, pp. 273–294.

3. Peter Gourevitch, *Politics in Hard Times: Comparative Responses to International Economic Crises* (Ithaca: Cornell University, 1986).

recovery from the Great Depression; indeed, actual budget deficits were often larger in countries where political leaders espoused financial orthodoxy. Hence efforts to explain why some countries undertook cautious and ineffectual fiscal-stimulus programs during the 1930s, while others did not, are unlikely to increase our understanding of the political preconditions of economic recovery. Recent work suggests that Britain's recovery was rapid and sustained in international comparison, even though it was driven more by a permissive monetary policy than by an expansive fiscal policy.[4]

But more to the present point, Gourevitch himself concedes that, over the medium term, policy convergence was a more striking outcome of the economic crisis of the 1930s than policy divergence. Britain embraced full employment as a major goal of macroeconomic policy with fewer reservations than most other industrial nations after 1945, even though the City retained much of its political influence and farmers continued to make up a miniscule proportion of Britain's working population. Gourevitch also concludes, much as we do, that the economic policies of Nazi Germany had a good deal in common with those of the democratic countries, which were governed by quite different political coalitions and interest group aggregations. In sum, Gourevitch's model is designed to identify and explain divergence in policymaking, but in his empirical work he found convergence.

Much the same can be said of the conclusions of Gourevitch and other exponents of the coalition-centered approach regarding policymaking since the early 1970s. There is no question that differences in the ideological orientation of governments, and the interests they represented, accounted for significant differences in economic and policy outcomes in the short term. In the wake of the Conservative Party's electoral victory in Britain in 1979, Ronald Reagan's election to the presidency in the United States in 1980, and the formation of a center-right government in Bonn in 1982, it seemed clear that where conservative political parties held office, and where monetarist economic views held sway, governments would be more likely to embrace restrictive macroeconomic policies in order to fight inflation, regardless of the consequences for employment levels and growth. Conservatives in Britain and America also were likely to be more aggressive in reducing or eliminating social-welfare programs and more likely to acquiesce in, or even promote, the decline in union power. By way of contrast, it appeared that countries

4. Temin, *Lessons from the Great Depression*, pp. 107–8 and *passim*; Barry Eichengreen, *Golden Fetters: The Gold Standard and the Great Depression, 1919–1939* (New York: Oxford University, 1992); Barry Eichengreen, "The origins and nature of the Great Slump revisited," *Economic History Review* 45 (1992), no. 2, pp. 213–239.

where socialist or social-democratic parties remained in power would continue to maintain their commitments to full employment and the welfare state. But beginning with socialist France's shift to a restrictive macropolicy stance in 1982–83, ideological and coalition-centered explanations for policy outcomes have become less and less plausible. What needs to be explained today is not why Ronald Reagan and Margaret Thatcher have advocated monetarism, financial openness, abdication of government responsibility for economic growth and employment, and the rollback of the welfare state, but why socialists in France and Spain and social democrats in Norway and Sweden have adopted essentially similar policies, albeit with greater hesitation and less enthusiasm.

State- or institution-centered approaches appear to be equally unsuited to explaining policy convergence. Exponents of these views argue that the behavior of policymakers is heavily influenced by the organization of the polity and economy. They stress that formal rules, compliance procedures, and standard operating practices structure the relationship between individuals in various units of the polity and the economy. In their view, the organization of policymaking affects the degree of power that any one set of actors has over policy outcomes, as well as influencing actors' definitions of their own interests.[5]

Two institutionalist arguments gained prominence in seeking to explain differences in economic policy outcomes among nations since the early 1970s. The neo-corporatist school focused on labor-market organization. Countries with centralized, neo-corporatist labor relations, it was argued, could use incomes policies as an instrument of macroeconomic policy coordination alongside fiscal, monetary, and exchange-rate policies. As a result, they were more successful in simultaneously achieving the "magic quadrangle" of price stability, external balance, growth, and full employment, whereas these goals appeared to be mutually exclusive for countries without such institutional capacity.[6]

Another institutionalist argument that has enjoyed a certain currency explains differences in inflation rates over longer periods in terms of the

5. Peter Hall, *Governing the Economy: The Politics of State Intervention in Britain and France* (New York: Oxford University, 1986), p. 19 and *passim*; Kathleen Thelen and Sven Steinmo, "Historical institutionalism in comparative politics," in Sven Steinmo, Kathleen Thelen, and Frank Longstreth, eds., *Structuring Politics* (New York: Cambridge University, 1992).

6. Examples include, Manfred G. Schmidt, *Wohlfahrtstaatliche Politik unter bürgerlichen und sozialdemokratischen Regierungen* (Frankfurt a.M.: Campus, 1982); David R. Cameron, "Social democracy, corporatism, labor quiescence, and the representation of economic interests in advanced capitalist society," in John H. Goldthorpe, ed., *Order and Conflict in Contemporary Capitalism* (New York: Oxford University, 1984); Wolfgang Blaas and Alois Guger, "Arbeitsbeziehungen und makroökonomische Stabilität im internationalen Vergleich," in Peter Gerlich, Edgar Grande, and Wolfgang C. Müller, eds.,

degree to which the central banks has enjoyed autonomy from pressures emanating from the executive and legislative branches of government. According to this view, independent central banks will be more stability-oriented, yielding lower rates of inflation; less-independent central banks will produce wider swings between restrictive and accommodative monetary policies in cycles determined by the timing of political elections, yielding higher average rates of inflation. John Goodman has applied this argument to macroeconomic policy in Germany, France, and Italy from 1973 to 1990. He concludes that Germany, with the most independent central bank, has had the lowest inflation rate, while France, with the least independent central bank, has experienced the most fluctuation in monetary policy. In his view, Italy lies somewhere between, in terms of both macroeconomic stability and the institutional independence of the central bank.[7]

The problem with both of these arguments is that they afford little insight into the preconditions for, and causes of, major institutional change of the sort that took place in the two periods of movement under discussion here. Neo-corporatist institutions may well have endowed governments with greater room for maneuver in macropolicy (in the fortunate countries which had them) through the mid- to late 1970s; but why have these institutions broken down everywhere since the early 1980s? Similarly, assuming that Goodman is correct in his argument that independent central banks are more successful than dependent central banks in fighting inflation, why did nearly all industrialized nations reduce the independence of their central banks after 1931, and why has a movement in the opposite direction developed in many countries in recent years? Institution-centered arguments appear to be plausible so far as they go, but they fail to specify the circumstances that lead to institution-building in the first place. Hence they are more useful for examining periods of economic and political stability than periods of radical change, and more suitable to explaining differences in policy regimes across nations than to explaining processes of policy convergence.

A third approach in comparative political economy that has attracted a certain amount of attention in recent years, and that was developed to meet some of the deficiencies of coalition- and institution-centered explanations noted above, explores the "political power of economic ideas."

Sozialpartnerschaft in der Krise. Vergleich (Vienna: Böhlau, 1985); Peter Katzenstein, *Small States in World Markets: Industrial Policy in Europe* (Ithaca: Cornell University, 1985); Fritz Scharpf, *Crisis and Choice in European Social Democracy* (Ithaca: Cornell University, 1991).

7. John B. Goodman, *Monetary Sovereignty: The Politics of Central Banking in Western Europe* (Ithaca: Cornell University, 1992).

According to this approach, a major change in the theoretical paradigm through which economic problems and policy options are understood can open up new possibilities for forging political and interest-group coalitions, as well as provide legitimacy for policy innovation and institution building.[8]

The assumptions underlying this approach are well summarized in the famous passage in the concluding notes to John Maynard Keynes's *General Theory of Employment, Interest and Money* where he observes that:

> the ideas of economists and political philosophers, both when they are right and when they are wrong, are more powerful than is commonly understood. Indeed the world is ruled by little else. Practical men, who believe themselves to be quite exempt from any intellectual influences, are usually the slaves of some defunct economist. Madmen in authority, who hear voices in the air, are distilling their frenzy from some academic scribbler of a few years back. I am sure that the power of vested interests is vastly exaggerated compared with the gradual encroachment of ideas.[9]

According to this view, a revolution in economic thought occurred during the 1930s, with Keynes's *General Theory* being the most systematic exposition of the new theoretical paradigm. On the institutional level, this revolution in economic theory provided the justification for macropolicies oriented toward growth and full employment, and for a more flexible system of international exchange rates than had existed under the gold standard. The importance of stabilizing demand in Keynesian macroeconomics also justified strengthening trade unions and expanding social and welfare transfers. Similarly, the ascendency of the monetarist paradigm in economic theory since the mid-1970s, closely followed by the proliferation of supply-side theories, has provided the intellectual justification for a more restrictive macropolicy stance, cutbacks in public services and welfare transfers, and renunciation on the part of governments of responsibility for rates of economic growth and full employment.

There is no doubt that important changes in economic theory accompanied institutional change and policy innovation during both of the periods of movement with which we are concerned here. However, a closer look at the key reforms of the 1930s and 1940s and of the 1970s and 1980s suggests that the connection between changes in economic ideas, on one

8. Peter A. Hall, ed., *The Political Power of Economic Ideas: Keynesianism across Nations* (Princeton: Princeton University, 1989). It should be noted that Hall and his colleagues designed the research project that yielded this volume to test the "political power of economic ideas" hypothesis and that many of them emerged from their study rather skeptical of its explanatory power, much as we are.

9. John Maynard Keynes, *The General Theory of Employment, Interest, and Money* (New York: Harcourt, Brace, Jovanovich, 1953), p. 383.

hand, and changes in policy stance and institutional capacity, on the other, is too tenuous to justify the causal explanations posited by the "political power of economic ideas" school.[10]

Consider, for example, the impact of Keynesianism on economic policymaking during the 1930s and 1940s. A widely accepted, although reductionist, reading of the policy implications of the *General Theory* is that in a severe slump such as the Great Depression government deficits may be the only effective means of raising demand and hence bringing about economic recovery. Consequently, according to this view, fiscal policy should be used as an instrument of macroeconomic policy and government budgets should be balanced over the business cycle rather than the calendar year. Not surprisingly therefore, political scientists in search of the impact of Keynesian theory on economic policy have looked for evidence of the use of fiscal stimulus.[11]

The results suggest something very much less than a Keynesian revolution in economic policymaking during the 1930s and 1940s. Two industrialized nations did embark on massive deficit spending programs during the Great Depression: Nazi Germany and authoritarian Japan. However, in neither country can the break with fiscal orthodoxy be attributed to Keynesian theory. It is true that the United States and Sweden embarked more timidly on fiscal stimulus programs during the 1930s; here Keynes's ideas influenced public debate at the time (although Sweden had its own champions of fiscal expansion in the Stockholm school economists). However, as was noted above, the very modest budget deficits run by Sweden and the United States were too small to have made a significant macroeconomic contribution to recovery. As Temin puts it: "The 1930s were not a test of Keynesian theory because Keynesian policies were not used."[12]

Several recent studies of recovery from the Great Depression have argued, persuasively in our view, that in most or all of the major economies, the single most important factor in bringing about recovery

10. Charles P. Kindleberger notes that the debate between "Keynesians" and "monetarists" "did not have its origin in the 1920s or 1930s, as many students of the subject think, but can be traced back to the seventeenth century and beyond." *A Financial History of Western Europe* (Boston: George Allen & Unwin, 1987), p. 6.

11. On the reductionist interpretation of Keynesianism see Walter Salant, "The spread of Keynesian doctrines and practices in the United States," in Hall, ed., *The Political Power of Economic Ideas*, pp. 27–51. For examples of efforts by political scientists to unearth evidence of the use of fiscal stimulus in the 1930s, see Gourevitch, *Politics in Hard Times*; Margaret Weir and Theda Skocpol, "State structures and the possibilities for 'Keynesian' responses to the Great Depression in Sweden, Britain, and the United States," in Peter B. Evans, Dietrich Rueschemeyer, and Theda Skocpol, eds., *Bringing the State Back In* (New York: Cambridge University, 1985), pp. 107–163.

12 . Temin, *Lessons from the Great Depression*, p. 108.

from the Great Depression was the shift from restrictive to expansionary monetary policy as one country after another explicitly or effectively abandoned the gold standard. Not just Keynes and his followers but a wide range of more orthodox economists became advocates of cheap money as the 1930s progressed. For example, the Bank of England, which remained a bastion of theoretical opposition to Keynes's ideas throughout the decade, formulated and implemented a cheap-money policy after 1932, which brought about early and sustained economic recovery in Britain.[13]

There is no denying that Keynes's ideas had a profound impact on the economics profession in much of the industrialized world after World War II. However, the principles of Keynesian demand management, and in particular the central role of fiscal stimulus as a recession-fighting instrument, were by no means accepted universally within the industrialized world in the immediate aftermath of World War II. In a handful of countries, notably Britain and Sweden, policymakers were influenced by Keynes's ideas about macroeconomic management early on. However, the problems they faced in the aftermath of World War II were very different from those facing the industrial nations in the 1930s. The main problem confronting policymakers in postwar Britain and Sweden was excess, not insufficient, demand. Governments in both countries modulated the size of budget *surpluses* during the early postwar years in order to fine-tune the economy. Meanwhile, in many continental nations, including France, Italy, and Germany, policymakers were more concerned with supply problems than demand management, and they often remained skeptical about the utility of deliberately running government deficits as an instrument of macroeconomic policy. It was not until well into the 1960s that policymakers in much of continental Europe showed much interest in countercyclical fiscal policies. On the level of policymaking and implementation, therefore, the heyday of Keynesian macroeconomic theory was in the waning years of the *trente glorieuses*, not at the beginning.[14]

Thus while there was policy convergence in the 1930s and 1940s across nations, it was not around Keynes's ideas, at least not in the reductionist sense in which they are often represented. This is not to say that in the broader sense, Keynes's influence has not been profound, if difficult to measure. The subdiscipline of macroeconomics, and many of the basic

13. Temin, *Lessons from the Great Depression*; Eichengreen, *Golden Fetters*.

14. Pierre Rosanvallon, "The development of Keynesianism in France"; Marcello de Cecco, "Keynes and Italian economics"; and Christopher S. Allen, "The underdevelopment of Keynesianism in the Federal Republic of Germany," all in Hall, ed., *The Political Power of Economic Ideas*, pp. 171–193, 195–229, and 263–289.

instruments of econometric analysis and national accounts keeping were a product of the Keynesian revolution. As A. C. Pigou, one of Keynes's more prominent academic critics in the 1930s put it after the war:

> Those of us who disagree in part with his analysis have, nevertheless, undoubtedly been affected by it in our own thinking; and it is very hard to know exactly where we stood before. Not a little of what we now believe ourselves to have known all along, it may well be we owe to him.[15]

Moreover, the growing ascendancy of Keynesian theory in the postwar era tended to justify, *ex post facto*, a number of policy changes and institutional reforms that had been undertaken earlier. On the most basic level, Keynes's thought tended to justify government intervention to stabilize the economy. It also legitimized the reorientation of monetary policy to include high or full employment and/or high rates of economic growth as central goals. It justified the more flexible system of international monetary relations set up at Bretton Woods, as well as the principle that domestic economic stability should not be sacrificed to maintenance of exchange-rate parities. It may have contributed to the willingness of officials to tolerate budget deficits and creeping inflation. But if our objective is to explain policy convergence across nations during the 1930s and 1940s, the Keynesian revolution in economic thought is a slender reed.

If anything, it would be even more difficult to ascribe the sea change in social and economic policy orientation since the mid-1970s to "the political power of economic ideas." There is no doubt that the recent policy reorientation has been accompanied by the proliferation of economic doctrines hostile to Keynesianism, including monetarism, the rational-expectations school, supply-side economics, and even arguments in favor of return to a gold exchange standard. Common to all of these economic theories is an emphasis on how market imperfections, notably as a result of state intervention in the economy and producers' associations (cartels, trade unions, etc.), diminish efficiency and produce suboptimal economic outcomes. Hence the new economic theories advocate reducing the size of government, cutting back entitlement programs, deregulation, breaking up or diminishing the power of trade unions, and eliminating barriers to the flow of goods and finance: in brief the return to the market or laissez-faire.[16]

Among the new directions in economics, monetarism clearly has been the most influential tendency. Nobel Prize laureate Milton Friedman

15. "The economist," in *John Maynard Keynes 1883–1946* (Cambridge, 1949), p. 21, cited in Peter Hall, "Introduction," Hall, ed., *The Political Power of Economic Ideas*, p. 4.

16. On the proliferation of economic doctrines hostile to Keynesianism, see Paul Krugman, *The Age of Diminished Expectations: U.S. Economic Policy in the 1990s* (Cambridge Mass.: MIT, 1990), pp. 81–83.

comes closest to wearing the mantle of Keynes as chief theoretical exponent of the "counter-revolution in economic theory." Central bankers in several key nations, including Germany, Britain, and the United States, adopted monetary targeting during the 1970s as suggested by monetarist theory. However, it would be difficult to characterize the change in monetary policy formation since the mid-1970s as a shift from Keynesianism to monetarism. According to Friedman and his disciples, central banks should be able to achieve price-level stability by abandoning discretionary policies and instead allowing the money supply to grow at a steady rate. The monetarists championed the autonomy of central banks, but they expected these institutions, once freed from political pressures, to formulate their policies almost automatically, through adherence to a few rules.[17]

However, central bank policy has remained as discretionary as ever. In the months following the breakdown of the Bretton Woods system in 1973, Germany was among the first nations to put the fight against inflation ahead of other goals in macropolicy formation. The Bundesbank undertook a "Copernican turn" in its monetary policy, shifting to an "almost brutally" restrictive stance immediately after fixed exchange rates were abandoned. It was the first central bank to publicly adopt monetary targeting, in December 1974. However, Germany's central bankers have always kept their distance from the theoretical monetarists. The quantity the Bundesbank targeted until 1988, *Zentralbankgeldmenge*, i.e., central bank money stock, differs from M1 or M2, as favored by the monetarists, and as a result the bank has been criticized by academic economists. In 1988 the Bundesbank switched to targeting M3, an even broader measures of money than CBM, M1, or M2. More importantly, Germany's central bankers have always maintained a pragmatic attitude toward quantitative targets, insisting that other indicators, including exchange rates, the balance of payments, and the level of business activity, must be taken into account as well. Otmar Emminger, vice president, and later president of the Bundesbank, was instrumental in the shift to monetary targeting; however, he never disguised his skepticism of the policy prescriptions of Friedman and his followers. Emminger insisted that changes in the velocity of circulation of money and other factors required central bankers to pursue discretionary policies, and he pointed to the radical swings in interest rates in the United States in the early 1980s as evidence of the harm that strict adherence to monetary targeting could bring. In his memoirs, after reviewing his disagreements over issues of principle with the academic monetarists, and the numerous occasions on which this gave

17. Patrick K. O'Brian characterized the proliferation of economic views hostile to Keynesianism as a counter-revolution, in "Britain's economy between the wars: a survey of a counter-revolution in economic history," *Past and Present* 115 (1987), pp. 107–30.

rise to public debate, Emminger went on to observe: "Nevertheless, I often found the dogmatic monetarists as invaluable support, particularly insofar as they made monetary policy easier to understand for the broad public." In other words, for Germany's influential central banker, monetarism was more useful as propaganda than as a guide to policy.[18]

When Britain and the United States shifted to a restrictive monetary policy in 1979, they also relied on monetary targeting. However, neither the Bank of England nor the Federal Reserve had much success in meeting their announced targets, and within three years both institutions had reverted to a more discretionary policy, although they maintained their inflation-fighting priorities. Peter Hall, who has studied the shift in British policy carefully, concluded that the Conservative government under Margaret Thatcher embraced monetarism

> primarily because of its attractions as political ideology rather than because of its persuasiveness as economic science ... the 1979 Conservative Government was able to resist many of the conventional pressures to revise its innovative economic policies precisely because it possessed a coherent economic philosophy. The monetarist vision provided a rationale for dismissing the pleas of businessmen, civil servants and trade unionists for economic mercy....[19]

A detailed account of the monetarist turn in the Federal Reserve's monetary policy in 1979 suggests that its motives were equally instrumental. On the basis of this evidence Paul Krugman has concluded:

> In retrospect, it seems clear what happened. The Federal Reserve was never monetarist. But it did need to win a major victory against inflation—both for the sake of the economy and to preserve its own treasured independence. It also knew that victory over inflation wouldn't come cheap.... The only reliable victory, in its view, would require a deep recession. The question was: How could the Fed persuade the country to swallow such bitter medicine?
>
> Monetarism was the perfect answer ....[20]

Krugman goes on to note that after the Fed abandoned monetary targeting and returned to a more discretionary policy

18. Otmar Emminger, *D-Mark, Dollar, Währungskrisen. Erinnerungen eines ehemaligen Bundesbankpräsidenten* (Stuttgart: Deutsche Verlags-Anstalt, 1986), p. 439. It was Emminger who characterized the floating of the mark against the dollar as a "Copernican turn," p. 253, and the restrictive monetary policy the Bundesbank adopted afterwards as "almost brutal," p. 254.

19. Hall, *Governing the Economy*, p. 276. See also Nigel Lawson, *The View from No. 11* (New York: Doubleday, 1993), pp. 76–87, 413–22, 447–57.

20. Krugman, *The Age of Diminished Expectations*, p. 84. See also William Greider, *Secrets of the Temple: How the Federal Reserve Runs the Country* (New York: Simon and Schuster, 1987).

> monetarists—Friedman in particular—routinely forecast a disastrous acceleration of inflation and/or a severe recession as a result of monetary instability. Yet the actual result has been remarkably smooth sailing.... There are still monetarists, but they almost seem like relics now. Milton Friedman's forecasts of doom were at first taken seriously, then ridiculed, then ignored.[21]

The experiences of other countries were similar. Reviewing the record of nine countries with monetary targeting, Argy, Brennan, and Stevens concluded that

> monetary targets were adopted as a tactical response to a particular economic situation, not as monetary rules.... Targets were never interpreted as monetary rules. Over-runs were not usually reversed; neither were under-runs, but they were far less frequent. The aggregates concerned were switched when considered necessary, and the targets themselves were ignored at times when other considerations intruded. Some countries eventually abandoned targeting altogether.[22]

In brief, monetarism may have provided theoretical justification for the shift in monetary policy stance in several nations during the 1970s, but it would be misleading to characterize these policy shifts as being driven by or adhering to a change in economic theory. Although the goals of monetary policy have changed markedly since the mid-1970s, there has been no consistent shift from discretionary to rule-based policy.

Many of the other policy prescriptions of the theoretical exponents of the return to laissez-faire have proved equally elusive. To the despair of economic liberals, government has proved intractable to shrinkage; nowhere within the OECD, not even in Thatcherite Britain or Reaganite America, did the size of state expenditure as a percentage of GDP contract appreciably in the late 1970s or 1980s. Initiatives to deregulate financial and other markets often led to new and unexpected forms of state intervention in the economy, with the U.S. savings and loan bailout being among the most conspicuous examples. From the present vantage point, it appears more appropriate to characterize the changing contours of state economic intervention during the last fifteen years as re-regulation than as deregulation.

In our view, therefore, the popular characterizations of the policy changes of the 1930s and 1940s as the "rise of the Keynesian welfare

21. Krugman, *The Age of Diminished Expectations*, p. 85.

22. Victor Argy, Anthony Brennan, and Glenn Stevens, "Monetary targeting: the international experience," *Economic Record* 66 (1990), no. 192, pp. 37–62. Citations pp. 37, 58. See also Charles Goodhart, "The conduct of monetary policy," *Economic Journal* 99 (1989), no. 396, pp. 293–346; and *idem*, "What should central banks do? What should be their macroeconomic objectives and operations," *Economic Journal* 104 (1994), no. 427, pp. 1424–36.

state" and the policy changes of the 1970s and 1980s as the "return to laissez-faire" are inadequate and even misleading descriptions of the policy convergence that took place across nations during these two periods. In neither era can the changes that took place be attributed to or explained by changes in economic theory.

It is interesting to note that scholars who have developed general explanations for states' policy responses to economic crisis during the 1930s have often come to conclusions opposite to those of scholars addressing similar issues during the 1970s. A common assumption in the literature on the Great Depression is that the economic crisis forced states to intervene massively in order to stabilize the economy. It was an easy step from this assumption to argue that, whereas crisis creates irresistible pressures for intervention, prosperity creates pressures for liberalization. Peter Temin has expressed this viewpoint perhaps most forcefully:

> Disorder breeds socialism.... The controls of socialism do well when times are bad, but they inhibit progress when times are good. Order therefore breeds capitalism.[23]

But in his study of French and British policy responses to the economic downturn after 1973, Peter Hall has come to the opposite conclusion. According to Hall, politicians and state officials have an incentive to expand intervention in the economy and take credit for prosperity during good times, but during bad times they are more likely to attribute economic problems to market forces beyond their control. In both Britain and France, the response to growing unemployment and lower rates of growth in the late 1970s and 1980s was a withdrawal from intervention in the economy and the renunciation of responsibility for growth and employment.[24] Although both Temin and Hall provide plausible accounts of the political processes during the respective periods they examine, they clearly do not rest on generalizable propositions. We need new arguments to understand policy convergence during the two "periods of movement" in question here.

Macropolicy Regime Changes

We believe that we can better understand a good deal of the policy changes that occurred during our two periods of movement by constructing a causal argument consisting of two linkages. The first linkage runs from cumulative and accelerating changes in nominal price levels to

23. Temin, *Lessons from the Great Depression*, p. 133.
24. Hall, *Governing the Economy*, pp. 281–2 and *passim*.

a shift in macropolicy orientation. In the early 1930s, a cumulative *deflationary* dynamic led to a shift in macroeconomic policy from defense of fixed exchange parities *à outrance* to policies oriented toward stabilizing prices and promoting economic recovery. In the 1970s and 1980s a cumulative *inflationary* dynamic led to a shift from growth- and employment-oriented macropolicies to an emphasis on fighting inflation. Using once again the mathematical metaphor referred to above, we see these two processes as having had reversed signs.

Although we are proposing an argument about political economy and not about economic theory here, it is clear that our analysis implies certain basic assumptions regarding economic theory. Specifically, our argument presupposes that full nominal price level flexibility can be highly disruptive, rather than leading to rapid adjustment and equilibrium, as in neoclassical views. This idea has a long lineage—from Thornton and Wicksell via Keynes and Fischer to Tobin, Temin, and Riese, and we do not mean to embrace any specific model within this general class.[25]

We can summarize our views of the disruptive effects of nominal price movements in the following terms. Expectations of falling prices depress demand, as purchases are postponed. Deflationary expectations are particularly disruptive in the areas of credit and finance, as they reduce the willingness to finance investment and increase incentives to hoard. The value of the collateral of debtors declines with respect to their money obligations. Firms and real estate owners may be driven into bankruptcy, taking with them the financial institutions that hold their debts, further propagating deflationary impulses through the economy. Declining demand and investment produce unemployment. If mass unemployment undermines trade unions' wage-setting capacity, deflation may become cumulative, unless and until the macroeconomic authorities intervene to break deflationary expectations.[26]

We see the inflationary process as a mirror image of deflation. Inflationary expectations lead consumers to accelerate purchases, increasing

25. Keynes, *The General Theory of Employment, Interest, and Money*; James Tobin, *Asset Accumulation and Economic Activity* (Chicago: The University of Chicago, 1980); J. Bradford De Long and Lawrence H. Summers, "Is increased price flexibility stabilizing?" *American Economic Review* 76 (1986), no. 5, pp. 1031–1044; Steven M. Sheffrin, *The Making of Economic Policy* (Boston: Blackwell, 1989), ch. 4; Thomas M. Humphrey, "Cumulative process models from Thornton to Wicksell," in Donald E. Moggridge, ed., *Perspectives on the History of Economic Thought: Volume IV: Keynes, Macroeconomics and Method* (Aldershot: Edward Elgar, 1990); K. Wicksell, *Interest and Prices* (New York: Kelley Reprint, 1965); Irving Fischer, "The debt deflation theory of great depressions," *Econometrica* 1 (1933).

26. Explanations featuring some or all of these mechanisms figure in the interpretations of the Great Depression produced by Fischer, "The debt deflation theory of great depressions";

effective demand, and putting additional upward pressure on prices. Rising prices encourage speculation, and eventually a flight from money into real assets, which disorganizes financial and asset markets. Rising demand causes labor markets to become tight, leading to nominal wage increases. In tight labor markets, even centralized trade unions tend to lose control over wage bargaining. A cumulative process can ensue, unless macroeconomic policymakers act to break inflationary expectations.

The second linkage in our argument runs from changes in macropolicy orientation to other aspects of economic and social policy. The shift to growth- and employment-oriented macropolicies during the 1930s involved decoupling domestic financial markets from the deflationary pressures propagated through the gold standard. This created the necessary preconditions for more extensive regulation of national financial markets. Regulation of financial markets, in turn, allowed (although it did not require) states to construct the institutional capacity for implementing selective industrial policies on the micro level.

Likewise, the reorientation of macropolicy to break deflation and promote recovery strengthened the position of labor and provided the necessary preconditions for neo-corporatist bargaining among the social partners. In order to break the fall in nominal prices and wages, many governments during the 1930s actively promoted producer cartels, which set prices and output levels among manufacturing firms; agricultural marketing boards, which set minimum prices for key commodities; and labor law, which strengthened the wage-bargaining position of trade unions. Even Nazi Germany froze nominal wages in 1933, in order to break the downward wage-price spiral set in motion by Brüning, after independent trade union organizations had been dismantled and outlawed. Finally, the change in macropolicy orientation created a more permissive environment for the dramatic expansion of the welfare state.

The shift to an inflation-fighting macropolicy stance since the mid-1970s has had equally important implications for other aspects of economic and social policymaking. The liberalization of financial markets was a crucial element in this shift. This has been particularly true in countries where extensive systems of financial controls allowed the state to ration credit selectively to various classes of borrowers at below-market prices. As Sofía Pérez points out in her contribution to this volume, in some countries, notably France and Spain, politicians and administrators discovered that

---

Keynes's theoretical and journalistic writing; Temin, *Lessons from the Great Depression*; Harold James and Ben Bernanke, "The Gold Standard, deflation and financial crisis in the Great Depression: an international comparison," in R. Glenn Hubbard ed., *Financial Markets and Financial Crises* (Chicago: University of Chicago, 1991), pp. 33–68; and Barry Eichengreen, *Golden Fetters*.

the political choices involved in allocating disinflation through credit rationing were too hard and that they either preferred to accomplish this unpleasant task through, or could accomplish it only through, the imposition of high real interest rates on a nondiscriminatory basis. In other countries, notably Norway and Sweden, the buildup of inflationary expectations was accompanied by the emergence of black and grey credit markets on the fringes of the regulated, official markets, rendering the use of credit ceilings as an instrument for implementing restrictive policies increasingly unviable. In addition, many European countries both inside and outside the snake, and later the EMS, have attempted to import price stability by tying their currencies to an external anchor, notably the German mark. In order to make these policies more effective, they liberalized international financial transactions as well as domestic credit markets.

The shift in macropolicy priorities to the fight against inflation has also weakened trade unions. This was due in part to rising rates of unemployment that these policies have produced. Moreover, in countries such as Sweden and Norway where centralized neo-corporatist bargaining between trade unions, employers' federations, and government representatives took place, monetary policy generally accommodated the outcome of wage bargaining and fiscal policy. In recent years, in contrast, central banks have reserved to themselves the prerogative to adopt on short notice more restrictive policies to combat inflation or to defend exchange rates, even if this nullifies the expected effects of negotiated incomes policies on the unemployment rate. Since the macroeconomic effects of centralized wage bargaining have become less predictable, it is not surprising that the collective-bargaining process has succumbed increasingly to centrifugal pressures. Finally, the shift to a more restrictive macroeconomic environment has induced states to reduce budget deficits by cutting back social and welfare expenditure.

In brief, we argue that the two sea changes in economic policymaking that we examine were driven not primarily by new economic ideas, changes in political power relations, or the organizational resources of societal actors, but rather by efforts to reverse cumulative, destabilizing dynamics in the movement of nominal prices. Accelerating changes in nominal prices led to changes in macropolicy stance, which in turn produced changes in regulation and microeconomic policies. Thus the primary causal arguments we build run from macro to micropolicy, and not the other way around. Consequently, the concept of macroeconomic policy regime, and changes therein, is central to our argument.

Our argument is built upon the exploration of two major shifts in macroeconomic policy orientation followed by, and closely associated with, changes in the regulation of national financial markets during the past sixty years. Of course macroeconomic policies are subject to continuous change; over the course of this era in all industrial nations there were innumerable shifts from more restrictive to more expansive macropolicy stances and back again. However, we believe that shifts in the general orientation and final goals of macroeconomic policies are relatively infrequent; indeed, we identify only two during this period. We refer to such shifts in policy stance as regime changes.

The terms policy regimes and regime changes are widely used in the contemporary political economy literature. Our usage is derived from Peter Temin, who in turn drew upon the work of Thomas J. Sargent, one of the leading exponents of the rational expectations school. Sargent used the term to build an argument about how a dramatic action by the public authorities could change expectations in the marketplace so quickly that the economy could reverse direction, with very minor costs of readjustment.[27] Temin took up his term, but modified it significantly in the process. Following Sargent, Temin sought to identify an underlying macropolicy regime:

> The regime is an abstraction from any single decision; it represents the systematic and predicable part of all decisions. It is the thread that runs through the individual choices that governments and central banks have to make. It is visible even though there inevitably will be some loose ends, that is, some decisions that do not fit the general pattern. These isolated actions have little impact because they represent exceptions to the policy rule, not new policy regimes.[28]

However, Temin, who is not an adherent of the rational expectations school, believed that bringing about a change in the expectations of market actors about price movements often involved considerable real economic costs. Moreover, whereas Sargent had focused almost exclusively on expectations about prices, Temin was interested also in expectations about demand.[29]

In discussing recovery from the Great Depression, Temin argued that, within each industrial nation, a major turning point in macropolicy regime could be identified at some point during the 1930s, when the authorities abandoned the restrictive policies meant to preserve external balance and set out to promote or facilitate domestic economic expansion. For Britain this occurred between September 1931, when it went off gold, and the spring of 1932, when the authorities adopted a cheap-money policy to promote domestic recovery. Several smaller countries

27. Thomas J. Sargent, "The end of four big inflations," in Robert E. Hall, ed., *Inflation: Causes and Effects* (Chicago: University of Chicago, 1983).

28. Temin, *Lessons from the Great Depression*, p. 91.

29. Ibid., pp. 91–92.

heavily dependent on Britain for trade, including some of the Commonwealth countries, Sweden, and Denmark, decided soon afterwards to float their currencies with the pound; most of them adopted a cheap-money policy within a few months as well. In Germany the regime change occurred after the Nazi takeover in January 1933. The previous governments headed by Papen and Schleicher, it is true, had taken a few expansionary measures, including tax incentives for hiring new workers, limited public works projects, and housing subsidies. But Temin insisted, and we agree, that a strong and clear signal that macropolicy would be oriented to new goals was made only by the Nazi leadership. For Temin, all of the industrialized nations underwent regime changes of this sort between the fall of 1931 and the fall of 1936, when France, the Netherlands, and Switzerland, the last holdouts in the gold bloc, abandoned their exchange-rate parities.[30]

We have used Temin's discussion as the springboard for our own concept of macropolicy regimes and regime changes, and we accept his periodization for the regime changes of the 1930s. In comparison with Temin, however, we have adopted a much more expansive definition of macropolicy regimes. Indeed, we mean to argue that since the 1920s only three macropolicy regimes can be distinguished in Western Europe and North America: the interwar Gold Standard, from the early- to mid-1920s to the early- to mid-1930s; a growth regime, which lasted from the mid-1930s to the mid-1970s through the early 1990s (depending on the country); and a disinflationary regime, which has been in place since then.

We believe that each of these regimes exhibits distinct characteristics; however, in terms of the priority of growth and employment versus price stability, and accordingly also in terms of the position of the central bank within the policymaking process, the first and the third regimes exhibit several fundamental similarities—on this more below.

We define regimes in terms of (1) goals and (2) the particular assignment of policy instruments to achieve these goals. The following table sets out in schematic fashion the main characteristics of the three macropolicy regimes of relevance to our discussion:

30. Ibid., pp. 93–106.

TABLE 1.1 Three Macropolicy Regimes Across Industrialized Europe: Goals and Instruments.

I. Interwar gold standard (1920s–mid-1930s)

Macropolicy

Goal: Maintenance of exchange-rate parities. It was assumed that maintaining exchange-rate parities would guard against inflation and that domestic price flexibility (usually downward) would secure external balance.

Instruments: Restrictive monetary policy, largely achieved through adjustment of discount rates. Conservative fiscal policy. Loan-financed public spending was acceptable when the proceeds were spent on capital investment, but budgets were brought into balance again when exchange-rate parities were challenged on the markets.

Micropolicies

Goal: Employment and growth.

Instruments: Largely hortatory. By enhancing international competitiveness, a greater share of world markets would be captured by domestic firms, and unemployment would be exported. In product markets, governments encouraged mergers among firms and investments as means of fostering productivity gains ("rationalization"). In labor markets, governments promoted greater "flexibility" (i.e., downward pressure on nominal wages).

II. High-growth and -employment regime (1930s–1970s)

Macropolicy

Goal: Combining high growth and/or high or full employment with relative price stability and external balance.

Instruments: Flexible monetary policy. Real interest rates were kept low to encourage investment. Exchange rates were adjusted from time to time to compensate for differences between national rates of inflation and to bring trade balances into equilibrium. Mildly expansionary fiscal policies. The size of state budgets relative to national economy increased considerably. Some countries adopted countercyclical fiscal policies. In all countries transfer payments stemming from social and welfare programs tended to stabilize demand during cyclical downturns. High levels of public investment buttressed business confidence that major recessions were unlikely. However, most countries avoided secular increases in the ratio of the public debt to GDP.

Micropolicies

Goal I: Keeping inflation in check in an expansionary macroeconomic environment.

Instruments: (In some countries, notably the Nordics, the Low Countries, Austria, and Germany) Incomes policy. Wage increases were tied to productivity gains. Wage restraint prevented full employment from leading to an inflationary wage-price spiral. (In some countries, notably France, Spain, Norway, and Sweden) Selective credit rationing. Inflationary pressures that otherwise would have been generated by low interest rates were contained by credit ceilings and by other forms of administered credit allocation.

Goals II–III: (In some countries, notably France and Norway) Modernization; (in some countries, notably Italy and Norway) regional redistribution of growth and employment.

Instruments: Industrial policies, based on financial controls, tax incentives, subsidies, and the regulation of trade to promote modernization and regional redistribution.

Goal IV: (In all countries) Some redistribution of income from the wealthy to the poor.

Instruments: Unemployment insurance, social security, health insurance, income support, housing subsidies, education grants.

III. Disinflationary regime (mid-1970s–present)

Macropolicy

Goals: Fighting inflation as a first priority. As much growth and employment as are compatible with stabilizing nominal price levels.

Instruments: Restrictive monetary policy. Real interest rates must be kept sufficiently high to break inflationary expectations and to prevent their resurgence. Effective transmission of interest-rate signals through the credit markets requires dismantling administrative credit controls. In many countries fixing the exchange rate of the national currency to an external anchor, notably the German mark, with its reputation for price-level stability, reinforces the credibility of the anti-inflationary policy. Making the external anchor effective requires dismantling restrictions on international capital flows.

Fiscal policy is difficult to characterize across nations. The recessions induced by the onset of anti-inflationary monetary policy tend to push budget deficits up. Some countries have tried to cut back deficits as part of macroeconomic stabilization policies or to reduce the "crowding-out" of private investment as part of supply-side growth policies. Others have either failed to cut back budget deficits or have deliberately used expansionary fiscal policies to offset or moderate the effects of restrictive monetary policies. The medium-run trend everywhere appears to be toward a more restrictive fiscal policy stance.

Micropolicies

Goal I: Keeping unemployment as low as possible and achieving as much growth as possible under the constraints set by macropolicy orientation.

Instruments: Improving the balance of trade as a means of capturing a greater share of world markets for domestic firms and exporting unemployment abroad; in product markets, incentives to enhance competitiveness of national firms, emphasis on investment, increasing productivity. In labor markets, restoring "wage flexibility."

Goal II: Preventing unemployment and slow growth from leading to social disintegration.

Instruments: Managing job losses by encouraging early retirement of older workers through pension incentives; repatriation of foreign "guest workers," if necessary through manipulation of emigration laws; use of schools and training programs as holding tanks to slow arrival of younger workers on job markets; development of retraining programs; preserving some of the social and welfare benefits instituted earlier under the high-growth and -employment regime.

It must be stressed that our definition of policy regimes does not imply a dichotomy between intervention and laissez-faire.[31] All three regimes described above are interventionist; to repeat, the differences

31. At this juncture, it also may be useful to distinguish our concept of policy regimes from two familiar economic models, the Phillips Curve and the Mundell-Fleming model. Like the Phillips Curve, our analysis posits trade-offs between employment levels (and growth rates) on the one hand, and inflation rates on the other. However, the Phillips Curve is a short-term model. It assumes that the capital stock is fixed. Our concept of macropolicy regimes, in contrast, is a long-term model. We do not by any means wish to suggest that the trade-offs between inflation and unemployment remain stable over time. Moreover, the whole point of our discussion of cumulative price movements is to explore their impact on investment, and thus lies outside the Phillips Curve framework.

Like Mundell-Fleming, our model is meant to illuminate the relationship between policy goals and instruments. However, Mundell-Fleming is also a short-term model that assumes price stability, whereas our model is meant to elucidate policy shifts driven by price-level instability. See J. M. Fleming, "Domestic financial policies under fixed and floating exchange rates," *IMF Staff Papers* 9 (1962), no. 3, pp. 369–80; R. A. Mundell, "The monetary dynamics of international adjustment under fixed and flexible exchange rates," *Quarterly Journal of Economics* 74 (1960), no. 2, pp. 227–57; and "Capital mobility and stabilization policy under fixed and flexible exchange rates," *Canadian Journal of Economics and Political Science* 29 (1963), no. 4, pp. 475–85.

involve goals and the assignment of instruments to achieve goals. The core issue differentiating the regimes we define involves the policy assignments of central banks. Under both the interwar gold standard and the contemporary disinflationary regime, the priorities of monetary policy were and are holding inflation in check and maintaining external balance, and the main instrument at the disposal of central bankers was and is interest-rate policy. Under the growth regime, however, fighting inflation was often the task of incomes policies and/or selective credit rationing. In the neo-corporatist countries, trade unions assumed responsibility for macroeconomic stability by negotiating and enforcing centralized collective bargaining agreements that imposed wage restraint on their members. By keeping wage increases at or below the level of productivity increases, the trade unions prevented full employment from triggering wage-price spirals, allowing central banks to hold interest rates steadier and at lower average levels. In countries that had adopted extensive controls on national financial markets, incomes policies could be supplemented or substituted by credit rationing or administered credit ceilings. Briefly put, the growth regime relied on monetary and fiscal policy to stimulate demand, and thereby promote growth and employment, while it used labor-market policies and regulation of financial markets to curb inflation; the interwar gold standard and disinflationary regimes relied and rely primarily on monetary policy to fight inflation and maintain external balance, and on supply-side policies, including tax cuts and other investment incentives, to promote growth and employment.

Nigel Lawson, Chancellor of the Exchequer under Margaret Thatcher from 1983 to 1989, articulated the distinction between the two most recent macropolicy regimes in almost identical terms in his Mais Lecture to the City University Business School in June 1984:

> The conclusion on which the present Government's economic policy is based is that there is indeed a proper distinction between the objectives of macroeconomic and microeconomic policy, and a need to be concerned with both of them. But the proper role of each is precisely the opposite of that assigned to it by the conventional post-War wisdom. It is the conquest of inflation, and not the pursuit of growth and employment, which is or should be the objective of macroeconomic policy. And it is the creation of conditions conducive to growth and employment, and not the suppression of price rise, which is or should be the objective of microeconomic policy.[32]

Both of the processes of regime change under examination here began with abrupt changes in the policies of central banks. As we will

32. Quoted in Lawson, *The View from No. 11*, pp. 414–5.

discuss in greater detail below, changes in regulation, labor market policies, and social policies occurred much more slowly. In the 1930s, changes in central bank policy were undertaken in response to the collapse of the gold standard and a cumulative deflationary dynamic which threatened to disorganize economic activity and destabilize domestic politics. As was noted above, the leader was Britain, which went off gold in September 1931 and discovered a few months later that it could use the room for maneuver created by the removal of the external constraint on monetary policy to lower domestic interest rates in order to promote economic recovery. Between September 1931 and September 1936 the other European countries followed Britain off gold *de facto* or *de jure*; all adopted more expansionary macroeconomic policies.[33]

The regime changes of the 1970s and 1980s, similarly, began with an abrupt change of course in central bank policy. Switzerland and Germany led the way, executing "Copernican turns" in monetary policy after the fixed dollar parity was abandoned in early 1973. Prior to then, the commitment to fixed exchange rates had prevented German and Swiss central bankers from acting forcefully to break inflationary expectations; but after the decoupling of the mark and franc from the dollar, the central banks of these two countries were able to raise real interest rates sharply, allowing the mark and the franc to appreciate against the dollar and other currencies. Between 1974 and 1990 the other nations of Europe followed suit. The Netherlands and Austria followed Germany's lead, pegging their currencies to the mark. By 1979 accelerating inflation in the United States and Britain led these nations to adopt restrictive monetary policies as well.[34]

With the world's two most important reserve centers, the United States and Germany, both holding real interest rates high in order to curb inflation (and, in the case of the United States after 1981, in order to attract capital from abroad), other nations seeking to buck the trend toward restrictive macroeconomic policies found their microeconomic institutions for fighting inflation under additional pressure. The expansionary macroeconomic policies pursued by France's newly elected socialist government in 1981 produced large trade deficits, capital flight, exchange-rate

33. On Britain's decision to leave gold, and the subsequent reorientation in macropolicy stance, see, in addition to the sources cited above, Dianne B. Kunz, *The Battle for Britain's Gold Standard in 1931* (New York: Croom Helm, 1987); and R.S. Sayers, *The Bank of England, 1891–1944* (New York: Cambridge University, 1976), pp. 387–430. For Britain's trading partners that followed it off gold, see Eichengreen, *Golden Fetters*.

34. On Germany and its trading partners, see Emminger, *D-Mark, Dollar, Währungskrisen*; on Britain, see Hall, *Governing the Economy*; and Lawson, *The View from No. 11*; on the United States, see Greider, *Secrets of the Temple*.

depreciation, and accelerating inflation. This led the French to engineer their own macropolicy regime change in 1982–3.[35]

By the mid-1980s, the last holdouts adhering to the growth regime in Europe were the Nordic redoubts of social democracy, Sweden and Norway. Thanks to their extensive batteries of domestic and external financial controls, their ability to achieve wage restraint through centralized collective bargaining, and their success in maintaining competitiveness on foreign markets through devaluations and productivity increases, the Norwegians and Swedes managed to maintain their commitments to full employment and growth-oriented macroeconomic policies for several years longer than the rest of Europe. However, in the end, they too were constrained to engineer a regime change in macropolicy stance. A social democratic government in Norway initiated a "turning operation" in 1986, which anchored the krone to the German mark. In order to bolster credibility in their commitment to monetary austerity, the authorities dismantled international financial controls. Domestic financial markets had been largely deregulated already, during the early 1980s, because of the explosive growth of grey financial markets alongside the regulated sector. The final step in instituting the new course was the *de facto* pegging of the krone to the ECU in October 1990. The impact of these measures on the economy was harsh. Unemployment climbed from 2.1 percent in 1987 to 5.2 percent in 1990. Norway's banking sector faced crisis as falling real estate prices reduced the value of borrowers' collateral and as business and personal bankruptcies mounted.

Similar events played themselves out in Sweden. The Swedish version of the "turning operation" occurred in 1990, when the Riksbank adopted exchange-rate stability as its highest priority. The Swedes too felt constrained to give up full employment as a policy objective. As was the case in Norway, Sweden had largely deregulated domestic financial markets in the course of the 1980s, in response to the proliferation of grey financial markets beyond the purview of the regulators. In 1989, as a part of the macroeconomic stabilization program, they completed the process of financial deregulation by terminating foreign-exchange controls. Here too, the upshot of the regime change was a sharp jump in unemployment and a liquidity crisis in the banking sector.[36]

What finally drove both Scandinavian nations to abandon the growth regime was accelerating inflation. Through much of 1980s their successes

35. Michael Loriaux, *France after Hegemony: International Change and Financial Reform* (Princeton: Princeton University, 1991); Goodman, *Monetary Sovereignty*; Hall, *Governing the Economy*. See also Pérez's contribution to this volume.

36. Lars Jonung, "Riksbankens Politik 1945–1990," in Lars Werin, ed., *Från ränteregliering till inflationsnorm* (Stockholm: SNS, 1993).

in keeping unemployment low had been purchased with higher-than-average rates of domestic price inflation, and by the late 1980s the situation was getting out of hand. Because of tight labor markets, centralized wage agreements began to break down, undermining the efficacy of incomes policies. At the same time, the use of credit rationing as an instrument of macroeconomic restraint was undermined by the explosion of grey credit markets. In other words, both of the chief microeconomic instruments of macroeconomic regulation at the disposal of policymakers in the Nordic countries—credit rationing and wage restraint—were disintegrating simultaneously. The authorities concluded that they would have to resort to high real interest rates and austerity in order to break inflationary expectations, even if it meant provoking a recession.[37]

The motivations of policymakers in undertaking the first regime change we describe appear at first glance more transparent than in the second case. Accelerating deflation in the 1930s produced a catastrophic decline in economic activity and threatened to undermine, and in some cases actually did undermine, political institutions and regimes. In the course of the 1970s and 1980s, in contrast, the turnaround to a restrictive policy regime occurred long before inflation reached levels at which the macroeconomic costs would appear to have become unacceptably high. There was a certain amount of "flight into real values," such as speculative real estate purchases in Scandinavia, which threatened to distort certain asset markets. But in summing up the recent literature on the impact of inflation on economic activity, Paul Krugman has observed

> it is one of the dirty little secrets of economic analysis that even though inflation is universally regarded as a terrible scourge, most efforts to measure its costs come up with embarrassingly small numbers.[38]

There are of course also the redistributive effects of inflation which need to be considered. Since these redistributive effects are unpredictable, as well as unjustifiable by social, political or economic norms, and in the final analysis are the result of government policy, the greatest cost may be the "loss of commonwealth." Against such losses must be put the costs of halting or slowing inflation, estimated by Krugman to have amounted to 20 percent of one years' GNP in the United States in the early 1980s, as well as the loss of commonwealth created by the rise of unemployment and the slowing of growth.[39]

37. Ton Notermans, "The abdication from national policy autonomy: why the macroeconomic policy regime has become so unfavorable to labor," *Politics and Society* 21 (1993), no. 2, pp. 133–167.

38. Krugman, *The Age of Diminishing Expectations*, p. 52.

39. The phrase "loss of commonwealth" is Charles S. Maier's, "The politics of inflation in the twentieth century," in Fred Hirsch and John H. Goldthorpe, eds., *The Political Economy*

We are inclined to conclude that alongside the loss of commonwealth another intangible factor must be set in order to explain the aversion not just of Thatcherite conservatives and Germany's independent central bank to inflation but also of social democratic policymakers in Scandinavia: the loss of control over the economy. Long before inflation reached levels that threatened to depress aggregate economic activity, it threatened to destroy the economic steering capacity of states, providing the immediate impetus for the regime changes we describe. As inflationary expectations grew, central bankers discovered that moderate rises in interest rates were interpreted by the markets as an indication that even more inflation lay ahead, and consequently stimulated, rather than depressed, the demand for money. Accelerating inflation put regulatory systems in full conflict with market incentives. This stimulated evasion, undermining the effectiveness of regulation. Firms and banks became confident that they would never be denied rediscounting facilities because of macroeconomic policy imperatives, and they shaped their financial plans accordingly. Centralized trade union federations lost the ability to enforce wage restraint on their members in an environment characterized by tight labor markets and rising prices. The regime changes of the 1970s and 1980s, therefore, reflected not only the preference of policymakers for price stability but also their desire to reestablish control over the evolution of key macroeconomic indicators. But control could be established only at a price, namely a fundamental reordering of the goals of the old policy regime as well as the reassignment of policy instruments to attain goals. The imperative of reestablishing control over key instruments of economic policymaking goes a long way toward explaining policy convergence across nations with very different governing political coalitions and ideological orientations during the course of the 1970s and 1980s.

Domestic and International Factors in Two Regime Changes

It has been widely debated whether the shift to restrictive macroeconomic policies on the part of nearly all of the industrialized nations since 1973 has been driven primarily by domestic or by international factors. There are essentially two lines of argument that ascribe preeminent importance to international forces. The first sees the process as having

---

of Inflation (Cambridge Mass.: Harvard University, 1978), pp. 37–71, cited phrase p. 41. For Krugman's estimates, see *The Age of Diminishing Expectations*, pp. 56–57.

been driven by the internationalization of finance. According to this view, the institutional capacity of individual countries to insulate domestic markets from international financial flows has deteriorated inexorably during the postwar era. The growth of the Eurocurrency markets since the mid-1960s and the multinationalization of financial institutions and corporations have made it increasingly difficult for governments to regulate international financial transactions.[40] Michael Stewart has gone on to argue that the internationalization of finance has imposed a deflationary bias on the world monetary system, since capital will flow to the countries with the most restrictive policies.[41]

In our view, there is no denying the trend toward greater financial openness, and the mechanism Stewart describes certainly has been at work. However, there are two issues yet to be resolved here. One is whether these processes were the essential ones in bringing about the macropolicy regime changes we examine—about this, more later. The other is whether internationalization forced deregulation or deregulation led to internationalization.

Arguments such as Stewart's assume a secular historical trend toward financial integration, that crossed some sort of threshold during the late 1960s or 1970s, leading to a narrowing of the constraints under which national monetary policy is set. We feel that a longer view of the history of international financial flows suggests that internationalization has been a discontinuous process, driven more by policy than by innovations in information and communications technologies or inexorable changes in factor mobility brought about by economic development. International capital flows were already quite developed by the end of the nineteenth century, and they reappeared quickly after the dismantling of exchange controls at the end of World War I. Indeed, according to some measures, financial openness during the 1920s was at about the same level as during the 1970s and 1980s, and much higher than during the 1950s and 1960s. International financial flows were reduced by regulations imposed during the 1930s and 1940s, and in our view their resurgence has been due in no small measure to the relaxation of financial regulation, at first gradually, and then more rapidly beginning in the 1970s.[42]

40. Jeffry A. Frieden, "National economic policies in a world of global finance." *International Organization* 45 (1991), no. 4, pp. 425–451.

41. Michael Stewart, *The Age of Interdependence: Economic Policy in a Shrinking World* (Cambridge, Mass.: MIT, 1984).

42. See Eric Helleiner, *States and the Reemergence of Global Finance* (Ithaca: Cornell University, 1994); Brendan Brown, *The Flight of International Capital: A Contemporary History* (London: Routledge, 1987); Robert Zevin, "Are world financial markets more open? If so why and with what effects," in Tariq Banuri and Juliet B. Schor, eds., *Financial Openness and National Autonomy* (New York: Oxford University, 1992).

In our judgement the weakest version of the internationalization-of-capital argument assigns primary importance to technological innovation. Progress in information and communications technologies, it is true, has permitted twenty-four-hour trading on world stock exchanges and currency markets, and rapid financial transfers; but are there compelling reasons to assume that new technologies could not be harnessed to serve the regulators as effectively as the traders? One critic of such arguments has noted recently that electronic money transfers tend to leave more traces behind them than paper transactions.[43]

The second, and in our judgement more significant argument that assigns central importance to international factors in bringing about macropolicy regime changes is that monetary policy in smaller or more peripheral economies is held hostage to the reserve centers, at least when the latter adopt restrictive policies. According to this view, domestic factors may be of primary importance in macroeconomic policy formation within the reserve centers, eventually within a single country with hegemonic status in the international monetary system; the remaining nations, however, have no choice but to adjust their policies accordingly, short of opting out of international trade and payments networks altogether. In a striking twist on this argument, John Cornwall has argued that even though several small European nations, including Austria, Sweden, and Norway, were relatively successful in fighting inflation with incomes policies during the 1970s, they were forced to follow the lead of the reserve centers, that is, Germany and the United States, in adopting a high interest rate policy, especially after 1979. In the long run, this brought about an unravelling of neo-corporatist institutions and the abandonment of incomes policies. Cornwall further asserted that nations without centralized collective bargaining had no choice but to break inflation through restrictive macroeconomic policies: either the hegemon has incomes policies and a growth- and employment-oriented macropolicy or no nation does.[44]

There is no question that the macroeconomic policies of the reserve centers constrain the choices available to other nations. Hansjörg Herr's contribution to this volume examines the mechanisms whereby these constraints operate in detail. Countries without effective foreign exchange controls will be particularly affected by a shift to restrictive policies in the reserve centers. The failure of France's Keynesian stimulus program in 1982 under the weight of rising trade imbalances, capital flight, and

43. Fred Block, *Revising State Theory: Essays in Politics and Postindustrialism* (Philadelphia: Temple University, 1987), p. 216.

44. John Cornwall, *The Theory of Economic Breakdown: An Institutional-Analytical Approach* (Cambridge, Mass.: Blackwell, 1990).

accelerating inflation and the shift to a policy of *rigueur* is an excellent case in point. But were the macropolicy options of all of the industrialized nations constrained by U.S. and German policies as completely as Cornwall and others have suggested?

It is precisely because of the insights they afford into this question that the policy trajectories of the two Scandinavian laggards in the recent regime change become so interesting. When real interest rates in the reserve centers skyrocketed after 1979 and the world economy spun into recession, the Nordic countries were strikingly successful in preserving external balance and full employment, at least for a time. As was noted above, they maintained international competitiveness through strategic devaluations. However, effective foreign exchange controls did not prevent wealth holders in the Nordic countries from undertaking readjustments in their portfolios in response to accelerating inflationary expectations. Real estate prices soared. There was a flight into debt to finance speculative purchases of real assets. Productive investment stagnated. The growth- and full-employment regime in the Nordic countries was destroyed by the acceleration of domestic inflationary pressures not because of the erosion of control over international capital flows. It is significant that Sweden and Norway dismantled their domestic financial controls first. Exchange controls were abolished not because the Swedish and Norwegian authorities had lost control over international financial transactions but because their central banks opted for fixed exchange parities in order to make credible their commitment to an inflation-fighting regime.[45]

It took only five years, from September 1931 to September 1936, for all of the nations of Europe to engineer fundamental reorientations in their macropolicy stances in response to the Great Depression. The time window during which the most recent round of macropolicy regime changes occurred was much larger by comparison: thirteen years elapsed between the Bundesbank's "Copernican turn" in 1973 and Norway's "turning operation" in 1986, and it was not until the early 1990s that the Nordic countries consistently embraced restrictive policies. In our view, this suggests not only that tolerance thresholds for inflation differ more widely across nations than for deflation but also that the international propagation mechanisms for deflationary impulses in the 1930s were a good deal stronger than for the inflationary impulses in the 1970s and 1980s. Indeed, we would go so far as to argue that, at least for some well-regulated and competitive national economies, domestic inflationary pressures, not

45. Notermans, "The abdication from national policy autonomy." See also his exchange with Jonathon Moses: Moses, "Abdication from national policy autonomy: what's left to leave?" and Notermans, "Social democracy in open economies," *Politics and Society* 22 (1994), no. 2, pp. 125–148, 149–164.

international pressures, were of decisive importance in forcing the recent macropolicy regime changes.

To turn to the regime change of the 1930s, there is no doubt that the gold standard was the primary mechanism for propagating deflationary impulses. But to stop at that would beg the question of why policymakers across Europe chose to tie themselves to the mast of the international gold standard to begin with. In the case of nations with weaker currencies, particularly those that experienced hyperinflation in the wake of World War I, it was clear that adherence to the gold standard was forced upon them by outsiders as a necessary precondition for receipt of international stabilization loans. The League of Nations sponsored missions to set up or reconstruct central banks in East-Central Europe during the early 1920s, and its foreign advisors insisted on independent central banks and on fiscal and monetary orthodoxy.[46]

But why did the neutral nations, which had built up strong net-creditor positions during the war, and the Allies, who had access to international capital markets even before they adopted fixed exchange parities, return to gold as well, often at considerable cost to domestic output? In our view, domestic political considerations played a large role in the embrace of the gold standard. The inflationary effects of wartime budget deficits were magnified everywhere by postwar wage-price spirals. The return to fiscal and monetary orthodoxy, including an international monetary system based on fixed exchange rates and gold, was seen as a crucial step in the restoration of price-level stability within the domestic economy. In our view, it would not be an exaggeration to state that the return to gold during the 1920s was driven as much by domestic economic policy concerns as it was by the exigencies of reconstructing the international economy. The fact that there was a good deal less political determination to lower tariff barriers during the 1920s, and that international trade grew much more slowly during that decade than international capital flows, tends to support this proposition.[47]

Our aim in laying so much stress on the domestic wellsprings of macropolicy regimes and regime changes is not to deny that the international monetary system frequently constrains the choices of policymakers;

46. On Norman's international financial diplomacy, see Sayers, *The Bank of England*, pp. 153–210. For an illustration of how Norman could force even an ex-Ally like Italy to modify its laws in order to conform with his vision of central bank independence, see Marcello De Cecco, "Introduzione" to De Cecco, ed., *L'Italia e il sistema internazionale, 1919–1936*, Collana Storica della Banca d'Italia, Serie Documenti, vol. VI (Bari: Laterza, 1993), pp. 3–103, esp. 70–83

47. Eichengreen, *Golden Fetters*; Kenneth Mouré, *Managing the Franc Poincaré: Economic Understanding and Political Constraint in French Monetary Policy, 1928–1936* (New York: Cambridge University, 1991).

rather it is to stress the *immanence* of the key dilemmas in the political economy of advanced industrial states that we explore to the *national economy*. A counterfactual thought experiment should illustrate our point. Imagine a one-country world, with a single central bank. We could easily envisage in such a world an alternation between inflation-fighting and growth regimes such as we describe, the one leading to a deflationary, and the other to an inflationary, dynamic. In our judgement this would hold true even if our hypothetical single country were endowed with a high level of institutional capacity, including centralized collective bargaining and the ability to implement incomes policies. The elimination of international economic and monetary relations would not remove the core policy tensions.

Of course in the real world the structure of international monetary relations does shape macropolicy formation within individual countries. To put it in Herr's terms, the fact that the international monetary system consists of a hierarchically structured set of national currencies with different store-of-value qualities is not irrelevant to the propagation of inflationary and deflationary impulses, nor to possibilities for establishing and preserving relative price-level stability and high employment and/or economic growth.

International constraints are hardest for the non-reserve currency nations when resisting the general direction of policy in the reserve centers exacerbates domestic monetary tensions. For example, the depreciation of sterling after 1931 and of the U.S. dollar after 1933 greatly augmented the difficulties facing the holdouts within the gold bloc, since it reduced the competitiveness of their exports on international markets and redoubled speculative challenges to their exchange parities. This in turn forced them to keep interest rates high and stimulated further price deflation. By way of contrast, central bankers in Germany and Switzerland welcomed the depreciation of the dollar against their currencies after 1973, since they wanted to raise interest rates in order to choke off domestic inflationary expectations. The same proposition holds true in reverse. Britain could tolerate the depreciation of its currency against the dollar between September 1931 and early 1933 with equanimity, since the higher prices it paid for dollar imports contributed to domestic reflation, which was desirable under the circumstances. For France in 1982–3, however, the depreciation of the franc against the mark and dollar merely exacerbated the domestic inflation problem. In sum, nations often can resist international monetary disorder emanating from the reserve centers, but only provided that they have their own houses in order.

Macropolicy Regimes and Financial Regulation

It is now time to turn our attention to the consequences of macroeconomic policy regimes and regime changes for selective micropolicies. Our analysis suggests that both deflation and inflation tend to disorganize financial systems in the long run: inflation produces a flight out of money, while deflation leads to hoarding. Indeed, the disorganization of financial markets is one of the crucial forces driving the macropolicy regime changes we describe. Consequently, the restructuring and re-regulation of financial markets has tended to follow major shifts in macropolicy orientation.

With the collapse of the gold standard between 1931 and 1936, financial openness lost its function as an anchor for domestic price level stability. The new macropolicy regime was compatible with a much greater degree of national financial isolation and with more extensive use of financial instruments in the implementation of selective micropolicies. However, the extent to which the change in macropolicy regime spilled over into microlevel regulation depended critically on a host of contingent national political and institutional factors. As a result a wide diversity in national regulatory systems developed. Moreover, the changes in regulation and micropolicy took place much more slowly than the change in macroregime; they usually involved complex legislation, which was often preceded by lengthy study and deliberation.

In the wake of the collapse of the gold standard, national policymakers faced two immediate assignments in the area of financial regulation. The first was to insulate domestic credit markets from international pressures, which had proved so deleterious under the gold standard. The dictatorships, which maintained their old gold parities at least nominally, adopted the most extensive systems of international financial regulation. Since their currencies became hopelessly overvalued, all international financial transactions were centralized in state agencies and tightly regulated. Trade was organized through bilateral clearings, much of it being negotiated on the basis of barter agreements rather than monetary transactions. Although the democratic nations remained committed to multilateral trade and payments, at least until World War II broke out, they too regulated currency markets and international financial transactions more tightly than before. Following the example of Britain, with its Exchange Equalization Fund, they created institutions that intervened on the exchange markets to manage the float of national currencies.

The second objective of financial regulation during the early 1930s, which is discussed at length by Forsyth and Kregel in their respective essays in this volume, was to deal with the wreckage of the banks and industrial firms that had collapsed during the Great Depression and to make similar bank failures less likely in the future. This was a particularly serious problem for continental nations with mixed or universal banking systems, which had proven particularly vulnerable during the economic downturn. Banking regulation and supervision was significantly expanded and reformed throughout much of Europe, and the regulatory structures set up in the 1930s remained in place with little modification until the 1970s. The exigencies of rearmament and war added additional layers of financial regulation, some of which would be stripped away and some of which would remain after the end of World War II.

In the aftermath of World War II, government planners defined an entirely new set of tasks for financial regulatory systems. As Pérez discusses in her essay in this volume, policymakers in France during the late 1940s and in Spain during the late 1950s made credit controls the centerpiece of national industrial policies designed to achieve economic modernization. The planners used their extensive controls over the national credit system to channel loans at below-market interest rates to selected firms and sectors. During the 1950s Norway and Sweden established similar controls over the banking system. In the case of the Nordic countries, however, credit rationing was used as an instrument of social policy, not industrial policy, with the main objective being the expansion of low-cost housing construction.

Since the 1970s there has been a broad trend toward liberalization of financial markets. Many of the controls set up during the 1930s have been modified or eliminated. We find it difficult to reduce all of these measures to a common denominator or to bring all of them into the analytical framework developed here. However, we do want to argue that at least one set of related changes in financial regulation across several European nations is directly related to the shift to a disinflationary macropolicy regime, namely, the dismantling of selective credit rationing systems.

Notermans and Pérez identify two major reasons for the collapse of administered credit systems since the 1970s: evasion and the high political costs of administering disinflation. Policymakers in all four of the countries that possessed such systems examined here—France, Spain, Norway, and Sweden—initially considered their extensive batteries of financial controls as useful weapons, certainly not hindrances, in the fight against inflation. By limiting credit expansion through the imposition of ceilings on new lending, these nations sought to brake monetary expansion without resorting to high interest rates, with their predictably depressive effects on economic activity. However, in all four countries evasion eroded the efficacy of financial controls. French and Spanish banks reacted to restrictions on their rediscounting facilities at the central bank by issuing new forms of debentures to raise money for their industrial clients. They thus created money without recourse to the central bank, defeating the efforts of the latter to control monetary aggregates. In Norway and Sweden, efforts to limit the growth of the money supply through the imposition of credit controls produced an explosion of lending on the part of nonbanking financial institutions that were not subject to credit controls and that had previously played a marginal role in national financial systems. Efforts to extend banking regulation to these institutions simply led to the proliferation of new varieties of nonbank financial institutions, offering ever more exotic financial products. In all four countries regulators concluded that the costs of enforcing controls that worked directly against market incentives were unacceptably high.[48]

The second problem facing the regulators was the political cost of imposing disinflation through the administrative machinery. Particularly in France and Spain, officials discovered that cutting back lending to firms and banks that had long maintained close relations with the state machinery was a painful proposition. It became clear that breaking inflationary expectations would require bankruptcies, restructurings, and layoffs; when politicians and administrators concluded that it was no longer possible to postpone dealing out this bitter medicine, they chose to do so through the more impersonal mechanism of high market interest rates, rather than rationing available credit on a case-by-case basis. Considerable differences in the structure of national banking systems have survived the shift to a disinflationary macropolicy regime; however, credit rationing systems appear to have become universally a casualty of the macropolicy regime change.

Macropolicy Regimes and Corporatism

The *de jure* or *de facto* abandonment of gold and the shift in macroeconomic policy, especially monetary policy, to promotion of economic recovery beginning in 1931 was supported by administrative measures undertaken to halt and reverse falling prices and wages. Three sorts of legislative initiatives were common to a large number of industrialized countries: (1) state promotion of producer cartels to stabilize the prices of

48. Notermans, "The abdication from national policy autonomy"; Pérez's essay in this volume. British authorities never tried to use credit controls as an instrument of selective micropolicy. However, after 1958 they did require the clearing banks to make special deposits as an instrument of credit control. As Kregel's essay in this volume points out, use of the "corset" encouraged the growth of a secondary credit market beyond the purview of the regulators—the same pattern of regulatory evasion discernable in the French, Spanish, Norwegian, and Swedish cases. The "corset" was abolished by the Thatcher government in 1980.

manufactured goods; (2) state promotion of agricultural marketing boards to stabilize prices and farm incomes; and (3) changes in labor legislation that facilitated the organization of trade unions and/or established minimum nominal wages.

In many nations, interventions designed to stabilize the prices of particular goods or the incomes of particular groups, notably farmers, occurred even before the gold standard was abandoned. For example, in much of continental Europe policymakers isolated national cereals markets behind high tariff walls and tried to stabilize farm income from the late 1920s on, even as they sought to drive down industrial wages and nonfarm prices and to maintain their exchange rate parities. This resulted in a mix of macro- and micropolicies with incompatible objectives, which in some cases endured for several years. In discussing this period of policy experimentation, Karl Polanyi aptly observed that: " ... in the struggle to retain it [the gold standard], the world had been unconsciously preparing for the kind of efforts and the type of organizations necessary to adapt itself to its loss."[49]

Policy initiatives to stabilize manufacturing and agricultural prices, farm incomes, and nominal wages required organization and coordination of the relevant interest groups. The manner in which interests were organized, notably the mix of state compulsion and associational autonomy, differed widely across nations, with the trade unions in particular faring very differently under dictatorships than under democracies. Still, we feel that it does not require too much forcing of the historical evidence to extend Bo Rothstein's characterization of the agricultural and labor policy initiatives in the early 1930s in Sweden as the "formative moment" of corporatism to the rest of Europe as well.[50]

It is of course clear that the emergence of organized interests long predated the Great Depression. This is certainly true of cartels. German industry was heavily cartelized already on the eve of World War I. The famous Reichsgericht (Supreme Court) decision of 1897 had made cartel agreements legally binding and enforceable in the courts. Elsewhere in Europe cartels had spread before 1914 as well, particularly in coal mining, iron and steel making, chemicals, armaments manufacturing, engineering, and sugar refining. Outside of Germany, cartel agreements rarely enjoyed legal sanction, but neither were they prohibited. The armaments boom during World War I tended to intensify interfirm cooperation in price-fixing, collective bargaining, and marketing. Many of these cartel-like

49. Karl Polanyi, *The Great Transformation: The Political and Economic Origins of Our Time* (Boston: Beacon, 1957), p. 27.

50. Bo Rothstein, "Explaining Swedish corporatism: the formative moment," *Scandinavian Political Studies* 15 (1992), no. 3, pp. 173–91.

agreements collapsed during postwar reconstruction, but the slow economic growth that characterized the years after monetary stabilization during the 1920s generally led to new efforts of manufacturers to reach agreements fixing prices, limiting output, and dividing markets. Under conditions of depressed domestic demand and intense international competition, however, it proved increasingly difficult to organize price-stabilizing agreements on a voluntary basis.

What was new about the Depression years was the degree of state involvement in promoting and enforcing cartel agreements, and the strikingly international character of the movement toward compulsory cartelization. Not only Nazi Germany (July 1933) and fascist Italy (June 1932) issued broad legislation authorizing the creation of compulsory cartels; even the British state, despite its strong laissez-faire traditions, imposed a compulsory cartel on the coal industry (1930) and played an active part in the cartelization of cotton, iron and steel, and shipbuilding in following years. Government-supported agreements in these sectors regulated output, prices, and market shares and used the proceeds of fees levied upon individual firms to purchase and scrap excess capacity. Tariffs and import quotas were introduced to bolster the cartels. Compulsory cartelization in the Netherlands, another nation with a long laissez-faire tradition, was envisaged by the Wet op het Verbindend Verlaren van Bedrijfsovereenkomsten in 1935. In France, legislation that would have given the government broad powers to organize and enforce compulsory cartelization was proposed twice, in 1932 and 1935, although neither of these bills ever became law. The second general cartel law was passed by the Chamber, but failed in the Senate. Nevertheless, French governments subsequently issued a series of decree laws that created compulsory cartels in individual industries, including sugar refining, potash, shoemaking, and fishing. Even the United States temporarily abandoned its traditional hostility to cartel-like arrangements by promoting business organization under the National Recovery Act in 1933.[51]

51. On German cartels, see Franz Neuman, *Behemoth: The Structure and Practice of National Socialism, 1933–1944* (New York: Harper, 1966), pp. 261–274 and *passim*; Schweitzer, *Big Business in the Third Reich*. On cartelization in Italy, see Felice Guarnieri, *Battaglie economiche fra le due guerre* (Bologna: Il Mulino, 1988), pp. 373–388 and *passim*. On Britain, see Sidney Pollard, *The Development of the British Economy, 1914–1980*, 3rd rev. ed. (Baltimore: Edward Arnold, 1983), pp. 98–107; George C. Peden, *British Economic and Social Policy: Lloyd George to Margaret Thatcher* (Oxford: Philip Allan, 1985), pp. 103–107; Steven Tolliday, *Business, Banking, and Politics: The Case of British Steel, 1918–1939* (Cambridge, Mass.: Harvard University, 1987); and R. Roberts, "The administrative origins of industrial diplomacy: an aspect of government-industry relations, 1929–1935," in J. Turner, ed., *Businessmen in Politics: Studies of Business Activity in British Politics, 1900–1940* (Exeter, N.H.: Heinemann, 1984), pp. 93–104; Samuel Beer, *Modern British Politics* (London:

Economic historians have generally taken an unfavorable view of cartelization during the 1930s. Franz Neumann's characterization of German cartels as a system of organized waste was accepted not just by American administrators during the postwar Occupation but also by most scholars subsequently. This is not the place to assess the microeconomic efficiency of cartels; however, if we assume that the immediate overriding problem facing national economies in the early 1930s was halting the collapse of nominal prices, and the disorganization of national economies that this created, as an emergency measure cartelization must be seen in a more favorable light.

Legislation to support agricultural prices and farm income was, if anything, even more pervasive than cartelization in manufacturing. It was often in this area that the trend toward state-sponsored corporatism first manifested itself; as was noted above, legislation protecting agriculture often preceded the abandonment of gold. For Rothstein the formative moment in the development of Swedish corporatism was June 1932, when a compulsory marketing board for milk was created and milk prices were fixed. He notes that the legislation in question was passed prior to the elections that swept the Social Democrats into power, where they would remain almost continuously for the next half century, hence also prior to the famous "cow trade" or alliance between Social Democrats and the Farmers' League (1933). Indeed, it was introduced by a government headed by the Liberals, and the bill was supported by Conservatives as well, in addition to the Farmers' League. Despite their longstanding opposition to state intervention in the economy, and particularly to compulsory regulation of markets, the Conservatives defended the bill in Parliament by arguing that the economic survival of the dairy farmers was at stake: "one must in some measure set one's misgivings in principle aside. Necessity trumps law."[52]

Necessity trumped laissez-faire traditions across Europe, and extensive regulation of the agricultural sector became the norm. In Britain, the Agricultural Marketing Act of 1931 allowed two-thirds of the producers of any agricultural commodity to prepare a scheme for organized marketing, including price maintenance. However, since this legislation did not give the marketing boards control over output and imports, it proved ineffective. The Agricultural Marketing Act of 1933 remedied these deficiencies: boards could now regulate output, and the government was authorized to support such schemes with tariffs or import quotas. Under

---

Faber and Faber, 1965). On France, see Alfred Sauvy and Anita Hirsch, *Histoire économique de la France entre les deux guerres* (Paris: Economica, 1984), vol. II, pp. 97–125.

52. Rothstein, "Explaining Swedish corporatism," p. 181.

the provisions of this act, milk, potato, and bacon and pig marketing boards were established. Meanwhile, the Wheat Act of 1932 gave farmers a guaranteed price, with taxpayers making up the difference between it and the market price.[53]

In France, too, the web of agricultural regulation gradually tightened during the 1930s. A law of 15 August 1936 created the Office national interprofessionnel du blé (later Office national interprofessionnel des céréales, or ONIC), which allowed the government to control prices, output, and imports. In Norway, marketing boards for eggs, vegetables, milk and butter, pork, meat, and fish were established between 1929 and 1937; the Netherlands regulated wheat, dairy products, pork, and agricultural imports between 1931 and 1933; in Italy the main agricultural products were thoroughly regulated by 1933.[54]

Shortly after it came to power, the Nazi regime in Germany created the Reichsnährstand (Reich Food Estate or RNS) to standardize markets and to fix prices through regional boards. The immediate impetus was the large harvest of 1933, which threatened to produce another round of falling prices. By 1935 the Nazis had discovered that the RNS apparatus was equally useful for keeping prices down in an expansionary macroeconomic climate, to the dismay of peasants who had earlier welcomed agricultural regulation.[55] Other measures widely adopted across nations to stabilize farm income included various forms of debt relief and credit subsidies.

Intervention in the markets for agricultural products and manufactures set an important precedent for labor-market legislation in the democratic countries. During the heyday of the gold standard, policymakers in many democratic countries tended to view trade unions as a cause of the crisis. Under the regime of fixed exchange rates, it was widely argued that economic adjustment was blocked because trade unions made nominal wages downwardly inflexible. Such views informed the labor policies of the Liberal-led coalition that governed Sweden until 1932; they influenced the Conservative government's policies during the coal miners' strike in Britain in 1926; and they lay behind Brüning's deflationary emergency decrees during the twilight of Weimar.

53. Peden, *British Economic and Social Policy*, pp. 102–3; Pollard, *The Development of the British Economy*, pp. 85–6.

54. Sauvy and Hirsch, *Histoire économique de la France*, vol. II, pp. 66–77; Guarnieri, *Battaglie economiche fra le due guerre*, p. 373 and *passim*; I.J. Brugmans, *Paardenkracht en Mensenmacht. Sociaal-economische Geschiedenis van Nederland 1795–1940* (Leiden: Martinus Nijhoff, 1983); Oistein Hveding, *Landbrukets Gjeldskrise i Mellomkrigstiden* (Oslo: Statens Lånekasse for Jordbrukere, 1982).

55. Harold James, *The German Slump: Politics and Economics, 1924–1936* (New York: Oxford University, 1986), pp. 355–7.

But once governments began organizing agricultural and industrial interests to stop the collapse of nominal prices, it was possible to take a more benign view of the role of trade unions. In the course of the 1930s, legislation strengthening the power of the unions was enacted in Scandinavia and the Low Countries. The Wagner Act of 1935 had a similar purpose in the United States. In France the Matignon Accords in June 1936 not only strengthened the unions but gave the state a central role in the collective-bargaining process. In Britain there was no important labor legislation during the 1930s, but the trade unions at least held their own, and the Treasury accepted the arguments that Keynes had made during the 1920s that efforts to force down nominal wages significantly in a democracy would prove counterproductive.

As was noted above, it was in the area of labor relations that the greatest cross-national variation in policymaking during the 1930s can be discerned, with the dictatorships and the democracies taking very different paths. Fascist Italy entered the Depression with a highly corporatist and highly repressive system of labor relations. Independent trade unions had been suppressed, and the fascist union federation had been given a monopoly on labor representation under the Palazzo Vidoni accords in 1925. During the "battle of the lira," Mussolini used the tight control these agreements gave him over labor markets, backed up if necessary by castor oil and the club, to roll back nominal wages substantially. Brüning's fourth emergency decree law of December 1931, which imposed both price cuts on cartels and across-the-board wage reductions, in effect transformed the "societal corporatism" of the Weimar Republic into something rather like the authoritarian "state corporatism" of fascist Italy.[56]

Thus the fascist or authoritarian variety of corporatism was first used to promote deflation, not reflation, and the adoption of these labor-market *institutions* must be seen as neutral in terms of our model of macropolicy regimes. However, the *goals* to which they were applied changed with the macropolicy regime change. After the Nazis came to power, they established a system of labor relations loosely modeled on the Palazzo Vidoni Accords. In May 1933 independent trade unions were abolished and all workers were forced to join the Deutsche Arbeitsfront. The macropolicy objective of the regime, however, was promotion of recovery, not deflation,

56. On fascist Italy's labor policies, see Adrian Lyttleton, *The Seizure of Power: Fascism in Italy, 1919–1929*, 2nd ed. (Princeton: Princeton University, 1987), esp. pp. 308–332; Vera Zamagni, "La dinamica dei salari nel settore industriale," in Pierluigi Ciocca and Gianni Toniolo, eds., *L'economia italiana nel periodo fascista* (Bologna: Il Mulino, 1976), pp. 329–378; Gianni Toniolo, *L'economia dell'Italia fascista* (Bari: Laterza, 1980). On the distinction between "authoritarian" and "societal" corporatism, see Phillipe Schmitter, "Still the century of corporatism," in Phillipe Schmitter and Gerhard Lehmbruch, eds., *Trends toward Corporatist Intermediation* (Beverly Hills: Sage, 1979), pp. 7–52.

and in May 1933 the regime also froze wages at current levels, terminating the long downward drift in nominal wages initiated by Brüning. Arthur Schweitzer reports that this measure had the particularly ardent support of small businesses in the less organized sectors, since

> Many employers suddenly discovered that unionized wage rates had put a floor under the prices of their products. They realized to their surprise and dismay that when, in a severe depression, union wage rates are abolished, wage rates do not decline only to a "natural" equilibrium rate.... Thus, instead of realizing an advantage from the abolition of unions, producers experienced extreme price competition in product markets.[57]

Fascist Italy in effect enlisted its wage-setting institutions to end the deflation in a similar manner. The final round of across-the-board wage cuts was undertaken in April 1934. Thereafter, nominal wages were held steady, while the fixing of manufacturing and agricultural cartel prices terminated the deflation. The rearmament boom associated with the Ethiopian War, 1935–6, brought about economic recovery. During the upswing, the German and Italian dictatorships used their extensive economic powers to keep both nominal and real wages from rising appreciably. The point that needs to be stressed here, however, is that in the absence of independent trade unions both dictatorships put a floor under nominal wages in order to brake the deflation.[58]

The most significant long-term changes in the relationship of the state to organized interests were in the areas of agricultural and labor-market policy. The trend toward cartelization in manufacturing, by contrast, was largely reversed after the end of World War II. The United States was probably the first nation to terminate its flirtation with organized capitalism. By 1935 the Supreme Court had already ruled the National Recovery Act unconstitutional, and with it legislative support for cartels. In postwar Europe U.S. officials were relentless advocates of free competition and anti-cartel laws. They used the leverage Marshall Plan aid gave them to promote the liberalization of inter-European trade, which in turn created an unfavorable environment for cartels. Powerful voices were raised in Europe too against the "economic Malthusianism" that had dominated the 1930s. Although organized markets persisted in some important economic sectors, the European Coal and Steel Community being the most significant example, in an era of rising prices and high economic growth

57. Schweitzer, *Big Business in the Third Reich*, pp. 400–401.

58. On Nazi labor policy, in addition to Schweitzer, see Tim Mason, *Sozialpolitik im Dritten Reich: Arbeiterklasse und Volksgemeinschaft*, 2nd ed. (Opladen: Westdeutscher Verlag, 1978); Tilla Siegel, "Lohnpolitik im nationalsozialistischen Deutschland"; Tilla Siegel, "Wage policy in Nazi Germany." On labor policy in the Italian recovery, see Guarnieri, *Battaglie economiche fra le due guerre*, pp. 431–2 and *passim*; Zamagni, "La dinamica dei salari."

cartels were widely viewed as impediments to innovation and productivity growth and were seldom given government support.[59]

In contrast, the highly regulated agricultural regime that came into being during the 1930s enjoyed a much longer life. Nearly all industrialized nations maintained an extensive battery of controls over their farm sectors, including trade restrictions, subsidies, and marketing boards. Agricultural protection was incorporated into the European Economic Community framework through the Common Agricultural Policy (CAP).[60]

The defeat of the fascist powers in the war brought about convergence in labor relations across Western Europe after 1945. The rights of trade unions were strengthened nearly everywhere, and union membership often reached historical highs. In Scandinavia, the Low Countries, and Austria, centralized wage bargaining was coordinated with macroeconomic policymaking for the first time.

The shift to a disinflationary macropolicy regime during the 1970s and 1980s has by no means led to the systematic reversal of the labor legislation and agricultural policies of the 1930s and 1940s. Conservative governments headed by Reagan in the United States and by Thatcher in Britain did attribute responsibility to the trade unions for the economic problems besetting their respective economies, and did take measures, including legislative initiatives, designed to weaken the power of organized labor. On the European continent, however, political leaders have largely avoided openly anti-union policies. Nevertheless, the high rates of unemployment produced by the shift to more restrictive macroeconomic policies have weakened the power of trade unions almost universally.

Macropolicy Regimes and Social Policy

The dramatic expansion of social security and welfare provision in Europe after World War II was supported by macroeconomic policies

59. On Germany's anti-cartel law, see Volker R. Berghahn, *The Americanization of West German Industry, 1945–1973* (New York: Cambridge University, 1986). For an excellent recent argument emphasizing the liberalizing aims of US economic policy in Europe, see J. Bradford De Long and Barry Eichengreen, "The Marshall Plan: history's most successful structural adjustment program," In Rudiger Dornsbusch, Wilhelm Nölling, and Richard Layard, eds., *Postwar Economic Reconstruction and Lessons for the East Today* (Cambridge, MIT, 1993), pp. 189–230. On the European Coal and Steel Community, see Alan Milward, *The Recontruction of Western Europe, 1945–51* (Berkeley: University of California, 1984); Alan Milward, *The European Rescue of the Nation-State* (Berkely: University of California, 1992), esp. 46–118; and John Gillingham, *Coal, Steel, and the Rebirth of Europe, 1945–1955: The Germans and French from Ruhr Conflict to Economic Community* (New York: Cambridge University, 1991).

60. Milward, *The European Rescue of the Nation-State*, pp. 224–317.

oriented toward growth and employment. Esping-Andersen has described the connection between macropolicy and welfare regimes in compelling terms:

> Perhaps the most salient characteristic of the social democratic [welfare] regime is its fusion of welfare and work. It is at once genuinely committed to a full-employment guarantee, and entirely dependent on its attainment. On the one side, the right to work has equal status to the right of income protection. On the other side, the enormous cost of maintaining a solidaristic, universalistic, and de-commodifying welfare system means that it must minimize social problems and maximize revenue income. This is obviously best done with most people working, and the fewest possible living off of social transfers.[61]

Moreover, the transfer payments associated with the welfare state and unemployment insurance tended to stabilize demand during economic downturns in postwar Europe. As we noted above, acceptance of Keynes's idea that recessions should be combatted by deficit spending was anything but universal in postwar Europe; nevertheless, even in the absence of widespread doctrinal conversion to Keynesianism, the built-in countercyclical features of unemployment insurance and other social transfer payments gave a countercyclical profile to fiscal policy.

The dovetailing of postwar macropolicies and social welfare policies allowed European nations to avoid the bitter experiences of Germany in 1930 and Britain in 1931, when efforts to defend the gold standard led officials to cut social welfare payments drastically, producing political crises. The collapse of the Great Coalition, the exit of the Social Democrats from government, and the transition to rule by emergency decree under Chancellor Brüning was produced by a funding crisis in Germany's unemployment insurance fund, the "jewel" of Weimar's welfare state.[62] Significantly, Hjalmar Schacht, Germany's central bank president, was one of the most influential advocates of fiscal austerity, believing that confidence in the exchange parity of the mark could be maintained only by drastic cuts in government spending.

A similar drama was played out in London in the summer of 1931, although the political consequences were less catastrophic. In Britain, too, a government containing representatives of the left was confronted in 1931, by its financial advisers, with the choice between defending the pound and making deep cuts in social spending, including unemployment benefits. The government fell, and the Labour party split over the issue, with most of its members going into opposition, although Ramsay

61. Gøsta Esping-Andersen, *The Three Worlds of Welfare Capitalism* (Princeton: Princeton University, 1990), p. 28.

62. The expression is Abraham's, *The Collapse of the Weimar Republic*, p. 233.

MacDonald, the Prime Minister, and Philip Snowden, his Chancellor of the Exchequer, chose to retain their positions and administer fiscal austerity in a new cabinet supported by the Conservative Party.[63]

It was obvious to the architects of the postwar expansion of the European welfare state that the reforms they advocated would require either a more expansionary international economic environment or the insulation of the domestic economy from international trade cycles and capital flows. Paul van Zeeland, the future Prime Minister of Belgium, wrote a book about this subject in 1935.[64] It was a leitmotif of British negotiators during their talks with American officials leading up to the Bretton Woods conference on the reconstruction of the international monetary system in 1944. During these talks, British newspapers openly speculated about the implications of American proposals for the revival of international trade and currency convertibility on the Beveridge Plan.[65] Such concerns reflected a tendency to make international monetary policy conform to domestic social and economic policy, and not the other way round. The outcome was a compromise, which John Gerard Ruggie has characterized as embedded liberalism:

> unlike the economic nationalism of the thirties, it would be multilateral in character; unlike the liberalism of the gold standard and free trade, its multilateralism would be predicated upon domestic interventionism.[66]

In other words, the imperatives of building and sustaining welfare states directly influenced macroeconomic policy debates and played an important role in the creation of a more flexible system of international monetary relations after World War II, in place of the gold standard.

Since the 1970s social welfare provision has come under attack in Europe for a variety of reasons, many of them not directly related to macroeconomic policy imperatives: the unresponsiveness of large public bureaucracies to the needs of their clients; the negative effects of government programs on the incentive structure of welfare recipients; the

63. The best account of the crisis of the Labour government led by MacDonald in 1931 may be L.P. Thompson-McCausland's unpublished typescript, "History of the 1931 Crisis," Bank of England, Historical Archive, G15/29 2504/5. See also Dianne B. Kunz, *The Battle for Britain's Gold Standard in 1931*.

64. Paul van Zeeland, *La crise de l-étalon-or: confrontation de sa forme classique avec les méthodes et les buts de l'économie contemporaine* (Paris, 1935), cited and discussed in Milward, *The European Rescue of the Nation-State*, pp. 340–1.

65. Richard N. Gardner, *Sterling-Dollar Diplomacy in Current Perspective: The Origins and the Prospects of Our International Order* (New York: Columbia University, 1980), pp. 95–6 and *passim*.

66. John Gerard Ruggie, "International regimes, transactions, and change: embedded liberalism in the postwar economic order," in Stephen D. Krasner, ed., *International Regimes* (Ithaca: Cornell University, 1983), pp. 195–231, cited passage on p. 209.

decline in national solidarity, and so forth. Moreover, to observe that in an era of slower economic growth taxpayers and voters have become less inclined to support programs that redistribute income to marginalized groups at the bottom of the social hierarchy is merely to state the obvious.

Nevertheless, some of the difficulties facing the contemporary welfare state can be traced directly to the macropolicy regime change. Even a relatively poor society may support social welfare provision that gives citizens the opportunity to withdraw from labor market participation under certain conditions (the decommodification of labor, in Esping-Andersen's terms) and that sustains demand during economic downturns if it is locked in a deflationary spiral or if past experience suggests deflation is a serious danger. Even a relatively wealthy society may seek to roll back social welfare programs that ratchet labor costs upward and that sustain demand during economic downturns, if fighting inflation becomes the primary goal of macroeconomic policy. With the shift to a disinflationary macropolicy regime in recent years, the compromise of embedded liberalism has broken down, and many of the policy dilemmas of the 1920s are re-emerging.

Some Conclusions: The Strengths and Limitations of the Macropolicy Regimes Concept

Deriving the full heuristic benefits of concepts in the social sciences requires that their limits and well as their explanatory potential be explored in detail. We have set out to demonstrate that many aspects of social and economic policymaking in the industrial nations of Western Europe since the early 1930s can be better understood within a single framework by examining the structural imperatives of macropolicy regimes. We have also suggested that macropolicy regime changes can be best understood as being driven by the imperative of maintaining an acceptable degree of price stability.

In the area of financial regulation, we have argued that the shift to a growth regime during the early 1930s opened up the possibility for much more extensive regulation on the micro level than had been the case under the interwar gold standard. Not all European nations chose to regulate extensively, however—Britain perhaps least of all. Among the nations that did develop extensive state controls over the financial sector, the timing and goals of intervention varied considerably. France and Spain developed credit-rationing systems in the late 1940s and late 1950s, respectively, in order to promote industrial modernization; Norway and Sweden developed similar credit controls during the 1950s to divert financial resources into housing construction. Other variables must be examined in order to explain differences in the uses of selective micropolicies across nations; several of the essays in this volume explore these differences and their causes.

We have also argued that the shift to a disinflationary macroregime in the 1970s and 1980s forced the dismantling of credit-rationing systems. Restrictive monetary policy conducted in isolation by the central bank proved a more effective means of achieving disinflation than administered and negotiated credit ceilings. We have also suggested that macroeconomic policy objectives were responsible for the dismantling of external financial controls in many nations. Once the traditional domestic arrangements for containing inflation began to fail, many European countries substituted an external anchor in the form of a fixed exchange rate with the German mark. But once containment of domestic inflationary pressures by means of an external anchor had become the main policy task, exchange controls, which had been explicitly designed to allow individual countries to pursue policies deviating from those of their neighbors, lost their rationale.

While the need to combat inflation forms the core rationale of the change in macroeconomic policy, as well as financial and labor market regulation, this is not to say that every initiative in these fields since the mid-1970s can be traced to macroeconomic policy imperatives. Despite the basic trend toward policy and regulatory convergence, significant cross-national differences remain, and explaining these differences falls outside of the framework proposed here. For example, the architects of Britain's Big Bang had other concerns, as Kregel's essay in this volume points out. Moreover, the liberalization of financial regulation has not led to convergence in national financial systems. The structure of corporate ownership, and the structure of the supply side of capital markets, particularly the role of institutional investors, account for persistent differences across nations. The origins and consequences of these differences are explored in the essays of Kregel and Vitols.

In the area of social policy, we have argued that the expansion and stability of the postwar welfare states required the adoption of growth-oriented macropolicies. The shift to a disinflationary macropolicy regime since the mid-1970s has put welfare states on the defensive everywhere. However, differences in the generosity and institutional foundations of welfare states persist, and our argument cannot shed much light on these national differences.

With regard to labor markets, we believe that the shift to growth-oriented policies strengthened the bargaining position of workers (after 1945, organized labor) everywhere. It constituted a necessary, but not sufficient condition for the high density of corporatist relations that developed in the Low Countries and Scandinavia. The recent shift to a disinflationary macropolicy regime has tended to undermine centralized collective bargaining and incomes policies.

We have built our argument in order to explain broad processes of policy convergence across nations during two periods of institutional and policy innovation. Significant differences in institutional capacity and policy orientation across nations survived both of the macropolicy divides we examine. Several of the contributions to this volume explore these differences; in order to do so they call upon additional variables.

A more significant limitation of our argument is that it does not explain fully the timing and causes of the deflationary and inflationary nominal price movements that triggered the policy changes we explore. We do not claim to have developed a comprehensive explanation for why the containment of inflation through microeconomic instruments failed during the 1970s and 1980s. Nor have we explained why the pre-1914 gold standard did not produce deflationary pressures as severe as those that developed beginning in the late 1920s.

It is important to add that we have proposed neither a comprehensive explanation for the Great Depression, nor for the long postwar economic expansion, nor for the downturn since 1973. We do hold the view that macropolicy orientation itself influences economic growth rates. However, a full account of long-term economic trends would require the study of a myriad of micro- and macroeconomic factors that lie well outside the scope of our project.

What we have sought to analyze are the circumstances under which policymakers have instituted macroeconomic regime changes, and the implications of these regime changes for other aspects of economic and social policymaking. We have argued that economic policymakers ultimately must give preference to price stability over other goals, including full employment and/or high economic growth and the preservation of fixed exchange rates. Our approach creates a single common framework, within which two sea changes in economic policymaking, in the 1930s and 1940s, and in the 1970s and 1980s, can be understood. We rest our case on the proposition that this framework yields valuable insights in its own right about the role of the state in the economy.

Acknowledgments

The authors would like to thank Marion Berghahn, Peter Hall, Hansjörg Herr, Harold James, Carl Kaysen, Jan Kregel, Arno J. Mayer, Paul Pitman, and Peter Temin for comments on earlier drafts of this essay.

Chapter 2

A Sea Change in Economic Governance Across Europe, 1931–1948

Douglas J. Forsyth

Introduction[1]

This essay discusses changes in the goals, instruments, and institutional setting of monetary policymaking and financial regulation in Britain, France, Germany/West Germany, and Italy between 1931 and 1948 (1957 in the case of West Germany). The collapse of the gold standard in 1931 set in motion an era of unprecedented change in monetary policymaking and financial regulation that continued through the Depression, war, and early postwar years. By 1948 a seventeen-year era of unprecedented innovation in financial regulation drew to a close in Britain, France, and Italy. The situation remained unsettled somewhat longer in West Germany, notably as a result of U.S. efforts during the Occupation after World War II to decentralize both the central bank and the major commercial banks. In Germany, therefore, it is necessary to take the story through 1957, when the central bank, the Deutsche Bundesbank, was rechristened and recentralized and Germany's three great universal banks, Deutsche Bank, Dresdner Bank, and Commerzbank, were reconstituted from the nine (initially thirty) constituent parts into which the American authorities had tried to divide them. With allowances for the peculiar conditions obtaining in

1. I would like to thank Monika Dickhaus, Harold James, Charles S. Maier, Ton Notermans, and Paul Pitman for commenting on earlier drafts of this essay.

Germany, it can be argued that the roughly seventeen-year era of institution-building and policy innovation was followed by thirty-odd years of remarkable stability in the institutional setting and basic orientation of monetary policy and financial regulation. As Sabino Cassese has observed, the financial institutions set up in the 1930s and 1940s enjoyed a long life; only within the last decade and a half have they been altered substantially.[2] This essay therefore is concerned with the forces driving change during a period of upheaval, experimentation, innovation, and institution-building, which was followed by a long era of stability and prosperity. Despite marked differences in monetary policy formation and financial regulation across nations, an attempt will be made here to understand diverse national experiences within a common analytical framework.

This transformation in policymaking is best understood as a set of first-order and second-order changes. The first-order changes consisted in the reordering of the goals of monetary policymaking and the instruments assigned to achieve them. Changes in monetary policymaking in turn created opportunities for, although they did not necessarily require, a set of second-order microeconomic changes in regulation of the financial sector, including tighter regulation and closer supervision of commercial banking; foreign exchange controls; selective credit controls; the nationalization of formerly private banks; the creation of new public financial institutions; and financial market segmentation. In all four countries, microlevel innovations in at least some of these areas were undertaken between 1931 and 1948. Moreover, all four countries adopted new statutes governing their central banks. Taken together, these changes represented a regulatory divide and created the preconditions for a major reordering of the role of the state in the economy.

The argument developed here rests on a particular view of the causes of Great Depression, and of the mechanisms of recovery from it, a view which has been proposed recently by Barry Eichengreen, Jeffery Sachs, and Peter Temin, among others. It can be briefly stated as follows: The Great Depression was caused by a cumulative deflationary dynamic, which in turn was an unintended consequence of the institutional logic of the interwar gold standard. The gold standard operated in an asymmetrical manner. Countries with balance of payments surpluses were under no obligation to expand domestic money supplies; instead, they also could allow foreign exchange reserves to accumulate at the central bank. Countries in deficit, however, were obliged to impose monetary

2. Sabino Cassese, "The long life of the financial institutions set up in the thirties," *Journal of European Economic History*, Special Issue on Banks and Industry in the Interwar Period, 13 (1984), no. 2, pp. 273–294.

contraction, usually through raising interest rates. This asymmetry created a cumulative deflation as the exchange rates of one country after another were challenged on the financial markets, forcing these countries to tighten monetary policy. Expectations of falling prices produced a collapse in investment and output and undermined the stability of national banking systems.[3]

Delinking from gold allowed policymakers to reorder the priorities of macroeconomic policy, permitting economic recovery. This process began in September 1931 when Britain abandoned its gold parity. Within a few months, by the spring of 1932, the British authorities took advantage of the relaxation of the external constraint to lower the Bank of England's discount rate, in stages, from 6 percent to 2 percent. This had the intended effect of stimulating a revival in investment and economic activity. Within six years most other advanced industrial nations, including the three countries discussed in this essay, followed Britain in *de facto* or *de jure* abandonment of gold and in reordering their macroeconomic priorities to promote recovery.

The object here is to explore the implications of the *economic* model outlined above for our understanding of the *political economy* of the Depression, war, and postwar years in comparative context. The argument proposed here is that the collapse of the gold standard marked the transition between two macropolicy regimes that can be distinguished across nations. The key differences between these two macropolicy regimes lay in the *goals* of monetary policy and in the *instruments* assigned to achieve these goals. The *gold standard regime* assigned primary importance, in the formulation of monetary policy, to maintenance of fixed exchange-rate parities; the main instrument assigned to achieve this task was manipulation of the discount rate. It was followed by a *growth regime*, which sought to combine high levels of output, employment, and growth with price stability and external balance. Under this regime, the impact of monetary policy upon growth and employment was never ignored. Microeconomic instruments, including direct controls on production and wages, rationing, voluntary incomes policies, voluntary restraints on bank lending, and financial controls, often were assigned the task of fighting inflation. The orientation of fiscal policy varied more widely across time and across nations. Since no common denominator in fiscal policy can be identified, it is essentially irrelevant

3. Barry Eichengreen and Jeffrey Sachs, "Exchange rates and economic recovery in the 1930s," *Journal of Economic History* 40 (1985), no. 4, pp. 925–946; Peter Temin, *Lessons from the Great Depression* (Cambridge, Mass.: MIT, 1989); Barry Eichengreen, *Golden Fetters: The Gold Standard and the Great Depression, 1919–1939* (New York: Oxford University, 1992); Barry Eichengreen, "The origins and nature of the Great Slump revisited," *Economic History Review* 45 (1992), no. 2, pp. 213–239.

for the definitions of macropolicy regimes proposed here. All four nations passed from the gold standard to the growth regime between 1931 and 1936.[4]

The process of micro re-regulation of national financial systems took much longer than the basic shift in monetary policy orientation. Changes in monetary policy created the preconditions for more extensive regulation of national banking systems and capital markets, but they did not require them. Financial regulation in the countries considered here was driven by several different motives. First, in Germany and Italy the Depression had produced major bank failures, and it was necessary to clear away the wreckage and reconstruct national financial systems. In all four countries, the difficulties of banks during the Depression induced the authorities to extend banking supervision and to redefine the lender-of-last-resort responsibilities of central banks in a more expansive sense. Second, since the primary or sole assignment of monetary policy was no longer achievement of external balance, foreign exchange controls were adopted to isolate national financial markets from international influences, which under the gold standard had limited national policy autonomy. On the domestic front, European nations also created new regulatory instruments to control the creation of commercial bank credit as alternatives to the use of interest-rate policy to fight inflation. Third, postwar planners utilized financial controls as key instruments of economic modernization programs and regional development policies.

Thus the lengthier process of financial re-regulation was the product of policy objectives that arose during and after World War II, as well as directly out of the Depression. It was the result of complex legislation, often preceded by lengthy study and debate. The objectives of financial re-regulation varied more widely across nations than the goals of monetary policy. National financial systems retained or acquired distinctive characteristics.

The four countries selected for study here were by no means unique with respect to the changes they undertook in monetary and financial policy orientation. Indeed, all of the advanced industrial nations, in North America and Japan as well as in Europe, passed through regime changes of the sort described above during the 1930s and 1940s. Britain, France, Germany, and Italy have been singled out for study here not because of their uniqueness but because of the author's regional specialization as a Europeanist and because their study is supported by his linguistic abilities. They also constitute the four largest economies and polities in Western Europe. Moreover, the significant differences that existed among these four nations

4. See also the essay by Forsyth and Notermans in this volume.

during the period in question—in political regimes and fortunes in war, in the specifics of macroeconomic policymaking, in the structure of national banking systems and capital markets, and in the processes of institution-building—afford a broad test in comparative perspective of the concepts of macropolicy regimes and regimes changes advanced in this essay and in the accompanying essay by Forsyth and Notermans.

Macropolicy Regimes

As was noted above, the argument set out here regarding institution-building and policy innovation during the 1930s and 1940s is predicated on the logical and temporal primacy of change in the orientation of monetary policy. It assumes that, beneath the diversity in macroeconomic policy formation across nations, two underlying regimes can be discerned; the shift from one to the other meant crossing a regulatory divide and redefining the role of the state in the economy.

Students of international monetary relations often define monetary regimes in terms of the rules, norms, and procedures governing international monetary policy. In these terms, the interwar gold standard can be characterized as a monetary regime. The Bretton Woods system of flexible fixed exchange rates that came into being after World War II would be another regime, according to this logic. The intervening years might be termed an era of chaos or a floating exchange-rate regime.[5] It is important to underscore that the distinction being made here is quite different. The core of the concept proposed here consists in the *goals* assigned to central bank policy and in the *instruments* employed to achieve these goals.[6]

The gold standard was a regime in this sense not because of the norms, rules, and procedures governing international monetary relations but because each nation adhering to gold made defense of fixed exchange rates the primary goal of monetary policy, and interest rate policy was the primary instrument assigned to achieve that goal. This argument also posits a fundamental unity in macropolicy orientation across nations after the collapse of gold, from the 1930s through the long postwar expansion.

Such unity may strike the reader as counterintuitive: the paths of exit from gold were many; the macroeconomic policy objectives of nations

5. John Gerard Ruggie, "International Regimes, Transactions, and Change: Embedded Liberalism in the Postwar Economic Order," in Stephen D. Krasner, ed., *International Regimes* (Ithaca: Cornell University, 1983), pp. 195–231; Robert O. Keohane, *After Hegemony: Cooperation and Discord in the World Political Economy* (Princeton: Princeton University, 1984); Michael D. Bordo and Forrest Capie, "Introduction," in Bordo and Capie eds., *Monetary Regimes in Transition* (New York: Cambridge University, 1994), pp. 1–12.

6. See the essay by Forsyth and Notermans in this volume.

beginning in the late 1930s were far from identical; twists and turns in monetary policy formation within individual nations occurred repeatedly; a variety of exchange-rate systems succeeded one another. The case for underlying continuity and for the existence of a transnational high-growth and -employment macropolicy regime will be made here by examining three issues. First, the exits from the gold standard will be considered. The four countries in question admittedly followed very different paths away from gold, and the ensuing economic recoveries occurred at different times and in different manners. Nevertheless, a common set of policy imperatives can be identified. Changes in the goals and instruments of monetary policymaking are the red thread that links various national experiences together. Second, the manner in which the four nations dealt with the monetary overhang produced by World War II will be explored. Despite considerable diversity in stabilization policies, none of these four nations blocked inflationary expectations after the war primarily through a restrictive monetary policy enforced through high interest rates, such as was followed after World War I (and once again after 1973). Third, the compatibility of Germany's postwar monetary policy with the growth-oriented macropolicy regime described in this essay will be examined. In contrast to Britain and France, which are often considered to have pursued growth- and full-employment-oriented macroeconomic policies after World War II, Germany is usually depicted in the literature as having pursued an inflation-averse, hard-currency strategy. The objective here is to show that even Germany's postwar monetary policy can be understood within the conceptual framework of the high employment/high growth regime.

Exits from Gold

This section describes briefly the very different paths by which the four nations abandoned gold and reoriented their macroeconomic policies to achieve recovery in output and/or employment. The object is not to provide detailed accounts of economic policymaking in the four countries concerned but merely to sketch in enough background information to permit the development of an argument about the common elements underlying these experiences.

Britain was the first of the four nations to abandon the gold standard and reorient monetary policy to the promotion of economic recovery. In April 1925 Britain had returned to its prewar gold parity. Like the other nations that pegged their currencies to gold in the 1920s, Britain hoped the metallic standard would provide an external anchor hindering price inflation. The decision to return to prewar parity, despite a significant rise in the domestic price level since 1914, was driven largely by the preoccupation with restoring London as an international financial center. Treasury and Bank of England officials recognized that a significant deflation would be necessary to bring British prices into line with those obtaining in other nations so that exports could recover and the current account could be brought into equilibrium. Their effort to encourage a rollback in nominal wages led to the government's confrontation with the miners' union in 1926 and an abortive general strike, but nominal wages proved remarkably resistant to downward pressures. Monetary policy remained relatively restrictive until the crisis of the pound in 1931, with nominal interest rates held exceptionally high in secular perspective. Unemployment stayed above 10 percent. In keeping with orthodox views on appropriate macroeconomic policy, budgets were balanced, at least until the onset of the Depression brought about an inevitable fall in revenues and increases in social transfer payments.[7]

The pound came under strong speculative pressure in the summer of 1931, following the banking crisis in Germany. The Bank encouraged the Labour government in office at the time to take drastic measures to cut the government's budget deficit in order to restore investors' confidence in sterling. Labour split over the issue in August, and a new national coalition was assembled, which included the fiscal conservatives within the Labour Party, Liberals, and Conservatives. The monetary policy followed by the Bank of England during the crisis year was less consistently orthodox. Bank rate was raised to 4.5 percent by summer, which may be considered rather high, given that the domestic economy was falling into a deep recession and the discount rate in New York was at 1 percent. The classical remedy for blocking an external drain, in any event, would have been to raise interest rates still higher. This the Bank of England declined to do, fearing that higher rates would have the opposite of the desired effect, panicking the markets and intensifying, rather than abating, the flight of capital from London. The Bank also hoarded its gold reserves in the crisis.[8]

7. D.E. Moggridge, *British Monetary Policy 1924–1931: The Norman Conquest of $4.86* (New York: Cambridge University, 1972); Susan Howson, *Domestic Monetary Management in Britain, 1919–38* (New York: Cambridge University, 1975); Sidney Pollard, *The Development of the British Economy,* 1914–1980, 3rd rev. ed. (Baltimore: Edward Arnold, 1983), pp. 98–107; George C. Peden, *British Economic and Social Policy: Lloyd George to Margaret Thatcher* (Oxford: Philip Allan, 1985).

8. R.S. Sayers, *The Bank of England, 1891–1944* (New York: Cambridge University, 1976); Dianne B. Kunz, *The Battle for Britain's Gold Standard in 1931* (New York: Croom Helm, 1987); L.P. Thompson-McCausland, "History of the 1931 Crisis," unpublished typescript, Bank of England, Historical Archive, G15/29 2504/5.

In late September the pound was floated. For the first few months after gold was abandoned, Treasury and Bank officials feared that depreciation would produce inflation, and raised interest rates to 6 percent. By the spring of 1932, however, the authorities decided that there was no significant inflationary danger. They took advantage of the relaxation of the external constraint to lower interest rates in order to encourage domestic economic recovery.

An Exchange Equalization Fund was established to manage the float of sterling; far from seeking to regain the old gold parity, when the pound began to rise on the markets again in 1932, Bank and Treasury officials applied downward pressure on the exchange rate, rebuilding their foreign-exchange reserves in the process. A multitude of trade restrictions were introduced, including tariff increases and import quotas for specific goods. Imperial preference created favored access to British markets for Commonwealth nations and the Empire. Nevertheless, British exchange and trade policy during the 1930s preserved a significant degree of openness and multilaterlism. This was reversed after the outbreak of war in 1939. Foreign-exchange controls were introduced in 1939, which effectively isolated the sterling area from the rest of the world. Trade was bilateralized.

But returning to the break with gold in the early 1930s once maintaining fixed exchange rates was no longer the overriding priority in macroeconomic policy formation, Bank and Treasury officials came to view a moderate reflation of nominal prices for commodities and manufactured goods as desirable. In conformance with this logic, the government broke with longstanding laissez-faire traditions by supporting compulsory cartelization and price-fixing schemes in industry and agriculture. Bank and Treasury officials now accepted that nominal wages could not be pushed downward without producing unacceptable levels of social conflict; however, they hoped that the recovery of prices would run ahead of wages, allowing real wages to fall. The national governments during the 1930s continued to pursue a conservative fiscal policy. They sought to contain budget deficits as much as possible in order to sustain business confidence and avoid crowding out private investment. These policies appear to have met with considerable economic success. In comparison with other nations, Britain recovered precociously from the Depression after 1932. The average rate of economic growth between 1932 and 1938, in fact, was not only higher than during the 1920s but also higher than during the Edwardian era. The one bleak spot in this picture was unemployment, which never fell below 10 percent prior to the rearmament boom at the very end of the decade.

Germany followed a very different path away from gold. The value of the German mark had been pegged to gold in 1924 as part of the stabilization measures taken to end hyperinflation. After stabilization, interest rates in Germany were held consistently above the levels prevailing in the reserve centers, New York and London. Since Germany ran a current-account deficit during most of the period it was on gold, high interest rates were necessary to attract foreign capital. Rigid reserve requirements (40 percent of the note circulation) were written into the Reichsbank's statutes in order to impose narrow limits on monetary expansion. State budgetary policy, at least at the federal level, was conservative. The Reichsbank was forbidden from making advances to the treasury. Through 1926 the Reich ran substantial budget surpluses; the reemergence of relatively small deficits as a result of the economic downturn beginning in 1928 created considerable anxiety among officials and politicians. In 1930 controversy over the budget deficit wrecked Weimar's Great Coalition and led to emergency rule under Chancellor Brüning. Brüning embarked on a determined program of budget cuts in order to eliminate deficits. In addition to his program of "fiscal deflation," Brüning sought to stabilize Germany's financial position by imposing a series of cuts in wages and cartel prices through emergency decrees.[9]

The first step in Germany's exit from the gold standard occurred in the summer of 1931 in the wake of a major banking crisis. The government imposed foreign-exchange controls and negotiated standstill agreements with Germany's creditors, which froze certain classes of foreign claims on German assets. Despite the relaxation of the external constraint created by these measures, the Brüning government renewed its efforts to force down the price level and balance the budget. Although Brüning and his two successors as Chancellor during the twilight of the Weimar Republic undertook isolated expansionary policies—subsidies to farmers, tax rebates to firms that hired new workers, the financing of modest public-works programs through rediscounts of bills issued by parapublic organizations with the central bank—they were not prepared to contemplate a dramatic reordering of the priorities of macroeconomic policy.[10]

A decisive change in macropolicy regime came only with Hitler's accession to power in January 1933. The Nazi Party had assigned great importance to achieving full employment. Within the first few months of Hitler's rule, the new government adopted a series of administrative measures designed to reverse price deflation. Agricultural marketing

9. Karl Erich Born, *Die deutsche Bankenkrise 1931: Finanzen und Politik* (Munich: Piper, 1967); Harold James, *The Reichsbank and Public Finance in Germany, 1924–1933: A Study of the Politics of Economics during the Great Depression* (Frankfurt a.M.: Knapp, 1985); Knut Borchardt, *Perspectives on Modern German Economic History and Policy* (New York: Cambridge University, 1991), pp. 143–203.

10. See Peter Temin's brief but excellent discussion of German monetary policy in *Lessons from the Great Depression*, pp. 100–103.

boards were established that fixed minimum prices for farm products. State support was extended for compulsory cartelization and price-fixing schemes. Wages were frozen at current levels (i.e., further reductions were blocked) following the destruction of independent trade unions. Once the price level ceased to fall, and showed signs of moving upwards again, these same administrative tools were used to keep inflation in check.

External balance was secured by tightening exchange controls and centralizing international payments under government supervision. Commercial agreements bilateralized trade in subsequent years. Credit controls were instituted, and interest rates were set at below-market rates, creating a credit queue. Monetary and fiscal policy were reoriented toward financing the government's work-creation programs and later rearmament. In order to disguise the extent of departure from orthodoxy in the formulation of fiscal policy, the Nazi government adopted the system of "soundless" finance (geräuschlose Finanzierung). This consisted in the expansion of a practice introduced in the final phase of the Weimar Republic, whereby parapublic agencies issued paper eligible for rediscount at the central bank. State budget deficits appeared to be manageable, and the expansion of note circulation appeared to be the result of an increase in self-liquidating commercial credit. Minimum gold- and foreign-exchange reserve requirements for the central bank were suspended.[11]

Thus under the Nazis monetary and fiscal policy were reoriented to promote recovery of output and employment, and later rearmament. Inflation was kept in check with microeconomic instruments, notably wage and price controls. External balance was secured by controls on trade and international payments.

Like the British, the Italians returned to gold (in 1927) at an exchange parity that deliberately overvalued their currency for prestige reasons. Unlike the British, the Italians had a set of microeconomic instruments at their disposal that allowed them to force the level of prices and wages downward effectively. Among these instruments were castor oil and the club. In effect, the fascist government used its dictatorial powers to force across-the-board reductions in wages and prices. Gianni Toniolo aptly has characterized these measures as the only original contribution of fascism to economic theory and practice.[12]

11. Harold James, *The German Slump: Politics and Economics, 1924–1936* (New York: Oxford University, 1986); Arthur Schweitzer, *Big Business in the Third Reich* (Bloomington: Indiana University, 1964); Eckhard Wandel, "Das deutsche Bankwesen im Dritten Reich (1933–1945)," in Ernst Klein, et al., *Deutsche Bankengeschichte*, vol. 3 (Frankfurt a.M.: Knapp, 1983).

12. Gianni Toniolo, *L'economia dell'Italia fascista* (Bari: Laterza, 1980), p. xii and *passim*; Franco Cotula and Luigi Spaventa, "Introduzione," in Cotula and Spaventa, eds., *La politica monetaria tra le due guerre, 1919–1935*, Collana storica della Banca d'Italia, Serie

Even the fascists found it difficult to deal with erosion in the stability of Italy's major commercial banks under the impact of debt deflation, however. In the course of 1930–32 the Banca d'Italia tied up most of its resources in the rescue of the country's banking system. Fortunately, the extent of these operations limited the Bank's ability to impose further monetary contraction on the economy.[13]

Fascist Italy was remarkable among the four countries considered here in that the reorientation in macroeconomic policy was not driven primarily by a desire to promote economic recovery or reduce unemployment. Unlike their Nazi counterparts, the Italian fascists did not believe their legitimacy or authority rested upon their ability to overcome the Depression. Rather, a consistent reversal in macropolicy occurred in December 1934 or January 1935 only as preparations for the Ethiopian War got underway. In Italy, more than anywhere else, rearmament drove recovery, and it did so from the very beginning.

From the time of the banking crisis until preparations for war got underway in earnest, the government pursued contradictory policies. On the one hand, the regime continued to exert downward pressure on wages and salaries through April 1934, when the last round of administrative cuts were announced. A growing balance-of-payments deficit after the British devaluation in September 1931 was countered by higher tariffs and trade controls. Italy's imports were forced down to the level of its steadily diminishing foreign-exchange earnings. On the other hand, beginning in 1931–32, the government promoted the formation of compulsory manufacturing cartels and agricultural-marketing boards in order to stabilize prices in various sectors.[14]

After serious preparation for the Ethiopian War commenced, the contours of the new macropolicy regime emerged with greater clarity. No further attempts to depress wages were undertaken. Budget deficits were tolerated. In December 1934 foreign-exchange controls were imposed, removing the external constraint on monetary policy. Italy abandoned the gold standard formally only in October 1936, a week after the devaluation

---

documenti, vol. VIII (Bari: Laterza, 1993), pp. 1–206; Jon S. Cohen, "The 1927 revaluation of the lira: A study in political economy," *Economic History Review*, 2nd Series, 25 (1972), no. 4, pp. 642–654; Roland Sarti, "Mussolini and the Italian industrial leadership in the Battle of the Lira 1925–7," *Past and Present* 47 (1970), pp. 97–112; Renzo De Felice, "Lineamenti politici di quota 90," *Nuovo Osservatore* 50 (1966), pp. 374–376.

13. Gianni Toniolo, ed., *Industria e banca nella grande crisi 1929–1934* (Milano: Etas Libri, 1978); Douglas J. Forsyth, "The rise and fall of German-inspired mixed banking in Italy, 1894–1936," in Harold James, Håkan Lindgren, and Alice Teichova, eds., *The Role of Banks in the Interwar Economy* (New York: Cambridge University, 1991), pp. 179–205.

14. Felice Guarnieri, *Battaglie economiche fra le due guerre* (Bologna: Il Mulino, 1988).

of the French franc, but it had ceased acting according to the logic of the gold standard much earlier.

France was the last of the four countries considered here to stabilize its currency (in 1928) and the last to abandon the gold standard regime. Reluctance to abandon gold was no doubt strengthened by the prolonged monetary and financial instability that had characterized the French economy prior to the stabilization of the exchange rate, and by the comparatively favorable economic conditions that prevailed after the return to gold.[15] In contrast to the British and Italians, the French chose a gold parity that undervalued their currency. Consequently, after 1928 France ran a large current-account surplus and accumulated formidable gold reserves. The favorable external situation allowed the Banque de France to keep its discount rate at comparatively low and steady levels during a period in which Bank of England was very much "under the harrow," in the words of its governor. To be sure, monetary policy in France was conducted according to classical tenets after the stabilization. Émile Moreau, the governor of the Banque de France, described the role of his institution in the following terms: "It is the monetary function: to assure at all times the convertibility of the bank note into gold—the common base of all credit. The other roles are, to my mind, of secondary importance."[16] Fiscal policy was equally orthodox. France ran budget surpluses from 1926 through fiscal 1929/30. Indeed, if one takes into account the Caisse d'amortissement, a sinking fund set up to retire government debt, the budget did not fall consistently into deficit until 1933.[17]

During the early 1930s, the Depression caught up with France. Economic output declined after June 1930. Declining output had the usual effect of depressing government revenues and increasing social-transfer outlays. Successive French governments mounted valiant efforts to balance budgets but failed to keep up with the downward spiral in revenues. As other nations devalued, the franc became overvalued, reducing France's share of export markets, which were declining anyway because of the general contraction of economic activity, rising tariffs, and the imposition of other trade restrictions worldwide. More importantly, after the devaluation of the dollar in 1933, gold began flowing out of France, forcing the Banque de France to raise interest rates, particularly in 1935–36. Perhaps inspired

15. Kenneth Mouré, *Managing the Franc Poincaré: Economic Understanding and Political Constraint in French Monetary Policy, 1928–1936* (New York: Cambridge University, 1991), pp. 274–80. Mouré identifies a number of additional factors; the two mentioned here seem decisive.

16. Émile Moreau, *Souvenirs d'un Gouverneur de la Banque de France. Histoire de la stabilisation du franc (1926–1928)* (Paris: Génin, 1954), p. 170, quoted in Mouré, *Managing the Franc Poincaré*, p. 122.

17. Mouré, *Managing the Franc Poincaré*, p. 160.

by the Duce and Chancellor Brüning, Prime Minister Pierre Laval sought and obtained emergency decree powers in June 1935 to impose sweeping price and wage cuts. At the same time, Laval launched a program of public works to create employment, contradicting his efforts to lower prices.[18]

The policy incongruence that emerged during Laval's government was reinforced after the Popular Front took office in May 1936. Léon Blum's government announced its intention to pursue an ambitious social agenda and stabilize farm income. The sit-down strikes in the metalworking firms surrounding Paris and the Matignon Accords between employers and workers brokered by the Prime Minister on 7 June 1936 implied substantial raises in nominal wages. Throughout the spring and summer, Blum reiterated his opposition to a devaluation of the currency, despite the fact that the rest of his economic program was in full conflict with his exchange-rate policy. An acceleration of the external drain ensued, and in September 1936 France devalued. Following the devaluation, interest rates were lowered and monetary policy was assigned the task of promoting domestic economic recovery. Government support for compulsory cartelization and price-fixing schemes in some manufacturing sectors and in agriculture was intensified and was used consistently to keep prices from falling.[19]

As this brief discussion indicates, not only were the defections from gold in the four countries considered here spread over six years; significant variation characterized the policies these countries followed after leaving gold. Perhaps the most important differences divided the two democracies from the two dictatorships. From the time they left gold until the outbreak of World War II, Britain and France remained committed to at least a degree of multilateralism in trade and payments. Germany and Italy, in contrast, imposed tight controls on foreign-exchange transactions and conducted their trade within bilateral agreements. The two dictatorships also imposed far more extensive controls on their domestic economies, including forced savings requirements for individuals, firms, and financial institutions, and extensive wage and price controls. After the outbreak of war, in any case, the French and British emulated their fascist opponents in imposing pervasive controls on domestic and international financial flows.

But even prior to the outbreak of war, there was a good deal of common ground in the responses of all four countries to the Great Depression. At some point under the interwar gold standard, each of the four countries had sought to depress the general price level through monetary contraction and

18. Ibid., pp. 178–83.

19. Ibid., pp. 237–73; Alfred Sauvy and Anita Hirsch, *Histoire économique de la France entre les deux guerres* (Paris: Economica, 1984), vol. II, pp. 97–125.

fiscal retrenchment, supplemented in the three continental nations by administrative measures calling for blanket price- and wage-cuts. After breaking with gold, all four nations used administrative measures, including agricultural-marketing boards and compulsory cartelization to break the downward drift of prices. After breaking with gold, all four undertook a reorientation of monetary policy away from defense of fixed exchange rates to promotion of recovery of output and/or employment. Germany and Italy used microeconomic instruments—wage and price controls—to fight inflation beginning in the mid-1930s; Britain and France followed suit during the war.

Differences in fiscal-policy orientation were much greater. Until the eve of World War II, Britain sought to avoid large budget deficits in order to maintain investors' confidence in sterling and the economy. France, Germany, and Italy tolerated budget deficits, although the latter two nations, in particular, sought to conceal their size through suppression of published information about public accounts and through various forms of financial legerdemain.

Coping with Postwar Monetary Overhangs

The manner in which policymakers dealt with postwar monetary overhangs is an important test case for the macropolicy regimes concept put forward in this essay and elsewhere in this volume. The macropolicy regime changes described above, 1931–36, occurred in response to a prolonged deflation. In the aftermath of World War II, in contrast, policymakers throughout Europe faced significant inflationary pressures. All of the European belligerents, to some degree, had financed the war effort by running the printing presses. Moreover, the mobilization of industry to produce armaments resulted in a dearth of consumer goods, which was destined to persist until production could be reoriented from military to civilian needs. On the continent these difficulties were exacerbated by the destruction and disruption of economic activity wrought by the fighting, which caused production to fall far below prewar levels. In brief, at the end of the war all four countries discussed here had to cope with significant monetary overhangs, that is, accumulated purchasing power far in excess of available goods. Insofar as the authorities allowed the monetary overhang to express itself as open inflation, it threatened to produce a wage-price spiral with a cumulative dynamic.[20]

20. On postwar monetary overhangs, see Rudiger Dornbusch and Holger Wolf, "Monetary overhang and reforms in the 1940s," *National Bureau of Economic Research Working Papers* no. 3456 (1990).

In its essential respects, the situation policymakers confronted was analogous to conditions after World War I. What is striking, however, is how differently the authorities reacted after the end of World War II. Following World War I, one government after another embraced the orthodox financial doctrine of balanced budgets and monetary contraction, the latter brought about by a dear-money policy on the part of the issue banks, as the cure for inflation. Britain acted as trailblazer on this path to monetary stabilization. The British government began running budget surpluses in the second half of 1919, and the Bank of England shifted decisively to a policy of dear money in November 1919, when the discount rate was raised from 5 percent to 6 percent; when inflation continued, it was raised to the unusually high level of 7 percent in April 1920. Although observers in subsequent years widely concurred in attributing to these policies the deep recession that gripped Britain following the break in world raw-materials and shipping prices in the summer of 1920, officials at the Bank and the Treasury at the time were convinced of the soundness of their actions, particularly in light of the persistence of inflation and other symptoms of monetary disorder on the continent.[21]

Continental policymakers initially were reluctant to submit to the stern medicine taken by their English counterparts. Some of them were more inclined to attribute the postwar inflation to supply problems rather than to lax monetary and fiscal policies. Among them was Francesco Saverio Nitti, minister of the treasury in Italy from 1917 to 1919, and prime minister from 1919 to 1920. Nitti argued that a return to orthodox monetary and financial policy prior to the recovery of production and trade would be impossible. He wanted to continue the wartime regime of rationing and of controls on wages and prices to restrict purchasing power during a transition period, during which output would be allowed to recover. Similar views were held in France by Etienne Clémentel, the Minister of Commerce, and in Germany by Walter Rathenau, the Reconstruction Minister, and Wichard von Moellendorf, Undersecretary of Economics. Nitti and Clémentel also hoped that generous credits from Britain and the United States would be forthcoming for continental nations until their traditional sources of foreign-exchange earnings had recovered. But the proponents of a planned economy were frustrated. Not only did the Anglo-Americans wind up financial assistance to their continental allies quickly after the armistice; but throughout the continent there was massive opposition on the part of interest groups and public opinion to the continuation of rationing and other wartime controls. The rapid dismantling of these microeconomic instruments left them with

21. Susan Howson, "The origins of dear money, 1919–1920," *Economic History Review*, 2nd Series, 26 (1974), no. 1., pp. 88–107.

few alternatives to monetary and fiscal policy to fight inflation. This experience would serve as a lesson to policymakers after World War II, when wage and price controls and rationing were widely retained.[22]

The abolition of direct controls did not rule out the use of credit rationing as an alternative to dear money as an instrument for blocking monetary expansion and inflation. This was indeed an alternative that tempted many continental central bankers struggling to cope with inflation after World War I. At the Brussels Monetary Conference in September-October 1920, G. Vissering, the head of Netherlands Bank argued, against the views of the Bank of England's representative at the conference, that dear money was a blunt instrument for curbing price inflation. It would act, he believed, as a "burden upon legitimate productive undertakings."[23] Vissering favored combining selective controls on credit expansion with low interest rates: money would be kept cheap, but priority would be given to borrowers who could increase rapidly the supply of vital goods.

Many continental issue banks had acquired considerable experience in the use of informal credit rationing before the Great War. They had been more reluctant than the Bank of England to use changes in the discount rate as the normal instrument of monetary management. Interest-rate changes were kept in reserve to respond to major crises, such as large gold outflows. Selective credit rationing, that is, varying the criteria for loans and rediscounts as a means of influencing the total volume of the issue bank's lending portfolios and hence general credit conditions, was used as a more subtle instrument for intervention on the money markets.

A number of continental nations tried credit rationing, in the manner advocated by Vissering, in order to stop postwar inflation. Among them was Italy in 1920–21. In the short run, the Italian policy was successful; the money stock in Italy ceased expanding in 1920 and even contracted mildly over the next two years. Prices fell back.[24] However, inflation and monetary growth resumed in 1922, and after Mussolini's Pesaro speech in July 1925 the authorities resorted to dear money as the chief domestic instrument in their effort to establish "quota 90" as the lira's fixed gold parity. Sooner or later, policymakers throughout the continent, including Vissering and the Italians, came around to the British point of view. Budget

22. On Nitti, see Douglas J. Forsyth, *The Crisis of Liberal Italy: Monetary and Financial Policy, 1914–1922* (New York: Cambridge University, 1993), esp. pp. 178–82, 199, 230–2, 239, 270; on Clémentel, see Marc Trachtenberg, "A new economic order: Etienne Clémentel and French economic diplomacy during the First World War," *French Historical Studies* 10 (1972), no. 2, pp. 315–341; on Rathenau and Moellendorf, see Gerald Feldman, *The Great Disorder: Politics, Economics, and Society in the German Inflation, 1914–1924* (New York: Oxford University, 1993), esp. pp. 80, 88, 113–5, 126, 132–3, 137–41, 143–5, 148, 155–6.

23. Quoted in R.S. Sayers, *The Bank of England*, vol. I, p. 154.

24. Forsyth, *The Crisis of Liberal Italy*, pp. 135–8, and *passim*.

deficits and cheap money apparently produced uncontrollable inflation and, if carried to extremes, as the German experience in 1922–23 seemed to indicate, even hyperinflation. Monetary stabilization in all three continental countries considered here—in Germany in 1924, in France in 1924–27, in Italy in 1925–27—was accomplished with dear money.

Although the four countries discussed here pursued very different policies in dealing with their monetary overhangs after World War II, the rejection of dear money as the primary policy instrument for checking inflation, and the preoccupation with avoiding a protracted deflation and a deep recession, are common denominators. Everywhere there was a determination to avoid what were now perceived to be the mistakes of the 1920s.

In Britain, a National Debt Enquiry (committee) was set up in early 1945 to consider monetary and financial policy during a transitional period that was expected to follow the war. The committee assumed that a recession would follow a boom about two years after the end of hostilities, much as had been the case after World War I. Among the committee members was John Maynard Keynes. Keynes himself had been a "dear money man" in 1920 but he now felt that nominal interest rates had to be held steady and at low rates after the war to guard against deflation, recession, and unemployment. During the postwar boom, inflationary pressures could be repressed by keeping wartime controls in place:

> all controls—rationing control, raw material control, new issue control, bank credit control and high taxation control must be retained in principle for a period of at least two years and only gradually relaxed as and when consumer goods become available in greater quantities.
>
> If the vast bulk of purchasing power which must necessarily exist at the end of the war, is released in psychological conditions necessarily surrounding the end of the war, the result cannot be different from what it was in 1919 to 1921.[25]

Keynes's argument that excess purchasing power should be blocked until supply caught up with demand echoed Nitti's arguments in 1920. The difference was that after World War II British officials held on to the regulatory instruments that had been dismantled so quickly after World War I. The continuation of rationing, combined with price controls, kept inflation for essential items in check. In exchange, the trade unions exercised wage restraint. Moral suasion exercised by the Bank of England on the commercial banks restrained the growth of bank credit. Britain tried

25. Note by Keynes, 7 January 1942, quoted in Susan Howson, *British Monetary Policy, 1945–51* (New York: Oxford University, 1993), p. 43. Keynes put forward similar ideas in his papers for the National Debt Enquiry in 1945. See Howson, *passim*. On Keynes as a "dear money man" in 1919–20, see Susan Howson, "'A dear money man'?: Keynes on monetary policy, 1920," *Economic Journal* 83 (1973), pp. 456–64.

to use controls on international trade and capital flows to supplement its domestic anti-inflationary policy instruments. However, U.S. insistence that sterling convertibility be restored as quickly as possible (by 1947) and the demands of Commonwealth nations, colonies, and other friendly nations that the sterling balances that they had accumulated in wartime be unblocked as quickly as possible made these instruments less effective that the British would have liked. In addition to controls and wage constraints, the authorities used fiscal policy to fight inflation. Wartime tax policy was structured to allow the government to dose the release of purchasing power after the end of hostilities; taxpayers accumulated credits, which the government gradually unblocked as the supply of consumer goods expanded. Beginning in fiscal 1947/48, the government modulated the size of budget surpluses to match aggregate demand with available resources.[26]

Monetary policy, in contrast, was rather expansionary. Postwar interest rates were extremely low. The Bank of England's discount rate had been set at 2 percent (historically the lowest level for bank rate) during most of the war, and the yields on long-term treasury securities were not allowed to climb above 3 percent. In 1945–47 Hugh Dalton, Chancellor of the Exchequer in the Labour government, tried, albeit unsuccessfully, to drive interest rates even lower. But even after the failure of Dalton's "cheaper money" policy, bank rate was held at 2 percent, and market quotations for long-term treasury securities were not allowed to climb above net yields of 3.75 percent until 1950. Monetary expansion was rather brisk during Dalton's tenure at the Treasury; it slowed considerably after that, despite the fact that nominal interest rates remained very low. Despite the accommodative monetary policy, the rise in retail prices was held to 4.4 percent annually between 1945 and 1950.[27]

After the Tory electoral victory in October 1951 (and following renewed inflationary pressures after the outbreak of the Korean War), R. A. Butler, the new Chancellor of the Exchequer, announced the "return to the prewar use of a flexible monetary policy." Bank rate was brought up to 4 percent in March 1952. However, even under the Conservatives, employment and growth continued to be taken into account, along with inflation and external balance, in the formulation of monetary policy. There may have been a return to a flexible monetary policy in 1952, but there was scarcely a return to dear money.[28]

Germany's postwar monetary overhang was considerably greater than Britain's, and its strategy for dealing with it, that is, a monetary reform

26. Howson, *British Monetary Policy, 1945–51*.
27. Ibid., p. 156 and *passim*.
28. Ibid. Butler is cited on p. 9.

that involved a currency exchange and a write-off of most assets and financial claims in the old currency, correspondingly drastic. However, a common element linking British and German policy was the concern to avoid macroeconomic policies that would lead to deflation and recession.

This concern already was expressed in Ludwig Erhard's famous memo of February 1944, an early and influential plaidoyer for monetary reform. The future Economics Minister observed that the Reich's debts, which already exceeded 300 percent of national output and had been monetized by the central bank to a significant degree, could never be funded in a normal manner. But open hyperinflation, in his judgement, could be avoided by currency reform. Erhard argued that the highest priority in carrying out a reform should be the recovery and growth of the German economy.[29]

In this respect, at least, the monetary reform implemented under Allied military government in June 1948 fully conformed to Erhard's vision. The elimination of the monetary overhang through a write-off avoided many of the undesirable macroeconomic consequences both of dear money and of hyperinflation. If dear money generally favors creditors over debtors and reduces demand by diminishing both investment and consumption, the redistributive impact of the German currency reform of 1948 had exactly the opposite effects. As Henry Wallich put it, the monetary reform

> made few concessions to social equity. No great effort was made to temper the economic wind to shorn creditors and savers.... The counterpart of the toughness of the reform was the aid it gave to the active forces of the economy. It raised production incentives by keeping down the burden of carrying the unproductive part of the population—pensioners, owners of savings, old people, people unable to fend for themselves. By wiping slates clean it favored entrepreneurs, businessmen and debtors at the expense of fixed-income receivers and creditors.[30]

Under the terms of the reform, the debts of the former Reich government, other state agencies, and the Nazi Party were declared void. Most other assets and claims denominated in Reichsmarks were converted into the new currency at a ratio of 100:6.5., above an allowance of DM 60 per person. DM 40 of this allowance was paid out immediately, while the rest was temporarily blocked. Wages, salaries, state pensions, and rents were

29. Ludwig Erhard, *Kriegsfinanzierung und Schuldenkonsolidierung. Faksimiledruck der Denkschrift von 1943/44* (Frankfurt a.M.: Propyläen, 1977). See the brief but excellent discussion of Erhard's memo in Christoph Buchheim, "Die Währungsreform 1948 in Westdeutschland," *Vierteljahrsheft für Zeitgeschichte* 36 (1988), no. 2, pp. 189–231.

30. Henry C. Wallich, *Mainsprings of the German Economic Recovery* (New Haven: Yale University, 1955), p. 71–2.

converted on a 1:1 basis. The Allies left it to the new German government to draw up legislation compensating savings bank depositors, private-pension holders, and various other groups injured by the currency reform, and to levy the necessary taxes to fund the compensation scheme.[31]

Following the currency reform, the monetary authorities in Germany had to contend with significant inflationary pressures on two occasions, in late 1948/early 1949 and once again beginning in the second half of 1950, after the outbreak of the Korean War. On both occasions, the Bank deutscher Länder (BdL), the new central bank set up under the Allied military authority, used credit rationing, not dear money, as the primary instrument to restrain monetary growth.

The first significant spurt of inflation occurred just six months after the currency reform. The immediate impact of the reform was a dramatic improvement in the economy. The new currency was accepted, and dis-hoarding of goods took place, producing a spurt of economic growth. Prices rose briskly, too, however. By the end of the year, industrial raw materials had increased 26 percent, producers' prices 14 percent, retail food prices 18 percent, and clothing 35 percent. Sellers began to withhold goods from the market again in anticipation of additional price increases; the currency reform threatened to unravel. In contrast to prices, nominal wages remained relatively stable, an important anchor for the currency reform but also a source of growing social discontent. The main causes of the inflation were the unblocking of additional RM assets according to the terms of the reform and the rapid expansion of bank credit, from virtually zero.

The BdL held bank rate steady at 5 percent, the level obtaining at the time of the currency reform. Instead, Germany's central bank took three steps to brake inflationary expectations: it increased reserve requirements for commercial banks from 10 percent to 15 percent; it refused to discount bank acceptances (as opposed to rediscounts) except for a few specific purposes; and it requested that commercial banks limit their total loan volume to the level of 31 October 1948.

The policy was not particularly restrictive. The credit ceilings were lifted in March 1949, and the restrictions on the rediscounting of acceptances were terminated in May. The discount rate was cut, in stages, to 4 percent between May and July; by September reserve requirements were restored to their original level. During the fifteen months of disinflation, from January 1949 to March 1950, the money supply continued to expand. Economic growth slowed from the levels achieved immediately after the

31. In addition to Buchheim and Wallich, on the German currency reform see also Eckhard Wandel, *Die Entstehung der Bank deutscher Länder und die deutsche Währungsreform 1948. Die Rekonstruktion des westdeutschen Geld- und Währungssystems 1945–1949 unter Berücksichtigung der amerikanischen Besatzungspolitik* (Frankfurt a.M.: Knapp, 1980).

currency reform, but industrial output still managed to rise by 23 percent. Unemployment grew during these fifteen months, but largely because of the influx of refugees; the number of industrial workers actually increased.

The restrictive measures taken by the BdL to curb inflation in 1948–49 were so mild that economic historians generally have assigned equal or greater weight to factors independent of the central bank in accounting for the slowing of price increases. These include the arrival of Marshall Plan aid, the incipient downturn in world commodity prices, the emergence of budget surpluses as a result of the higher revenues accruing from higher national income after June 1948, the end of the influx of balances blocked by the currency reform, and the slowing of consumer purchases because of the growing gap between wages and prices.[32]

Further evidence of the central bank's reluctance to press monetary restraint to the point that economic growth would be compromised can be adduced from its willingness to support a government stimulus package, which was prepared in early 1950 but never completely implemented as a result of the boom that got underway after the outbreak of the Korean War. The stimulus program envisaged a tax cut in June, along with a work-creation and housing program. The BdL promised to support the latter by rediscounting up to DM 2 billion in credits associated with it, in effect monetizing public expenditure.[33]

After the outbreak of the Korean War, Germany again faced significant inflationary pressures. The situation was compounded by a severe balance-of-payments crisis, which threatened to undermine Germany's program of trade liberalization and force it to violate the terms of the newly founded European Payments Union. In other words, not just domestic price stability but other important government economic objectives, as well as Germany's international economic relations, were called into question by the deterioration of the trade balance. This time, in October 1950, the BdL raised interest rates substantially, increasing the discount rate from 4 percent to 6 percent and the Lombard rate from 5 percent to 7 percent. Despite the emergency, the rate increases were highly controversial. The Chancellor (Adenauer) and the Ministers of Finance (Fritz Schäffer), and Economics (Erhard) attended the Central Bank Council meeting where the decision was taken; Adenauer and Schäffer spoke against raising interest rates for fear of the effect on growth and employment, but to no avail.[34]

32. Buchheim, "Die Währungsreform 1948 in Westdeutschland"; Wallich, *Mainsprings of the German Economic Recovery*, pp. 73–87.

33. Wallich, *Mainsprings of the German Economic Recovery*, pp. 85–6.

34. Otmar Emminger has left a good account of this meeting in *D-Mark, Dollar, Währungskrisen. Erinnerungen eines ehemaligen Bundesbankpräsidenten* (Stuttgart: Deutsche Verlags-Anstalt, 1986), pp. 54–6.

This represented the highest nominal interest rates imposed by a central bank in the four countries considered here during the era of postwar reconstruction. It may appear to contradict the thesis being advanced here, namely that dear money was consistently eschewed by central bankers during the reconstruction era. However, two additional factors must be considered. First, inflation was running at about 12 percent at the time of the rate hikes, meaning that real interest rates charged by the central bank remained significantly negative. High as German interest rates appeared to contemporaries, therefore, they would hardly meet our definition of dear money. Second, even during the Korean crisis the BdL relied primarily on credit rationing, not on interest rate policy, to break inflationary expectations. In late January 1951 the BdL instructed commercial banks to reduce the volume of their loan portfolios by a total of DM 1 billion. The central bank exercised a high degree of selectivity in enforcing the measure. Certain credits, for example, for exports and agriculture, were exempt from the ceilings, and a certain amount of flexibility was used in setting the credit ceilings for individual institutions. It was not altogether clear that this degree of intervention in the internal affairs of the commercial banks even was permitted by the BdL's statutes; it certainly created acute discomfort among the central banker executives. Otmar Emminger noted in his memoirs that the measures proved highly effective but recalled that BdL officials at the time hoped they would never again be constrained to undertake similar measures.[35]

Currency reforms with features comparable to the measures taken in Germany in June 1948, including substantial write-offs of old monetary assets, were proposed, but never implemented, in Italy and France. In these two countries, the principal exponents of monetary reform were politicians of the left: in Italy, Mauro Scoccimarro, the Communist Finance Minister in De Gasperi's first government, and in France the Radical Pierre Mendès-France. In both cases the proponents of monetary reform proposed to achieve both an end to inflation by reducing the money stock and a confiscatory tax on wealth accumulated during the war. In both countries the redistributive purposes of the monetary reform were politically contentious and contributed to the rejection of the proposals by the coalition governments that held power after liberation. Instead, in both France and Italy the monetary overhangs inherited from the war were eliminated by allowing inflation to rage—until 1947 in Italy, until at least 1948 in France. However, both countries ultimately managed to stabilize prices and reverse inflationary expectations without resorting

35. Wallich questions the legitimacy of the BdL's measures in *Mainsprings of the German Economic Recovery*, p. 77. On Emminger's wish that the measures never need be repeated, see *D-Mark, Dollar, Währungskrisen*, p. 57.

to dear money. Credit rationing, rather than high interest rates, was the key policy instrument in both countries' anti-inflationary programs.[36]

Italy stabilized first. At first glance Italy might appear to be the weakest case for the argument being made here, namely that European nations universally pursued growth-oriented monetary policies after World War II. After all, Luigi Einaudi, the Banca d'Italia's first postwar governor and the architect of its anti-inflationary policy in 1947–48, was a distinguished economist, a leading proponent of the quantity theory of money, and a critic of Keynes. His monetary policy was judged to be unduly restrictive by the U.S. ECA (Marshall Plan) advisers at the time, and it has been the object of severe criticism by Keynesian economists since then. Einaudi has been charged with having produced an unnecessarily severe deflation and with having used Marshall Plan aid to build up the central bank's exchange reserves instead of achieving the maximum possible levels of domestic investment.[37]

But in comparison with Mussolini's monetary stabilization policies from 1925 to 1927, what is striking about the "Linea Einaudi" in 1947–48 is its comparative mildness, particularly the avoidance of dear money. The main instrument of monetary restriction employed by Einaudi was the imposition of minimum reserve requirements for the commercial banks that went into effect at the end of September 1947. Reserves levels were set sufficiently high that the volume of bank credit was not cut, but a ceiling was placed on further credit expansion. After the reserve limits were reached, commercial bankers could expand the total volume of their credit only by attracting additional deposits. Accompanying the imposition of the reserve ceilings, the discount rate was raised, but only

36. Among the many discussions of Mendès-France's policies, noteworthy is François Bloch-Lainé and Jean Bouvier, *La France restaurée, 1944–1954. Dialogue sur les choix d'une modernisation* (Paris: Fayard, 1986), *passim*. On Scoccimarro's proposals in Italy, see John Lamberton Harper, *America and the Reconstruction of Italy, 1945–1948* (New York: Cambridge University, 1986), pp. 48–55; Enzo Piscitelli, "Del cambio o meglio del mancato cambio della moneta nel secondo dopoguerra," *Quaderni dell'Istituto Romano per la Storia d'Italia dal Fascismo alla Resistenza* 1 (1959), pp. 9–88; Bruno Foa, *Monetary Reconstruction in Italy* (New York: King's Crown, 1949), pp. 88–96 and *passim*.

37. Marcello De Cecco offered a scathing critique of the "linea Einaudi" in "Economic policy in the reconstruction period, 1945–1951," in, S.J. Woolf, ed., *The Rebirth of Italy 1943–50* (London: Longman, 1972), pp. 156–180. He has since come to a more favorable view of Menichella's policy. See his "Keynes and Italian Economics," in Peter A. Hall, ed., *The Political Power of Economic Ideas: Keynesianism across Nations* (Princeton: Princeton University, 1989), pp. 195–229. In defence of the deflation of 1947–48 see also Paolo Baffi, "Via Nazionale e gli economisti stranieri, 1944–53," *Rivista di Storia Economica*, nuova serie, 2 (1985), no. 1, pp. 1–45; and Mario Arcelli, "Commento alla relazione di Guido Carli: 'Donato Menichella, Governatore della Banca d'Italia,'" in Banca d'Italia, *Donato Menichella: Testimonianze e studi* (Bari: Laterza, 1986), pp. 61–73.

moderately, from 4 percent to 5.5 percent (inflation was running at 7.5 percent *per month* during 1946–47).

The impact of these measures on inflationary expectations was sudden and dramatic. The black market exchange value of the lira turned around almost immediately, gaining against the dollar and the pound (but in late November the authorities reduced the official parity of the lira against the dollar to stimulate exports). A boom in stock prices stopped in its tracks; wholesale prices declined by 15 to 20 percent and retail prices by 12 percent between October 1947 and March 1948.

To be sure, there was an economic price to be paid for the reversal of inflationary expectations. Many firms and individuals that had based their plans on the expectation that inflation would continue, and that plentiful credit would be available, found themselves strapped for resources. Black market interest rate soared. A wave of bankruptcies ensued, and the rate of unemployment rose. Output fell by 15 percent from its peak in October 1947.

In order to ameliorate the impact of the limits on bank credit expansion, the government intervened directly in aid of distressed firms in strategic economic sectors. Lit. 50 billion was allocated in subsidies to aid the reconversion and modernization of the mechanical industries. The Treasury advanced another Lit. 10 billion to the state industrial holding company IRI and raised its capital from Lit. 12 billion to Lit. 20 billion, later to Lit. 60 billion. Subsidies and special credit facilities for other manufacturing sectors or special interest groups were also introduced. Albert O. Hirschman, an economist working for the Federal Reserve at the time, wryly observed that Einaudi's "orthodox" policy, "actually led to more State intervention in, and greater State control of, Italian economic life."[38] As a result, the money stock actually expanded during the credit crunch. The difference was that firms and individuals could no longer count upon receiving plentiful credit and hence became more cautious about expansion. The budget

38. Albert O. Hirschman, "Inflation and deflation in Italy," *American Economic Review* 38 (1948), no. 4, pp. 598–606; cited passage, p. 604. Most of the figures given above are from Hirschman. On monetary stabilization in postwar Italy, in addition to the sources already cited, see Alessandra Casella and Barry Eichengreen, "Halting Inflation in Italy and France after the Second World War," in Michael D. Bordo and Forrest Capie, eds., *Monetary Regimes in Transition* (New York: Cambridge University, 1993), pp. 312–345; Marcello De Cecco and Francesco Giavazzi, "Inflation and stabilization in Italy: 1946–1951," in Rudiger Dornbusch, Wilhelm Nölling, and Richard Layard, eds., *Postwar Economic Reconstruction and Lessons for the East Today* (Cambridge, Mass.: MIT, 1993), pp. 57–81; Sergio Ricossa, "Introduzione," to Sergio Ricossa and Ercole Tuccimei, eds., *La Banca d'Italia e il risanamento post-bellico, 1945–1948* (Bari: Laterza, 1992); Paolo Baffi, "Memoria sull'azione di Einaudi (1945–1948)," in Paolo Baffi, *Testimonianze e ricordi* (Milan: Scheiwiller, 1990), pp. 59–78; Friedrich A. Lutz and Vera C Lutz, "Monetary and foreign exchange policy in Italy," *Princeton Studies in International Finance* no. 1, (Princeton: Princeton University, 1950).

remained in deficit, so there was no anti-inflationary fiscal policy, such as Britain and Germany adopted. Indeed, given that public resources were used extensively to compensate for the financial distress caused by commercial lending restrictions, this was virtually inevitable.

The negative effects of the deflation on workers were confined almost exclusively to the nonunionized sectors of the economy. Since December 1945 workers in the unionized sectors of the economy had been protected against the erosion of real earnings through inflation by a comprehensive wage escalator (*scala mobile*). The existence of the scala mobile was no doubt a major incentive to the authorities to bring inflation under control. A new agreement in November 1947 between employers and the trade unions gave workers almost complete protection against deflation as well. According to the agreement, wages were to be maintained at current levels, so long as the cost of living did not drop by more than 8 percent; wages were to be reduced less than in proportion to the cost of living for decreases of the latter between 8 percent and 20 percent. Moreover, a ban on dismissals of unionized workers remained in effect.

The recession produced by Einaudi's deflation was short-lived. By the spring of 1948, less than six months after the imposition of the reserve requirements, output and investment began to recover. Some observers have argued that recovery would have gotten underway even sooner, if it had not been for the uncertainty surrounding the outcome of the political elections in April, which produced a landslide victory for the Christian Democrats and a decisive defeat of the Communists and Socialists. Under these circumstances, it is difficult to argue that macroeconomic policy was unduly restrictive. Indeed, Einaudi and Donato Menichella, his successor as governor of the Banca d'Italia, must have had Mussolini's dear money policy in 1925–27 in mind as a negative model in 1947–48. Their positive model, presumably, was the Banca d'Italia's successful use of credit rationing to break inflation (temporarily) in 1920–21. The introduction of minimum reserve requirements gave them a more effective instrument for resisting bank credit expansion; in 1920–21 the Banca d'Italia had had little direct influence on the lending practices of the major commercial banks until they were forced to apply to the central bank for substantial rediscounting credits. Throughout 1947–48 Banca and Treasury officials were determined to limit the negative impact of monetary stabilization on output and employment. Even a traditionalist economist like Einaudi was anxious to avoid prolonged recession and dear money.[39]

39. On the preoccupation of Donato Menichella, Einaudi's successor as Governor of the Banca d'Italia, to avoid a prolonged recession on the order of 1925–27, see Franco Bonelli, "Menichella e la storia bancaria italiana," in Banca d'Italia, *Donato Menichella. Testimonianze e studi*, pp. 215–221.

Monetary stabilization in France was a far more tortuous process than in Italy. Decisive measures to check inflation were not taken before the fall of 1948, and during the Korean War inflation resumed again. As was noted above, Mendès-France's proposals for a currency reform were rejected by the coalition government that took office under De Gaulle after the liberation. The views of Mendès's chief rival in the cabinet, Finance Minister René Pleven, on how to cope with inflation were described by one of his admirers in the following terms:

> Maintaining that it was the volume of production that should adjust to the volume of money in circulation, and not the other way around, the present minister places his faith in the renewal of France, exhorting it to great efforts. Thus, it has been said that the Pleven Plan is more inspired by Stakhanov than by Poincaré [who as Prime Minister presided over the stabilization of the franc in 1926–28].[40]

Perhaps Pleven was a "Stakhanovite" in his emphasis on recovery of output as the remedy for the monetary overhang. However, Pleven's policies were also "Keynesian" in their aim to bring about euthanasia of the rentier. Money in postwar France was even cheaper than in Britain. Until December 1946 the discount rate of the Banque de France was 1–5/8 percent, and the rate of return on bonds between 3.6 percent and 4.6 percent. Since retail prices doubled from liberation to the end of 1945 and went up another 80 percent in 1946, "any notion of a real rate of interest was deprived of meaning."[41]

Prior to the fall of 1948, such efforts as there were to halt inflation were halfhearted. In early 1947 a monocolor Socialist government under Léon Blum decreed a general reduction in prices by 5 percent and announced its intention to lower prices by another 5 percent within sixty days. But even though wage and price controls were in place, enforcement was ineffective, and after a brief pause the inflationary process resumed, with retail prices rising by another 60 percent between March and December 1947.

As in Italy (and Germany after the currency reform in June 1948), the expansion of bank credit was a significant element driving the inflationary process forward. The French imposed reserve requirements on the commercial banks at about the same time that the Italians did, but in contrast to Italy, commercial bills were considered to be short-term, liquid assets and hence not subject to the lending ceilings. Not surprisingly therefore,

40. Pierre Lormel, *L'expérence Pleven e le contribuale français* (Paris: Editions du Chêne, 1945), p. 31, quoted in Michael Loriaux, *France after Hegemony: International Change and Financial Reform* (Princeton: Princeton University, 1991), p. 107.

41. Jean-Pierre Patat and Michel Lutfalla, *A Monetary History of France in the Twentieth Century* (Basingstoke: Macmillan, 1990), p. 124.

the main result of the reserve requirements was the expansion of the commercial bill portfolios of the banks, *pari passu* with the contraction of operations subject to the restrictions, such as advances against collateral.

In early 1948 a government headed by Robert Schuman, in which René Mayer served as Finance Minister, introduced new anti-inflationary measures. Ffr. 5,000 bills were retired from circulation, without compensation to the holders—a very modest form of currency write-off, and thus a faint echo of Mendès-France's earlier proposal for monetary reform. A forced loan on business, which took the place of a wealth tax proposed in 1945, was imposed at the same time. For a few months once again, inflation slowed; but by the summer it had resumed its gallop.

At the end of September 1948 the Banque de France made a more determined effort to break the growth of bank credit. Ceilings on rediscounts at the central bank were set individually for every bank. For some banks, the ceilings were close to the level of rediscounts at the time; for other institutions, where the level of rediscounts at the time the measures were taken was considered to be unusually low for some reason, some room for additional expansion was granted. At the same time, commercial banks were obliged to keep minimum holdings of treasury paper at 95 percent of the level they held on 30 September; they were required to invest 20 percent of new deposits in treasury securities. This was not in itself a drastically restrictive measure, since the average ratio of treasury securities to deposits among commercial banks was 28 percent at the time. However, it made it impossible for the banks to run off their holdings of treasury securities in order to acquire additional funds for loans to the private sector. Significant exceptions to the rediscount ceilings were granted, the most notable of which was for medium-term obligations issued by the Crédit National to finance investments called for by Jean Monnet's Plan for Industrial Reequipment and Modernization. Meanwhile, the discount rate, which had been allowed to creep up slowly from its low level at the end of 1946, was set at 3 percent at the time these measures went into effect.

The disinflationary policies introduced by the Banque de France in the fall of 1948 were even milder than those of the Banca d'Italia a year earlier. As was the case in Italy, bank credit and the money stock never ceased expanding; but in contrast to Italy there was no significant downward drift in nominal prices, nor a recession. Output continued to expand after credit rationing went into effect, although at a slower rate. Short-term interest rates were kept quite low, although nominal yields on thirty-year mortgages and other long paper rose to 7 to 8 percent. In June 1950, on the eve of the Korean War, the discount rate was put back to 2.5 percent. Even so, the rate of increase in retail prices fell from 58 percent in

1948 to near zero in the first half of 1950. In light of the moderation of the monetary restraint exercised by the Banque de France, it is not surprising that economic historians have attributed the fall in inflation to causes that lay outside the purview of the central bank: the recovery of output, which relaxed pressure on prices, the arrival of Marshall Plan aid, the break in international commodity prices, the growing gap between retail prices and wages, and so forth.

Inflation resumed in France after the outbreak of the Korean War. Once again the chief instrument employed by the Banque de France to rein in inflationary expectations was the tightening of rediscount ceilings. At the same time, the discount rate was raised—from 2.5 percent to 3 percent in October 1951, and to 4 percent in November 1951. Thus in France, as in Britain, the Korean War marked the return to an active interest-rate policy. However, credit rationing remained the primary instrument for imposing monetary restraint, and nominal interest rates remained moderate.[42]

To summarize the above discussion, despite the many differences in the policies pursued by Britain, Germany, Italy, and France to cope with monetary overhangs after World War II, it is possible to identify a set of common preoccupations and concerns guiding policymakers in all four countries. The determination to avoid recession, and particularly to avoid creating a recession as the by-product of anti-inflationary policies, was pervasive. In particular, there was a general reluctance to use dear money as the primary instrument of an anti-inflationary policy and to assign to interest-rate policy the sole task of fighting inflation. Instead, a wide range of alternative inflation fighting instruments were deployed.

Britain used direct controls, that is, rationing and price controls, supplemented by voluntary wage restraint and voluntary restraint in the expansion of bank credit by commercial bankers to curb private expenditure in the early postwar years. After 1947, budget surpluses were used as an additional inflation-fighting instrument. Throughout, money was kept cheap. In Germany purchasing power was reduced by a massive write-off of monetary assets and claims. The German monetary reform favored debtors over creditors, and entrepreneurs over rentiers: in these respects its effects were (intentionally) directly the opposite of a policy of dear money.

All three continental nations used credit rationing instead of dear money as the chief instrument to control the expansion of bank credit. The degree of government intervention in the credit-rationing process

42. Additional sources on monetary stabilization in postwar France include: Henri Koch, *Histoire de la Banque de France et de la monnaie sous la IVe République* (Paris: Dunod, 1983); M.A. Kriz, "Credit control in France," *American Economic Review* 41 (1951), no. 1, pp. 85–106; Albert O. Hirschman and Robert V. Rosa, "Postwar credit controls in France," *Federal Reserve Bulletin* 35 (1949), no. 4, pp. 348–360.

varied from country to country. Germany and Italy imposed reserve requirements on the commercial banks but let them choose how to allocate credit among their clients. The Italian government compensated for the restrictions on commercial bank lending with a variety of highly selective programs of direct state subsidies. In France the state intervened more directly in the credit-allocation process, setting lending ceilings for individual banks and setting priorities in the types of bills eligible for rediscount with the central bank.

By the early 1950s all four countries were actively varying short-term interest rates to influence key macroeconomic variables; but in all four, growth and employment, as well as price-level and exchange-rate stability, were important objectives taken into account in the formulation of monetary policy. Monetary policy in all four countries contrasted markedly with stabilization policies after World War I. During the 1920s all four countries considered here ultimately turned to dear money as the primary instrument for fighting inflation. In contrast to monetary policy, no common denominator can be identified across nations in fiscal policy after World War II. Britain and Germany ran budget surpluses to support their monetary stabilization policies; Italy and France continued to run deficits. The red thread identifying macropolicy regimes and linking policy orientation across nations must be sought in monetary, not fiscal, policy.

A Monetary Sonderweg *in Postwar Germany?*

Germany is often depicted in the literature as the one major European country that consistently resisted a growth-and full-employment-oriented, and thus inflationary, monetary policy throughout the postwar era. As a result of the horrific experiences with hyperinflation following both world wars, Germany is alleged to have become uniquely inflation-averse. Germany's commitment to monetary stability, it is often argued, is institutionally anchored in its independent central bank. This idea of a German postwar monetary *Sonderweg* has been actively promoted by the Bundesbank itself in official publications and in the work of prominent bank officials. Central bank autonomy was indeed introduced by the Occupation authorities with the creation of the Bank deutscher Länder in 1948, and it was explicitly confirmed in the Bundesbankgesetz (Central Bank Law) of 1957. One former Bundesbank official has argued proudly that no central bank in the world, the U.S. Federal Reserve included, has its independence so firmly anchored in its statutes as the Bundesbank.[43]

43. Emminger, *D-Mark, Dollar, Währungskrisen*, p. 27. See also Deutsche Bundesbank, *Währung und Wirtschaft in Deutschland, 1876–1975* (Frankfurt a.M.: Knapp, 1976).

Moreover, the Bundesbank's primary assignment is defined as "safeguarding the currency." Although this formulation is rather ambiguous, it clearly excludes full employment and high economic growth as primary goals of the central bank. Indeed, on at least one occasion during the long gestation of the Bundesbankgesetz, from 1949 to 1957, the Wissenschaftliche Beirat des Wirtschaftsministeriums (Advisory Council of the Economics Ministry) recommended that the Bank's assignment be defined in broader terms that would have included full employment and economic growth, price-level stability, and external balance—but this language was rejected in the final bill. The Bundesbank's statutes instruct it to cooperate with the government in attaining the latter's economic policy objectives, but only insofar as this is compatible with the Bank's primary mission of "safeguarding the currency." As noted, the Bank is explicitly independent of government direction.[44]

Consequently, Germany's formal institutions suggest that it represents an exception to the argument put forward here, according to which growth and/or employment, in addition to price-level stability and external balance, consistently were accorded equal weight in monetary policy formation after the collapse of the gold standard. The historical record might be taken to support German exceptionalism as well, since over most of the period after the Korean crisis Germany had lower inflation than the other major European countries and usually lower inflation than the United States, too. But a closer examination of German monetary policy raises significant questions about the validity of the monetary *Sonderweg* thesis.

The problem with the idea of German monetary exceptionalism lies in the "currency dilemma" described by Otmar Emminger: the conflict between maintenance of the mark's fixed exchange rate and fighting inflation domestically. Germany's comparative success in fighting inflation caused the mark to become undervalued with respect to the British pound and the French franc from the mid-1950s on; by the late 1950s or early 1960s, at the latest, it was undervalued with respect to the dollar as well. The undervaluation of the mark was a major cause of Germany's structural export surpluses. The repatriation of export earnings, in turn, undermined the Bundesbank's efforts to restrain domestic monetary expansion. Beginning in the mid-1950s, raising interest rates often had a perverse effect in Germany, since it attracted capital from abroad, leading

44. On the Bundesbank's autonomy, see Carl-Ludwig Holtfrerich, "Relations between monetary authorities and governmental institutions: The case of Germany from the 19th century to the present," in Gianni Toniolo, ed., *Central Banks' Independence in Historical Perspective* (New York: de Gruyter, 1980), pp. 105–159; on the gestation of the Bundesbankgesetz, see Volker Hentschel, "Die Entstehung des Bundesbankgesetzes 1949–1957. Politische Kontroversen und Konflikte," *Bankhistorisches Archiv* 14 (1988), no. 1, pp. 3–31; no. 2, pp. 79–115.

to monetary expansion rather than contraction. This perverse effect was aggravated by the end of the decade, at the latest, by recurrent waves of speculation on the revaluation of the mark.

The German "monetary dilemma" represented not only an impediment to the Bundesbank's "*Stabilitätspolitik*" but also a very substantial limitation on the independence of the central bank, since the government, and not the Bank had final authority in setting the exchange rate. By 1956 many German economists, including Emminger, who worked for the central bank, had reached the conclusion that, short of imposing severe trade restrictions, revaluation was the only effective instrument available to Germany to fight inflation.[45]

Yet throughout the 1950s and 1960s, successive German governments were exceedingly reluctant to revalue. The 5 percent revaluation in 1961 and the 10 percent revaluation in 1969 were considered by inflation hawks to be too little too late. Against the pro-revaluation camp were ranged Germany's powerful export interests. Robert Pferdmenges, the president of the German Banking Association, Hermann Abs, chairman of Deutsche Bank, and Fritz Berg, the president of the Federation of German Industry, were strong opponents of revaluation. They were the closest economic advisors of Adenauer during his long tenure as Chancellor. After Adenauer's retirement, Germany's export lobby could rely on the opposition to revaluation of Franz Josef Strauss, the influential president of Bavaria's conservative party, the Christian Socialist Union (CSU).[46]

Even within the central bank there was powerful opposition to revaluation. Wilhelm Vocke, president of the Direktorium (executive committee) of the Bank deutscher Länder from 1948 to 1957, liked to summarize the goals of his monetary policy as being avoidance of both inflation and revaluation. Emminger has written in his memoirs that Vocke simply failed to comprehend the "German monetary dilemma," and at least in public Vocke denied the existence of a conflict between defending the mark's exchange parity and fighting inflation. Karl Blessing, President of the Bundesbank from 1958 to 1969, presided very reluctantly over two revaluations. Only a few months before the first revaluation in 1961, he threatened to resign rather than accept a change in the mark's exchange parity. Both of these individuals, along with many of their colleagues in the Central Bank Council in the first two postwar decades, had begun their professional activity with the Reichsbank. The memory of Germany's chronic balance-of-payments difficulties during the interwar years was

45. Emminger, *D-Mark, Dollar, Währungskrisen*, pp. 78–84.

46. Ibid., pp. 109, 134, 151, 161, 170, 224, 261. On the revaluation in 1961, see also Hugo M. Kaufmann, "A debate over Germany's revaluation, 1961: A chapter in political economy," *Weltwirtschaftliches Archiv* 103 (1969), no. 2, pp. 181–212.

etched indelibly in their minds, and they were nearly as concerned as Adenauer and Strauss about maintaining Germany's strong export performance. The vagueness of the Bundesbank's mandate, to "safeguard the currency," allowed them to give preference to maintaining the exchange-rate parity above maintaining domestic price level stability (and hence giving preference to high growth and full employment) when these two goals began to come into conflict in the late 1950s.[47]

All of this changed with the collapse of Bretton Woods and with the first oil shock in 1973. The transition to floating exchange rates removed the most significant constraint on the autonomy of the central bank, precisely at the moment when inflationary pressures accelerated. After 1973 the Bundesbank consistently put the fight against inflation ahead of other policy goals. Germany's inflation rate also was further below the OECD average during the turbulent decade following the breakup of Bretton Woods than it had been during the 1950s and 1960s. It was in the years after 1973 that the Bundesbank justifiably earned its reputation for autonomy and monetary austerity; reports of a German monetary *Sonderweg* prior to then, in contrast, have been much exaggerated.

The Regulation of Financial Markets

In the wake of the collapse of the interwar gold standard, policymakers in all four countries considered here substantially expanded public regulation of financial markets and institutions. The reordering of macroeconomic policy objectives was an important precondition for many of these legislative initiatives. Under the gold standard, financial openness served as an anchor for domestic price level stability; thus the logic of the macropolicy regime implied that domestic and international financial flows be left as free as possible. Once the authorities abandoned the gold standard, they were free to regulate domestic and international financial transactions in pursuit of a variety of alternative policy goals.

Three major motives can be discerned in the new wave of financial regulation. First, policymakers sought to create greater stability in national banking systems. Their immediate concern was to deal with the chaos caused by bank failures during the Great Depression. This problem was particularly acute in nations with mixed or universal banks, including Germany and Italy, where individual institutions practiced both commercial and investment banking. But even Britain and France suffered

47. Emminger, *D-Mark, Dollar, Währungskrisen*. On Vocke, see esp. pp. 90–93; on Blessing's threat to resign in 1961, pp. 117–8.

some bank failures during the Great Depression, and all four countries extended banking supervision and adopted more expansive views of the lender-of-last resort responsibilities of the central bank in response.

A second motive driving financial regulation, now that growth and employment had become important objectives in setting interest rate policy, was the need to create new policy instruments to secure external balance and fight inflation. Policymakers sought to insulate domestic financial markets from international capital flows, which had acted as a powerful constraint on monetary policy formation under the gold standard. On the domestic front, selective credit controls, including credit ceilings, rediscount ceilings, and variable minimum reserve requirements, were introduced as alternative or supplementary inflation-fighting instruments to interest rate policy. Third, in the wake of World War II, financial regulation was used as a key instrument in interventionist economic modernization and regional development programs.

The Expansion of Bank Supervision and the Lender-of-Last-Resort Responsibilities of Central Banks

Nearly every nation adhering to the gold standard experienced a wave of bank failures in the late 1920s and early 1930s. As one nation after another imposed monetary contraction to defend gold parities, price levels fell, investment nearly ceased, and economic activity declined. The negative effects on bank balance sheets due to this decline in business activity was exacerbated by the mechanism of debt deflation, that is, the decline in the value of the nonmonetary assets that served as collateral against bank loans, relative to the banks' monetary liabilities vis-à-vis depositors. This effect was particularly acute in countries that had mixed or universal banking systems, including Germany and Italy. The lengthier maturity structure of the loan portfolios of universal banks made them particularly vulnerable to debt deflation. In both countries, all of the major commercial banks essentially failed, and ended up in state hands as a result of rescues.[48]

In addition to debt deflation, a second factor that contributed to the severity of the banking crisis of the early 1930s was the rapid integration of national and international financial markets since the late nineteenth century. In 1931 policymakers discovered that the loss of confidence in

48. Irving Fischer, "The debt deflation theory of great depressions," *Econometrica* 1 (1933). On the particular vulnerability of universal banks to debt deflation, see Pier-Luigi Ciocca and Gianni Toniolo, "Industry and finance in Italy, 1918–1940," *Journal of European History*, Special Issue on Banks and Industry in the Interwar Period, 13 (1984), no. 2, pp. 113–36.

one financial institution or group of institutions could set in motion a general panic that could bring down an entire national financial system and even spread to other countries. Prior to the late nineteenth century, the highly segmented structure of national and international credit markets had sharply limited the danger of such contagion.

In all four of the countries under consideration here, national financial markets arose gradually in the course of the late nineteenth and early twentieth centuries through the merger of highly segmented sectoral and regional credit markets. This was the case even in Britain, the seat of the world financial center and the home of the industrial revolution. P.L. Cottrell has pointed out recently that a national financial market emerged in Britain only as a product of the merger of country and city banking, which was brought about by the great amalgamation movement among the joint-stock banks, between the late 1870s and 1920.[49] Prior to then, the London financial market, with its focus on international trade and finance, and with its complex interlinkages between the Bank of England, the great merchant banks, and discount houses, was a world apart from the country bankers who operated in the industrial districts of the Midlands and the North. In France, it took the growth of the great banques des depôts, beginning in the 1870s, as well as the extension of the Banque de France's provincial network, to create the semblance of a national financial market, and this process was far from complete by the outbreak of World War I.[50] In Germany, Berlin emerged as an important financial center only after unification. The great German universal banks were even slower than their English and French counterparts in developing national branch networks: as late as 1913, the nine Berlin Grossbanken had a total of only 145 independent branches, excluding suburban suboffices, of which ten belonged to the Deutsche Bank, Germany's largest private bank, and forty-nine to the Darmstädter Bank, which had the most extensive branch network of the big Berlin banks.[51] The largest commercial banks in Italy were, if anything, behind the German banks in asserting their predominance. The failure of the largest two commercial banks in the country, the Credito Mobiliare and the Banca Generale, in the early 1890s slowed the process of financial consolidation. Two new banks, the Banca Commerciale Italiana and the Credito Italiano, were founded by German-led international banking syndicates in 1894 and

49. P.L. Cottrell, "The Domestic Commercial Banks and the City of London, 1870–1939," in Youssef Cassis, ed., *Finance and Financiers in European History, 1880–1960* (New York: Cambridge University, 1992), pp. 39–62.

50. Jean Bouvier, *Un siècle de banque française* (Paris: Hachette, 1973).

51. P. Barrett Whale, *Joint Stock Banking in Germany* (London: Macmillan, 1930), p. 31 and *passim*.

1895, respectively. Together with the Banco di Roma and the Banca Italiana di Sconto, they held around 16 percent of the total assets of the Italian banking system on the eve of World War I; the Commerciale operated the largest branch network, with a total of fifty-four offices (including suburban suboffices).[52] A peculiarity of the Italian system was the fragmentation of financial centers. The two German-inspired institutions had their headquarters in Milan, and this city's stock exchange was the most active in Italy; but the central bank and the third and fourth largest commercial banks were headquartered in Rome. This geographical separation reflected fundamental tensions between the central bank and the leading private institutions.

Not only were integrated national financial markets still a relatively recent development on the eve of the Great Depression; an international monetary system was also a product of the late nineteenth century. Only after the major continental powers followed Britain in adopting a pure gold standard (Germany in 1871, France and Italy essentially in 1873, the United States in 1879, Russia in 1898), and only after the general expansion of international trade beginning in the 1870s, were more intensive links between national financial markets forged. It must be emphasized that the growing integration of financial markets in this era was the direct result of the adoption of a macropolicy regime that relied on international openness as an anchor for domestic price stability.

There were a few harbingers of the growing vulnerability of increasingly integrated financial markets prior to the Great Depression: the Baring Crisis in 1890, in which the losses of a leading English merchant bank on Argentine bonds threatened to paralyze the London financial markets; the New York Stock Exchange crisis in 1907, which caused considerable distress on money markets as far away as Berlin and Milan; the breakdown in international payments upon the outbreak of the European war in 1914. But it took the European banking crisis and the collapse of the interwar gold standard in 1931 to bring home to central bankers and government authorities the full implications of several decades of rapid financial integration.[53]

Prior to the Great Depression, banking was not very carefully regulated in any of the four countries under consideration. In nineteenth-century

52. Umberto Bava, *I quattro maggiori istituti italiani di credito* (Genoa: Valugani, 1926), p. 79 and unpaginated statistical appendices.

53. On the Baring crisis and the crisis of 1914, see Marcello De Cecco, *The International Gold Standard: Money and Empire*, 2nd ed. (London: Pinter, 1984); on the crisis of 1907 in Italy, see Franco Bonelli, *La crisi del 1907. Una tappa dello sviluppo industriale in Italia* (Turin: Fondazione Luigi Einaudi, 1971); on 1907 in Germany, see Whale, *Joint-Stock Banking in Germany*, pp. 128–131. On the transmission of banking panics, see Peter Temin, "Transmission of the Great Depression," *Journal of Economic Perspectives* 7 (1993), no. 2, pp. 87–102.

Europe, the main legal impediments to the expansion of banking were restrictions on the formation of joint-stock companies. Thus in England a general prohibition on joint-stock companies was in place until 1826, and in order to protect the Bank of England's monopoly in London, joint-stock banks could not be founded within sixty-five miles of the capital until 1833. Even after this barrier fell, English joint-stock banks were allowed to join the London clearing (giving them access to the payments facilities maintained by the Bank of England) only beginning in 1854. In 1862, the liability of shareholders was limited to the capital they subscribed, further encouraging the formation of joint-stock companies. In France, each joint-stock corporation, including banks, required individual approval until company laws were liberalized in 1863 (for companies with less than Ffr. 20 million in share capital) and 1867 (for all companies). In Prussia, company laws were liberalized in 1869, and Prussia's liberal legislation was extended throughout the territory of the newly constituted Reich after 1871. Italy's unification between 1859 and 1870 similarly extended Piedmont's liberal company laws throughout the peninsula. Everywhere, the liberalization of company law produced an explosion of new bank foundings. By the early 1870s, most banks in all four countries were subject to few legal or regulatory requirements that went beyond ordinary company law unless they engaged in certain specialized activities, such as note issuing (in all four countries), mortgage underwriting (in Germany), or retail savings deposit-taking (Germany and Italy).[54]

It is true that the leading bankers in all four countries developed notions about what constituted sound banking practices in the decades prior to World War I and that traditions of self-regulation developed in each country. Some aspects of banking policy became the object of public debate, and leading institutions could feel compelled to modify their practices as a result of public discussion. Further, central banks and governments could exert informal pressure on private banks to make them conform to certain minimum standards; indeed, on a number of occasions the threat of legislation induced private banks to change their policies in order to forestall formal regulation. Thus in 1919, in order to ward off anti-trust legislation, the five big joint-stock banks in England announced they would not effect any additional mergers among themselves; in 1912 and once again in 1928, following negotiations with the Reichsbank, the big German banks agreed to disclose more information at more frequent intervals on their balance sheets; and in 1918 Italian bankers signed a private agreement with the

54. A good survey of the liberalization of company law in nineteenth-century Europe and the rise of joint-stock banking can be found in Karl Erich Born, *Geld und Banken im 19. und 20. Jahrhundert* (Stuttgart: Kröner, 1977). On France, see also Bouvier, *Un siècle de banque française*.

Minister of the Treasury committing themselves to cooperate with the Banca d'Italia, the government, and with each other in floating public loans, in fixing active and passive interest rates, and in other areas of policy.[55]

There were considerable national variations in the banking regulation introduced after 1931. In its bank law of 1936, Italy gave its regulators very extensive discretionary powers. Even before the Great Depression, Italy had experienced a series of major bank panics with destabilizing macroeconomic effects (the early 1890s, 1907, 1921–23), and the Italian authorities were determined not to let it happen again. Well before the Great Depression, in 1926, Italy introduced limited banking supervision. In 1930–32, when these measures proved inadequate, much tougher norms were adopted. Banking supervision was placed in the hands of a Committee of Ministers. An inspectorate was created, chaired by the Governor of the Banca d'Italia, which was to carry out the Committee's directives. The Committee was authorized to close branches or institutions; to set active and passive interest rates; to decide reserve ratios, as well as ratios of own to outside resources; and to decide the use to which deposits exceeding such ratios would be put. It could demand approval in advance for certain types of lending operations; it could decide what proportion of profits should be set aside as reserves; it could fix maximum limits for individual loans; and it could specify the procedures for reducing exposure when these limits were overstepped. Norms could be adopted for all banks, for specific categories of banks, or for individual institutions.[56]

In sum, the law of 1936 gave the Italian government almost unlimited power over the banking sector. Although the work of technocrats, and not of Fascist Party ideologues, this legislation very much reflected the totalitarian ambitions of the regime. However, during the final years of the dictatorship the vast powers the 1936 banking law assigned to the Committee of Ministers, and hence to the government, were exercised in actual fact by the inspectorate, and hence by the Governor of the Banca d'Italia. In 1947 the Committee of Ministers was abolished, and the inspectorate formally became a dependency of the Banca. Needless to say, the inspectorate gave the Banca d'Italia considerable leverage over Italy's financial system and hence over economic policy in general.[57]

55. On the British agreement of 1920, see Sayers, *The Bank of England*, vol I, pp. 238–239; on the German agreements, see Whale, *Joint-Stock Banking in Germany*, pp. 133, 282; on the bank accord in Italy, see Forsyth, "The Rise and Fall of German-Inspired Mixed Banking in Italy," p. 191.

56. Franco Belli, "Le leggi bancarie del 1926 e del 1936–1938," in Banco di Roma, *Banca e industria fra le due guerre*, vol. 2, *Le riforme istituzionali e il pensiero giuridico* (Bologna: Il Mulino, 1981), pp. 203–268.

57. Belli, "Le leggi bancarie del 1926 e del 1936–1938"; Giangiacomo Nardozzi, *Tre sistemi creditizi. Banche ed economia in Francia, Germania e Italia* (Bologna: Il Mulino, 1983).

In addition to vastly expanding the government's (later the central bank's) powers of regulation and supervision, in 1933–34 the Italian authorities nationalized the country's three major commercial banks, which had effectively failed. They were reorganized as Banche di Interesse Nazionali (Banks of National Interest or BIN), and their ability to engage in industrial promotion was sharply curtailed. In the course of the Depression, the commercial banks effectively had turned into industrial holding companies by buying up the stock of client firms. As a result of bank rescue operations in 1931–33, the state found itself in possession of most of the country's manufacturing capacity. These firms were assigned to a state holding company, the Istituto per la Ricostruzione Industriale or IRI in 1933. The IRI received direct annual grants from the state, but its chief means of finance was the sale of state-guaranteed, tax-exempt obligations. Although the IRI had some success in placing its securities with the general investing public, large blocks of obligations were also taken up by the savings banks and other public banks. Thus in its efforts to overcome the chronic instability that its system of private universal banks had produced, Italy completely restructured its capital markets and acquired the largest state-owned manufacturing sector outside of the Soviet Union.

In contrast to Italy's banking law, the Reichsgesetz über das Kreditwesen (KWG) of 1934 adopted a much more limited, rule-based system of bank regulation in Germany. There were three main features of the KWG: the size of credits to individual customers was restricted in proportion to the share capital of the banks; reserve requirements were instituted; and permission was required for opening new branches. Another law required banks to disclose more detailed information on their balance sheets. Banks also were required to submit annual reports by independent auditors.[58]

The main features of the KWG were incorporated in the decentralized supervisory authorities established by the Länder governments in the western Occupation zones after World War II. In 1961 another KWG recentralized the supervisory authority (Bundesaufsichtsamt für das Kreditwesen), which was attached to the government rather than the Bundesbank. The main outlines of the new law followed the legislation of 1934. One exception was that the government could no longer regulate bank branching; in 1958 Germany's highest court had ruled that restrictions on opening branches limited competition and was hence inadmissible. A few additional innovations were introduced after a spate of bank failures in 1973–74: the Aufsichtsamt was authorized to conduct audits at its discretion; certain foreign-exchange transactions were regulated more

58. Wandel, "Das deutsche Bankwesen im Dritten Reich"; Karl Erich Born, *Die deutsche Bankenkrise 1931: Finanzen und Politik* (Munich: Piper, 1967); Nardozzi, *Tre sistemi creditizi*.

tightly; the rules on large loans were stiffened a bit; and a liquidation bank (Likobank) was set up to bolster the voluntary deposit insurance schemes run by the three banking sectoral peak associations. In its main features, however, banking regulation in Germany still follows the pattern set in 1934.[59]

In contrast to Italy, there was little interest in Germany—during the final phase of the Weimar Republic, under the Nazis, or after World War II—in radically changing the mixed banking system. Most policymakers attributed the banking crisis of 1931 either to errors on the part of individual bankers, to the severity of the Depression, or to the failure of the Reichsbank to exercise its lender-of-last-resort responsibilities. The banking legislation of 1934 did not envisage the break-up of the universal banks; they were reprivatized during the late 1930s. The efforts of U.S. Occupation authorities to impose a decentralized and segmented American-style banking system on Germany were equally unsuccessful. The separation of investment and deposit banking was never effected; and the Federal Republic allowed the regional branch offices of the old universal banks, which the Americans had divided into separate institutions within the various Länder, to reamalgamate into three institutions with nationwide branch networks in 1957–58.[60]

This does not mean, however, that Germany's banking system survived the Depression and the war unchanged. Prior to 1931 Germany's universal banks engaged in company promotion by making nominally short-term loans to start-up firms, and the loans were rolled over repeatedly. Once these firms achieved an acceptable degree of financial stability, the universal banks acted as underwriters of stock issues, which often allowed them to recover their investment. In other words, they served as intermediaries between stockholders and firms. After World War II, the German stock market never recovered its former vitality. The currency reform of 1948 reduced the book value of German firms to well below what their market value would become as a result of the ensuing economic recovery. The postwar tax code penalized share ownership. In this environment, the universal banks redefined themselves as financial intermediaries by collecting time deposits from individuals and firms and by

59. Hans E. Büschgen, "Zeitgeschichtliche Problemfelder des Bankwesens der Bundesrepublik Deustchland," in Klein, et al. eds., *Deutsche Bankengeschichte*, vol. 3, pp. 349–409; Helmut Mayer, *Das Bundesaufsichtsamt für das Kreditwesen* (Düsseldorf: Droste, 1981).

60. On the reamalgamation of the big commercial banks and the central bank, see Theo Horstman, *Die Alliierten und die deutschen Grossbanken. Bankenpolitik nach dem Zweiten Weltkrieg in Westdeutschland* (Bonn: Bouvier, 1991); Manfred Pohl, "Die Entwicklung des privaten Bankwesens nach 1945. Die Kreditgenossenschaften nach 1945," in, Ernst Klein et al., eds., *Deutsche Bankengeschichte* (Frankfurt a.M.: Knapp, 1983), pp. 205–276.

issuing long-term, fixed-interest-bearing loans to corporate borrowers. Thus the practice of universal banking in Germany was radically transformed between 1931 and 1948, but it was not transformed by the regulatory and supervisory legislation.[61]

France's banking regulation rests on laws adopted in 1941 (under Vichy) and 1945 (after liberation). The regulatory authority, the Commission de Contrôle, contained representatives of the Banque de France, the government, and, after 1950, the association of bankers. Since 1945, owing to the nationalization of the deposit banks (banques des depôts), most bank deposits have been held by state-owned institutions. Both the deposit banks and the investment banks (banques des affaires), which were left in private hands by the nationalization legislation of 1945–46, were subjected to rather intrusive supervision.[62]

In contrast to the three continental nations discussed here, Britain did not create a formal supervisory authority during the 1930s and 1940s. Indeed, supervision remained highly informal and was limited to certain categories for which the Bank of England had come to accept ultimate financial responsibility. This applied mainly to the City of London, and in particular to the merchant banking houses that were members of the Accepting Houses Committee and to the discount houses that maintained close relations with the Bank. As for other institutions, John Fforde, the Bank of England's official historian, observes that it was assumed that, if a clearing bank or a British overseas bank got into serious trouble, the Bank would intervene, by arranging either a merger or some other form of reconstruction. However, the Bank's resources were clearly inadequate to mount a major rescue operation, and the use of Treasury funds inevitably would have raised the question of more formal banking supervision. The Bank could discuss liquidity problems with the clearing banks through the Finance Houses Association, but its moral suasion must have been weaker here than with the acceptance and discount houses. Smaller provincial banks, along with the hire-purchase credit firms that sprang up in increasing numbers in the 1950s, were under no form of supervision whatsoever. Britain's conservative commercial banking traditions had prevented major institutions from folding during the 1930s; but the informal and noninclusive style of supervision that survived World War II invited speculative excess on the fringes of the system, and it was only a matter of time before such excesses led to bankruptcies and more formal regulation.[63]

61. See the essay by Jan Kregel in this volume.

62. Koch, *Histoire de la Banque de France*, esp. pp. 39–75.

63. John Fforde, *The Bank of England and Public Policy, 1941–1958* (New York: Cambridge University, 1992), pp. 749–779.

In addition to regulation, however, another innovation contributed to the greater stability of banking systems in the postwar era: a more expansive conception of the responsibilities of the central bank (and ultimately the state) as the lender-of-last-resort.

Walter Bagehot's classic description in *Lombard Street* (1873) of the duty of the lender-of-last-resort to lend freely, but dearly, to the money market in times of distress, and to prevent the failure of a single bank from setting in motion a global crisis of confidence in the credit system, was well known to European central bankers on the eve of the Great Depression.[64] In some fashion, all four of the institutions discussed here recognized their responsibilities as lenders-of-last-resort. However, their understanding of these responsibilities was much more limited before 1931 than it has become since. The Bank of England had perhaps the longest experience in dealing with financial panics, and its behavior was of course the object of Bagehot's famous essay. But as was noted above, the Bank traditionally confined its commitments to the maintenance of stability in the City of London. When Baring's, a major merchant bank, got into trouble in 1890, the Bank came to its assistance; when the Bank of the City of Glasgow went under in 1878, the Bank took no action. Collapse of the latter institution inflicted considerable pain on the economy of Clydeside, but it did not disrupt the City of London.[65] But growing financial integration induced the Bank to rethink its obligations during the interwar years.

In 1928 William Deacon's Bank, a smaller clearing bank with head offices in Manchester and interests in the Lancashire cotton industry, was on the verge of failure. Fearing that panic might spread through the northwest, the Bank undertook a cash infusion and subsequently arranged William Deacon's merger with the Royal Bank of Scotland. A year later (1929–30) the Bank headed up a rescue syndicate that included several large clearing banks to bail out a British overseas bank, the Banca Italo-Britannica. In September 1931, just when Britain was about to go off gold, the Bank of England was compelled to step in again to rescue another overseas bank, the Anglo-South American Bank. These interventions subtly expanded the Bank of England's lender-of-last-resort responsibilities, and postwar developments would expand them even more.[66]

For Germany, the lesson that financial integration required a more expansive definition of lender-of-last-resort responsibilities was learned

64. Walter Bagehot, "Lombard Street" in, Norman St. John-Stevas, ed., *The Collected Works of Walter Bagehot*, vol. IX (London: The Economist, 1978).

65. De Cecco, *Money and Empire*; Cottrell, "The Domestic Commercial Banks and the City of London, 1870–1939."

66. For all three episodes, see Sayers, *The Bank of England*, vol. I, pp. 253–267.

more painfully. There had been a spate of bank closings after 1873 and another round of bank failures in 1901. The Reichsbank did not intervene in any of these episodes, and panic did not spread to other institutions. Central bank authorities seem to have made a distinction between their responsibility to supply liquidity to the money market during periods of generalized stress (which they did) and their responsibility to rescue individual institutions that were experiencing difficulty due to mismanagement or excessive risk-taking (which they refrained from doing). The leading private bankers appear to have supported this policy. Indeed, both in the 1870s and again in 1901, stronger institutions acted quickly to capture the deposit base and solid industrial and commercial clients of the failed banks. Germany's private bankers seem to have regarded the failure of their principal competitors more as an opportunity than as a threat to their own stability.[67]

There is evidence that such attitudes and assumptions were at work during the banking crisis in 1931. The Danatbank, which had embarked on an ambitious program of company promotion and lending to municipalities during the 1920s, felt the squeeze first. Harold James reports that Oscar Wassermann, the head of Deutsche Bank, was still referring to the banking problem as "the Danat issue" as late as 6 July 1931, just a week before his own institution was forced to ration payments to depositors. Neither Wasserman nor Luther, the Reichsbank President, seem to have understood until it was too late that the failure or even rumors of the impending failure of a single major Berlin bank would trigger a generalized panic among the depositors of all of the big banks.[68]

Another crucial factor in the German banking crisis derived directly from the macroeconomic constraints imposed by the gold standard. The rigid metallic and foreign-exchange reserve requirements written into the Reichsbank's statutes in 1924 restricted its ability to inject liquidity into the German banking system in 1931. When Germany's banks began experiencing substantial deposit withdrawals in the spring of that year, they obtained liquidity through rediscounting operations with the Reichsbank. The Reichsbank's note issue swelled dangerously close to the maximum levels allowed by its reserves, and since this information was published regularly, creditors of the German banking system were alerted to the fact that the Reichsbank would either have to restrict its lending to the banks soon, endangering their survival, or repudiate its own reserve requirements, putting into jeopardy the convertibility of the mark. Thus

67. Whale, *Joint-Stock Banking in Germany*, pp. 9–35, 180–181.

68. James, *The German Slump*, p. 310; James, *The Reichsbank and Public Finance*, pp. 197–198, and *passim*. See also Born, *Die deutsche Bankenkrise 1931*.

the Reichsbank's increasingly difficult reserve situation aggravated the banking crisis.[69]

The experiences of the 1930s seem to have produced a more expansive interpretation of the responsibilities of the Banque de France as lender-of-last-resort as well, although the dynamic was somewhat different. In France none of the largest deposit or merchant banks failed during the Depression. However, quite a few regional and local banks were forced to close their doors, creating much bitterness in the affected regions and towns. The branch offices of the Banque de France often competed directly with local institutions for business, and observers found that the Banque was unduly aggressive in absorbing the clienteles of failed small banks that it had refused to aid.[70] Under the new banking regime set up in the 1940s, the authorities encouraged consolidation within the banking system, and hence the acquisition of smaller banks by larger institutions, but they no longer permitted institutions to fail. At the same time, the Banque de France all but halted its direct lending operations to nonbank customers in order to concentrate on its role as bankers' bank.

Among the four central banks discussed here, the Banca d'Italia probably went into the Great Depression with the most expansive understanding of its lender-of-last-resort responsibilities. The Banca had already had considerable experience with banking panics, most recently in the early 1920s. In December 1921 a depositors' run forced one of the largest commercial banks in the country, the Banca Italiana di Sconto, to close its doors. The Banca d'Italia attempted to organized a rescue syndicate, but this effort failed due to reluctance of the two leading rivals of the Sconto, the Banca Commerciale Italiana, and the Credito Italiano, to give the central bank unreserved support. A moratorium on withdrawals by the Sconto's depositors was declared. Ultimately, they received only a fraction of their original deposits, spread out in installments over several years. But despite the partial losses suffered by depositors, the Banca d'Italia was drawn into a costly liquidation of the Sconto's assets. The failed bank's ailing debtors included several large industrial firms, among them Ansaldo and Alfa Romeo, which were too big to be allowed to fail, and the central bank assumed responsibility for nursing them back to health. In the Sconto debacle the Banca d'Italia had the worst of both worlds: it failed to prevent the deflationary consequences of a major bank failure, but at the same time it was forced to lock up its own resources in a costly and drawn-out liquidation. When a depositors' run began on a

69. Born, *Die deutsche Bankenkrise 1931*, p. 183 and *passim*.

70. Jean Bouvier, "Monnaie et banque d'un aprés-guerre àl'autre: 1919–1945," in *Histoire économique et sociale de la France*, t. 4, vol. 2 (Paris: Presses universitaires françaises, 1980), pp. 687–728, esp. p 713.

second large commercial bank (the Banco di Roma) in late 1922 and early 1923, Bonaldo Stringher, the Banca d'Italia's director, was determined to save it, regardless of the expense and despite the lack of solidarity of the other large commercial banks.[71]

Partly as a result of this bitter experience in the early 1920s, Italy avoided spectacular and destructive depositors' runs and bank moratoria during the Great Depression, such as occurred in other countries with mixed banking systems, notably Germany and Austria. Both of Italy's remaining major universal banks, the Banca Commerciale and the Credito Italiano, essentially failed in the course of 1930–31 and had to be rescued with the support of the state and the central bank; but they failed silently, and their rescues were negotiated behind closed doors.[72]

To summarize the arguments made above, in all four countries bank regulation was stiffened during the 1930s and 1940s and central banks adopted more expansive understandings of their lender-of-last-resort responsibilities because increasingly integrated financial systems faced increasing vulnerability to destabilizing shocks.

New Policy Instruments for Achieving External Balance and Fighting Inflation.

Following the *de facto* or *de jure* abandonment of the gold standard between 1931 and 1936, all four countries considered here ceased using interest-rate policy as the primary instrument for achieving external balance. Two alternative strategies for managing international trade and financial transactions emerged during the 1930s. Germany and Italy brought nearly all foreign-exchange transactions under close government supervision. Foreign trade was increasingly bilateralized, with much of it effectively being carried out on a barter basis. Britain and France relied more heavily on manipulation of the exchange rate to achieve external balance after their respective departures from gold. They sought to maintain at least a degree of multilateralism in their trade and payments until the outbreak of World War II. However, once the war broke out in 1939, they in effect emulated the fascist nations by

71. On the collapse of the Sconto and the rescue of the Roma, see Forsyth, *The Crisis of Liberal Italy*; Anna Maria Falchero, *La Banca Italiana di Sconto, 1914–1921: Sette anni di guerra* (Milano: Angeli, 1990); Luigi De Rosa, *Storia del Banco di Roma*, vol. 2 (Rome: Banco di Roma, 1983) (privately published, restricted distribution); De Alberto Stefani, *Baraonda bancaria* (Milano: Edizioni del Borghese, 1960).

72. Gianni Toniolo, "Crisi economica e smobilizzo pubblico delle banche miste (1930–1934)," in Toniolo, ed., *Industria e banca nella grande crisi 1929–1934* (Milano: Etas Libri, 1978), 284–352.

imposing extensive controls on foreign-exchange transactions and by managing trade on a bilateral basis.

All four countries initially imposed extensive foreign-exchange controls as an emergency measure. Germany introduced controls first, in July 1931, in the wake of the banking crisis and the Standstill Agreements with its foreign creditors. Italy established a foreign-exchange monopoly in December 1934 in response to a deteriorating trade balance and external pressure on the lira. This was also the month in which serious preparations for the war in Ethiopia got underway. As was noted, Britain and France imposed exchange controls immediately following the outbreak of the war in September 1939. However, once exchange controls were in place, their continued existence was taken for granted; indeed, controls of one sort or another remained in place more or less uninterruptedly in all four countries for the next forty years.[73]

The idea of utilizing exchange controls as a means of insulating domestic economic policymaking from international pressures appears repeatedly in the economic position papers of the opposition Labour Party in Britain from the early 1930s on. In June 1935, Evan Durbin and H.V. Berry prepared a draft memo on the financial policy of a future Labour government which presupposed that foreign-exchange controls would be introduced.[74] Keynes also favored exchange controls, both as an instrument for preserving external balance and as a means of securing a higher level of domestic investment in Britain. National government as well as Treasury and Bank of England officials, in contrast, were reluctant to extend government regulation in such a significant manner, or to create the formidable bureaucratic machinery that administering exchange controls would have required, at least during peacetime. But even they accepted the inevitability of controls once war broke out, and a consensus soon developed within the wartime coalition government that controls would be maintained after the end of the conflict.[75]

There were many parallels in the evolution of thought in France regarding exchange controls. The Popular Front included the imposition

73. On international capital controls, see John B. Goodman and Louis W. Pauly, "The obsolescence of capital controls? Economic management in an age of global markets," *World Politics* 46 (1993), pp. 50–82; Alexandre Lamfalussy, "Changing Attitudes Towards Capital Movements," in Francis Cairncross ed., *Changing Perceptions of Economic Policy: Essays in Honor of the Seventieth Birthday of Sir Alec Cairncross* (New York: Methuen, 1981), pp. 194–217; Joseph Gold, "International Capital Movements under the Law of the International Monetary Fund," *IMF Pamphlets Series* 21 (1977); Alec Cairncross, *Control of Long-term International Capital Movements* (Washington, D.C.: Brookings Institution, 1973).

74. Howson, *British Monetary Policy, 1945–51*, pp. 72–73.

75. Ibid., *passim*.

of exchange controls in its electoral program in the spring of 1936. During the summer of 1936, however, economic experts inside and outside of the public administration dissuaded Léon Blum from imposing exchange controls. A common argument was that rigid controls of exports, imports, and capital movements represented "economic fascism," whereas devaluation of the franc and preservation of multilateral trade and payments would align France with the Western democracies, notably America and Britain. Blum's commercial attaché in Berlin prepared a report on the German experience with exchange controls that suggested it would take up to a year before the system became effective and that a large bureaucracy would be required to run the system. In the face of expert advice to the contrary, Blum demurred. Nevertheless, in France after September 1939, as in Britain, postwar planning was based largely on the assumption that exchange controls would remain in place.[76]

In the Anglo-American negotiations that led up to the Bretton Woods agreement, Keynes placed great importance on the ability of member nations to impose exchange controls. Article VI of the agreement, while it obliged members to avoid restrictions on current external payments (i.e. payments for goods and services) as soon as their general balance of payments situation allowed them to do so, explicitly allowed members to control both short- and long-term capital movements. In fact, the agreement envisaged that the resources of the IMF might prove inadequate to finance large capital outflows from a member nation experiencing balance-of-payments difficulties, and that the IMF itself therefore might require nations requesting its assistance to impose capital controls. In his speech in support of the agreement to the House of Lords on 23 May 1944, Keynes hailed these provisions as a major vindication of British interests:

> Not merely as a feature of the transition, but as a permanent arrangement, the plan accords to every member Government the explicit right to control all capital movements. What used to be a heresy is now endorsed as orthodox. In my own judgement, countries which avail themselves of this right may find it necessary to scrutinize all transactions, so as to prevent evasion of capital regulations. Provided that the innocent, current transactions are let through, there is nothing in the plan to prevent this. In fact, it is encouraged. It follows that our right to control the domestic capital market is secured on firmer foundations than ever before, and is formally accepted as a proper part of agreed international arrangements.[77]

Prior to the restoration of convertibility of the major European currencies in 1958, all four of the nations considered here imposed controls

76. Mouré, *Managing the Franc Poincaré*, pp. 237–8, 242–3.
77. Quoted in Gold, "International capital movements under the law of the IMF," p. 11.

not only on capital movements but also on current account. After 1958, Britain, France, and Italy retained controls on capital outflows as an instrument for maintaining external balance. By that time Germany had no need of controls on outflows, since its position as a structural surplus nation was already well established. However, beginning in 1961 Germany imposed controls on capital inflows in order to maintain control over domestic monetary growth. The measures taken included the prohibition of sales of domestic money market paper, and the prohibition of interest payments on mark deposits to nonresidents. These measures were lifted after revaluation of the mark in March 1961, but they were reintroduced in the late 1960s when speculation in favor of revaluation resumed on a large scale.

In addition to foreign-exchange controls, following World War II the three continental nations discussed here introduced a variety of selective credit controls as anti-inflationary instruments, including flexible minimum reserve requirements, ceilings on central bank rediscounts, and loan portfolio ceilings. The effectiveness of these instruments depended, at least in part, upon the existence of foreign-exchange controls, since without such controls domestic borrowers could circumvent domestic credit restrictions by borrowing on foreign capital markets.

Usually the object of employing selective instruments was to restrict the total volume of bank credit without raising the general structure of interest rates. Hence banks were to be induced to ration credit according to criteria other than price. In practice this often required that the instruments referred to above be utilized in conjunction with other forms of government intervention, including exemptions from the controls on particular types of loans, direct subsidies to firms that could no longer obtain bank loans, interest-rate subsidies for particular classes of loans, moral suasion exercised upon the banks not to raise interest rates, and interest-rate caps.

France and Italy made the most extensive use of selective credit instruments after the war. This use was facilitated by the nationalization of the major commercial banks in both countries and by the very extensive regulatory powers vested in the inspectorate in Italy, and in the Commission de Contrôle and the Trésor in France. Authorities in Germany were far more reluctant to use selective credit policies; indeed, Henry Wallich questions whether the imposition of credit ceilings in October 1948 and again in October 1950 was actually legal under the statutes of the Bank deutscher Länder, although he notes that these actions were not seriously questioned.[78]

In Britain during the era of postwar reconstruction, selective credit control was limited to the Bank of England's exercise of moral suasion

78. Wallich, *Mainsprings of the German Economic Revival*, p. 77.

on the clearing banks. Several economists working at the Treasury during Labour's tenure in office, most notably Robert Hall and Douglas Jay, wanted to draw up more formal controls on the expansion of bank credit following continental models, but they failed to overcome the resistance of the Bank of England to such measures. The Treasury exercised direct control over securities issues on the London market, however, through the Capital Issues Committee. The Treasury used its authority to control the total volume of new security offerings and to give preference to issues that conformed with broader policy directives, such as promotion of exports (beginning in 1945) and rearmament (in 1951).[79]

Selective Credit Controls As an Instrument of Developmental and Regional Policies.

The third broad motive for regulatory intervention in the financial sector was promotion of growth and regional development. Such concerns took on greater importance after World War II. The most radical innovator was France. Postwar French reformers were convinced that their financial system had failed to achieve adequate levels of industrial and infrastructural investment between the wars. Being one of the last nations to abandon the gold standard, France's economy had recovered slowly and imperfectly from the Great Depression. Moreover, swift defeat in 1940 at the hands of an enemy perceived to be more technologically and economically advanced, and the steady decline of the French economy under Vichy, inevitably put economic growth and modernization at the top of the postwar political agenda.

The radical transformation of the financial system and the assignment to the state of significant developmental functions was aided by the fact that France's business community in general, and its banking community in particular, emerged from depression and war with its reputation and influence badly damaged. Businessmen and bankers were not very visible in the ranks of the Resistance, and at least some of their number had collaborated openly with Pétain and Hitler. The left, momentarily ascendant after 1945, never forgave the *haute banque* for the Banque de France's withdrawal of support from the Cartel des Gauches in 1924. In 1936 the Popular Front stripped the Banque's private shareholders of much of their power; in 1945 they were stripped of their shares as well. The nationalization of the Banque, the major commercial banks, and

79. Howson, *British Monetary Policy, 1945–51*, pp. 228–36, 250–3, 284–5, 335–7, and *passim*; Fforde, *The Bank of England and Public Policy*, pp. 638, 641–3, 687, and *passim*.

insurance companies, as well as the expansion of the state's regulatory powers in 1945, was intended to prevent the "*mûr d'argent*" from once again obstructing reform.[80]

However, it was only through a piecemeal process of trial and error that Jean Monnet and his staff of planners discovered that the regulatory authority over the financial system introduced by legislation in 1936, 1941, and 1945, much more than the nationalizations, had created the most effective instruments for implementing indicative planning. The implementation of planning through selective credit policies required Monnet and his associates to forge an alliance with the Ministry of Finance and its senior bureaucrats, notably François Bloch-Lainé, the Director of the Trésor, where regulatory authority over the financial sector was vested. The creation of this alliance was not altogether straightforward. Monnet waged a long battle with Bloch-Lainé over control of the Fonds de Modernisation et d'Equipement (FME), which was given disposition of the Marshall Plan counterpart funds in 1948–49. The Ministry of Finance won this jurisdictional battle, but its functionaries embraced the modernization program of the planners, transforming the Trésor, in the words of one scholar, "from being a bank for the government into being a bank for the economy."[81]

Although an extended discussion of France's selective credit policy would be out of place here, the development of several key instruments can be outlined briefly. One crucial instrument was making certain types of medium-term (up to five years) finance bills eligible for rediscount by the Banque de France. The relevant legislation was introduced by De Gaulle's provisional government in May 1944, on the eve of the Normandy landings. Private banks seeking access to the rediscounting facilities of the central bank for loans of this nature had to obtain a signature from the Crédit National, one of the public financial institutions under the control of the Trésor. The legislative guidelines for rediscountable bills were exceptionally vague, specifying only that they should be "destined to develop the means of production of an enterprise"; this allowed the Trésor maximum discretion in setting priorities for the expansion of medium-term credit. The minimum reserve requirements and credit ceilings introduced in 1948 and 1950, referred to above in the discussion of anti-inflationary policies in the era of postwar reconstruction, did not apply to medium-term bills carrying the signature of the Crédit National.

80. On the eclipse of business and banking influence after the liberation, see Bloch-Lainé and Bouvier, *La France restaurée*, pp. 213–244.

81. John Zysman, *Governments, Markets, and Growth: Financial Systems and the Politics of Industrial Change* (Ithaca: Cornell University, 1983), esp. pp. 104–133. The quote is on p. 106.

In the early postwar years other types of "transformable" medium-term credit were introduced as well; all of them required the signature of one of several public banks controlled by the Trésor.

A second key instrument of selective credit policy, as noted above, was the FME, which managed the counterpart funds generated by the Marshall Plan. The Trésor distributed these resources to state-owned and private firms in support of the Monnet Plan's investment program. In 1955 they essentially were replaced by the Fonds de Développment Economique et Social (FDES), the resources of which came directly from the state budget. By using FDES funds to subsidize interest rates on loans rather than making loans or grants outright, the Trésor could influence the flow of investment capital greatly in excess of its own resources.

A third major instrument of selective credit allocation was the use of the resources of the state-owned banking sector, including the savings bank network, and its parent institution, the Caisse des Depôts et Consignations, the postal savings banks, major specialized organizations, including the Crédit National, the Crédit Agricole, and the Crédit Foncier de France. All of these institutions pre-dated World War II; however, particularly from the early 1950s on, the state made more aggressive use of the resources raised by the public banks from depositors and through bond issues to support its investment program. The financial resources under the direct control of the state were further augmented by the imposition of reserve requirements in 1948, which required banks to invest certain proportions of their assets in state securities.[82]

The state's control over the newly nationalized commercial banks was less direct, since the relevant legislation had preserved managerial autonomy. However, the extensive battery of financial controls and incentives at the disposal of the Trésor allowed it to exercise significant influence on the investment decisions of nationalized commercial banks as well as the investment banks which had remained in private hands.

This is not the place to assess the contribution of indicative planning to France's rapid economic growth in the first three postwar decades. In any case it is clear that other European nations, including Italy and Germany, which made less extensive use of financial controls as instruments of economic planning, achieved high rates of growth as well. What is important to stress in the context of this essay is, first, the reorientation of the goals of interest-rate policy to achieve high rates of growth and employment, and second, the deployment of new regulatory instruments to maintain external balance (i.e., exchange controls), and to fight inflation (reserve

82. Patat and Lutfalla, *A Monetary History of France in the Twentieth Century*, pp. 122–4, 143–6 and *passim*. On selective credit allocation in France, see also Loriaux, *France After Hegemony*, and the essay by Sofía Pérez in this volume.

requirements, rediscount ceilings, credit ceilings) were necessary preconditions for the "classic" system of French indicative planning based on selective credit allocation.

As we have seen, the bank reforms in Italy in 1933–34, gave the public authorities regulatory powers over the financial sector at least as extensive as those in France. There were also planning enthusiasts in postwar Italy, including politicians such as Republican Party leader Ugo La Malfa and Christian Democrat Ezio Vanoni, and public officials, including Pasquale Saraceno and Oscar Sinigalia. However, both the public administration and successive cabinets were too fragmented in Italy to draw up and implement a comprehensive investment program. The public role in postwar investment, it is true, was massive. State-guaranteed bond issues by parapublic corporations, including the IRI, the Istituto Mobiliare Italiano (IMI), and the ENI (Ente Nazionale di Idrocarburi) dominated the securities markets. Nearly the entire banking sector was in public hands, including the savings banks (Casse di Risparmio), the major commercial banks (the three Banche di Interesse Nazionale, or BIN, nationalized in 1933–34), important regional institutions (Banco di Napoli, Banco di Sicilia, Monte dei Paschi in Siena, etc.), and Mediobanca, an institution created in 1945–46 to take over the investment banking functions formerly exercised by the universal banks. But despite this massive public presence, in comparison with France, there was less coordination between macroeconomic policy and investment policy in Italy, and less use of regulatory instruments to achieve selective credit allocation.[83] An exception was the policy of blocking the expansion of bank credit and channeling subsidies and subsidized credit to particular industries and sectors in 1947–48, as discussed above. In addition, the maintenance of fairly tight controls on capital exports may have sustained the level of domestic investment during much of the postwar era. But otherwise, the principle causal argument proposed in this essay, which links changes in macropolicy orientation to regulatory change, explains less about postwar capital formation and investment policy in Italy than it does in France.

The authorities in Italy did use selective credit controls as an instrument of regional policy, however. In the 1950s, the Banca d'Italia favored the regional savings banks (Casse di Risparmio) in allocating permits for opening new branches over the big deposit banks (BIN). The

83. Harper, *America and the Reconstruction of Italy, 1945–1948*; Andrew Shonfield, *Modern Capitalism: The Changing Balance of Public and Private Power* (New York: Oxford University, 1965), pp. 176–92; Alan R. Posner, "Italy: dependence and political fragmentation," in Peter J. Katzenstein, ed., *Between Power and Plenty: Foreign Economic Policies of Advanced Industrial States* (Madison: University of Wisconsin, 1978), pp. 225–254.

Banca feared that excessive expansion of the BIN would drain resources from the poorer regions of the country into the more developed areas, reinforcing economic dualism. Moreover, during the 1950s the government created a series of regional investment banks, the so-called Mediocrediti Regionali, to supplement the activity of Mediobanca, which focused its attention on the largest firms in Italy's industrial triangle.[84]

Britain made relatively moderate use of financial regulation to support selective intervention in financial markets. As was noted above, the Bank of England used moral suasion to encourage the clearing banks to favor investments in export industries and rearmament in the early postwar years. The Capital Issues Committee regulated new stock and bond issues, using similar selective criteria. Controls on foreign portfolio and direct investments were rigid, and probably effective.

The Bank of England also presided over the creation of two new parapublic investment banks, which were intended to help meet the investment needs of larger and smaller industrial firms, respectively. The two institutions in question, the Financial Corporation for Industry (FCI—for big firms) and the Industrial and Commercial Finance Corporation (ICFC—for small firms) opened their doors in 1945. Their share capital was subscribed by the Bank, merchant banks, and the leading investment trusts. They were to be equipped with research staffs, similar to the German universal banks. They were envisaged as instruments with which the Bank could formulate and implement an industrial policy in cooperation with industrialists and leading merchant bankers. By all accounts, these initiatives did not produce a major transformation of the banking system or of the structure of capital markets in Britain.[85]

In Germany even less use was made of financial regulation to pursue selective credit allocation, apart from the selective imposition of credit ceilings during the Korean crisis in 1951, discussed above. This is not to say the German government made no use of financial instruments to pursue industrial policies after World War II. A public investment bank, the Kreditanstalt für Wiederaufbau, was established in 1948–49 to make investment loans with the counterpart funds generated by Marshall Plan aid. The Hermes program provided public loan guarantees for export credit. On the regional level, the Landesbanken, which functioned as central banks to the (public) savings institutions, often pursued regional industrial policies, at times in cooperation with Land governments.[86]

84. Nardozzi, *Tre sistemi creditizi*, pp. 54–63.

85. Fforde, *The Bank of England and Public Policy*, pp. 704–727.

86. Hans-Hermann Francke and Michael Hudson, *Banking and Finance in West Germany* (New York: St. Martin's, 1984). On the use of selective credit allocation by the Landesbanken as an instrument of industrial policy, see Richard Deeg, "Banks and the State in

However, none of these forms of public intervention depended crucially on the changes in macropolicy regime and regulatory system that occurred in the 1930s and 1940s, and thus they fall outside of the argument developed here.

Conclusions

The object of this essay has been to explore common ground across four nations in the transformation of the goals, instruments, and institutional setting of macroeconomic policymaking and financial regulation, from the collapse of the gold standard in the early- to mid-1930s through the era of reconstruction after World War II. The arguments proposed here concern political economy; however, their persuasiveness rests upon the validity of the economic analysis of the causes of the Great Depression, and the mechanisms of recovery from it, put forward recently by Eichengreen, Sachs, and Temin, among others. According to this interpretation, the Great Depression was caused by a cumulative deflationary dynamic unleashed by the asymmetrical manner in which the interwar gold standard functioned. Countries with balance-of-payments deficits were required to restore equilibrium by adopting deflationary macroeconomic policies, while countries in surplus stood under no obligation to pursue expansionary policies. This asymmetry set in motion a process in which one country after another adopted macroeconomic policies that produced falling investment, demand, and employment. Delinking domestic monetary policy formation from gold was the essential precondition for economic recovery.

Once this analysis of the economics of the Great Depression is accepted, three core propositions regarding the political economy of the Depression, war, and postwar years can be adduced: they are the subject of this essay. The first proposition is that the collapse of the gold standard was the crucial event that set in motion the most profound transformation of the role of the state in the economy in the twentieth century. The wave of institution-building that followed emanated outward from the reordering of macroeconomic policy and the regulation of the financial sector in response to three great challenges that quickly followed one another: recovery from the Great Depression, rearmament and war, and postwar reconstruction and modernization.[87]

Germany: The Critical Role of Subnational Institutions in Economic Governance," PhD. dissertation, Dept. of Political Science, MIT (1992).

87. The periodization scheme for major institutional change proposed here dovetails with Karl Polanyi's arguments in *The Great Transformation: The Political and Economic Origins of Our Time* (Boston: Beacon, 1957). Polanyi, too, dated the "great transformation" of

The second major proposition is that the transformation of macroeconomic policymaking assumes logical and temporal primacy over changes in selective microeconomic policies and financial regulation.[88] The transformation in the goals of macroeconomic policy—from maintenance of exchange-rate parities under the gold standard, to seeking to combine high levels of economic growth and/or employment with price-level stability and external balance after gold was abandoned—was a necessary but insufficient precondition for the more intrusive regulation of the financial sector that all four countries considered here introduced in the course of the 1930s and 1940s (less in Britain than on the continent). This essay suggests that there was considerably greater variation across nations in the regulatory innovations introduced in this period than in the goals and instruments of monetary policy formation. Regulatory change occurred in order to accomplish three crucial goals. First, all four nations sought to restore or augment the stability of their banking systems by extending regulation and supervision and by adopting a more expansive interpretation of the lender-of-last-resort responsibilities of the central bank. Second, selective controls over international capital flows and domestic lending and securities issues were adopted. These microeconomic instruments were employed to maintain external balance and check inflation, allowing interest-rate policy to be set in order to promote growth and employment. Third, selective credit allocation was used in France to promote national, and in Italy regional, economic development.

The third major proposition is that changes in the goals and instruments of monetary, not fiscal, policymaking constitute the red thread that

---

the state's role in the economy in the twentieth century from the collapse of the gold standard in 1931. He contrasted the "conservative twenties" with the "revolutionary thirties." It is at odds with the periodization proposed by Charles S. Maier in "The Two Postwar Eras and the Conditions for Stability in 20th-Century Western Europe," *American Historical Review* 86 (1981), no. 2, pp. 327–367, which argues that the years immediately following the two world wars were the decisive periods of institutional change.

88. This interpretation is at odds with much of the recent literature on the American New Deal, which posits a more radical "administrative" or "regulatory" New Deal during the initial years of Roosevelt's presidency, followed by a more liberal "Keynesian" or "macroeconomic" New Deal after the recession of 1937. See Alan Brinkley, "The New Deal and the Idea of the State," in Steve Fraser and Gary Gerstle, eds., *The Rise and Fall of the New Deal Order, 1930–1980* (Princeton: Princeton University, 1989), pp. 85–121; Margaret Weir and Theda Skocpol, "State structures and the possibilities for 'Keynesian' responses to the Great Depression in Sweden, Britain, and the United States," in, Peter Evans, Dietrich Rueschemeyer, and Theda Skocpol, eds., *Bringing the State Back In* (New York: Cambridge University, 1985), pp. 44–77. Scholars working in this tradition completely ignore the transformation in monetary policymaking after the United States left gold in 1933. The macroeconomic revolution they identify consisted in the use of fiscal policy to promote macroeconomic stabilization.

runs through the transformation of macroeconomic policy formation in all four of the countries discussed here.[89] Considerable differences in fiscal policy orientation are identifiable across nations, and no common denominator can be established. A "fiscal policy revolution" may have taken place in some nations after World War II; however, the monetary policy revolution that took place between 1931 and 1936 was not only more generalized, taking place throughout Europe and indeed throughout the industrialized world, but also the necessary if insufficient precondition for the complex regulatory changes that followed it in the course of the 1930s and 1940s.

89. This argument is at odds with much of the literature that seeks to identify a "Keynesian" transformation in economic policymaking in the advanced industrial states at some point during the 1930s or 1940s. See the essay by Forsyth and Notermans in this volume.

Chapter 3

The International Monetary System and Domestic Economic Policy

Hansjörg Herr

Introduction

Monetary economies exist within an international context characterized by the given international monetary system and a hierarchy of currencies. The international monetary system can restrict the scope of domestic economic policy, or it can serve to increase the scope of domestic economic policy and become a vehicle of domination between states. It is therefore not possible to adequately analyze domestic economic policy without taking into account international relations. This is the point of departure for the following analysis.[1]

The section below examines the connection between price-level stability and high employment, and the third section analyzes the mechanisms of monetary dominance between countries. The fourth section outlines the working mechanisms of international monetary systems. The fifth section offers an interpretation of developments in the international monetary system since World War II, and the final section examines possible future developments.

Price-Level Stability and Employment

Employment and Inflation

In general, maintaining price-level stability in monetary economies requires unemployment. An increasing employment rate eventually leads,

1. Translated by Silke Tober and Dominic Kahn. I would like to thank Douglas Forsyth, Ton Notermans, and Silke Tober for many helpful comments.

via market forces, to wage increases that exceed increases in productivity and initiate a wage-price spiral.[2] Trade unions do not necessarily play a leading role in a wage-price spiral. The inflationary process is fueled by wage increases in excess of negotiated wages resulting from a high demand for labor. Unions merely take these market-determined wages into consideration during the next round of wage negotiations to maintain their own legitimacy.[3] Given an accommodating monetary policy, inflation is a cumulative process (Keynes 1930; Dornbusch/Sturzenegger/Wolf 1990). This is not merely a consequence of the underlying wage-price spiral. Inflation inevitably leads to a flight into tangible assets and an increase in the velocity of the national currency. As a result of fiscal lags, inflation may furthermore increase the budget deficit, which the government might then be forced to finance by printing money (Olivera 1967; Tanzi 1977). It is especially likely that budget deficits will escalate if taxes and other state revenues are not raised in line with inflation. Even low rates of inflation therefore contain cumulative elements, which are reinforced by an increase in inflation.

If an inflationary process is not stopped, it leads to the successive erosion of the monetary system and thus destroys the coherence of the national economy as parallel currencies emerge and economic processes are demonetized. Even if positive real interest rates are maintained through high nominal interest rates and through a reduction of the duration of debt contracts, economic agents cannot discount the possibility of negative real interest rates in the future, or of a complete breakdown of the monetary system or currency reform. Inflation therefore always increases economic uncertainty and erodes economic agents' confidence in the monetary system. The inevitable outcome is a collapse of domestic investment activity and economic growth because a flight into tangible assets implies a refusal to finance and participate in productive processes. Relative price level stability is a necessary condition for a stable monetary economy, because only a relatively stable price level can preclude cumulative processes and encourage economic prosperity by means of high investment. During an inflationary process, central banks face the uncomfortable choice of either accommodating inflation or initiating a

2. Keynes (1930) stressed the key role that profit inflation, due to excess demand in the commodity market, can play in initiating an inflationary process. The increase in the price level is likely to trigger a wage-price spiral, that is, income inflation, and thus start a cumulative process.

3. The West German unions, for example, following a policy of wage restraint, were under pressure to reestablish their legitimacy at the end of the 1960s given wildcat strikes resulting in wage increases beyond negotiated wages. The demand for higher wages in the early 1970s was thus at least in part a result of the unions' attempt to defend their legitimacy (Scharpf 1987).

stabilization crisis.[4] In order to keep the economy functioning coherently, central banks will in the end be left with no option but to induce a stabilization crisis and consequently unemployment.

Although the conflict between price-level stability and high employment also emerges in a closed economy, it is significantly heightened by international processes. This is because foreign currencies serve as a yardstick for measuring domestic price-level stability. Because of the relatively low transaction and carrying costs, foreign currencies are far better than domestic tangible assets as stores of value. A flight into foreign currencies results in a currency depreciation-inflation spiral, which then reinforces the wage-price spiral (Bilson 1979). It is important to note that changes in the exchange rate resulting from a collapse of confidence in the national currency can lead to an explosive increase in inflation. If the state has liabilities denominated in foreign currency, there exists an additional inflation potential, since real currency depreciation increases the state's debt-service burden and may widen the budget deficit (Sachs 1986). In sum, the conflict between price-level stability and high employment usually manifests itself as a conflict between exchange-rate stability and high employment.

Restrictions on capital movements can slow down inflation by generating additional transaction costs. They cannot, however, bring the underlying inflationary mechanism to a halt—even if there are no loopholes. If economic agents are prevented from increasing their portfolio share of foreign assets, the flight into tangible assets intensifies and further fuels inflation. Restricting capital movements can be beneficial if the domestic price level is essentially stable and capital flight is exclusively motivated by interest-rate differentials and political considerations. Furthermore, restrictions on capital movements limit the extent to which domestically borrowed funds can be exported.

Incomes Policy

The specific domestic conditions determine how susceptible individual countries are to inflation and influence the speed with which policymakers react to inflation and currency depreciation. The more favorable the institutional and political conditions for productivity-oriented wage developments, the smaller the conflict between high employment and price-level stability. The combination of expansive monetary policy and productivity-oriented wage increases is the foundation for stable accumulation (Scharpf

4. The term "stabilization crisis" refers to the decline in production and employment resulting from anti-inflationary monetary policy.

1987, 212ff.). Most monetary economies require a certain minimum level of unemployment,[5] which creates the necessary labor-market conditions for relative price-level stability.

Under conditions of high employment there are several methods that can be used to encourage productivity-oriented increases in money wages:

a) Given an explicit or implicit social contract, incomes policy can be used to establish a nominal wage anchor. A nominal wage anchor requires specific institutional and socioeconomic conditions. In particular, it requires trade unions and employers' associations capable of coordinating pay increases. Such coordination can take the form of centralized wage negotiations, as in Austria, or wage settlements in key industries or key enterprises that are subsequently adopted in general, as in the Federal Republic of Germany and Japan (Soskice 1990). A social contract furthermore presupposes that unions and employers' associations are able to curtail wage increases in excess of negotiated wages. This is necessary because incomes policy implemented in an environment of high employment has to continuously work against market forces that induce wage increases.

b) Incomes policy is rarely effective in the absence of an exogenous mechanism of monetary discipline. In principle an independent central bank is always able to guarantee the internal and external value of its currency. If unions, employers' associations, and the government adapt their behavior to exogenously determined monetary policy, a regime of cooperative economic policy can emerge. From a game-theoretic perspective, the threat to maintain price-level stability at all costs provides the central bank with the advantage of the first move (Scharpf 1987, 176). If, on the other hand, especially unions and employers' associations do not yield to the central bank—because, for example, institutional or political conditions render them unable to pursue a macroeconomic strategy—a conflict of interests resulting in high unemployment is the probable outcome. The Federal Republic of Germany provides a typical example of the first case, in that trade unions usually subordinate their policies to that of the Bundesbank; the early 1970s saw one of the rare exceptions.

c) The position of a weak central bank can be strengthened by means of a nominal exchange-rate anchor, that is, by pegging the exchange rate to a stable currency. Domestic economic agents are then faced with a rigid external constraint that results either in a modification of their behavior or, in the event of inflation, unemployment (Giavazzi/Pagano 1988). For

5. During recent years attempts have been made to determine a *non-accelerating inflation rate of unemployment* (NAIRU) and explain the particular domestic reasons for the different unemployment rates necessary to prevent cumulative wage-price spirals (Metcalf 1986; Layard 1990). The NAIRU concept has monetarist characteristics, as it analyzes not the conditions for price-level stability, but for a constant rate of inflation.

> example, nominal exchange-rate anchors were adopted by southern European countries and more recently Scandinavian countries to augment the credibility of domestic monetary policy and compel trade unions and employers' associations to cooperate. In these cases, the German mark, as the European key currency, served as the anchor. Ultimately, a nominal exchange-rate anchor can be maintained only if domestic economic policy is successfully subordinated to the external constraint. Otherwise, any nominal anchor will inevitably give way. A nominal crawling peg appears to be a compromise between establishing an external constraint and maintaining a certain flexibility in domestic economic policy. If, however, growing internal pressure (indicating a stabilization crisis) rapidly leads to nominal exchange-rate adjustments, economic agents will soon realize that the exchange rate does not, in fact, present an external constraint, and the exchange rate will no longer function as a stability anchor. Only a one-time exchange-rate adjustment, as part of a stability-oriented reform package, or a nominal crawling peg with low nominal rates of devaluation,[6] can serve to reduce the costs of stabilization (Herr/Westphal 1991).

In the absence of a successful incomes policy a country has to accept high unemployment if it wants to stop a wage-price spiral and establish price-level stability. The level of unemployment compatible with price-level stability is dependent on the particular institutional and political conditions prevailing in the country in question. A high unemployment rate does not deprive unions of their function. On the contrary, unions have the important task of preventing decreases in money wages and cumulative deflation. In the event of rising unemployment, market processes also give rise to the danger of an erosion of the nominal wage anchor. In this case, if nominal wages lose their rigidity a process of cumulative deflation can be checked only with great difficulty.

The Conflict Between High Employment and External Equilibrium

Although an effective incomes policy is a necessary condition for high employment, it is not a sufficient one. It would therefore be shortsighted to attribute the problem of unemployment solely to the conflict between high employment and price-level stability. Even in the absence of wage inflation, central banks may be forced to act restrictively with a view to external equilibrium. A chronic current-account deficit that forces the central bank to act restrictively may emerge if the respective country

6. A real exchange-rate anchor aimed at stabilizing the real exchange rate amounts to an indexation of the nominal exchange rate and may reinforce inflationary processes.

continually experiences stronger economic growth than its trading partners. The more expansive the international economic climate, the more favorable are the external conditions for internal economic growth. Although in the face of a restrictive world economy it may be possible to increase the scope for domestic economic growth through real devaluation, this would drastically increase the demands made on incomes policy, since trade unions would have to tolerate increases in the price level without corresponding increases in nominal wages. In theory, it is possible for individual countries to evade a given negative external influence if the development of nominal wages matches the macroeconomic situation. In this case, however, incomes policy becomes the decisive macroeconomic policy instrument. Unions and employers' associations become interventionists able to offset any economic disturbance through changes in the level of nominal wages[7]—a scenario unlikely to persist in the longer run.

The more stable the initial price level, the easier it is for incomes policy to stabilize the price level under conditions of high employment. An international monetary system with fixed exchange rates is therefore substantially more conducive to incomes policy than a regime with flexible exchange rates and strong exchange-rate fluctuation. Accordingly, the breakdown of the Bretton Woods system and the two oil-price shocks in the 1970s were at least partly responsible for the failure of incomes policy during that period (Bosworth 1991). An example of the mutual support of incomes policy and nominal exchange-rate stabilization is provided by Austria, which since 1973 has pegged the schilling to the German mark.

The policy objectives of governments, and in particular central banks, are more complex when taking the external environment into consideration. A central bank may, for example, strive for a surplus on the current account, whether out of precaution or a thirst for power. As demonstrated by Britain and Germany after World War I, deflation may be accepted for external reasons, although it could hardly be interpreted as a domestic economic goal. For Germany it was rational to avoid devaluation so as not to increase the foreign debt in real terms; Britain returned to the gold standard at its prewar parity because its main competitor, the United States, did not have to change the parity of the dollar, and because Britain wanted to reestablish the position of dominance the pound had enjoyed before World War I.

7. "The notion of a reverse wage-price mechanism, which makes wage policy responsible for stabilizing the price level, suggests monopolistic behavior on the part of unions and sees them as non-market-conforming interventionists" (Riese 1993, 14) (The translation is ours —ST/DK).

Mechanisms of Monetary Dominance

The Quality of a Currency As a Store of Value

Individuals acting in the present are faced with a given past and an uncertain future.[8] They therefore have the desire to transfer wealth from the present to the future in a reliable store of value. Given economic stability, money and other nominal assets fulfill the store-of-value function. National currencies differ in their stability and therefore in their quality as a store of value. The internal and external stability of a currency are intimately related. Exchange-rate stability can be viewed as a criterion for evaluating the efficiency of domestic stabilization policies. More specifically, it indicates whether the central bank's monetary policy is successfully inducing economic agents to hold a sufficient part of their wealth in the form of domestic nominal assets (Riese 1986, 247). The exchange rate is first and foremost an asset price that converts between domestic and foreign wealth. If a country is experiencing a depreciation-inflation spiral and the central bank pursues an accommodating monetary policy, there is no endogenous limit to the increase in the exchange rate. Continual currency depreciation, especially in an inflationary environment, destroys confidence in the future stability of a currency and induces portfolio adjustments which in no way reflect purchasing-power parity.

The stability of a currency ultimately is contingent on monetary policy, which in turn is influenced by the specific conditions prevailing in a given country. It is assumed here that monetary policy dominates all other macroeconomic policies. Monetary policy is able to counteract the potentially positive effects of an expansive fiscal policy by raising the rate of interest above the expected rate of profit and inducing a crisis. Likewise the central bank may raise unemployment to a level that prevents wage inflation. The assertion that monetary policy dominates obviously presupposes that the central bank can act autonomously and that monetary policy is not subordinated to fiscal policy or nominal wage developments. High budget deficits do not prevent the central bank from enforcing price-level stability; there will, however, be the possibility of an extreme crowding-out with declining investment and growing unemployment. It is also assumed that monetary restriction does not lead to an endogenous escalation of budget deficits, as this destroys the independence of the monetary policy. Restrictive monetary policy may generate

8. General equilibrium theory explicitly states the conditions that have to be satisfied if there is to be no uncertainty: either universal future markets or rational expectations based on objective probabilities are required for the future to merge with the present (Hahn 1981). However, universal future markets do not exist, and economic agents attach subjective, not objective, probabilities to future events.

political turmoil and thereby erode the power of the central bank, even if it is institutionally independent. On a political level, a "game of chicken" involving monetary and fiscal policy may therefore end to the disadvantage of monetary policy. A game of chicken involving trade unions and the central bank is also possible if trade unions bring about an increase in nominal wages despite a nonaccommodating monetary policy. Unemployment will consequently rise. In contrast to fiscal policy, which is faced with an endogenous growth of budget deficits during a stabilization crisis, trade unions lose some of their strength in a stabilization crisis, so that a reduction in nominal wage increases is brought about through market processes. However, political factors may nonetheless force the central bank to adopt an accommodating monetary policy.

If the central bank fights inflation early and without creating a longer-term accumulation crisis, the money it issues will be internally and externally stable and a high-quality store of value. If, on the other hand, the central bank begins to combat inflation only when erosion of the national monetary system is already discernible (i.e., when a flight into relatively stable currencies and tangible assets is taking place), and if stabilization produces serious economic and political crisis, the national currency will be a low-quality store of value. In most cases a low store-of-value quality is reflected in the internal and external depreciation of the currency and in a relatively high variance of all economic variables. This high variance results from the late initiation of a stabilization crisis that causes all economic variables to change erratically (Okun 1971; Fischer 1981; Padoa-Schioppa/Papadia 1984). Stable nominal variables do not automatically produce a high-quality store of value. If nominal stability is bought with high interest rates and economic stagnation the quality of a currency remaines low—because, for example, the uncertainty about the future value of the currency is high. In addition, a low store-of-value quality usually limits the freedom of disposal of a currency, since countries with unstable currencies tend to impose restrictions on capital movements. It should be noted that the free disposal of a depreciating currency may even be limited when capital movements are not regulated, because economic agents inevitably incur large losses when they try to change out of an unstable currency once depreciation has taken place.[9]

Actual and, above all, expected monetary policy determine the quality of a currency. Economic agents do not jump, like marionettes, to a

9. Full convertibility is usually defined as the absence of restrictions on capital movements. Such a definition of convertibility is economically meaningless because it ignores the question of currency stability. Following the usage at the time of the gold standard (Bloomfield 1959), it is maintained here that, from an economic viewpoint, the only useful definition of convertibility is the free disposal of a currency given its external stability.

new equilibrium or a new equilibrium path[10] after a change in monetary policy. They continuously attempt to anticipate fundamental policy changes. Expectation formation with respect to monetary policy cannot be explained entirely by economic factors. Economic agents also assess the specific market constellation of individual countries; that is, they assess the political, social, and institutional situation, taking into account the degree of independence of the central bank and the coherence and character of economic policy pursued by dominant social groups.

Since an assessment of the economic situation in a country is dominated by expectations, confidence in the economic policy of the central bank and other economic policymakers plays a critical role in determining the quality of a currency as a store of value. Economic theory has rightly assigned the reputation and credibility of monetary policy a central place in monetary theory (Blackburn/Christensen 1989). The task economic agents face in forming expectations is simplified by the fact that, at least in the medium term,[11] the market constellation of a given country is characterized by a certain rigidity because conditions particular to a given country can be changed neither easily nor at will. Likewise, it is not possible to simply copy institutions and regulations without changing their character. If a country adopted the model of an independent central bank on which the Bundesbank is based, this would by no means imply that the Bundesbank's monetary policy would be copied as well. Because of their rigidity, market constellations affect the expectations of economic agents. In this context one can support the Keynesian thesis that in a world with an uncertain future rational economic agents assume that past and present developments will persist in the foreseeable future (Keynes 1936, 128). Only in the event of obvious structural breaks do expectations suddenly change. It follows that the effects of economic policy, such as expansive fiscal policy, cannot be deduced in general but only within the context of a particular structure of expectations (Lucas 1976). The following remarks serve to clarify this idea.

In general, expectations of future monetary stability can be generated only by a past record of successful stability-oriented policy (Klein 1978). The history of the German mark provides a good example of this because the Bundesbank has built up the mark's reputation since the 1950s by combining continual current-account surpluses with a strong aversion to

10. Dornbusch (1976) developed one of the most renowned models that treats economic agents like marionettes by combining the long-run purchasing-power parity theory with the short-run interest-rate parity approach.

11. The medium term is a period between one and several decades.

nominal devaluation. Price-level stability was enforced even against the interests of the government, when necessary (Emminger 1986; Spahn 1988). Since the early 1950s, the market constellation of the Federal Republic of Germany has been characterized by a continuous nominal decrease of the mark's trade-weighted exchange rate without eroding the surplus on the current account.[12] Although temporary devaluation against the dollar and yen—the two other currencies of international importance—were tolerated, any weakness with respect to other currencies—especially European currencies—was resolutely counteracted. The economic policy of the Federal Republic of Germany established the mark as a currency of international importance.

In rare cases it may be possible that a convincing promise to create monetary stability will decisively increase the reputation of a currency. This was exemplified by the high value of the dollar for several years following the restrictive monetary policy in the United States after 1979 and the election of President Reagan one year later. The strength of the dollar was maintained despite several interest rate cuts after mid-1982 and the narrowing of interest rate differentials vis-à-vis other international reserve currencies. Economic agents apparently assumed that Reagan's inauguration would bring the transition from the market constellation of a weak dollar to a market constellation in which the external value of the dollar is rigorously defended by economic policymakers—which proved not to be the case.

The recent history of Latin America as well as Central and Eastern Europe clearly illustrates, however, that the promise of stability-oriented policy does not automatically entail a change in the market constellation. Stability programs designed to overcome a market constellation of high budget deficits, inflationary monetary policy, and a weak currency may be met by a "wait-and-see" attitude on the part of economic agents that would then contribute to the failure of such programs through continued capital flight and persistently low investment (Dornbusch 1990). The wait-and-see attitude leads to a "tyranny of the status quo" (Dixit 1992, 109), because the widespread belief that a given country will remain in the market constellation of a weak currency will lead to a situation in which policymakers are forced to revert to inflationary economic policy.

12. The Bundesbank quickly combatted current-account deficits by implementing restrictive policy measures. This was most apparent in 1981 when the Bundesbank predicted a general crisis of confidence in the mark and reacted with a "drastic break in interest rate and liquidity policy" (Deutsche Bundesbank 1981, 5; the translation is ours - ST/DK), thereby producing a deep recession. Subsequent to German unification, a current-account deficit emerged, which cannot be reduced as easily as those in previous periods. One cannot completely exclude the possibility that the shock of unification will alter Germany's market constellation.

Economic Dominance and the Scarcity of Money

Relations of economic dominance and submission between monetary economies depend, first, on differences in the real economy[13] and their relative political and military might and, second, on the relative scarcity of the national currencies. Only the second aspect is analyzed in this section, assuming the effect of the other to be neutral. In a two-country model, assuming a flexible exchange rate and an equilibrium constellation characterized by exchange-rate stability and identical interest rates in both countries, two reaction patterns are possible if the store-of-value quality of one of the currencies changes, for examples due to an increase in the expected rate of inflation. If interest rates do not change, the currency that is expected to be more unstable will, *ceteris paribus*, immediately depreciate. The exchange rate will then reflect the new relation between the store-of-value qualities of the two currencies. In a dynamic context, this scenario is not very realistic because the country that allows its currency to depreciate aggravates its inflation problem and destroys confidence in its currency. The result may be a devaluation-wage-inflation spiral and a devaluation-capital-flight-devaluation spiral. The country in question will therefore generally have to impose restrictive monetary policy measures to prevent the erosion of its monetary system. In particular, the nominal exchange rate will have to be stabilized in order to fight inflation and bolster confidence in the national currency. In this case the new relation between the store-of-value qualities of the currencies will be reflected in an interest-rate differential and a constant or slightly adjusted exchange rate. The country whose currency has the higher store-of-value quality then has a relatively low interest rate, while the interest rate in the country whose currency has the lower store-of-value quality is relatively high.

The relationship between the two countries described above is one of dominance and submission. The country whose currency has the lower store-of-value quality will align its interest rate with that of the other country. In the case of an increase in interest rate on the part of the dominant country, the dominated country, to maintain stability, will also be forced to raise its interest rate. If the dominant country lowers its interest rate, the dominated country will follow suit in order to take advantage of the possibilities for economic growth. Dominance thus implies the freedom to set one's monetary policy autonomously and thereby delimit monetary policy and economic growth in other countries. Relations of

13. The term "real economy" is taken to comprise the size of a given country (population, gross domestic product, territory) and its technological development (general level of productivity, use of high technology, research and development, etc.).

dominance and submission between countries are brought about by differences in the stability of the national currencies. The country that is able to secure the highest scarcity of its currency, that is, the highest value stability, dominates the country whose currency is less scarce or, in the extreme case, permanently threatened by a loss of its money functions.

Institutionally fixed exchange rates hardly modify this mechanism. A higher rate of inflation leads to trade deficits. If the visible trade deficit exceeds a given surplus on invisible trade, or if invisible trade is in deficit as well, the result is a current-account deficit that can be financed only through a reduction of international reserves and/or by inducing capital imports. As reserves are necessarily limited, a country with inflation and increasing current-account deficits will have to raise its interest rate and improve its current-account balance by reducing domestic growth. Even if net capital imports increase, this does not change the asymmetry of the adjustment mechanisms, because climbing interest rates curb domestic demand and production.

The above implies a rejection of the Mundell-Fleming model (Fleming 1962, Mundell 1968). Given fixed exchange rates, the Mundell-Fleming model assigns to expansive fiscal policy the task of generating sufficient effective demand for full employment, while an increasing rate of interest is supposed to induce capital imports high enough to finance emerging current-account deficits. If the interest elasticity of capital imports is inadequate—which it inevitably is in the case of a country with a low-quality currency—the effects of restrictive monetary policy will outweigh the effects of expansive fiscal policy. If a country with a low-quality currency attempts, despite rising interest rates, to stabilize production by increasing fiscal impulses, it will be faced with a constellation of escalating budget deficits that will increasingly restrict the scope of fiscal policy. Italy and Belgium in the 1980s provide instructive European examples of this case.

Stability-Oriented Mercantilism and Dominance

Mercantilism, economic dominance, and the instability of international monetary systems are interrelated. Mercantilism is defined as an economic policy that results in continuous current-account surpluses. Lasting current-account surpluses can be the outcome of a competitive real exchange rate—providing global protection—or of tariff and non-tariff barriers, or of low domestic growth relative to that of the world economy. With respect to the store-of-value quality of a currency, the particular development of the nominal exchange rate associated with the current-account surplus is

TABLE 3.1 The Two Types of Mercantilism and Their Characteristics

<table>
<tr><th></th><th colspan="2">Stability-Oriented Mercantilism</th><th>Devaluation-Oriented Mercantilism</th></tr>
<tr><td>Definition</td><td colspan="2">Current-account surplus combined with stable exchange rates or currency appreciation</td><td>Current-account surplus combined with devaluation</td></tr>
<tr><td rowspan="2">Instrument</td><td colspan="2">• stable unit labor costs
• sterilization policy of the central bank</td><td rowspan="2">• moderate increase in unit labor costs
• high level of trade barriers
• restrictions on capital movements</td></tr>
<tr><td>• low level of trade barriers
• free capital movements</td><td>• high level of trade barriers
• restrictions on capital movements</td></tr>
<tr><td>Effect</td><td>• high store-of-value quality of the currency
• reserve currency
• low growth</td><td>• high (export-led) growth
• high store-of-value quality of the currency</td><td>• high (export-led) growth with (at most) moderate inflation</td></tr>
</table>

of paramount importance. If lasting current-account surpluses are realized in combination with nominal exchange-rate stability or even currency appreciation, one can speak of stability-oriented mercantilism. If, on the other hand, current-account surpluses are attained by means of nominal devaluation, we are dealing with devaluation-oriented mercantilism. With regard to economic dominance and the instability of the international monetary system, stability-oriented mercantilism is of particular importance. An overview of the various types of mercantilism is given in Table 3.1.

The market constellation of stability-oriented mercantilism hinges on a stable internal price level resulting from noninflationary wage increases. High productivity growth typically supports the existence of stable unit labor costs. This constellation produces a high store-of-value quality of the currency of the mercantilist country. As a consequence, stability-oriented mercantilist countries are characterized by relatively low nominal and real interest rates, whereas countries with current-account deficits and weak currencies are typically forced to have relatively high nominal and real interest rates so as to import enough capital to finance their deficit.

The lower the store-of-value quality of the currency of a net-debtor country, the higher the probability that its liabilities are denominated in foreign currency—provided that loans are granted at all. Because creditors do not provide loans in unstable currencies, countries in the Third World and in Central and Eastern Europe are unable to obtain loans denominated in their own currencies. The United States, on the other hand, is able to incur debt in its own currency despite the fact that it is a net-debtor country with current-account deficits.

For a country with a stability-oriented mercantilist policy there is always the danger that the store-of-value quality of its currency may become so high that capital imports destroy its mercantilist position by causing the currency to appreciate greatly despite low interest rates. The central bank can reduce this threat by creating "artificial" capital exports, that is, by building up its international reserves and thus reducing the pressure on its currency to appreciate.[14] This is possible insofar as the central bank's intervention in the foreign-exchange markets can be sterilized. Interventions can be compensated for by a reduction in other components of the monetary base, if they increase the monetary base to a greater extent than desired by the monetary authorities. It is only when capital imports become too large that the central bank has to accept an appreciation of its currency or an unwanted increase in the monetary base. It should be noted that mercantilist sterilization policies may be carried out within any given exchange-rate system.

A good example of mercantilist stabilization policies is provided by the Bundesbank. Market pressure on the mark to appreciate was met with measures to delay or mitigate the appreciation. Manifestations of this were the enormous buildup of international reserves resulting from sterilization operations in the 1950s and 1960s, the delayed revaluation of the German mark in 1961, and the renewed buildup of international reserves in 1976-78, 1985-87 and 1992-94. On the whole, the Bundesbank thus favors a policy of nominal-exchange-rate stabilization, whereby moderate appreciation is tolerated for reasons of domestic economic stability. Japan and Taiwan provide additional examples of mercantilistic sterilization policies.

If stability-oriented mercantilism is combined with low trade barriers and free capital movement, the currency of the mercantilist country will develop into an international reserve currency. This constellation is likely to have negative repercussions on domestic economic growth. If the mercantilist country fails to preserve the surplus on the current account despite low wages and high productivity because its currency strongly appreciates, policymakers may induce a stabilization crisis. This lowers imports and stimulates exports in the medium term, thereby improving the current account.

In a dynamic context a mercantilist nation may fail to realize a current-account surplus vis-à-vis countries with weak currencies. The restrictive pressure exerted on those countries may be so great that they do not incur a current-account deficit—either as a consequence of a

14. The granting of foreign aid produces similar effects.

coerced stabilization crisis or because there ceases to be a net import of capital. As a result, the country with the high-quality currency is unable to generate net capital exports despite low interest rates and thus undergoes an "appreciation crisis."[15] If it does not abandon its mercantilist policy, either restrictive policies in the countries involved will intensify or the international interest-rate structure will adjust, leading to deficits in countries with lower-quality currencies. The latter case presupposes that the national currencies of deficit countries inspire sufficient confidence to enable these countries to generate capital imports by means of high interest rates. In either case, the mercantilist policy will strengthen the dominance of the country with the high-quality currency and seriously restrict economic growth in the countries whose currencies have a lower store-of-value quality.

If all countries attempt to follow a stability-oriented mercantilist strategy, their economic objectives will be thoroughly incompatible and lead to a race for the most restrictive policy. The ensuing competitive currency appreciation constitutes an international negative-sum game that comes to a conclusion only when some countries give up their stability-oriented mercantilist strategy and subordinate themselves to the monetary dominance of other countries. The richer a country, the more effective is its anti-inflationary policy, and the greater its political tolerance of unemployment, the better are its prospects in this currency competition. It follows that the conditions prevailing in countries of the Third World and in the former planned economies are extremely unfavorable in the currency competition.

It should not be difficult to recognize the mechanisms of dominance described above within the European Monetary System (EMS) and in Europe as a whole. These mechanisms enabled the Federal Republic of Germany until German unification to maintain the high stability of the German mark, with only short interruptions, and to simultaneously build up its position as a net creditor. The mark became the key currency within Europe, and the Federal Republic of Germany was able to dominate the economic policies of other European countries—whether or not they were part of the EMS. As measures to shield the national economies were cut back during the 1980s (e.g., restrictions on capital movement and protectionist measures), the dominance of the mark became even more apparent. This intensified relationship of dominance can also be observed in several Scandinavian countries that liberalized their external relations for reasons of domestic policy and were in some cases exposed to severe external constraints. Consequently, most European countries

15. At the end of the 1970s and mid-1990s both the Federal Republic of Germany and Japan experienced such an "appreciation crisis".

perceived the West German policy of stability-oriented mercantilism as a hindrance to their own economic growth (see, e.g., Parboni 1981; Wyplosz 1988; or the Institute for Public Policy Research 1989). Efforts to further monetary integration account at least in part for the attempt to eliminate the monetary dominance of the Bundesbank by setting up a European central bank.

Stability-oriented mercantilism can be combined with trade barriers and exchange controls. The former enhance the global protection offered by the undervalued exchange rate, while the latter mitigate the pressure on the mercantilist country's currency to appreciate. Although the mercantilist country also has the higher-quality currency in this case, the regulations concerning trade and capital movement stand in the way of its currency becoming an international reserve currency. On the other hand, external regulations markedly improve the conditions for internal growth. Japan provides a typical example of this variant of stability-oriented mercantilism. It impedes imports primarily by means of nontariff barriers and only recently has started to allow free capital imports. This explains at least in part why, in spite of current-account surpluses, Japan began to acquire an international reserve currency position only in the mid-1980s and thus relatively late in comparison with Germany and why it was able to combine relatively high growth rates with current-account surpluses.

Despite the fact that current-account surpluses strengthen the store-of-value quality of a currency, a high-quality currency is not necessarily tied to current-account surpluses. If monetary policy enjoys high credibility, the reputation of the national currency can be maintained despite persistent current-account deficits and an international net debtor status. In this case it is assumed that a stabilization crisis will be induced if the currency weakens in order to confine current-account deficits to a level compatible with the stability of the national currency and not to create current-account surpluses. It is highly probable that a country whose currency functions as an international reserve currency is a perpetual net importer of capital and therefore able to maintain long-term current-account deficits. An equilibrium path is feasible when both the world economy and international wealth are growing and asset holders' preferences as well as the international structure of interest rates remain unchanged.[16] In this case the country with the leading currency still dominates; it does, however, enable countries with weaker currencies to be successful export nations and experience higher economic growth than they would have if the country with the leading currency had current-account surpluses. It thus improves their chances of becoming international net creditors and dominant in the

16. If the rate of increase in net capital imports is higher than the interest rate, it is even possible for the deficit country to sustain a perpetual trade deficit (Domar 1950).

currency competition. Net-creditor status is advantageous because debt service implies a continuous net inflow of foreign currency (Keynes 1913, 15ff.; Minsky 1979). For a net-creditor nation, furthermore, an increase in interest rates entails an automatic increase in the demand for its currency, which at the same time weakens the position of the net-debtor nations. The stronger the competitors are, the more a country's monetary dominance is threatened by the loss of its net-creditor status and the buildup of net foreign debt. It follows that, given a net-debtor position, monetary dominance generally can be maintained only if the country in question has additional advantages over its competitors that enhance the store-of-value quality of its currency. It is at this point that the comprehensive hegemonic status of a country comes into play (see "Stable and Unstable International Monetary Systems," below).

Contrary to widespread suppositions, it is not necessarily the primary goal of stability-oriented mercantilist policies to maximize domestic employment. A policy aimed at maximizing domestic employment would generate market-endogenous tendencies toward current-account deficits. Although a current-account surplus entails an export of unemployment, stability-oriented mercantilism tends to create a restrictive climate for the domestic economy because stabilization crises are tolerated to defend the current-account surplus. The above exposition reveals an important motive behind mercantilist economic policies. If current-account surpluses are realized as a result of stability-oriented mercantilism, the store-of-value quality of the currency of the given country improves. The country thereby creates the conditions to establish itself as an international financial center and for its currency to become an international reserve currency. It furthermore increases its economic and political dominance vis-à-vis other countries. Moreover, chauvinism, national prestige, and the attempt to reduce internal conflict by pursuing a national goal may be at the root of stability-oriented mercantilism (Frey 1984).

More defensive reasons can also motivate the pursuit of stability-oriented mercantilism. These are: the protection against the uncertainties of international economic developments and maintenance of as much autonomy in domestic economic policy as possible. Current-account surpluses make it possible to accumulate foreign-exchange reserves without a corresponding increase in foreign debt. They are therefore "a fault on the right side" (Robinson 1965, 206) and advantageous in case of international economic turbulence. A current-account surplus and international net-creditor status can also be interpreted as guarantors of a certain maneuverability within expansive fiscal policy (Herr 1991). However, the constellation of stability-oriented mercantilism may also emerge simply because the central bank (and the population) have a higher preference for price-level stability than do central banks in other countries.

Devaluation-Oriented Mercantilism

Devaluation-oriented mercantilism—the classic beggar-my-neighbor policy geared toward increasing domestic employment (Robinson 1937)—entails periodic devaluation with the aim of preserving or creating current-account surpluses and is therefore not aimed at enhancing the store-of-value quality of the national currency. This is to be distinguished from a one-time devaluation which improves the competitiveness of domestic producers and which may increase the reputation of the currency. If the exchange rate is successfully defended and a current-account surplus is maintained, a one-time devaluation can mark the beginning of stability-oriented mercantilism. Devaluation-oriented mercantilism can be successful only if specific domestic conditions exist. It is necessary that nominal wages are strictly controlled, that decreases in real income resulting from currency depreciation are accepted by the workforce, and that confidence in the relative stability of the national currency is maintained. A devaluation-oriented mercantilist strategy therefore is not feasible for countries with an inflation problem. The prerequisites for the success of devaluation-oriented mercantilism largely resemble those for successful stability-oriented mercantilism, the minimum requirement being that wage-price spirals and devaluation-inflation spirals are avoided. It follows that countries with a successful devaluation-oriented mercantilist policy tend to develop a constellation of stability-oriented mercantilism. Consequently, stability-oriented mercantilism is the standard type of mercantilism, whereas devaluation-oriented mercantilism is the exception and is likely to exist for only a short period of time.

The higher the rate of unemployment and the lower therefore the danger of inflation, the more favorable are the conditions for devaluation. If devaluation does not trigger a devaluation-inflation spiral, the threat of destabilizing capital flight drastically diminishes. It is therefore not surprising that competitive devaluations took place largely in the deflationary climate of the 1930s. Since the beginning of the 1970s the greater part of all devaluations served exclusively to reduce balance-of-payments deficits and therefore were not mercantilist by our definition. The depreciation of the yen at the end of the 1970s constitutes a rare exception (Herr/Spahn 1989).

Devaluation-oriented mercantilism is typically supported by tariff and nontariff barriers and restrictions on capital exports. This is because it primarily aims to increase domestic growth rather than the store-of-value quality of the national currency. This beggar-my-neighbor policy is not as destructive as policies of stability-oriented mercantilism. The latter involve rising interest rates, while the former is coupled with falling interest rates. If all countries attempted to run a stability-oriented mercantilist policy, an implosion of the world economy would follow. Devaluation-oriented mercantilist policies in all countries, on the other hand, would imply expansive monetary policies and lead to improved conditions for worldwide economic growth. This applies in particular when devaluation takes place in a noninflationary climate, as was the case in the 1930s (Eichengreen/Sachs 1985; Herr 1992).

Stable and Unstable International Monetary Systems

International monetary systems are characterized by a hierarchy of currencies. Currencies at the top of the hierarchy perform domestic money functions in the countries that issue them and international money functions[17] as well as domestic money functions in countries with disintegrating monetary systems. The bottom of the hierarchy is occupied by currencies that only partially perform certain domestic money functions, such as that of medium of transaction, but that are neither considered to be a reliable store of value nor used as the standard of value in loan contracts. The extent to which a currency performs certain money functions is determined by the decisions of economic agents. It cannot be dictated by the state.

In an international monetary system several international reserve currencies can coexist. There can, however, be only one leading currency at any given moment. The defining characteristic of the country with the leading currency is that it is able to determine the monetary policy of the entire international monetary system over a long period of time. If the key currency country implements restrictive policy measures, no other country can avoid increases in domestic interest rates. This also applies to flexible exchange rates, since currency depreciation can be tolerated only within limits, due to its inflationary effects and the necessity of sustaining confidence in the national currency. Above all, other reserve-currency countries have to avoid devaluation, because of the danger of substantial portfolio restructuring.

In a hegemonic monetary system, there exists an uncontested key currency. Although there may be other reserve currencies in addition to the key currency, none is able to replace the key currency. Given a multicurrency system, on the other hand, there are several reserve currencies with

17. Money fulfills international functions if it is used as an international standard of value, as a medium of payment in international purchase and debt contracts, and as an international store of value. As a result there will be a high demand for monetary assets denominated in a currency that performes international functions.

the potential to dominate monetary policy within the international monetary system. Even though one of the countries with a reserve currency dominates the international monetary system at any given moment, there is no key currency within a multicurrency system. The particular characteristics of a given international monetary system depend largely on the specific historic circumstances. Within a hegemonic monetary system, the ruling country not only dominates the monetary sphere but also has substantial economic, military, and political power based on its real economy. The strength of the real economy thus becomes part of the store-of-value quality of the currency. No leading economic and military power would permit a small country to dominate its monetary policy. In addition, an economically and militarily dominant country is viewed by economic agents as a "safe haven." It therefore can realize a certain import of capital even if its currency is unstable. The size of a given currency area and of the corresponding capital market is also a factor in determining the store-of-value quality of a currency, because it influences the degree of random fluctuation in economic variables (Swoboda 1968). In addition, a large market makes it impossible for big investors to provoke a currency depreciation in the process of shifting funds into a different currency, thus diminishing their own wealth.

In sum, the ruling nation in a hegemonic international monetary system has the distinguishing characteristic that one element of the store-of-value quality of its currency is independent of monetary policy and thus has to be recognized as exogenous by monetary theory. Monetary and nonmonetary factors of domination can reinforce each other; however, the hegemonic power also may take advantage of its nonmonetary dominance by relaxing its monetary discipline.

International monetary systems differ not only in that they are either hegemonic or multicurrency systems but also in the extent to which the countries belonging to a given monetary system pursue monetary policies that are functional on an international level. Within a hegemonic system the policy of the hegemonic power decisively shapes the monetary system. Within a multicurrency system, functional and dysfunctional policies go hand in hand with cooperation and noncooperation, respectively. A multicurrency system is extremely unstable if the major countries do not cooperate; cooperative policies can counteract the forces of instability. Table 3.2 summarizes the characteristics of the various types of monetary systems.

The most stable international monetary system is a hegemonic one in which the ruling country maintains the scarcity of its currency and tolerates a (limited) current-account deficit. In such a system there is no danger of competition for the leading-currency position. Indeed, the ruling

<table>
<tr><td rowspan="2"></td><td colspan="7">International Monetary Systems</td></tr>
<tr><td colspan="3">Hegemonic Systems</td><td colspan="4">Multicurrency Systems</td></tr>
<tr><td rowspan="2">Monetary and fiscal policy</td><td>functional</td><td colspan="2">dysfunctional</td><td colspan="2">noncooperative</td><td>cooperative</td><td>noncooperative</td></tr>
<tr><td>scarcity of the leading currency and nonmercantilist policy</td><td>mercantilist</td><td>inflationary</td><td>mercantilist</td><td>inflationary</td><td>nonmercantilist, noninflationary</td><td>autarkic</td></tr>
<tr><td>Level of tariff/ nontariff barriers and exchange controls</td><td>low</td><td colspan="4">low to middle</td><td>low</td><td>very high</td></tr>
<tr><td>Stable/unstable</td><td>stable</td><td colspan="4">unstable</td><td colspan="2">stable</td></tr>
<tr><td rowspan="2">Historic examples</td><td rowspan="2">• gold standard before WWI
• Bretton Woods system until the mid-1960s</td><td rowspan="2"></td><td></td><td>• gold standard after WWI</td><td></td><td rowspan="2"></td><td rowspan="2">• world economy after the breakdown of the interwar gold standard</td></tr>
<tr><td colspan="3">• post-Bretton Woods system</td></tr>
</table>

TABLE 3.2 Characteristics of Monetary Systems

nation promotes international economic expansion on the basis of the specific store-of-value quality of its currency. It is able to sustain current-account deficits without harming the store-of-value quality of its currency and therefore can avert the potential negative-sum game of competing mercantilist strategies (Padoan 1986). In addition, the hegemonic power is able to use noneconomic means to limit the mercantilist strategies of other countries. In a stable hegemonic monetary system, there are typically only a small number of trade barriers and exchange controls. The hegemonic power enforces free commodity trade and capital movement because this increases its dominance; at the same time, there are few reasons for deliberate international isolation in a stable world economy.

The gold standard before World War I in many respects approximated a stable hegemonic monetary system. In essence the gold standard was a pound sterling standard under British hegemony. Its stability was ensured by the uncompromising defense of the external value of the pound sterling through discretionary monetary policy that, coupled with the economic and military power of Britain, generated high confidence in the pound sterling (Goschen 1861; Bagehot 1873). This monetary policy was backed politically by Britain's key financial institutions, which determined the international orientation of economic policy and enforced the stability of the pound sterling (Polanyi 1944). Britain and the other leading industrial nations tolerated trade deficits, at least vis-à-vis countries at the bottom of the currency hierarchy, and thus stabilized international balance-of-payments transactions and improved the conditions for worldwide economic development (Ford 1962).

Although it may be in the self-interest of the hegemonic power to provide international economic stability (a public good), a corresponding monetary policy is in no way guaranteed (Kindleberger 1986). There are two possible scenarios in which the policy of the hegemonic power is dysfunctional for the world economy and obstructs economic growth worldwide. First, the hegemonic power may pursue a mercantilist policy. This generates a deflationary bias in the world economy, especially in the case of a stability-oriented mercantilist policy. But even devaluation-oriented mercantilism on the part of the hegemonic power creates problems, in that it either forces weaker countries to run current-account deficits—thus producing a balance-of-payments crisis—or destabilizes the key currency. This leads us to the second and more likely scenario of an inflationary key currency. This can come about if dominance leads to the exploitation of the key currency position, or if domestic political conditions force the hegemonic power to pursue an economic policy of "muddling through"—as exemplified by the United States since the mid-1960s. In both cases the international monetary system loses its stability anchor, with no other currency able to fulfill that function. If the key currency country pursues an inflationary policy, the international economy is exposed to inflationary tendencies, portfolio restructuring between currencies, and dramatic exchange-rate fluctuation. If the key currency country is then forced to induce a stabilization crisis—whether for domestic or for international reasons—it subjects the international economic system to both a restrictive policy and exchange-rate shocks. The high uncertainty inherent in an inflationary international monetary system retards economic growth due to low investment and cautious economic policies. An inflationary policy of the hegemonic power stimulates the emergence of other reserve currencies, which would otherwise be of no importance. Both the yen and the mark would have been considerably less important since the 1970s if the United States had preserved the scarcity of the dollar.

A dysfunctional policy on the part of the hegemonic power encourages the introduction of trade barriers and exchange controls as each country tries to shield its domestic economy from its disruptive effects. The hegemonic power itself will be inclined to introduce these restrictions if it has a devaluation-oriented mercantilist policy. Nonetheless, a disintegration of the world economy into separate and isolated blocks is improbable since this would be against the interests of the hegemonic power.

Because of its oligopolistic character a multicurrency system can produce more basic scenarios than a hegemonic system:

> a) A multicurrency system with several countries of comparable economic, political, and military strength is prone to trigger intense competition between currencies at the top of the currency hierarchy. If two or more nations strive for monetary dominance in a multicurrency system or are unwilling to submit to the monetary dominance of one country, then the store-of-value quality of the national currency becomes the decisive weapon in the currency competition. In a multicurrency system, the group of countries at the top of the hierarchy can become entangled in a mercantilist negative-sum game to attain current-account surpluses by means of a stability-oriented mercantilist strategy. This is the case because, in addition to exchange-rate stability, current-account surpluses are an important means of building up and maintaining the store-of-value quality of the national currency in the constellation sketched above. Current-account surpluses and net-creditor status reflect the scarcity of the national currency and improve the chances of protecting the domestic economy and winning the currency competition. In a hegemonic monetary system, the hegemonic power can tolerate a (limited) current-account deficit because it is only one of several factors that determine the store-of-value quality of its currency and because an alternative to the key currency does not exist. A leading country within a multicurrency system, on the other hand, is unable to tolerate such deficits. Perpetual current-account deficits and net-debtor status

necessarily weaken a position of dominance that rests exclusively on monetary factors. They are disadvantageous in the currency competition and ultimately pave the way for an economically similar country with a current-account surplus and net-creditor status to establish itself at the top of the currency hierarchy. As a result, balance-of-payments difficulties on the part of countries at the bottom of the currency hierarchy are much more likely than in a hegemonic monetary system. None of the countries with high-quality currencies can afford to run current-account deficits; these deficits are therefore concentrated in those countries at the bottom of the currency hierarchy. Historically, a pure multicurrency system has never existed. However, there have been international monetary systems characterized by intense currency competition. The classic example of a struggle for stability-oriented mercantilism is the currency competition after World War I that lasted until the collapse of the gold standard during the 1930s.

b) The interwar period also shows that the struggle between stability-oriented mercantilist countries can develop into a struggle for successful devaluation-oriented mercantilist policies if countries are politically forced to give up restrictive economic policies. The race for competitive revaluation or for devaluation, which generally last only for short periods of time, are not the only scenarios in a multicurrency system.

c) A third scenario is one in which specific national conditions and preferences result in only one country striving for monetary dominance and all other countries subordinating their economic policy to that country. Nonetheless, even a multicurrency system with a stable hierarchy of currencies is not quite comparable to a hegemonic monetary system. Since a position of dominance in a multicurrency system is based primarily on monetary factors, the dominant country must continuously "earn" its dominant role by maintaining the scarcity of the national currency and preventing a net debtor position from developing. The underlying bias of the international monetary system is thus a restrictive one even if an uncontested structure of dominance (temporarily) exists.

d) A further scenario emerges if no country of economic relevance strives for monetary stability or the second and third countries in the hierarchy periodically resort to inflationary policies. The stop-go policies of the leading countries in this scenario result in sudden changes in the relative store-of-value qualities of the different currencies and upset the international monetary system by generating destabilizing portfolio restructuring and exchange-rate changes, thereby impairing economic growth in the entire monetary system. A multicurrency system that is characterized by noncooperation encourages the introduction of trade barriers and exchange controls even more than a dysfunctional hegemonic system. There is therefore the danger that these restrictions on the part of individual countries and country groups become so extensive as to lead to the disintegration of the international monetary economy. The international monetary system that succeeded the Bretton Woods system has several features of a noncooperative multicurrency system. Inflationary developments in several countries coincided with stability-oriented and mercantilist policies on the part of other countries. Nonetheless, the post-Bretton Woods system cannot be characterized as a pure multicurrency system—at least not yet. The United States still holds a dominant position, and the dollar has (so far) no competitor that could displace it. Nevertheless, currency competition has intensified since the 1970s on the basis of diminished U.S. dominance and a periodic glut of dollars. The post-Bretton Woods system is at the threshold between a noncooperative multicurrency system and a dysfunctional hegemonic system.

e) The fifth scenario in a multicurrency system is characterized by economic cooperation between the economically most important countries. It is the most favorable scenario and at the same time the least likely. Many factors may impede international cooperation. Apart from the problems of insufficient information and the adherence to different economic models, there does not exist a supranational institution capable of organizing cooperation and penalizing breaches of contract. Models of rule-based cooperation presuppose that sovereignty in economic policy is largely transferred to a supranational institution. If this were not the case, there would be the constant danger that emergency regulations, which are unavoidable to counteract domestic shocks and special interests, would undermine the rules of the system. Although a country guilty of a breach of contract harms its reputation and has to reckon with countermeasures, it may nevertheless be welfare-maximizing to violate an agreement of cooperation due to the time inconsistency of optimal plans (Kydland/Prescott 1977). It is possible, furthermore, that one of the parties in the agreement is unable to pursue a coherent strategy or adhere to agreements because of specific political developments at home. More importantly, if the goals of the countries involved are incompatible, cooperation is impossible. This would be the case, for example, if all countries were striving to attain a dominant position or current-account surpluses to secure the quality of their respective currencies. The debate on cooperation suffers from the fact that the world economy is usually interpreted in terms of the prisoner's dilemma—a positive-sum game—where cooperation benefits all parties involved. However, the world economy is in many respects a zero-sum game and for individual countries, especially the dominant ones, cooperation may not be advantageous (Oudiz/Sachs 1984). A realistic variant, albeit one whose success is by no means guaranteed, is ad hoc cooperation on the part of the major countries in the multicurrency system at critical moments of international economic development (Dornbusch 1986; Kenen 1988).

f) The final scenario in a multicurrency system is that of economic dissociation. Within an unstable and restrictive multicurrency system, the benefits of integration may, for individual countries or country groups, be smaller than those of economic detachment (Krasner 1975). To be effective, the isolation would have to be very extensive. The breakup of the world economy in the 1930s into relatively autonomous economic blocks is an instructive example of this scenario.

If the dominance of a country is based primarily on monetary factors, the willingness of other countries to submit to it should be lower than in the hegemonic case. In a multicurrency system it is furthermore possible that a currency emerges unintentionally as a dominant currency. This may happen if a country attains current-account surpluses and net-creditor status as a result of "cautious" economic policies—especially a scarce-money policy—in view of the high uncertainty typical of a multicurrency system. Economic agents may then choose the currency of this country as the international reserve medium. The country in question is thus inevitably drawn into the oligopolistic relations between the leading currencies of the international monetary system. Overall, the likelihood of a restrictive and deflationary bias is greater in a multicurrency system than in a hegemonic system. This knowledge is not new: "Such a system [a multi-currency system], as is beginning to be understood, has a natural deflationary bias" (Hicks 1982, 274). "Gresham's law, which states that a system with two monies is unstable, is easily extended to the proposition that a world with two key currencies of equal worth, or of two key financial centres on a par, is equally unstable" (Kindleberger 1983, 87). Similar arguments are to be found in Vines (1980), Padoa-Schioppa/Papadia (1984), Thygesen (1985), Vandenbroucke (1985), Padoan (1986) and Herr (1992).

The Development of the International Monetary System Since World War II

The Bretton Woods System

The Bretton Woods system, established after World War II, was a hegemonic system with the dollar as the uncontested key currency and essentially fixed exchange rates. The tremendous economic, political, and military dominance of the United States after World War II can partially be explained by the weakening of all other industrial powers as a result of the war. It was therefore inevitable that the hegemonic position of the United States would diminish with time. Since the 1960s the United States' position of absolute economic and political dominance evolved into one of leadership (Kindleberger 1981; Keohane 1984). In addition, the United States contributed to the reduction of its own technological lead through the transfer of technology, predominantly in the form of direct investment (Strange 1976). Toward the end of the 1950s, restrictions on capital movements imposed in the 1930s were gradually lifted, so the mechanisms of an international monetary economy could only then begin to fully unfold.

The Bretton Woods system had a defect that later proved to be the primary cause of its instability. Prior to World War I, Britain, despite its hegemonic status, was forced to limit the availability of the pound sterling because the possibility of private gold exports and the obligation to exchange bank notes for gold acted as an external constraint. The Bretton Woods system did not possess a similar instrument for disciplining the U.S. Federal Reserve. On the contrary, central banks outside the United States were compelled to defend the exchange rate of the dollar, while the United States was not obliged to intervene. The rules of the game were such that a weakening of the dollar did not compel the country with the depreciating currency, but rather countries with hard currencies to intervene. The Bretton Woods system was therefore inherently unstable, since a lack of scarcity of the key currency implied the loss of its stability anchor and its structure made it easy for the United States to exploit the position of key-currency country.

The fear of a lack of international liquidity that would endanger international economic growth proved to be unfounded. On the contrary, since the early 1960s an excess supply of the dollar has developed, which, coupled with the reluctance of the United States to implement a restrictive economic policy, led to the breakdown of the Bretton Woods system. To preserve the system it would have been necessary to keep the dollar scarce after the mid-1960s. The socioeconomic conditions that existed after World War II, however, discouraged a scarce-dollar policy: there was a strong demand for full employment, economic policies were supposed to attain the "magic polygon" of economic goals, and the welfare state was to be expanded.

Economic policy in the United States during the 1960s was characterized by a highly expansive monetary and fiscal policy, which led to a stop-go policy—with clear emphasis on the go—toward the end of the Bretton Woods system. This policy was based on the "full-employment budget." Spectacular tax cuts under the Kennedy administration were followed by a simultaneous battle on two fronts under the Johnson administration: the escalating war in Vietnam and the intended transformation of the welfare state into the "Great Society" (Calleo 1980). Despite the increasing weakness of the dollar toward the end of the 1960s and a rush into gold and hard currencies—especially the Swiss franc and the German mark—U.S. fiscal and monetary policy continued to be expansive. Attempts to save the system by means of exchange-rate adjustments failed because even after the realignment the United States did not switch to a policy of stabilizing the dollar. Instead, the United States, under Nixon, relied on further nominal depreciation of the dollar and other countries—especially the Federal Republic of Germany, which was confronted with a tremendous inflow of capital—were not willing to subordinate themselves to what they saw as inflationary U.S. policy. Given the incompatibility of economic policy in the leading Western industrial nations, the introduction of flexible exchange rates and the final collapse of the Bretton Woods system in 1973 were inevitable.[18] However, currency blocs were formed, within which relatively fixed exchange rates and a regional leading currency exist, and which follow an external policy of joint float. The most important of these currency blocs is the European Monetary System. It was created in 1979 to succeed the not very successful European currency snake established immediately after the Bretton Woods system collapsed.

Bretton Woods did not fall apart because of weakness in the United States' real economy nor as a result of the liberalization of international capital movements, financial innovations, or the emerging off-shore and Euro-markets. It fell apart because of the lax monetary policy of the United States (Minsky 1979, 103). With the adoption of a strategy of dollar devaluation and the introduction of protectionist measures, U.S. economic policy developed characteristics of devaluation-oriented mercantilism at the beginning of the 1970s. The United States was thus unwilling or politically unable to guarantee the conditions necessary for a stable hegemonic monetary system, which include the scarcity of the key currency and the absence of nominal devaluation.

Instabilities in the 1970s and 1980s

Since the 1970s the international monetary system has been characterized by great instability. With respect to the key currency position of the dollar, two processes are of particular importance. First, the United States has been deliberately exploiting its special role within the international monetary system; second, characteristics of a multicurrency system have become discernible as the economic and political dominance of the United States is gradually declining. To explain monetary phenomena subsequent to the dissolution of the Bretton Woods system, the former is of greater relevance. The latter may, if at all, become important in the future.

The United States did not modify its economic policy subsequent to the collapse of the Bretton Woods system but rather continued its generally expansive and devaluation-oriented monetary policy during the 1970s. The Federal Republic of Germany, whose currency was the dollar's

18. Most economists did not view the transition to flexible exchange rates as destabilizing or as the lesser evil given inflationary U.S. policies. On the contrary, purchasing power parity theory taught that flexible exchange rates were an elegant instrument to balance the current account while at the same time maintaining autonomy in domestic economic policy

leading rival, stuck to its stability-oriented mercantilist strategy, thereby exerting pressure not only on other European currencies but increasingly on the dollar as well. When the U.S. current account slipped back into deficit in 1977, after surpluses in the early 1970s as a result of devaluations, Carter—like Nixon before him—pursued a devaluation strategy with the aim of reaching an external equilibrium without an internal crisis. In contrast to the period after 1985, the domestic conditions at the end of the 1970s were not conducive to a devaluation of the dollar. Inflation started to rise again in 1977, from its 1976 level of 6 percent, and finally reached double-digit rates. Confidence in the dollar broke down, resulting in a cumulative flight from the dollar, primarily into the mark and yen. This "queer spectacle" of U.S. economic policy produced a devaluation-inflation spiral with soaring rates of inflation and the increasing erosion of the key-currency position of the dollar (Minsky 1979).

Given this constellation, Carter—in an attempt to avert a domestic stabilization crisis—relied both on the willingness of other Western countries to cooperate and on political pressure to force the Federal Republic of Germany and Japan to switch to expansive economic policies. The objective was to bring the process of dollar-devaluation, which decidedly stimulated inflation, to a halt without resorting to a restrictive monetary policy. Although the German government turned to a moderately expansive policy, the Bundesbank remained uncooperative. Despite the fact that the U.S. adopted restrictive fiscal and monetary policy measures in the fall of 1978, the Bundesbank refused to support attempts to stabilize the dollar in any way (Emminger 1986, 384f.). Cooperation was still denied when Paul Volcker—a staunch supporter of tight monetary policy—was appointed President of the Federal Reserve. If the United States wanted to maintain the role of the dollar in the international economy, it had no choice but to induce a painful stabilization crisis. When the United States successively tightened its monetary policy in response to the persistent internal and external weakness of the dollar, the Bundesbank matched every increase in interest rates. This was the main obstacle to a rapid regeneration of the dollar vis-à-vis the mark in this period. Only toward the end of 1980, after the election of Reagan, did the dollar appreciate against the mark, while all other currencies, including the yen, had depreciated vis-à-vis the dollar one year earlier. By intensifying the currency competition between mark and dollar, the Bundesbank increased pressure on the Federal Reserve to further tighten its restrictive monetary policy. In this respect the Bundesbank shares responsibility for

(Friedman 1953; Johnson 1972). Shamefully few economists at that time doubted the merits of the transition to flexible exchange rates postulated by neoclassical monetary theory (some notable exceptions are Kindleberger 1969, Einzig 1970, Stützel 1978).

the deep economic recession at the beginning of the 1980s, brought about by internationally high interest rates. The motivation behind the Bundesbank's uncooperative behavior during this period is not clear. Emminger (1986), former President of the Bundesbank, emphasizes the Bundesbank's fear of renewed inflation. But there are many indications that the Bundesbank wanted to force the United States to adopt a policy of long-term dollar stabilization so as to halt the rise of the mark's importance as an international reserve currency. The latter was perceived as a disturbance because it curbed exports and increased exchange-rate turbulence.

On the whole, there was a "European-Arab revolt against American economic policy" toward the end of the 1970s (Calleo 1980, 796). The United States was unable to compel European countries, led by the Federal Republic of Germany, to introduce the economic policy it desired. The EMS, founded with the explicit goal of making European currencies more independent of the dollar, was perceived by the United States as a direct threat (Cohen 1979). In addition, the second oil price shock—itself a result of the dollar's depreciation—occurred in 1979 and increased the burden of inflation and current-account problems in all Western industrialized nations, especially in the United States.

The United States faced political and economic mayhem toward the end of the 1970s. For the first time since World War I, it was forced to implement restrictive policy measures in response to external factors and the escalating domestic inflation they brought about. Earlier, however, the United States had maintained a policy for a decade and a half that had resulted in a glut of dollars and sharply reduced the dollar's store-of-value quality.

In the early 1980s there were reasonable grounds to expect the United States to launch a stability-oriented policy, especially because in 1981 a president took office who had vowed to stabilize the dollar and the Pax Americana. Indeed, the regeneration of the dollar was accomplished surprisingly rapidly. As early as 1980 a period of dollar appreciation began that lasted until 1985. The relatively easy regeneration of the dollar, accompanied by drastic interest-rate cuts after mid-1982, clearly illustrates that the United States was still in a position to reactivate the dollar's role as key currency. There was no other currency that could have prevented its regeneration, although stabilizing confidence in the dollar required a period of extremely restrictive economic policy, accompanied by an expected revitalization of the real economy through deregulation and other supply-oriented policies of Reaganomics, and possibly a political and military strengthening of the Pax Americana.[19] A precondition for the dollar's renewed strength was the cutback in inflation in the

19. A case in point is the discussion of Eurosclerosis, which emerged at the end of the 1970s.

United States, which had climbed steeply in the late 1970s and had reached nearly 14 percent in 1980. The dollar's appreciation played an essential role in that the resulting effect on prices and real wages curbed nominal wage increases and thus lowered the costs of disinflation (Sachs 1985).

Reagan came to office with the promise of supply-side economics, including a balanced budget despite drastic tax cuts, but was unable to reach his economic goals. The intended policy, which did not represent a coherent economic strategy, gave way to an extremely expansive fiscal policy. The primary cause for the unintended results of U.S. macroeconomic policy was the deadlock between the White House and Congress (Sargent 1986). The White House wanted considerable tax cuts, while Congress blocked intended complementary spending cuts.

Starting in mid-1982 the United States had an expansive fiscal *and* monetary policy. In response to high budget deficits, above-average real growth, and the appreciation of the dollar until 1985, the U.S. current-account deficit grew continually. Within a few years it robbed the United States of its net-creditor status and transformed it into the world's greatest net-debtor nation. Countries with growing current-account deficits and expansive monetary and fiscal policies typically experience a depreciation of their currencies. Economic agents are generally not willing to finance increasing current-account deficits—not even at higher interest rates. Although the United States contracted international debt in its own currency and investors were thus faced with the "moral hazard" of dollar depreciation, U.S. capital imports increased so much that the U.S. current-account deficit escalated. Contracting debt abroad in the amount of the U.S. deficit can be accomplished only by a hegemonic key-currency country or a key-currency country that makes it credible that for the foreseeable future it can and will maintain a high store-of-value quality of its currency.

Although current-account deficits on the part of the key-currency country promote economic stability in a hegemonic monetary system and are not incompatible with a stable external value of the currency, even a key-currency country can withstand only limited current-account deficits without adversely affecting the stability of its currency. The huge and persistent twin deficits in the U.S. budget and current account since the early 1980s were bound to eventually lower confidence in the dollar. The renewed weakening of the dollar in 1985 was, therefore, hardly surprising. The only possible surprise was that the United States did not resort to a restrictive monetary policy after 1985, which would have been necessary to stabilize the dollar. Instead the United States once again relied upon a strategy of dollar depreciation, which then caused exchange-rate turbulence and the stock market crash of 1987 (Calleo/van Cleveland/Silk 1988). Nonetheless, this policy left the United States in a comfortable position. Unlike all other international net debtors, it was able to receive loans denominated in its own currency and thus pursue a strategy of currency depreciation without increasing its debt burden in dollars. The United States exploited this privilege of the key-currency country during the 1980s and thereby prolonged the instability of the dollar which had emerged in the 1960s.

The "rough landing" of the U.S. currency after 1985 was not anticipated by economic agents. An indication of this is the fact that the dollar gained in value despite shrinking interest-rate differentials (Krugman 1985). Although one could interpret the rise of the dollar until 1985 as an "irrational bubble" (Bliss 1985) that was bound to burst sooner or later, it seems more plausible that economic agents were mistaken in their estimation of future U.S. economic policy. They finally had to realize that the United States did not redirect economic policy under Reagan and was willing to stabilize the dollar only when confronted with cumulative instability.

It follows that after 1985 the United States, under Reagan, pursued a devaluation strategy to reduce current-account deficits, as it had done in the 1970s under Nixon and Carter. The decline of the dollar after 1985 also indicates that the United States was still in a position of dominance. As key-currency country, it did not have to subjugate its economic policy to international constraints to the same extent as other countries. The United States was able to leave the stabilization of the dollar's exchange rate to foreign central banks. The main difference between the situation following 1985 and that in the late 1970s was that the dollar's depreciation after 1985 did not take place in a climate of domestic inflation, so that it did not produce a cumulative wage-price spiral in the United States and inflation could be contained. In addition, falling energy prices after 1985 curbed the upward trend of prices. Finally, Western central banks, including the Bundesbank,[20] were much more cooperative with respect to dollar stabilization after 1985 than they had been in the late 1970s, and the dollar's decline was not accompanied by political erosion of the United States' international position.

Since 1985 the economic climate in the United States has been characterized by great uncertainty regarding the future development of the dollar's value. Nonetheless, high net capital imports continue to finance the U.S. current-account deficit. The import of capital cannot be explained solely by relatively high U.S. interest rates. As before, it is at

20. Disregarding political considerations, the domestic economic situation allowed the Bundesbank more latitude after 1985 than it had in the late 1970s. The conflict with expansive fiscal policy was resolved, and there were no signs of emerging inflation in the West German labor market. This is not to imply that the Bundesbank had no room for cooperation in the late 1970s.

least in part based on the specific store-of-value quality of the currency of the country dominating international economic relations.

The economic policy pursued by the United States can be interpreted as a strategy of short-term welfare maximization. This applies to the 1960s and 1970s, when the United States pursued domestic goals without considering external restrictions. The United States stabilized the dollar only during the serious internal and external crises of the late 1970s. It also applies to the 1980s when the United States built up substantial international debt denominated in its own currency and subsequently allowed the dollar to depreciate, thus reducing the value of assets held by foreign creditors expressed in their own currencies. It is therefore apparent that the economic policy of the United States in the 1970s and 1980s is not an expression of the continual decline of a key-currency country (Kindleberger 1985). Rather, it reflects the United States' exploitation of the internationally dominant role it still enjoys. The fact that the United States is still able to acquire international loans denominated in its own currency is a clear manifestation of this. Only with the loss of its ability to incur debt denominated in its own currency will the United States have lost its role as the key-currency country.

It would be shortsighted to attribute the instabilities of the international monetary system during the 1970s and 1980s solely to U.S. economic policy. Japanese and West German economic policy also had a disruptive influence on the international economy. These two countries, having the most important reserve currencies besides the dollar and being the largest net creditors in the world, pursued mercantilist strategies in order to sustain their trade surpluses. The mercantilism of these net-creditor nations implies that the export revenue of their debtors is insufficient to cover interest payments—a constellation that inevitably leads to insolvency unless the net-creditor nations export additional capital to enable debtor nations to service their debts. A mercantilist strategy on the part of the second and third countries in the currency hierarchy presents a problem for the international economy, because the current-account deficit of the key-currency country can only mitigate the effects of these mercantilist strategies. This deficit cannot be large enough to allow the rest of the world to earn a trade surplus. During the last decades, stable balance-of-payments transactions have thus been prevented primarily by Japan and the Federal Republic of Germany, which thereby created a restrictive bias for the world economy.

The countries of the Third World and the former planned economies are the most obvious losers in the battle against persistent current-account deficits and insolvency. Most developing countries had trade deficits during the 1970s and 1980s—more generally since World War II—thus succumbing to the mercantilism of industrial nations. Those industrial nations that have current-account deficits vis-à-vis Japan and the Federal Republic of Germany are determined to defend at least the surpluses they have with the countries of the Third World. The latter are the most poorly equipped to resist the mercantilist strategies of industrial nations. Their poverty is a great disadvantage in the race for the most restrictive economic policy, and domestic problems of inflation as well as foreign debt diminish their prospects in case of competitive currency depreciation. Similarly, most of the planned economies built up substantial foreign debt in the 1970s and have not managed to steer clear of insolvency problems during the transformation into monetary economies.

A Comparison of Developments in the 1930s and the 1970s/1980s

What distinguishes developments in the 1970s and 1980s from those in the 1930s? In my opinion there are two main differences. The first relates to the conduct of the key-currency country. In both periods the United States played the most important role in the international monetary system on the basis of its political and economic dominance. In the 1930s the United States, as key-currency country, had a mercantilist policy, in that it strove to attain current-account surpluses through protectionism and devaluation despite weak currencies on the part of all potential rivals. It thereby intensified the instability of the world economy (Kindleberger 1973). At the same time, until the final breakdown of the gold standard a number of countries did not take advantage of the increased scope for successful devaluation resulting from domestic deflationary developments. They thereby aggravated the deflationary pressure exerted by the international economy.

In contrast to the 1930s, when the United States refused to take responsibility for the world economy, U.S. economic policy has had a stabilizing effect since 1982. However, it should not be forgotten that in defending the dollar's stability the United States plunged the world economy into a deep crisis in the late 1970s. The costs of this stabilization crisis were enormous. They were borne not only by the developed industrial nations but also by the Third World in the form of reduced growth and high unemployment. The United States did, however, perform the function of international lender-of-last-resort during the financial instability of the 1980s —which, of cource was created largely by the United States itself—and stabilized the international economy by tolerating large current-account deficits. It would be a mistake to equate the developments after 1973 with those in the interwar period, despite flexible exchange rates and the high debt burden of the Third World. After the collapse of the Bretton Woods system, the countries with the major reserve currencies did not become involved in a mercantilist game to gain current-account surpluses. This constitutes a major difference with respect to the interwar period that can be attributed to the economic policy of the United States. Although the United States repeatedly has relied on the depreciation of the dollar since the early 1970s, its motivation was to reduce current account deficits and not to strive for current-account surpluses. In the 1980s the United States assumed the special role of key-currency country in that it accepted current-account deficits and acted as international lender-of-last-resort, thereby mitigating the negative consequences of the mercantilist strategies pursued primarily by Japan and the Federal Republic of Germany. If the United States had forced its current account into surplus via stabilization crises and protectionism during the 1980s, the world economy presumably would have fallen into a deflationary spiral, as it did in the 1930s.

The second main difference distinguishing the 1970s and 1980s from the 1930s relates to the conduct of the second and third countries in the currency hierarchy. In the 1970s and 1980s, the two most important international reserve-currency countries after the United States, the Federal Republic of Germany and Japan, followed a stability-oriented mercantilist policy and thus had a restrictive effect on the world economy. (Japan abandoned its stability-oriented mercantilist strategy once, in the late 1970s.) In the post-World War II era, devaluation-oriented mercantilism played a minor role and failed at an early stage due to inflation and capital flight. In the 1930s, on the other hand, devaluation-oriented mercantilism was very popular. Devaluation-oriented mercantilism has potentially expansive effects and was without doubt the decisive factor in overcoming the restrictive economic effects of the gold standard after World War I (Eichengreen/Sachs 1985). The gold standard was restrictive during the interwar period because Britain tried desperately to regain its key-currency position and because the policy of the United States, the new key-currency country, was dysfunctional for the world economy. The United States (and France, which had entered the gold standard with an undervalued currency) attracted a large part of the international gold reserves and neutralized the effects of these capital imports on domestic monetary policy. They thus intensified the deflationary competition for gold reserves which diminished only after the collapse of the gold standard (Eichengreen 1987). It is important to note that the devaluations in the 1930s took place in a deflationary environment with mass unemployment and little danger of inflation.

The End of Full-Employment Policy

North America and Western Europe began to abandon full-employment policies in the 1970s. In Europe this change in policy was initiated by the

Federal Republic of Germany in the early 1970s and is now being completed throughout the Continent. There are two reasons for this policy change: the failure of incomes policy and the destabilization of the international monetary system since the early 1970s. Most of the North American and European monetary economies were able to create full employment only temporarily. Until the late 1950s, unemployment could not be substantially reduced in most Western countries due to the economic disruptions caused by World War II. It then took only a decade until increasing worldwide inflation and exchange-rate turbulence compelled an increasing number of countries to abandon full-employment policies. Institutional and political conditions for price-level stability, and thus for nominal exchange-rate stability given full employment, vary considerably from country to country. Incomes policy as practiced in Austria and Scandinavia was not feasible in most other countries. In general, full employment was accompanied by creeping inflation with a tendency toward acceleration. In the late 1960s the potential danger of considerable inflation had grown in most countries.

Exchange-rate flexibility, introduced after the breakdown of the Bretton Woods system, brings with it specific additional sources of uncertainty (Riese 1986; Davidson 1982). Short-lived economic phenomena such as a price-level jump or an expansive fiscal policy could immediately destabilize capital movements and lead to cumulative changes in exchange rates. Within a confidence-inspiring system of fixed exchange rates with narrow margins of permitted fluctuation, minor changes in exchange rates give rise to stabilizing speculative activity.

The conflict between high employment and price level stability was aggravated by the instabilities of the international economy subsequent to the breakdown of the Bretton Woods system. These instabilities became a source of disruption for domestic economic development and increased the level of economic uncertainty. Given unstable international economic conditions, it is rational for countries to protect themselves from external shocks by means of generally cautious policies or even a stability-oriented undervaluation of their currencies. Above all, an unstable economic environment encourages policies that do not adversely affect the confidence of economic agents and provoke destabilizing portfolio adjustments. Inflation must then be fought from the outset, and there remains little room for incomes policy, which can never be as uncompromising and confidence-inspiring as a nominal exchange rate anchor and an independent central bank with the pledge to maintain price-level stability.

The fact that conditions for incomes policy worsened—as a result of dollar instability, exchange rate shocks, and oil price shocks—decisively affected economic development since the early 1970s. The lack of acceptance of real income reductions resulting from one-time price-level increases destroyed the basis for incomes policy in most countries. Since the late 1960s many attempts have been made to agree upon a social contract between employers' associations, trade unions, and government. Only in rare cases, however, has such a contract by itself been able to solve the problem of inflation.

In accordance with their diverse institutional and political conditions, individual Western industrial nations responded very differently to emerging inflation and exchange rate-problems during the late stages of the Bretton Woods system. The Bundesbank reacted by adopting the strongest measures of all Western central banks in the early 1970s. Despite relatively low rates of inflation but given a pronounced conflict with trade unions about wage increases, the Bundesbank induced a large-scale stabilization crisis, thus provoking one of the steepest declines in production in the history of the Federal Republic of Germany. In several other countries, policymakers were willing to produce a stabilization crisis only when cumulative erosion of the domestic monetary system was discernible, primarily in the drastic depreciation of the external value of the national currency. Great Britain, for instance, experienced monetary crises in 1972 and 1976, Italy in 1976, and France in 1976 as well as between 1981 and 1983. After a long period of hesitation even the United States was forced to produce a stabilization crisis when confronted with cumulative inflation and depreciation. Another group of countries already adopted a hard-currency policy in the 1970s by pegging the external value of their currencies to that of a stable currency. In Europe, the Netherlands and Austria chose to adopt the German mark as their nominal anchor at a very early stage. The method of reducing and controlling domestic inflation rates by means of a nominal exchange rate anchor became the dominant model in Europe, practiced by Italy, France, and Britain as well as the Scandinavian and southern European countries. On the whole, economic policy since the early 1970s has been aimed at stabilizing nominal exchange rates, controlling inflation, and shielding the domestic economy from external shocks. Consequently, the labor market dropped to the bottom of the priority list of economic policymakers.

In retrospect, the 1960s appear as a period of growing inflationary danger, while the 1970s brought the short-lived illusion of national autonomy through flexible exchange rates and the start of anti-inflationary policy. By the mid-1980s, market processes—in the extreme, monetary crises—had essentially forced policymakers in all Western monetary economies to recognize the primacy of relative internal monetary stability. In the 1980s monetary relations "normalized" as those labor-market conditions that encourage price-level stability and afford protection from international turbulence were reestablished. There are at present no indications that developments in the 1990s will mirror those of the 1960s. The instability of the international monetary system will in itself leave little room for full-employment policies. It is therefore to be expected that in the foreseeable future most of the developed monetary economies will exhibit a high level of unemployment. In retrospect developments in the 1960s were short-lived and offered scant prospect for macroeconomic stability.

The Future of the Dollar and European Monetary Integration

In the next few decades the dollar, the mark—or a new European currency—and the yen will most likely continue to dominate the international economy. Economically, politically, and militarily the United States is still by far the most powerful country and there is no reason why it should not be able to maintain successfully its international status for the foreseeable future if it implements a scarce-dollar policy. It would therefore be wrong to assume—even from a medium-term perspective—that there will be a transition from the international monetary system dominated by the United States, with the dollar at the top of the currency hierarchy, to an oligopolistic system, with several currency poles of comparable strength within a multicurrency system. Although the mark and yen have become the benchmark for judging the store-of-value quality of the dollar, at present there exists no currency that could displace the dollar internationally. Within a time span of several decades the world economy should increasingly tend toward a multicurrency system. Such long-term forecasts are, however, always subject to a high degree of uncertainty.

Of greater importance for the near future is that the United States has made clear that it is not willing or not able to subordinate its domestic policy to the goal of international monetary stability. It must be assumed that it will continue its policy of "benign neglect" as well as the exploitation of its privileged position within the international economy. As illustrated by events toward the end of the 1970s, in a situation with inflationary problems the United States' ability to pursue an economic policy with an exclusively domestic orientation is limited. It is, however, great enough to expose the other reserve-currency countries and those at the bottom of the currency hierarchy to disruptive shocks through changes in the relative scarcity of the dollar. It therefore seems that the world economy will have to adapt to the uncertainty of potentially destabilizing capital movements, periodic exchange-rate adjustments, and balance-of-payments crises.

If Japan further liberalizes its capital markets while maintaining its present economic policies, its chances of increasing the yen's significance as an international reserve currency are good. It is, however, improbable that the yen will become as important as the dollar in the foreseeable future. Japan has not built up a substantial currency block around the yen, nor does it have the political or military power to attain an internationally dominant position.

It is more difficult to judge the effects that European monetary integration will have on the international monetary system and on the role of the dollar. The transition from the European Monetary System to the European Monetary Union (EMU) with a single European currency could accelerate the development toward a multicurrency system. The economic, military, and political power of a Western European currency area would in no way be inferior to that of the United States. If a stable European currency is established—even if only by the EMS core countries—the dollar will be confronted with a dangerous competitor that will further constrain the maneuverability of U.S. economic policy. In such a scenario the possibility of an intense currency competition for the position of leading international currency—forced upon central banks by portfolio decisions on the part of asset holders—cannot be excluded. The emergence of cooperation is also conceivable because the United States' ability to exploit its position in the international monetary system is declining, which might increase its willingness to cooperate. If a minimum of cooperation cannot be established, the division of the world into separate economic blocs is likely.

Concerning the introduction of a single European currency, skepticism is warranted. Even if one were introduced, a high reputation and the ability to successfully compete with the dollar would by no means be guaranteed. The greatest economic danger of a single European currency is that it might give rise to economically peripheral regions. A region is particularly prone to becoming peripheral if its productivity increases are below average. Externalities, which Marshall (1920, 221) already characterized as "dependent on the general development of the industry," play an important role regarding the economic disadvantages of certain regions. There are many reasons for externalities that increase efficiency in economic centers—for example, a large labor market for qualified workers, adequate forms of cooperation between firms, successful regional corporatist structures, ample opportunity for on-the-job training, and an effective administrative setup. Proponents of currency union maintain that market pressure will lead those regions lagging behind to adopt the conditions of those regions that are economically ahead. Such convergence requires labor mobility and the elimination of specific regulations in different regions that, for example, obstruct efficiency. This viewpoint is not convincing. The innovative capabilities of economic regions depend on various conditions that differ from region to region and country to country. Regions cannot create adequate conditions rapidly even if supported by substantial regional policies. There is no reason to believe that countries entering monetary union with low innovative capabilities will therefore experience an accelerated development of productivity.

At least in the short term, wage differentials are the only instrument for maintaining the competitiveness of a region. It is extremely doubtful that nominal wages will be able to fulfill this function of regional policy. Controlling nominal wages on a regional level might be obstructed by labor mobility, which is contingent on regional differences in real wages and unemployment and which can hardly be checked within one currency area. More importantly, mechanisms of wage formation in Europe are subject to various national and political conditions that cannot be influenced by regional policy.

When a country with below-average innovative capabilities enters the monetary union, it has only one initial possibility of avoiding marginalization—it has only one game to play. If productivity and nominal wages do not adjust to the necessities of interregional competitiveness, it will be difficult to check the mechanisms that transform the country into a peripheral region. The possibility of discretionary exchange-rate adjustments thus implies the existence of a "safety net" that can be relied upon if economic developments in a country are not under control. A realignment coupled with a stabilization program may then facilitate adjustment or may even be necessary to make positive developments possible. The option of realignments is excluded in case of monetary union.

A likely consequence of a single European currency for all EMS countries is that the corresponding economic bloc would have a multitude of structural economic problems. A monetary union with all EMS countries might give rise to economically peripheral regions and concentrated centers of economic activity. Disagreement over regional and general economic policy issues alone could seriously interfere with a stability-oriented policy on the part of a European central bank (Riese 1989) and weaken the European currency. Such a development would ultimately limit the role of the dollar less than the existence of a strong German mark.

With the external shock of German unification in 1990, the danger of a transition to a new market constellation emerged in Germany: large budget deficits resulted from financial transfers to the new German states, and a current-account deficit emerged. German monetary policy, which persistently tightened until the fall of 1992, indicates that the Bundesbank is willing to defend the mark's international position even at the expense of increasing domestic (and European) unemployment. The Bundesbank's response to a potential weakness of the mark is thus the same as it was in 1950/51, 1965/66, and 1981/82. The difference is, however, that the current-account deficit did not disappear, and that the conflict between monetary policy and fiscal policy is likely to continue.

High interest rate policy in Germany after unification has had far-reaching consequences for the EMS. In the fall of 1992 it provoked realignments—for instance, a devaluation of the Spanish peseta—and even withdrawals from the EMS—in the case of Britain and Italy. It thereby destroyed the myth of invariable exchange rates and economic convergence within the EMS. After repeated monetary crises, the fluctuation bands of the European exchange rate mechanism were increased from ± 2.25 percent to ± 15 percent at the beginning of August 1993, amounting to the collapse of the EMS. Many countries that devalued their currencies, Britain and Spain, for example, were able to successfully reduce the external restrictive pressure because their problems of inflation had been sharply reduced during the 1980s. The Maastricht treaty on monetary union at the end of the 1990s has thus experienced another serious setback in addition to the political opposition in several potential member countries. In view of the economic problems to be expected in Europe and the prevailing economic and political climate, the failure of a monetary union with most of the EMS countries seems to be inevitable. It is conceivable that several European countries—Germany, France, Austria, Scandinavian countries, and the Benelux countries—will go ahead with monetary union in advance of other countries. In any case, the attempt by all EMS countries to fulfil the criteria of the Maastricht treaty to enter monetary union will reduce growth in Europe at least until the end of the decade.

There are few indications that Russia or one of the other large successor states to the Soviet Union will represent an internationally relevant economic pole even in the long run. On the contrary, it must be expected that most of the countries in transition will experience difficulties establishing monetary stability, which is a prerequisite for long-term economic growth. An international monetary system that would promote economic development in the Third World and the former planned economies is unlikely to emerge. Given the mercantilist strategies of Japan, the Federal Republic of Germany, and the economically successful East Asian countries as well as the probable future instability of the international monetary system, it appears that economic development will be possible only for individual countries but not in general.

References

Bagehot, Walter (1873). *Lombard Street*. Re-issued New York: Dutton, 1921.

Bilson, John *F.D.* (1979): "The Vicious Circle Hypothesis." *International Monetary Fund Staff Papers* 26: 1–37.

Blackburn, Keith and Christensen, Michael (1989): "Monetary Policy and Policy Credibility: Theories and Evidence." *The Journal of Economic Literature* 17: 1–45.

Blanchard, Oliver and Dornbusch, Rudiger (1984): "US Deficits, the Dollar and Europe." *Banca Nazionale del Lavoro Quarterly Review* 37: 89–118.

Bliss, Christopher (1985): "The Rise And Fall of the Dollar." *Oxford Review of Economic Policy* 2: 7–24.

Bloomfield, Arthur (1959): *Monetary Policy Under the International Gold Standard. 1880–1914*. New York: Federal Reserve Bank of New York.

Bosworth, Barry (1991): "Incomes Policies in Socialist Economies." in *Managing Inflation in Socialist Economies in Transition,* edited by Simon Commander, Washington D.C.:The World Bank, pp. 197–211.

Calleo, David P. (1980): "Inflation and American Power." *Foreign Affairs*, 59:781–812.

Calleo, David P., van Cleveland, H.B., and Silk, L. (1988): "The Dollar and the Defense of the West." *Foreign Affairs*, 66:846–862.

Cohen, Benjamin J. (1979): "Europe's Money, America's Problem." Foreign Policy, Nr. 35:31–47.

Davidson, Paul (1982): *International Money and the Real World*. London: Macmillan.

Deutsche Bundesbank (1981): *Geschäftsbericht für das Jahr 1981*. Frankfurt a.M.

Dixit, Avinash (1992): "Investment and Hysteresis." *Journal of Economic Perspectives*, 6: 107–132.

Domar, Evsey D. (1950): "The Effect of Foreign Investment on the Balance of Payments." *The American Economic Review*, 40: 805–826.

Dornbusch, Rudiger (1976): "Expectations and Exchange Rate Dynamics." *Journal of Political Economy*, 84:1161–1176.

——— (1986): "Flexible Exchange Rates and Excess Capital Mobility." *Brookings Papers on Economic Activity*. Washington D.C., No. 1/1986: 209–226.

——— (1990): "From Stabilization to Growth." *National Bureau of Economic Research, Working Paper No. 3302*. Cambridge, Mass.

Dornbusch, Rudiger, Sturzenegger, Federico, and Wolf, Holger (1990): "Extreme Inflation: Dynamics and Stabilization." *Brookings Papers on Economic Activity*, Washington D.C., No. 2/1990: 1–84.

Eichengreen, Barry and Sachs, Jeffrey (1985): "Exchange Rates and Economic Recovery in the 1930s." *Journal of Economic History*, XLV: 925–946.

Eichengreen, Barry (1987): "The Gold-Exchange Standard and the Great Depression." *Discussion Paper Number 1298. Harvard Institut of Economic Research*, Harvard University, Cambridge, Mass.

Einzig, Paul (1970): The Case Against Floating Exchange Rates. London: Macmillan.

Emminger, Otmar (1986): *D-Mark, Dollar, Währungskrisen. Die Erinnerungen eines Bundesbankpräsidenten*. Stuttgart: Deutsche Verlags-Anstalt.

Fischer, Stanley (1981): "Relative Shocks, Relative Price Variability, and Inflation." *Brookings Papers on Economic Activity*, Washington D.C., No. 2/1981: 381–431.

Fleming, Marcus (1962): "Domestic Financial Politics under Fixed and Floating Exchange Rates." *International Monetary Fund Staff Papers*, 9: 369–379.

Ford, Alec G. (1962): *The Gold Standard 1880–1914. Britain and Argentina*. Oxford: Clarendon Press.

Frey, Bruno (1984): "The Public Choice View of International Political Economy." *International Organizations*, 38: 95–111.
Friedman, Milton (1953): "The Case for Flexible Exchange Rates." in *Essays in Positive Economics,* edited by Milton Friedman, Chicago: University of Chicago, pp. 157–203.
Giavazzi, Francesco and Pagano, Mario (1988): "The Advantage of Tying One's Hands. EMS Discipline and Central Bank Credibility." *European Economic Review*, 32:1055–1082.
Goschen, Georg (1861): *The Theory of the Foreign Exchanges*. London.
Hahn, Frank (1981): "General Equilibrium Theory." in *The Crisis in Economic Theory,* edited by Daniel Bell and Irving Kristol, New York: Basic Books pp. 198–211.
Herr, Hansjörg and Spahn, Heinz-Peter (1989): *Staatsverschuldung, Zahlungsbilanz und Wechselkurs. Aussenwirtschaftliche Spielräume und Grenzen der Fiskalpolitik.* Regensburg: Transfer Verlag.
Herr, Hansjörg (1990): "Der bundesdeutsche und japanische Merkantilismus und seine Folgen." in *Wirtschaftspolitische Strategien. Probleme ökonomischer Stabilität und Entwicklung in Industrieländern und der Europäischen Gemeinschaft*, edited by Heinz-Peter Spahn, Regensburg: Transfer Verlag, pp. 113–138.
——— (1991): "International Constraints on Fiscal Policy: An International Comparison." in *Beyond Keynesianism. The Socio-Economics of Production and Full Employment,* edited by Egon Matzner and Wolfgang Streeck, Aldershot: Edward Elgar, pp. 161–181.
Herr, Hansjörg and Westphal, Andreas (1991): "Probleme der monetären Integration Europas. Das Europäische Währungssystem und die deutsche Vereinigung." in *Wirtschaftspolitische Konsequenzen der deutschen Vereinigung,* edited by Andreas Westphal and Hansjörg Herr and Michael Heine and Ulli Busch, Frankfurt a.M. and New York: Campus Verlag, pp. 75–114.
Herr, Hansjörg (1992): *Geld, Währungssystem und Währungswettbewerb. Die theoretische und historische Analyse einer internationalen Geldwirtschaft*. Frankfurt a.M. and New York: Campus Verlag.
Hicks, John R. (1982): "The Foundations of Monetary Theory." in *Money, Interest and Wages: Collected Essays on Economic Theory, Vol. II*, edited by John R. Hicks, Oxford: Oxford University, pp. 236–275.
Institute for Public Policy Research (1989): "The German Surplus: An Economic Problem in the New Europe." *Economic Study*, No. 2.
Johnson, Harry G. (1972): "The Case for Flexible Exchange Rates." in *Further Essays in Monetary Economics,* edited by Harry G. Johnson, London: Allen and Unwin, pp. 38–56.
Kenen, Paul B. (1988): *Managing Exchange Rates*. Royal Institute for International Affairs. London.
Keohane, Robert O. (1984): *After Hegemony*. Princeton: Princeton University.
Keohane, Robert O. and Nye, Joseph S. (1977): *Power and Interdependence: World Politics in Transition*. Boston: Little, Brown and Company.
Keynes, John M.(1913): *Indian Currency and Finance*. London: Macmillan.
——— (1930): *A Treatise on Money*. London: Macmillan.
——— (1936): *The General Theory of Employment, Interest and Money*. London: Macmillan.
Kindleberger, Charles P. (1969): "The Case for Fixed Exchange Rates." in *The International Adjustment Mechanism*. Federal Reserve Bank of Boston. Conference Series, No. 2, Boston.
——— (1973): The World in Depression, 1929–1939, Berkeley.
——— (1981): "Dominance and Leadership in the International Economy: Exploitation, Public Goods, and Free Riders." *International Studies Quarterly*, 25:242–254.

——— (1983): "Key Currencies and Financial Centres." in *Reflection on a Troubled World Economy* edited by Fritz Machlup, et al., London: Macmillan, pp. 75–90.

——— (1985): "The Dollar Yesterday, Today, and Tomorrow." *Banca Nazionale del Lavoro Quarterly Review*, 38: 295–308.

——— (1986): "International Public Goods Without International Government." *American Economic Review*,76: 1–13.

Klein, Benjamin (1978): "Competing Monies, European Monetary Union and the Dollar." in *One Money for Europe* edited by Michele Fratianni and Theo Peeters, New York: Praeger Publishers, pp. 69–94.

Kregel, Jan A. (1985): "The Supply-Side Approach in the United States—Reaganomics." in *Staat und Beschäftigung*, edited by Buttler et al., Institut für Arbeitsmarkt und Berufsforschung der Bundesanstalt für Arbeit, Nürnberg, pp. 101– 138.

Krasner, Stephen P. (1975): "State Power and the Structure of International Trade." *World Politics*, 27: 317–347.

Krugman, Paul R. (1985): "Is the Strong Dollar Sustainable?" in *The U.S. Dollar—Recent Developments, Outlook and Policy Options*. Federal Reserve Bank of Kansas City, Kansas City.

Kydland, Finn E. and Prescott, Edwards C. (1977): "Rules Rather Than Discretion: The Inconsistency of Optimal Plans." *Journal of Political Economy*, 85: 473–491.

Layard, Richard (1990): "Wage Bargaining and Incomes Policy: Possible Lessons for Eastern Europe". *Centre for Economic Performance*, Discussion Paper No. 2, London School of Economics.

Levine, Solomon B. and Taira, Koji (1985): "Japan's Relations: A Social Compact Emerges." in *Industrial Relations in a Decade of Economic Change,* edited by Juris Harvey, et al., Madison, Wisc., pp. 247–300.

Lucas, Robert E. Jr. (1976): "Econometric Policy Evaluation: A Critique." in *Carnegie-Rochester Series on Public Policy,* Vol. 1, edited by Karl Brunner and Alan Meltzer, Amsterdam.

Marshall, Alfred (1920): *Principles of Economics*, 8th ed. London: Macmillan.

Minsky, Hyman P. (1979): "Financial Interrelations, the Balance of Payments and the Dollar Crisis." in *Debt and the Less Developed Countries* edited by Jonathan D. Aronson, Boulder Colo: Westview Press, pp. 103–122.

Mundell, Robert A. (1968): *International Economics*. New York: Macmillan.

Okun, Alfred M. (1971): "The Mirage of Steady Inflation." *Brookings Papers on Economic Activity*, Washington D.C., No. 2/1971: 485–489.

Olivera, Julio (1967): "Money, Prices and Fiscal Lags: A Note on the Dynamics of Inflation." *Banca Nazionale del Lavoro Quarterly Review*, 20: 258–267.

Oudiz, Gilles and Sachs, Jeffrey (1984): "Macroeconomic Policy Coordination Among Industrial Economies." *Brookings Papers on Economic Activity*, Washington D.C., No. 1/1984: 1–75.

Padoa-Schioppa, Thommaso and Papadia, Francesco (1984): "Competing Currencies and Monetary Stability." in *Europe's Money,* edited by Rossi S. Masera and Robert Triffin, Oxford, pp. 79–110.

Padoan, Pier C. (1986): *International Financial Instability*. London: Croom Helm.

Parboni, Robert (1981): *The Dollar and Its Rivals*. London: New Left Books.

Polanyi, Karl (1944): *The Great Transformation*. New York.

Riese, Hajo (1986): *Theorie der Inflation*. Tübingen: Mohr.

——— (1989): "Geldpolitik bei Preisniveaustabilität. Anmerkungen zur Politik der Deutschen Bundesbank." in *Beiträge zur angewandten Wirtschaftsforschung,* edited by Heiner J. Ramser and Hajo Riese, Berlin: Springer Verlag, pp. 101–123.

——— (1992): "Bausteine einer Markttheorie der Transformation." in *Transformation in Mittel- und Osteuropa. Makroökonomische Konzepte und Fallstudien,* edited by Hansjörg Herr and Andreas Westphal, Frankfurt a.M. and New York: Campus Verlag, pp. 184–199.

——— (1993): *Das Grundproblem der Wirtschaftspolitik.* Free University Berlin, mimeo.

Robinson, Joan (1937): "Beggar-My-Neighbour Remedies for Unemployment." in *Contributions to Modern Economics*, edited by Joan Robinson, London: Blackwell, 1978, pp. 190–200.

——— (1965): "The New Mercantilism." in *Contributions to Modern Economics*, edited by Joan Robinson, London: Blackwell, 1978, pp. 200–212.

Sachs, Jeffery D. (1985): "The Dollar and the Policy Mix 1985." *Brookings Papers on Economic Activity*. Washington D.C., No. 2/1985:117–183.

Sachs, Jaffery (1986): "The Bolivian Hyperinflation and Stabilization." *National Bureau of Economic Research*, Working Papers No. 2073, Cambridge, Mass.

Sargent, Thomas J. (1986): "Reaganomics and Credibility." in *Rational Expectations and Inflation* edited by Thomas J. Sargent, New York, pp. 19–39.

Scharpf, Fritz W. (1987): *Sozialdemokratische Krisenpolitik in Europa*. Frankfurt a.M.: Campus Verlag.

Soskice, David (1990): "Wage Determination: the Changing Role of Institutions in Advanced Industrialized Countries." *Oxford Review of Economic Policy*, 6:36–61.

Spahn, Heinz-Peter (1988): *Bundesbank und Wirtschaftskrise*. Regensburg: Transfer Verlag.

Strange, Susan (1976): *International Economic Relations of the Western World 1959–1971*. Vol. 2: International Monetary Relations. London.

Stützel, Wolfgang (1978): *Volkswirtschaftliche Saldenmechanik*. 2nd ed., Tübingen: Mohr.

Swoboda, Alexander K. (1968): *The Euro-Dollar Market: An Interpretation*. Essays in International Finance, No. 64, International Finance Section, Princeton University.

Tanzi, Vito (1977): "Inflation, Lags in Collection, and the Real Value of Tax Revenue." *International Monetary Fund Staff Papers*, 24: 154–167.

Thygesen, Niels (1985): "Is the Multiple Currency a Destabilizing Factor?" in *The Political Economy of International Money: In Search for a New Order* edited by Loukas Tsoukali, London: Sage Publications, pp. 137–170.

Vandenbroucke, Frank (1985): "Conflicts in International Economic Policy and the World Recession: A Theoretical Analysis." *Cambridge Journal of Economics*,9: 15–42.

Vines, David (1980): "Competitiveness, Technical Progress and Balance of Trade Surpluses." *The Manchester School*, 48: 378–391.

Wyplosz, Charles (1988): "The EMS—From Success to Transition." in *Internationales Währungssystem und weltwirtschaftliche Entwicklung*, edited by Carl Dräger and Lothar Späth, Baden-Baden: Nomos, pp. 68–89.

Chapter 4

"Strong" States and "Cheap" Credit

Economic Policy Strategy and Financial Regulation in France and Spain

Sofía A. Pérez

The institutionalist approach to comparative political economy gained its current place in the field by responding to the question of how national economies adapted to the external shocks of the seventies. The first generation of "new institutionalists" argued that variation in the modes of adjustment observed across advanced industrialized countries was explained by fundamental differences in national institutional frameworks. One of the most important institutional variables identified in this literature was represented by differences in national financial systems and in postwar patterns of domestic financial regulation. These differences were captured in the early eighties by John Zysman (1983), whose three-way typology of national financial systems still serves as one of the principal works of reference on the role of financial systems for comparative political economists today. Like other work within the institutionalist literature, Zysman's typology was premised on the assumption that institutional attributes, reflecting national historical legacies, are relatively stable over time. Yet, this premise has been challenged by the unravelling of the cross-national pattern of regulatory divergence that Zysman captured.

Central to the framework proposed by Zysman was the emergence after World War II of distinctly interventionist forms of financial regulation in Europe. In Zysman's institutional model this phenomenon was typified by the "state-directed, price-administered" financial system found in France and Japan. Indeed, Zysman's typology revolved around the contrast between this type and the Anglo-Saxon, capital market-based financial system.[1] However, one of the central features of recent change in domestic patterns of regulation across Europe has been the abandonment of precisely such a regime of selective credit regulation not only in France but also in Spain, where the French model had been adopted in the early sixties.

This essay focuses on the role of selective credit regulation in postwar financial regulatory regimes. It proposes that the choice of whether to extend state discretion over credit allocation, and, equally important, of how to instrumentalize such discretion, is an important aspect of the two postwar regulatory divides.[2] It suggests that the pattern of cross-national regulatory divergence captured by John Zysman was a historical phenomenon, one that crystallized only after World War II, and was undermined by the end of the postwar economic boom. It argues that the emergence and later abandonment of a regime of selective credit regulation in two countries, France and Spain, was closely tied to the choice of a particular macroeconomic growth strategy, which was itself made possible by an exceptional economic context (both domestically and externally). Change in that economic context starting in the late sixties rendered such a growth strategy nonviable, changing the policy imperatives of governments and leading to the abandonment of interventionism. Contrary, however, to a market-driven view of domestic financial reform (see, for example, Dollar and Frieden 1990; Frieden 1991), I argue that the fundamental reasons for the abandonment of the old regulatory regime lay in the political consequences of interventionism for state elites, not in technical economic constraints or increased sectorial pressures in favor of liberalization. This is also reflected in the lack of market-conforming convergence in those countries where interventionism was abandoned.

The essay is organized into six sections. The first discusses the pattern of regulatory change in the two countries that are the focus of analysis, France and Spain, as well as the contrast with two shadow cases, Italy and Germany, whose financial systems have exhibited greater continuity. The second and third sections provide an explanation of such regulatory divergence among these four countries in the postwar period. The fourth section discusses the role of international factors in explaining the divergence. The fifth in turn discusses the impact of international change on domestic financial regulation in France and Spain. The last section takes

1. Zysman's typology also included a third type: the German model of a private-bank-organized credit market. With the decline of the "state-directed" model, the attention of political economists has now shifted onto the contrast between this third type and the Anglo-Saxon model. See, for example, Vitols, in this volume.

2. See the ch. 1 by Forsyth and Notermans.

up the issue of whether the abandonment of interventionism reflects a trend toward market-driven, international regulatory convergence.

Change and Continuity in Domestic Financial Regulation

This essay seeks to explain the unravelling of the postwar pattern of cross-national regulatory divergence in Europe by focusing on one aspect of such change, namely the abandonment of the postwar regime of selective credit regulation in France and Spain. The dependent variable that will concern us is therefore a historical sequence, one that entails the emergence of a distinct pattern of state-directed credit allocation in these two countries in the early postwar period and its subsequent dismantlement in the seventies and eighties. The regulatory regime at the heart of this sequence was typified by Zysman as the "state-directed, price-administered regime." However, this regime was not the only form of financial interventionism found in Europe during the postwar period. It constituted a "soft" model of interventionism that was closely associated with the institutions of indicative planning, and in which state discretion was exercised not (or not only) through direct state control of credit allocation but through selective regulation of credit to different users. I therefore will refer to this regulatory regime as the regime of "selective credit regulation," in order to distinguish it from another form of financial interventionism in which state elites exercised direct political control over credit allocation through state ownership of financial institutions. While the latter model (which was instituted in Italy) imposed state discretion in a more direct or "harder" way, it also tended to retain a more limited character than selective credit regulation as instituted in France and Spain. The cases of Italy ("hard" interventionism) and Germany (representing a noninterventionist form of credit regulation) are included as shadow cases to illuminate the discussion of France and Spain. Each of these shadow cases represents an alternative model of financial regulation, which, while distinct from each other, have demonstrated greater stability across the two regulatory divides treated in this volume. Before going on to explain the regulatory sequence defined above, the rest of this section offers a brief description of the course of financial regulation in the four countries. The point of departure is the type of financial system and regulatory framework found in these countries before World War II (the Civil War, in the Spanish case).

In both France and Spain, the main characteristic of financial regulation before the war was the conspicuous laxity of banking regulation and the absence of state discretion over the activities of the financial sector.

In the French case, the demise of the major industrial banks in the crises of the late nineteenth century left a financial sector dominated by large deposit banks. In contrast to the expired nineteenth century industrial banks, these banks shied away from industrial involvement and engaged only in short-term discounting of commercial bills that they were able to rediscount at generous terms with the Banque de France (Caron 1979; Patat and Lutfalla 1990, 14–15; Loriaux 1991, 111). In Spain, the repatriation of colonial capital that followed the military defeat of 1898 led to the creation of a number of private commercial banks at the turn of the century.[3] Unlike the progressive decapitalization that marred the French banking sector, the Spanish banks experienced a significant boom in the first three decades of the century and in some cases actively engaged in industrial promotion along the German model. Yet on the whole, and despite the universal character with which many of the institutions were founded, the Spanish banking sector exhibited the same propensity to engage only in short-term discounting. On the other hand, in both countries the stock markets played a significant, if insufficient, role in providing investment finance in the prewar period.

Contrary to widespread conceptions about the "statist" legacies of both of these countries, the role of the state was heavily constrained by the "liberal" orientation of the prewar political regimes—the Third Republic in France and the Bourbon Restoration (followed by the Second Republic) in Spain. With the exception of trade policy, which was characterized by a progressive increase in tariff levels, the predominant ideological orientation in the political class of both regimes was strongly hostile to state interference in the activities of private capitalists. This stance of "laissez-faire cum protectionism" (Kuisel; 1981) was clearly manifest in the area of financial regulation. While the banking sector was protected from foreign competition,[4] state authorities exercised no discretion over the allocation of its resources. A number of parapublic credit institutes were created in the twenties and thirties (the Crédit National and Crédit Agricole in France, the Banco de Crédito Industrial and Banco de Crédito Agrícola in Spain). Yet before the war, these institutions remained in private hands and their impact was strongly limited by the prerogative that private financiers exercised over their activities. Finally, both the Banque de France and the Banco de España also remained in private hands throughout the prewar decades and even engaged in open

3. Some of these banks were built on the defunct institutions created by French banking capital in the previous century to finance the building of railroads in Spain.

4. Protection was virtually complete in Spain, where the Banking Law of 1921 established a "status quo" in the sector, effectively allowing the existing banks to freeze entry into the sector.

competition with the private commercial banks (Kuisel 1981, 13–14; Olariaga 1960).

The war gave way to significant changes in these traditional regulatory regimes. In 1945, the de Gaulle government nationalized the Banque de France and gave the state a majority stake in the three largest commercial banks. However, according to most accounts, this partial nationalization did not produce any significant change in how the French financial system operated and in fact constituted a "natural" extension of the banks' progressive decapitalization over the course of the thirties. The banks were allowed to retain their corporate identities and, according to the principle of managerial autonomy, were able to operate in line with market principles and without political interference. Instead of direct political control of credit, a system of "soft" interventionism by way of the selective regulation of credit was therefore established. The two critical changes in this regard were (1) the creation of a National Credit Council to establish the guidelines for selective credit regulation and (2) the establishment of the practice of selective rediscounting of credit with the Banque de France.[5]

In time, this framework gave way to the creation of two distinct channels of privileged financing, or "privileged financing circuits." The first of these was the so called "Treasury circuit," whereby financial institutions, most notably the savings banks, were required to deposit a part of their deposits with the Treasury, which in turn allocated these funds among semipublic credit institutes such as the Crédit National or Crédit Foncier, which provided lending to specific users. Because of a complicated crisscrossing of liabilities between the Treasury and various financial institutions, this circuit actually allowed the Treasury to create money of its own.[6] The second was the selectively regulated rediscounting of loans with the Banque de France. Though this second circuit was significant from the start, its importance in relation to that of the Treasury circuit increased progressively over the course of the sixties. On the whole, therefore, selective regulation was dominated by the element of selective expansion of credit rather than selective rationing. Indeed, generous rediscounting formed the basis for an implicit "guarantee of liquidity" to the banks, which allowed the latter to transform short-term deposits into long-term industrial lending.[7] This, however, was to change in the seventies, with the introduction of credit quotas (*encadrement du*

5. Before the war, the Banque de France had been allowed to rediscount only short-term discount bills. After the war this was extended first to long-term credits and eventually to specific users.

6. For a more detailed discussion, see Loriaux, 149–51.

7. For discussion, see Patat and Lutfalla, and Loriaux, 112–13.

crédit) which implied a tightening of the overall conditions under which credit was extended and a shift from rediscounting to rationing. In the mid-1980s, the framework of selective credit regulation was finally dismantled with the abandonment of the *encadrement* after 1985, giving way to a broad, market-oriented reform of the French financial system (see more below).

In Spain, the course of financial regulation after the Civil War had two broad phases. In a first phase, lasting from 1940 to 1960 and coinciding with the Franco regime's policy of economic nationalism, or *autarquía*, the prewar regime of a self-regulating banking cartel was reestablished. The cartel was institutionalized in the Banking Law of 1946, which recreated the Consejo Superior Bancario (CSB), granting it wide powers over all aspects of banking practices, while officially freezing entry into the sector (Muñoz 1969). The new regime also reestablished the prewar practice of *pignoración automática* (automatic collateral-lending to the banks on their purchases of public debt), whereby the public debt was monetized through the banks. Yet, in contrast to wide-spread controls over product markets, the Franco regime during this phase forewent any discretion over credit allocation. The principal change to the prewar regime of industrial finance came not in the area of financial regulation but in the form of the creation of the Instituto Nacional de Industria (INI) in 1941, which represented the first real challenge to the banking sector's position of control within the economy. However, unlike the Italian Istituto per la Ricostruzione Industriale (IRI), upon which it was theoretically modeled, the INI was prevented from taking a position within the financial system itself. Instead, its activities were strongly circumscribed to production in three basic industries—coal, steel, and energy.

The first significant change in the Spanish regulatory framework came with the end of the *autarquía* and the implementation of an IMF-sponsored stabilization plan in 1959. This shift coincided with the adoption of a more outward-oriented development strategy and French-styled indicative planning in 1961. While the *pignoración* was ended, the practice of selective central bank rediscounting was introduced in 1960. In 1962, both the Banco de España and the parapublic credit institutions were nationalized, and new banking legislation was introduced formally establishing a more segmented banking structure.[8] At the same time, a committee was established within the Ministry of Finance, though closely tied to the new Planning Commission, to set guidelines for selective credit regulation. And as in France two principal channels, or circuits, of

8. Commercial and industrial banking was formally separated, although in practice the legislation was amended in such a way that it allowed the Big Seven commercial banks to retain their universal character and charter their own industrial banks.

privileged financing were instituted: one through which financial institutions (principally the savings banks) were required to allocate a large portion of their deposits to the purchase of investment certificates, providing funds that were then allocated to specific users by the newly nationalized official credit institutions; the second consisting of special rediscount lines for commercial bank loans to specified users.

All in all, the construct of privileged financing and selective credit regulation contrived in Spain after 1959 closely resembled that established in France starting in 1945. As in France, the rapidly expanding rate of central bank liquidity to the banking sector meant that selective credit regulation was dominated by the element of rediscounting rather than rationing. In the Spanish case, such conditions lasted until 1971, when the special rediscount lines were replaced by compulsory investment coefficients forcing the banks to allocate specific proportions of their resources to specified users, thus effectively shifting to a system of credit rationing. This system was abandoned with the dismantlement of the compulsory ratios starting in 1977. However, as will be discussed further below, the abandonment of selective credit regulation came well before any significant efforts to reform the structure of the Spanish financial market.

Alongside the "soft" framework of selective credit regulation and privileged financing that characterized financial regulation during the postwar period in France and Spain, at least two other regulatory frameworks within credit-based systems can be distinguished in the European postwar context. The first of these, represented by Italy, is a form of political control over credit that, while more direct, avoided the subjugation of monetary policy instruments. The second, represented by Germany, is a noninterventionist framework of credit regulation that left decisions about the overall course of credit allocation up to private banks. As opposed to the regime of selective credit regulation in France and Spain, both the German and the Italian postwar frameworks represented relative continuity with the past in these countries and exhibited greater endurance in the last two decades.

The Italian postwar framework of credit regulation was defined by the banking law of 1936, which divided Italian financial institutions into, on one hand, those limited to short-term savings and lending and, on the other, those taking medium and long-term savings and charged with providing long-term lending. This division grew out of the massive crisis of the Italian banking system, which forced the state to take over a large number of banks (including the three largest commercial banks) in 1931, and led to the creation of the Istituto per la Ricostruzione Industriale (IRI) to administer the new Banks of National Interest in 1933. It reflected the failure of the system of universal banking in Italy, as it had been the Italian banks' excessive exposure to long-term industrial loans that had led to their massive failure. To avoid such instability, a special credit institution, the Istituto Mobiliare Italiano (IMI), was created to provide long-term industrial credit. The principal characteristic of the financial system created during the fascist period was therefore the dominant role of the state, which through the IRI and a number of publicly chartered banks controlled 67 percent of the total deposits of the banking system at the end of the war.

Despite its political origins, the fascist framework of financial regulation was fully maintained after the war; and it was extended with the creation of additional special credit institutions (such as Mediobanca) under the IRI. The most important difference in postwar regulation was the dominant role given to the Banca d'Italia in regulating the credit institutions. As has been pointed out by Shonfield, the postwar legal framework gave the Banca d'Italia the ability to impose a system of selective credit regulation, since a bank was required to obtain special permission from the central bank whenever it wanted to extend a loan in excess of 20 percent of its capital and reserves. However, "deeply antagonistic of the notion of any form of long-term planning dependent on their control of bank lending policies," central bank officials never developed such a system (Shonfield 1965, 181). Most important, Banca d'Italia officials were able to prevent the subordination of monetary policy instruments to industrial policy objectives.

Instead of the "soft" mechanisms of central bank rediscounting, financial interventionism in Italy thus depended on direct control by political authorities over the IRI's special credit institutions. Such control was used to channel investment to the IRI's enterprises in productive sectors but also for the more political objectives of financing development schemes in central and southern Italy (Shonfield 1965, 183; Nardozzi 1983, 60–61). Despite this overtly political character, this regulatory framework has exhibited greater endurance than the "soft interventionism" found in France and Spain. It was challenged, beginning in the late 1980s, by the government's decision to privatize some of the banks under the control of the IRI. However, these measures were part of a much broader privatization drive prompted by the political and fiscal crises in Italy rather than an independent drive toward financial liberalization.[9]

Finally, as illustrated by the German case, financial interventionism was not a universal phenomenon in Europe in the postwar period, even among credit-based financial systems. To be sure, some structures of

9. Beyond the privatizations, the Italian regulatory framework has experienced only marginal changes, most of which were required by European legislation. See OECD, *Economic Surveys, Italy 1995*, 52–3.

state-administered credit allocation were introduced in the period of reconstruction, the most important of which was the creation of the Kreditanstalt für Wiederaufbau (KfW), established to channel Marshall Plan funding for reconstruction. However, the state's role was circumscribed to acting at the margins, rather than structuring the overall course of investment in the FRG. Indeed, the regulatory framework created in Germany, as confirmed by the banking legislation of 1956–57, was essentially a self-regulating one, dominated by the three large universal banks, and closely resembling the framework of the prewar period. The organization of a national investment strategy was, with minor exceptions, left to the private banks, and, in the case of smaller enterprises, to the local savings banks system. In terms of its broad characteristics, this framework of financial regulation has experienced little modification up to the present time. Indeed, to the extent that change has occurred, it has come as a consequence of changes in European banking regulation, as in the recent imposition of limitations on the ownership of individual banks in nonfinancial firms.

Unlike the fluctuation in the Spanish and French regulatory frameworks, both the German and Italian systems of financial regulation have exhibited much greater stability since the interwar period. In the German case, such regulatory continuity extends even further back. This contrast will serve to instruct the following discussion, whose objective it is to explain the sequence of change represented by the emergence and subsequent abandonment of selective credit regulation in France and Spain.

Explaining the Postwar Pattern of Regulatory Divergence: Interventionist Abstention in Germany

As outlined above, one of the dimension of European postwar divergence in domestic regulatory regimes among credit-based financial systems was between state-directed and privately organized regimes of credit allocation. Although it included some elements of the former, the German postwar regulatory regime clearly represents the latter, with the federal government deferring responsibility for credit allocation to either the private banks or local authorities, and playing only a marginal role in supplementing financial institutions. In this, Germany stands apart from all three of the other cases discussed here. What explains this line of divergence represented by the abstention from interventionism in Germany?

The answer appears to lie in the domestic financial sector's perceived ability to autonomously organize and promote an adequate course of economic modernization. Economic reconstruction and modernization are tasks that require a substantial long-term horizon for investments, and thus also long-term financing. Credit-based financial systems are commonly viewed to be more capable of delivering such financing, because they avoid the "short-termism" associated with capital markets. However, the provision of long-term industrial credit by banks also involves transforming short-term deposits into long-term loans. This problem of "transformation" in industrial finance carries substantial risk for the financial stability of a banking sector. Where the banking sector is not capable of resolving it autonomously, the problem of transformation typically has drawn in the state in one form or another to either take over or dilute the risk of long-term finance. In this regard, the German banking sector stands apart from that of the other three countries treated here.

What sets the German case apart from the other three cases is foremost the fact that German postwar governments were not faced (anywhere to the same extent) with the task of remedying the domestic financial sector's inefficacy in providing an adequate level of long-term industrial finance. As has been widely noted, a critical aspect of the "privately organized" industrial policy course pursued in the FRG (Shonfield 1965; Zysman 1983; Katzenstein 1987; Hall 1986) was that long-term investment finance was achieved through a tightly strung relationship between German universal banks and large industrial firms in export sectors. The German banks resolved the problem of the provision of long-term finance in two ways. First, the banks raised a substantial amount of the financing they provided to industry on the capital market, thus diffusing the risk to their own accounts. Secondly, the ability of the German banks to engage in "transformation" without endangering their own stability is said to have rested on their ownership of shares in—and control of proxy votes on the supervisory boards of—the large firms to which they lent. This not only allowed them to monitor their borrowers but also placed them in a position to intervene in the management of these firms. Thus, the banks could develop a business strategy of foregoing short-term profits in favor of boosting the long-term business performance of their clients (Dyson 1986, 129–32).[10]

This model of "coordination by banker" has been identified as the backbone of Germany's postwar export-led growth strategy (Shonfield 1965), and reflects continuity with the pre-World War I experience, when the banks, originally chartered by emerging export industry, had played a central role in German mercantilism (Spindler 1984). To facilitate such a privately organized export strategy, postwar German banking legislation

10. As Josef Esser (1990) has noted, this characterization of the German investment model was more accurate for the earlier decades of the postwar period, as the importance of bank financing for industry decreased commensurately with an increasing capacity for self-financing in German industry. This capacity was comparatively high in the FRG from the 1960s on.

did two things. It maintained the independence of the central bank, as originally established by the Allies, yet went against Allied directives in reestablishing a nationally centralized, private universal banking system.[11] At the same time, postwar legislation also maintained the principle of self-regulation (Dyson 1986, 123), while direct state control over credit was strongly circumscribed. Aside from the provision of Marshall Plan funds through the KfW, privileged financing was largely limited to the provision of loan guarantees for export credit (the Hermes program). Privileged rediscounting by the Bundesbank was also limited to export-credits. Thus, the model of financial regulation that took hold in Germany reflects an early choice to forego direct state control over investment flows in favor of a negotiated strategy in which discretion was deferred to the main private actors.

Beyond its economic merits, this model of financial regulation also entailed political advantages for government authorities in postwar Germany. Excepting the return to universal banking, it was compatible with the liberal tenets of the Allied authorities and of a postwar domestic elite that was eager to disown the statist policies of the National Socialist past (Kloten et al. 1985).[12] The framework of financial regulation thus coincided with what Peter Katzenstein (1987) has described as the principles of a semisovereign state, in which state authority was vested in private or semiprivate actors. Such choices decreased the burden of accountability on political authorities and served in part to depoliticize economic policy. The decision to defer control over credit allocation to the banks was particularly important in this regard, because it kept investment decisions out of the political sphere and separated them from distributive politics. The banks also played a "central role ... in insulating the government from difficult and complex corporate problems," as illustrated most dramatically by the bank-led rescues of several corporate giants, such as AEG-Telefunken and Hapag-Lloyd in the early 1980s (Dyson 1986, 137; Dyson 1984).

The success of this privately organized financial system in Germany, however, presumed the exceptional expertise and organizational capacity of the German banks to shoulder the responsibility of organizing and

11. The Allies in 1946 broke up the branch networks of the Big Three universal banks into a series of successor banks, and imposed regional limitations on the activities of the banks. This de jure decentralization, however, was undermined by *de facto* integration among the successor banks over the following decade, and ended formally in 1956 (Sayers 1962, 56–57).

12. It should be noted that the measure of "organization" achieved within this negotiated policy framework went beyond that infused by the business strategies of the banks and entailed a significant measure of collusion with public authorities, both broadly, as in the undervaluation of the DM (see Kreile 1978), and more expressly, as in the discriminatory tax treatment of foreign direct investors (see Reich 1990). It was also supported by a far-from-liberal stance in trade policy (Milward 1984, 425–27).

providing long-term industrial finance.[13] Such capacity was lacking in all three of the other credit-based systems. In the French case, the large commercial banks that had come to dominate the financial sytem after the demise of the industrial banks proved unable to play an entrepreneurial role. This was illustrated both by the short-term nature of their lending and by the decapitalization that they suffered in the 1920s and 1930s, which had led to the creation of the Crédit National and had forced the state to begin the process of nationalization. In the Italian case, the banking sector developed along the "universal bank" line, yet the industrial exposure of the banks had led to massive failure in the 1930s and to the forced nationalization of the sector under the fascist regime. In the Spanish case, the private banks also developed as universal banks. Yet their industrial investments tended to be driven by speculative criteria and limited to highly protected sectors that offered monopolistic rents. The willingness of the Spanish banks to roll over their loans to industry was entirely premised on the automatic collateral lending from the central bank. The perceived inefficacy of this system was captured in the preamble to the 1941 launching of the INI, which argued that the existing private institutions were not the adequate ones to support the creation of new industries required by the "imperatives of national defense."[14]

In all three of these countries, the banking sector was unable or unwilling to resolve the problem of transformation autonomously, presenting a need for some form of state intervention to support the process of industrial finance. The German banks' ability to resolve this problem appears to have been exceptional, and the comparison to Italy and Spain suggests that it was not a simple function of regulatory institutions. The Italian universal banks perished precisely because they were too heavily involved in industrial finance and the task of transformation, illustrating the potential fragility of such a system. The Spanish universal banks, on the other hand, simply proved unwilling to promote industry where this did not involve extraordinary profit opportunities.

Lastly, it should also be noted that the ability of the German banks to provide an adequate level of industrial finance was contingent upon a broader confluence of circumstances. The most important of these circumstances seems to have been the competitive potential of the industrial sector itself. In the interwar period, when German industry experienced a period of relative decline, the same banks that had spearheaded German industrialization in the period from 1850 to 1914 stood accused of refusing to extend long-term credits and of exploiting their monopolistic position to

13. This capacity is also reflected in the German banks' exceptional industrial intelligence departments (Dyson 1986, 132).

14. Law of 25 September 1941, *Boletín Oficial del Estado* 280 (7 October 1941).

charge wide interest margins (Feldman 1991; James 1986). The performance of the German private-bank-led model after the war thus must also be seen in terms of the "relatively intact and technologically modernized basis of capital equipment" that Germany inherited in 1945 (Dyson 1984, 32) and the fact that the structure of German industry required "virtually no change" during the postwar boom period (Zysman 1983, 82).[15] These conditions contrast sharply with the task of catch-up modernization that the French and Italian postwar governments and the Franco regime faced. In these countries, the increase sense of economic backwardness produced by the war called for an increased state role in the economy, and in the French and Spanish cases, brought an end to the deference previously accorded to private bank initiative.

Explaining Divergence in Interventionist Regimes

The previous section focused on explaining one line of divergence in European regulatory regimes during the postwar period: that between systems in which the state exercised discretion over the allocation of financial resources, as in France, Spain, and Italy, and a privately organized model of financial allocation such as was instituted in Germany. The perceived inadequacy of private financial initiative to the task of economic modernization in the first three countries, and the character of that task have been highlighted as factors explaining this dimension of divergence. The abstention from interventionism in the German case is further explained by the political costs associated with the exercise of direct political discretion, and by the option of relegating responsibility to the private banks. The role of the state in Germany was limited to the immediate task of reconstruction and then was relegated to the margins, while primary responsibility for allocating investment capital was deferred to private institutions or local authorities.

As significant as the contrast between state-directed and privately organized credit regulation may be, there were equally significant differences in interventionist forms of regulation in postwar Europe. As discussed above, Zysman's typology of postwar financial systems typified only one form of financial interventionism: that associated with the broader regulatory concept of indicative planning. Consistent with that concept, interventionism in France and Spain did not center on a direct presence of the state in the credit market but rather on the creation of

15. See also Zysman (1983), 257, and Hardach (1980), 173. The competitive potential of German industry in the aftermath of the war is discussed in Stolper, Hauser, and Borchardt (1967), ch. 7.

privileged financing circuits in which credit was channeled through a combination of limited coercive measures (Treasury circuit in France, Official Credit Institutions in Spain) and positive incentives to financial institutions. Most important among the latter was the broad usage of selective central-bank rediscounting, which became the mechanism of choice over the course of the fifties and sixties. This use of rediscounting operated so as to provide an implicit "guarantee of liquidity" to the banking sector, diluting the banks' risk in providing long-term financing for industry. A central characteristic of this "soft" model of financial interventionism therefore was that it subsumed the central bank's instruments of monetary policy. This contrasts with the regulatory model established in postwar Italy, where privileged financing was provided by the state directly, while the central bank's rediscount window was not made subject to planning or industrial policy directives.[16] One illustration of this difference is offered in Table 4.1 (see page 217), which shows the differing proportion of claims on financial institutions in central bank assets.

I will argue that this difference between the Italian postwar regulatory framework and that instituted in France and Spain is critical in understanding the relative stability of the former and the abandonment of the latter in recent decades. The origin of this difference, I will suggest, lies in broad domestic political struggles over economic policy and strategy in the context of which these regulatory frameworks took shape.

Two factors were particularly important in shaping the differing character of financial interventionism in these countries. The first of these was the importance, in the domestic policy debates of the 1940s and 1950s, of a radical alternative that challenged the existing distribution of economic power in the economy. Such an alternative had important proponents firmly within the elite of the incipient postwar political regimes in France and Spain: members of the political Left who had formed part of the Conseil National de la Résistance (CNR) in the French case, the national-syndicalist wing of the Falange in the Spanish case. This political configuration meant that direct state control over the financial system, such as the Italian model involved, was associated with the radical alternative and was therefore seen as a major threat to the economic establishment. The second, related factor was the decision on the part of French and Spanish postwar authorities not to impose a course of domestic price stability in the immediate postwar period, which contrasts with the strong recessionary methods adopted by Italian governments beginning in 1947. This decision by French and Spanish authorities could ultimately only be rationalized through selective credit allocation.

16. Following the oil crisis, export-credit rediscount lines were temporarily established. However, this practice was the exception rather than the rule in Italy.

In both France and Spain, selective credit regulation and the broader framework of "indicative planning" with which it was associated were born as neoliberal alternatives to more radical modernization models. In both cases, the radical models were being advanced by individuals within the political regimes that emerged from the war, and they enjoyed sufficient ideological legitimacy to make it difficult for their opponents to dismiss them outright, without offering an alternative formula for achieving economic modernization. The radical alternatives entailed socializing ideals that threatened the position of established economic interests, and their proponents opposed the use of inflationary methods, which they regarded as benefitting the existing holders of economic power and hurting the interests of popular constituencies they themselves represented. Ironically, such similarities in the domestic political scene occurred in regimes as different as the emerging French Fourth Republic and the Spanish Franco regime.

In France, there was substantial division within the political leadership of the Resistance, and hence among those who held a claim to participate in the design of the French reconstruction effort. Such division had already been apparent before the end of the war within the CNR. It involved not only the line between Communist and non-Communists but also that between, on one hand, advocates of structural reform of socialist or syndicalist backgrounds and, on the other hand, neoliberal planners. Where the former foresaw a mixed economy based on socialist values and democracy in the workplace, the latter insisted on retaining free markets and private initiative as the basis for the postwar economy, with the state "acting on certain nerve centers of the economy, [so as to] reach fixed goals without being obliged to intervene at every level, or in every sector" (Hervé Alphand, quoted in Kuisel 1981, 162). These lines of division within the CNR replicated the ideological debate of the thirties, when neosyndicalist and neocapitalist planning proposals had proliferated. The debate over planning took on a left-right character in France, because it had been started with the designs for a syndicalist economy forwarded by the Confédération Générale du Travail (CGT) in the 1920s (See Kuisel 1981, chs. 3–6; Werth 1956, 230–31).

Within the provisional government of 1944, the drive for radical reform was led by Pierre Mendès-France, who had been finance commissioner of the Comité Français pour la Libération Nationale (CFLN) in Algiers and who was appointed to head the new Ministry for National Economy. Mendès-France's recovery scheme mixed socialist and technocratic ideals, calling for heavy taxation of illicit profits, a coherent program of nationalizations, and the imposition of strict rationing. Its centerpiece however, was a program of price and wage controls and a currency reform scheme involving the withdrawal of part of the existing currency pool. The immediate objective of this program was to curb the inflationary consequences of the wartime currency overhang. Yet, for Mendès, such stabilization was also a means for redressing the severe inequality in purchasing power that the existing distribution of bills and the dynamic of the black market produced in the immediate postwar period. In late March of 1945, however, de Gaulle decisively rejected Mendès' *ponction* (monetary drainage), accepting instead the plan of his Minister of Finance, René Pleven, to convert all bills on a one-to-one basis, "without freezing or retention" (Werth 1956, 248).

De Gaulle's decision not to deflate the currency pool and not to pursue a rigorous stabilization program in 1945 was, according to most accounts, a political one (Werth 1956; Rioux 1987, 65–66). Mendès-France's *ponction* represented a direct threat to the "hoarders of bills" and the "people with money." It was thus fervently opposed by the "economic powers that be," including the Banque de France, who "thought that France was 'not in a mood' to accept austerity" (Werth 1956, 247–49). Along with the economic establishment, the measure also directly threatened the other primary constituency of the French Right, the peasantry, since many peasants had managed to accumulate bills during the Occupation and thereafter through the black market.[17] Yet the political decision not to stabilize the currency pool implied, in turn, a particular economic logic, one espoused by Pleven, according to which price rises were a means to encourage production and "deflation would come by natural processes as soon as production could be expanded" (Wright 1948, 55). This economic logic of avoiding deflation, however, applied not only to the immediate decision of what to do with the existing currency pool. It became "France's financial policy for years to come" (Werth 1956, 246). If deflation was politically unacceptable to the government in 1945, it would not be less so in the following years. The result was a distinct macroeconomic growth strategy in France that was to endure through the 1950s and 1960s and that I here will call a "cheap-credit" strategy. The main principle of such a strategy was that "of stimulating investment above all else" (Hall 1986, 244), and in particular above price stability. It was premised on the notion that it was possible "to respond to the demand that excess liquidity generated by hastening the production of a commensurate supply of goods," so as to "bypass the need for monetary stabilization" (Loriaux 1991, 106). Ironically, given the redistributive implications of monetary stabilization in the French postwar context, such proto-Keynesianism was championed from what

17. Fear of peasant revolts and the opposition of the Banque de France are cited consistently in historical accounts of this period (Werth 1956, 248; Rioux 1987, 64–5).

was otherwise regarded as the seat of financial orthodoxy, the Ministry of Finance and the Treasury.

The creation of the postwar model of French financial regulation followed from the defeat of radical reform and from the adoption of a cheap credit strategy in at least two ways. First, the establishment of state discretion over credit flows, as entailed in the creation of the Treasury circuits and the special rediscount lines, was an integral part of the neoliberal model of indicative planning championed by Jean Monnet and adopted after Mendès-France's resignation. As such, it represented an alternative for directing resources toward the goal of modernization that avoided the more direct state control and socializing ambitions of radical planning models, and preserved the position of private capital in France. The confirmation of such a choice came with the banking nationalization of 1945, which broke with the CNR program in that it extended only to the three major commercial banks, and in that it preserved the corporate identity and managerial autonomy of these banks. Rioux notes that the nationalization legislation followed a confrontation between de Gaulle and the Left, with the latter pressing for complete state control of credit and investment, as called for by the CNR program. Instead the state's role was limited to a representative with a right to veto in each of the banks, and the National Credit Council was established, setting the institutional basis for selective credit regulation. As Rioux (1987) writes,

> The outcome clearly reflected the changed balance of political force: the choice of ministry to oversee the banking system, a task the Left had hoped would go to that of National Economy, in fact remained within the government; and the increasingly artificial distinction between deposit and commercial [investment] banks was formally maintained. The State now had effective control over credit, but its long-term capacity to direct investment was limited. (71)

On one level, state-directed credit regulation over a semi-private and managerially autonomous banking sector was thus offered politically as an alternative to the more direct control over the financial system sought by the Left. However, far from a simple token, the soft "interventionism" established after the war also served an important role in rationalizing the politically motivated macroeconomic course embarked upon in 1945. The choice to forego currency stabilization, and the cheap-credit growth strategy that followed from it, called for some mechanism to ensure that cheap credit would encourage investment rather than consumption, so as to avoid fueling a simple inflation. Indeed, only through the exercise of discretion could the macroeconomic decisions of 1945 be turned into a coherent strategy of modernization. In other words, selectivity was required to address the strategic imperative of expanding productivity in line with credit growth, so as to bypass deflation. This was necessary to make the gamble of 1945—that is, political stabilization through monetary expansion—pay off in the longer run. The choice to place politics ahead of economic vigor had served to consolidate the position of neoliberal planners and conservative political elites in the immediate postwar period. Thus, the model of indicative planning championed by Jean Monnet was directly associated with the proto-Keynesian growth strategy championed by Pleven from the Ministry of Finance. Planning was seen as the alternative to the deflationary course pursued by French governments in the thirties.

Finally, the regulatory framework of selective credit allocation also served a technical role in reconciling the French growth strategy with the need to maintain the external balance of the economy. As the choice not to deflate in 1945 was translated into economic strategy, "cheap credit" was turned from a macroeconomic choice into a strategic element of French policy. The regulatory consequence of this was a commitment to administratively determined interest rates. Over the medium-term, however, monetary expansion could not be allowed to consistently reach levels high enough to allow the low, administratively set interest rates to clear the credit market. This was illustrated early on by the rapid loss of reserves that France experienced over the course of 1945, forcing the first devaluation of the franc in December of that year, in which the currency lost over half its value. At such points, the instruments of selective allocation could be turned into a rationing mechanism used to resolve the imbalance between credit demand and supply, without having to raise credit rates.

Such use of credit rationing has in fact been identified as the most sophisticated aspect of French financial regulation, because it allowed French policymakers to reconcile apparently contradictory policy objectives (monetary restriction and low interest rates).[18] However, the evolution of financial regulation in France suggests that such technical refinement was achieved only gradually and in response to immediate necessity. Thus, Loriaux (1991) writes, for example, that "when in 1948, the fight against inflation began to assume greater importance, policymakers, rather than raise interest rates, imposed greater selectivity in the allocation of medium-term credits by approving fewer investment projects for rediscount" (114). The eventual technical merits of the French system of credit regulation therefore do not necessarily offer the most convincing explanation of its initial introduction. A simpler calculus of how to turn the politically motivated decision not to impose radical currency reform

18. See, for example, Cohen, Galbraith, and Zysman (1982).

into an economic modernization strategy appears to have been the original aim of postwar regulatory choices in France.[19]

The origins of French financial interventionism thus have been linked to the political choice by right-wing politicians not to deflate after the war, and to the "cheap-credit" growth strategy that followed from that choice. At the same time, the framework of "soft" interventionism established in France in 1945 satisfied the political need to offer a neoliberal alternative to the radical reform agenda that had been outlined by the CNR. Both sides of this explanation can be linked to the particular political configuration of the emerging French Fourth Republic and, in particular, to the efforts of the French right-wing political establishment to preempt a political challenge from the Left through the co-optation of popular constituencies. In this regard, the French postwar experience contrasts markedly with the course pursued by Italian governments during the first two decades after World War II.

As suggested above, the maintenance of the fascist model of financial regulation in postwar Italy was, as with financial interventionism elsewhere, legitimized in terms of the broad goals of economic modernization. In Italy, the character of state control over the allocation of credit was in fact much more direct and unambiguous than in France. Whereas the de Gaulle government maintained the corporate identity and managerial autonomy of the nationalized commercial banks in 1945, Italian postwar governments exercised a much more direct form of political control over credit through the special credit institutes of the IRI. However, direct control also implied that political discretion could be achieved without need for a comprehensive framework of selective credit "regulation" extending to institutions beyond the state's direct control. Nor did state-directed credit allocation come to subsume monetary policy instruments in Italy. The problem of transformation was resolved by having the state take over the riskiest kinds of industrial loans (i.e., long-term loans), rather than by providing the necessary liquidity to an independently managed banking sector.

The direct form of political control over credit allocation that characterized the Italian postwar financial system, coupled with more extensive direct control of industry through the IRI, in some ways approximates what would have been the radical alternative of financial regulation in France (and Spain, see below). Yet, paradoxically, such state-control was reestablished in Italy in the political context of the late forties and fifties,

19. This is also reflected in at least two technical histories of French monetary and industrial policy, both of which suggest that the objective of "selectivity" in French financial regulation followed from the choice against stabilizing the currency pool, and against deflation. See Patat and Lutfalla 1990; Sheahan 1965, 37.

in which the Left exercised far less influence over the domestic policy debate than in France. From 1947 on, when the Left was expelled from the ruling coalition, the Christian Democratic (DC) party, with the help of its centrist allies, came to exercise almost complete control over Italian politics. Helped also by a "buyer's labor market" and weak unions, it was, as Salvati (1985) notes,"able to confine working-class political forces to a role of hopeless opposition." This was the context in which Italy's postwar model of corporate finance and financial regulation was determined. "To the ideological conservatism and the heavy reliance on the Catholic hierarchy of the late 1940s and early 1950s new instruments of control were added as the state machine extended its scope" (513).

However, if the maintenance and expansion of political control over the financial system under right-wing Italian governments seems paradoxical in light of the postwar policy debate in France, its explanation follows directly from the political dynamics of right-wing hegemony (1947–1963) in Italy. As Sassoon (1986) notes, the exclusion of the Left meant that in Italy, the postwar policy debate was not "between `central planners' and neo-liberals but rather between the latter and the supporters of Keynesian intervention" (18). In 1947, with the appointment of Luigi Einaudi, the governor of the Banca d'Italia, as Budget Minister, this debate was settled in favor of those opposing any policies that would encourage wage growth. What followed was a "ruthless dose of credit control" that was imposed to end the inflationary consequences of wartime finances. Short of a simple stabilization episode, however, the measures of 1947 initiated a markedly deflationary policy course, the "Einaudi line," that lasted for almost two decades.[20] This use of deflationary methods to maintain wage competitiveness became the cornerstone of Italy's postwar export-led growth strategy. As a corollary, a large part of Italy's Marshall Plan funding was allocated to build up the Banca d'Italia's reserves, even against the objections of the ERP (European Recovery Program). At the same time, and despite its statutory subordination to the government, the central bank was placed in a position of *de facto* authority over monetary policy (Shonfield 1965; Sassoon 1986).

According to most accounts, what explains the option on the part of postwar governments in favor of the Einaudi line was the strong backing that such a policy had from Italy's northern industrialists, the main constituency of the Liberal Party to which Einaudi belonged.[21] The calculus of the DC leadership in placing Einaudi in charge went far beyond that of

20. For a more extensive discussion of Italian stabilization policies in the immediate postwar period, see Foa (1949).

21. See, for example, Sassoon (1986), 18–20.

the parliamentary alliance. As the Christian Democratic Prime Minister, De Gasperi, explained,

> Apart from our parties, there is in Italy a fourth party which may not have many supporters but which is capable of paralysing all our efforts by organizing the sabotaging of loans, the flight of capital and price rises. Experience has convinced me that it is not possible to govern Italy today without inviting into the new Government the representative of this fourth party, the party of those who have money and economic power. (quoted in Sassoon 1986, 19)

The paradox of an expansion in direct state control under right-wing Italian governments in the context of an otherwise highly market-oriented growth strategy reflects an accommodation in this right-center political coalition. If northern industrialists would have a veto over macroeconomic policy, the DC's political interests could be pursued through institutions that offered more direct political discretion in the economy. This was reflected in what Sassoon (1986) notes was "a clear vision of the specific role of the state: to intervene where private industry is reluctant to intervene and to do so on the basis of a low-wage policy" (9). Or, as Salvati (1987) writes,

> During the period in which the organized labor movement had been effectively excluded, a fairly simple relationship between private industrial interests and the Christian Democratic leadership had grown up. The government provided economic assistance to various sectors when needed and assured political stability, favorable labor market conditions, and unrestrained market freedom, while private industry furnished financial and electoral support and accepted a substantial public incursion into the manufacturing sector. There was no conscious model of economic planning and growth behind this extension of public ownership. The public firms fully accepted the choices of the market. But one of the driving forces was that of providing the party in office with a source of financial power and patronage that was independent of large industry and private capital. (515)

Such an accommodation within the Italian right-center coalition was strongly bolstered by the effective political exclusion of the Left. "After the expulsion of the Left from government and their electoral defeat in 1948, there were sufficient political guarantees for the private sector to tone down their opposition, which was essentially a political one: not against state intervention as such but against an intervention in which the forces of the Left would have had an important say" (Sassoon 1986, 23). The combination of deflation and patronage, moreover, promised to check the Left's political ascendance in the longer-run, a promise that held true until the early sixties.

The accommodation in postwar Italian policy also had direct implications for financial regulation. If, in order to maintain wage and export competitiveness, monetary instruments would not be available to defuse social conflict, then an expanded role for the state, and hence expanded discretion over resources for the DC itself, could serve to maintain political support. In this sense, discretion over credit through the IRI's credit institutes provided an ideal avenue of political patronage, as the resources these institutions allocated, namely credit, were more widely applicable than any other. On the other hand, the objective of not compromising the central bank's capacity to control credit implied that the problem of "transformation," so central to financing modernization, could not be achieved by providing the banking sector with an implicit "guarantee of liquidity." If this was so, then the risk of transformation would have to be taken over by the state directly, as it did through the state-owned credit institutes.

The politically determined character of macroeconomic policy strategy, and the role of the Left in the domestic policy debate, thus again appear as important determinants of postwar financial regulation. If the problems of modernization and transformation were as commanding in Italy as in France, the choice to embark on an export-led growth strategy precluded the soft form of state-directed credit regulation associated with French indicative planning. The Italian strategy's exclusive reliance on deflationary methods to maintain wage competitiveness (without the support of coordinated wage-bargaining enjoyed by the corporatist countries of northern Europe) nullified the possibility of achieving transformation by providing commercial banks with the necessary guarantee of liquidity. At the same time, the political defeat of the Left in the immediate postwar period meant that an expansion of direct state control in the economy was not considered as threatening as it was in France in the 1940s. Rather than preempting an immediate political victory by the Left, the aim of Italian postwar policy was to achieve an accommodation between the principal partners in the right-center coalition: Northern industrialists with an eye on their export markets and Christian Democratic politicians with a strong electoral base in the South. On the other hand, a deflationary policy course reduced the need for financial regulation to serve as an instrument of economic rationalization. Thus, Nardozzi (1983) notes that only 40 percent of the credits allocated by the public credit institutes during the period from 1962 to 1963 (a period of high investment activity among the firms of the "industrial triangle"), were allocated in the northwest. This, he suggests, "demonstrates that the supply of credit by the Institutes ... was determined not by the demand [for investment credit] (concentrated in the industrial triangle), but by the political criterion of *agevolazione*" (60).

However, perhaps the most telling illustration of the relationship between politically driven macroeconomic policy choices and financial regulation in the postwar period is offered by the Spanish case. As described above, and in contrast to France and Italy, financial regulation under the Franco regime underwent two distinct phases. From 1939 through 1959, it was marked by the paradox of the creation of the INI coupled with the reinstitution of the *pignoración automática* and by the complete absence of selectivity in the regulation of credit. This minimalist regulatory regime lasted for as long as the Franco regime's inward-oriented strategy of economic nationalism, or *autarquía*. The end of the *autarquía* with the stabilization plan of 1959 gave way to a new regulatory regime of selective credit regulation and "privileged financing circuits" that paralleled the French regulatory system in almost every respect. The adoption of selective credit regulation in Spain thus came as the corollary of the liberalization (both internal and external) of product markets.

In contrast to both the French and Italian governments of the immediate postwar period, the victorious Franco regime tackled the issue of stabilization of wartime finances directly through a currency conversion plan in 1939. To be sure, this was politically more feasible in the Spanish post-civil war context than in the French and Italian cases, as there were in fact two inflated currency pools in Spain, one issued in the Republican zone and one in the Nationalist zone. Currency reform thus was tackled by converting increases in bank account balances that had occurred during the war period in the Republican zone according to a regressing scale. This allowed lifting the freeze of Republican bank accounts. However, while the conversion reduced the increases that had occurred in the Republican zone to one-third, its net impact was nonetheless an overall increase in the currency pool (Paris Eguilaz 1949, 114). It did not, therefore, amount to a drastic stabilization operation, in comparison, for example, to the Einaudi credit control operation in Italy (or the German Währungsreform of 1948). More important, whatever stabilizing effect the conversion might have had on prices was effectively negated by the reinstitution of the *pignoración* for private bank subscriptions of public debt.[22]

The simplest reason for the reinstitution of the *pignoración* under the early Franco regime was to allow the state to monetize its debt through the banks, thereby expanding its own economic capacity. Yet, the *pignoración* was not the only option that the regime's leadership had for achieving this objective. Direct monetization through the Banco de España would have been a far more empowering route. As several economic historians have pointed out, the re-creation of the *pignoración* meant that state authorities gave up complete control over monetary

22. For discussion, see Ros Hombravella et al. (1978), 158–162.

magnitudes, ceding this to the private banks, who decided at what point to cash in their holdings of public debt (González 1979). Far from an assertion of state power, the re-creation of this monetary mechanism was therefore simply one more aspect of the reestablishment of the legal framework of 1921, which had created a state-sanctioned and virtually self-regulated banking cartel. This was confirmed in 1940, when the new regime officially decreed a "status quo," freezing entry into the banking sector.[23]

Within such a regulatory context, the main effect of the *pignoración* was to allow the banks to expand their assets, and their position of control in the economy, at virtually no cost. In a more specific sense, it allowed the banks to check the role that the state itself, through the newly created INI, could come to play in the industrialization drive. In this sense, it is significant that the INI had been created in part to assuage the national-syndicalist faction of the regime, whose leader, killed during the war, had advanced an agenda of radical reform, the centerpiece of which had been full nationalization of the banking sector. The *pignoración* constituted a politically opaque mechanism for allowing the banking sector to emasculate any radical potential in the INI. Its effect was highly inflationary credit growth during the forties and fifties, which the regime justified with reference to the German model of expansive war finance. As with the inflationary course adopted in France in 1945, such policies also served the Franco regime's political consolidation by fueling a vigorous black market and by diffusing the cost of wage increases insisted upon by the still prominent national-syndicalist faction.

However, this inflation-driven, inward-oriented model of industrialization proved to be self-limiting. As one economist of the national-syndicalist persuasion had warned, the main bottleneck turned out to be the economy's need for foreign exchange (Paris Eguilaz 1949). Crisis hit in 1958 when, following a 50 percent wage increase instituted by the national-syndicalist minister of labor in 1956, the banks proceeded to meet the surge in demand by ceaselessly cashing in their holdings of public debt for automatic collateral lending, creating an inflationary cycle over which the authorities had no control and leading to a rapid depletion of central bank reserves. The result of the crisis was a drastic cabinet reshuffle in 1958—in which neoliberal technocrats permanently displaced the national-syndicalist faction of the regime—the abandonment of the import-substitution model, and the adoption of the IMF-sponsored stabilization plan of 1959.

The stabilization plan marked the end of the *autarquía* and the adoption of a new outward-oriented development strategy. The principal elements of the policy change were liberalization of domestic prices, of

23. The "status quo" was turned into law by the Banking Law of 1946.

external trade, and of inward capital flows.[24] This was accompanied in the regulatory sphere by the adoption of French-style indicative planning, including the framework of selective credit regulation and privileged financing circuits described above. Yet, such a combination of product-market liberalization and the establishment of interventionist credit regulation appears contradictory. If the main thrust of the policy change was to be market-conforming, why did the liberalization of product markets not extend to the financial sector, but rather lead to increased interventionism?

In important respects, the answer to this puzzle parallels the analysis provided above for the French case. First, as in France, in the Spanish domestic policy debate of the late 1950s, French-style financial regulation represented an alternative to the more radical modernization strategy advocated by the regime's national-syndicalist wing. Notwithstanding its political defeat within the government in 1959, the national-syndicalist press continued to maintain an important voice in domestic circles after 1959. Because of the historical role of national-syndicalism in the regime's legitimizing discourse, such internal opposition could not be fully discarded. And as before the war, members of this press continued to criticize the power of the banks and call for nationalization of the sector.[25] The official subordination of the financial system as an instrument at the service of the National Plan served to placate such criticism. On the other hand, again as in France, the framework of neoliberal "indicative planning" established in Spain in the early sixties entailed a strong affirmation of the primary role of private capital in the economy. Thus, as a corollary of the creation of the Planning Commission in 1960, the INI was explicitly demoted to playing a role subsidiary to that of private initiative.[26]

As in France, therefore, the regulatory framework of indicative planning, and the "soft" financial interventionism that it implied, were offered politically as a neoliberal alternative to a more radical modernization strategy that enjoyed significant weight in the domestic policy debate. However, again as in France, this ideological dimension accompanied other, more active, reasons for the new interventionism. In adopting a framework of selective credit regulation, the Franco regime's technocratic planners were also seeking to redress the problems of the past, when untamed credit growth as determined by the banking sector had failed to result in productivity increases sufficient to avoid severe inflation. Yet, in contrast

24. Controls on outward capital flows continued in effect.

25. See, for example, the August 1949 (no. 16) issue of *Unión*, the January 29, 1950 issue of *La Hora*, and Velarde (1967, 622).

26. See Schwartz and González (1978). This ideological trade-off was also clear in the World Bank's first *Report on Spain*, which called for scaling down the INI's role and increasing the role of the Official Credit Institutions.

to the course charted by Italian governments, and despite the abandonment of import-substitution, the Franco regime's technocrats were unwilling to adopt a growth strategy based on the use of recessionary methods. Such a course was ruled out by the central objective of the Franco regime's technocrats: namely that of preserving the political order (see Anderson 1970).

The experience of the late fifties, when strikes in the industrial north had been seconded by student protest, advised strongly against the use of deflationary methods to repress wages. This was particularly so given that the neoliberal alternative promoted by the technocrats hinged on relations with the United States and the EEC, and hence ruled out a return to the more extreme political repression of the forties. The French strategy of allowing cheap-credit growth while using indicative planning to rationalize the allocation of credit thus offered itself as a natural course of action for the technocrats. As in France, this policy choice was picked up in the new regulatory framework in the form of low, administratively set credit rates, further augmenting the need for some sort of rationing mechanism. Selective credit regulation thus also clearly played a strategic role, that of providing a means for directing credit to the most productive activities in order to rationalize an expansionary monetary policy. This expansive orientation is captured in Tables 4.1 and 4.2, which show the proportion of claims on banks in the central bank's assets and inflation rates in the four countries.

The comparison of the French, Italian, and Spanish cases offered here suggests that there were two interrelated determinants of the form that interventionism took in the postwar period: (1) the significance in the domestic policy debate of proposals for a radical modernization strategy that would have implied a primary role for state, rather than private, initiative; and (2) the choice between, on one hand, an export-led growth strategy that relied on deflationary methods to impose domestic price and wage stability and, on the other, a cheap-credit strategy that sought to force the rate of growth by placing the rate of investment above the objective of price stability. In France and Spain, the "soft" framework of financial interventionism and privileged financing circuits represented a neoliberal alternative to the more radical, and socializing, planning models of the French Left and the national-syndicalist wing within the Franco regime. In Italy during the 1940s and 1950s, the Left was largely ejected from the policy debate, and it was Christian Democratic governments that chose to maintain and appropriate the framework of financial regulation that had been constructed during the fascist period. Given the Left's political weakness during this period, such a role for the state was not perceived to entail a significant threat for right-wing politicians or their private constituencies.

This political and ideological dimension of the construction of different regulatory regimes was an important one. If state control over the economy had not been associated with the socializing aims of a radical Left, and if modernization was the principal objective, neoliberal technocrats in France and Spain might well have opted for the Italian model, which allowed for control over allocation without compromising monetary policy. If the Left had been in a stronger political position in Italy, right-wing politicians there might well have sought to limit state control over the economy. However, by itself such an explanation fails to account fully for the establishment of interventionist frameworks under right-wing governments in France and Spain. As has been suggested above, financial interventionism in these countries also clearly served a practical role, that of rationalizing an expansionary macroeconomic policy orientation that was itself chosen for fundamentally political reasons. Such an expansionary policy course called for some mechanism to direct credit to productive users as a way of bypassing deflation and making the expansionary gamble pay off in the longer-run. At the same time, an expansionary credit course allowed state authorities to resolve the problem of "transformation" by providing the banking system with an implicit "guarantee of liquidity," making possible the "soft" framework of interventionism. This, on the other hand, was ruled out in Italy, where the policy decision to impose deflation in 1947, and to maintain domestic price stability thereafter took precedence. Finally, it should be noted that such a macroeconomic constraint on financial regulation would also have applied to the German case, had the problem of "transformation" in corporate finance in the FRG not been resolved by the private sector.

Postwar Macroeconomic Strategy and the International Economic Order

So far, it has been argued that one of the central causes for divergence in postwar regulatory regimes in Europe is to be found in differences in the macroeconomic growth strategies that regulatory regimes were meant to support. The framework of selective credit regulation established in France and Spain—which minimized direct state control over the financial system and relied heavily on an implicit "guarantee of liquidity" to the banking sector—was both contrived to support, and made possible by, an expansionary monetary policy orientation. On the other hand, such a regulatory model was precluded by the antiflationary strategy pursued in Italy and Germany, where the emphasis placed on price stability proscribed a subordination of monetary policy instruments to industrial policy objectives.

The character that financial interventionism took thus was strongly conditioned by the broader economic policy strategy within which it was embedded. Yet, the range of available policy strategies, and in particular the viability of the "cheap credit" strategy pursued in France and Spain, depended in significant measure on an exceptional set of international economic conditions that offered extensive leeway for an expansionary monetary course. Such conditions were particularly important in the French and Spanish cases, given that neither country had the type of labor market institutions that would have made it possible to achieve wage restraint through nondeflationary methods, as was possible in the corporatist countries of northern Europe. In this regard, the most important aspect of the international environment was, along with rapid international growth, the willingness on the part of the United States to provide the necessary liquidity to maintain the fixed-exchange rate system of Bretton Woods at the expense of its own export competitiveness.

The Bretton Woods regime facilitated a cheap-credit strategy in at least three ways: (1) by providing increased balance-of-payments leeway for monetary expansion in secondary economies; (2) by mitigating the domestic inflationary impact of monetary expansion in secondary economies; and (3) in the event of balance-of-payments crises, by allowing for the effective use of devaluations to restore the external balance. Critical to the attainment of these outcomes was the United States's willingness to support the exchange-rate system by moderating its own domestic policies, a condition that, starting in the mid-1960s, ceased to hold. Thus, it was not the formal monetary regime itself, but the underlying behavior of the dominant economic power, upon which conditions hinged.[27]

The single most important of these effects for secondary economies such as the French and Spanish was that of increasing the balance-of-payments leeway for monetary expansion. To a large extent, this effect was an intended one. As Gilpin (1987) writes, the Bretton Woods regime was meant to create "a world in which governments would have considerable freedom to pursue national economic objectives, yet the monetary order would be based on fixed exchange rates, in order to prevent the destructive competitive depreciations and policies of the 1930s" (131). The primary concern of the British and American architects of the postwar framework was allowing governments to pursue Keynesian growth strategies without undermining the prospects for international trade. Thus, the IMF was established to provide medium-term lending to countries experiencing balance-of-payments difficulties and to supervise

27. See the chapter by H. Herr in this volume.

exchange-rate adjustments so that countries "would not need to restrict imports to correct a balance of payments disequilibrium" (133).

In practice, however, the key to the maintenance of the fixed-exchange rate system lay in the combination of two phenomena that in the long-term would prove contradictory: the United States' commitment to keep the dollar convertible to gold at $35 per ounce, and its provision of ample liquidity to the world economy through its balance-of-payments deficits.[28] In one sense, these commitments implied a certain loss of policy autonomy for all involved parties. The United States forewent the option of manipulating its nominal exchange rate, while governments in secondary economies ceded a substantial amount of control over macroeconomic outcomes to the United States. "American monetary policy became world monetary policy," and "world liquidity became a function of the American balance of payments." However, precisely because this balance was "in frequent deficit from 1959 on," and because "the outflow of dollars provided the liquidity that greased the wheels of commerce" (Gilpin 1987, 133–4), this eased the balance-of-payments constraint on expansionary policies for America's trading partners. For those countries that sought to pursue a more, rather than less, expansionary policy course, the loss of formal autonomy was amply compensated in the form of added balance-of-payments leeway for monetary expansion.

For those countries pursuing a cheap-credit strategy, such as France and Spain, the loss of policy autonomy entailed by Bretton Woods thus constituted a nonbinding constraint. United States willingness to supply liquidity through its balance-of-payments deficits (and, before 1959, through the Marshall Plan and IMF) provided the foreign reserves necessary to expand domestic credit without immediate balance-of-payments crises. An expanding reserve base increased the balance-of-payments latitude for inflationary finance overall. This leeway was further expanded by the short-term assistance provided through the IMF, which supported the ability of countries such as France and Spain to carry out short, punctuated stabilizations without having to rely on fully recessionary methods. At the same time, given the U.S. economy's weight in the international economy, the progressive overvaluation of the dollar that followed from U.S. adherence to the N-1 condition mitigated the negative impact of higher-than-average inflation rates on French and Spanish export competitiveness.

28. The first condition was in part responsible for the second, since United States acceptance of the N-1 condition (allowing other countries to realign their exchange rates while itself foregoing that option) amounted to an attitude of "benign neglect toward [an] increasingly overvalued dollar and [a] declining trade balance" (Gilpin 1987, 138). The second condition would eventually undermine the credibility of the first, once the United States policy stance changed from "benign neglect" to exporting inflation.

The balance-of-payments leeway that the postwar order offered for domestic monetary expansion in secondary economies thus facilitated the cheap-credit strategy that was pursued in France and Spain from the standpoint of external constraint. At the same time, the fixed exchange-rate regime also worked to limit the domestic inflationary consequences of credit expansion in these countries, because the price of tradeables was kept down by price stability elsewhere. Thus, for example, while the difference in overall inflation between France and Germany for 1961–68 was 10 percent, the difference in the industrial-goods price index was only 3 percent, suggesting that Germany was absorbing some of the inflationary impact of credit expansion in France. On the other hand, as devaluations were used sparingly and only as a last resort during the Bretton Woods period, the fixed exchange-rate commitment also may have served to limit wage pressure in inflationary economies. Short of devaluation, the negative impact of inflation on an industry's international competitiveness was not redressed by way of exchange-rate adjustment, creating an incentive for both unions and employers to avoid wage and price increases. This was particularly important in countries such as France and Spain, which lacked the labor-market institutions to achieve wage restraint by other means.[29]

Finally, while the Bretton Woods regime eased the external constraints on an expansionary growth strategy and mitigated its domestic inflationary impact, it also facilitated such a strategy by rendering devaluations an effective instrument for trade adjustments once the external leeway had been exhausted. Because Bretton Woods created a framework in which devaluations were not negated by devaluations in other countries, and in which the speculative pressure on currencies was minimized in such a way as to make devaluations controllable, the positive effect of devaluations on exports was maximized in relation to the negative effect on inflation. Such devaluations had the effect of reversing real wage increases and of partially restoring the competitiveness that had been lost due to domestic price inflation.[30] However, while this is the most often noted advantage of the fixed exchange-rate regime, its importance in relation to the two other effects discussed above should not be overstated. The low incidence of devaluations during the Bretton Woods period in France and Spain suggests that devaluation was not the central element of postwar strategy.[31] Thus, most histories of the devaluations that were carried

29. It has been noted, for example, that in the absence of an effective incomes policy, the French government imposed price-controls as a way to increase pressure on employers to maintain wage moderation (Hall 1986, 247; Flanagan et al. 1983, 603).

30. This case has been made, in particular, in relation to the French devaluation that followed the Grenelle agreement of 1968. See Zysman (1983), and Hall (1985).

31. France devalued in 1958 and 1969, Spain in 1959 and 1967.

out suggest that, however useful, governments resorted to devaluations only when forced to do so by the loss of reserve.[32] Nonetheless, the very successful experience with devaluations in the late 1950s in both France and Spain meant that reliance on such an option-of-last-resort must have played an important role in the calculations of policy makers.

If the international monetary order of Bretton Woods provided a certain bias in terms of balance-of-payments leeway for monetary expansion, it remains an open question why other countries, such as Italy and Germany, eschewed inflationary industrial finance in the same international context. The question is particularly pertinent for Italy, where the state also was faced with the problem of fostering an adequate level of long-term investment finance. The answer is that, although Bretton Woods made it possible for governments to pursue an expansionary monetary policy course, such a course entailed important potential costs over the long run. As the events of the late 1960s would illustrate, the French and Spanish strategies implied a postponement of adjustment that hurt long-term export competitiveness and balance-of-payments performance. Such costs suggest that the inflationary strategy of modernization was pursued where the policy leeway created by Bretton Woods linked up with certain domestic political propensities.

As has been suggested above, the cheap-credit strategy of "transformation" in both France and Spain grew out of early policy choices that responded principally to domestic political needs. In time, such choices became embedded in national growth strategies, giving rise to a political "strategy of inflation." This allowed government officials to impose the costs of rapid modernization while diffusing social conflict by, as Peter Hall (1986) has written, "prevent[ing] any one group from claiming that the state has come down on the side of its opponents" (176). More specifically, inflation served to diffuse social conflict in two ways: The first was by undermining the political ability of traditional sectors, in particular agriculture, to oppose the shift of resources to more productive sectors. As Zysman writes for the French case, inflation served to "reduce the real value of the nominal level of protection and subsidy accorded to declining sectors," thus "silently facilitat[ing] an erosion of the position of traditional France which would not have been attempted by more open means" (143).[33] The second was the manner in which inflation limited

32. For example, Flanagan, Soskice, and Ulman (1983) point out that in 1968, when devaluation would have served to restore wage competitiveness following the Grenelle accord wage increases, de Gaulle rejected it for political reasons (611). Devaluation was instituted only the next year, when forced by capital flight and loss of reserves.

33. More specifically, Zysman distinguishes two ways in which an industrial policy based on credit regulation could produce the inflation that, in turn, served to undermine the ability

the extent to which labor could acquire an increasing share of the national income. Thus, rather than resort to full recessionary methods to limit wage-push inflation (as the Italian government did in 1963), the French and Spanish governments during the 1960s repeatedly opted for the use of credit expansion to erode the nominal wage gains that labor was able to achieve in negotiations with employers, and thus restore corporate profitability.[34]

However, if postwar economic conditions expanded the options available to governments as they pursued modernization, that environment began to change rapidly in the mid-1960s. Once U.S. domestic policy shifted from "benign neglect" to a more overtly inflationary course, it began to add to, rather than mitigate, inflationary pressures elsewhere. The expansive turn in the United States, combined with restrictions on bank activities in U.S. financial regulation, also boosted the growth of international financial markets in the sixties, increasing the mobility of short-term capital. Coinciding with greater competition in product markets from the other newly industrialized countries (NICs), such changes undid the policy leeway that the postwar economic order had sought to create for national economic policy, and led to calls for international monetary reform. The failure of that reform effort eventually led to the collapse of the Bretton Woods order.

---

of traditional sectors to resist change. The first, is the straightforward effect of an expansion in the money supply in order to both meet traditional sector demands and extend privileged financing to preferred sectors. The "additional" expansion became more apparent once the French switched to targeting monetary aggregates through credit ceilings yet allowed such credit ceilings to be lifted for credit to favored sectors. This implied an expansion of the money supply beyond the target, carried out to "defuse political conflict because traditional borrowers would not have to be denied directly the funds they sought" (140). The second is the way in which such targeted monetary expansion drove the dynamic of demand-shift inflation that resulted from the ability of labor and business in traditional sectors to defend existing wage and profit differentials, forcing growth sectors to bid up the differential in order to attract labor. "To provide everyone with money (thereby increasing the money supply) while giving favored users privileged rates is to facilitate an inflationary process of bidding for resources by the growing sector (143)."

34. In Spain, higher rates of inflation served to offset higher nominal wage increases, producing a slower rate of real wage increases than in France. But despite the regime's authoritarian character, labor unrest remained a continuous threat to the regime, one that was demonstrated by the wave of strikes in 1956–57. The traditional paternalistic social compact of the Franco regime is commonly understood to have been one in which labor relinquished political freedom in return for job security. Nevertheless, collective bargaining was partially legalized starting in 1958, and after 1962 collective wage agreements between employers and semiclandestine unions became widespread (Maravall 1978). While strong nominal wage increases during the 1960s were directly linked to past inflation (Espina 1990), deflation does not seem to have been a political option for the Franco regime, whose legitimizing ideological discourse centered on the principle of an organic society and a

Change in the international environment coincided with the progressive domestic exhaustion of the strategy of inflation in countries such as France and Spain. By the late 1960s, the large structural transformation that such a strategy had supported, in particular the shift of resources from agriculture to industry, had largely been achieved. Conversely, growth and modernization increased the ability of labor to exact wage increases, resulting in a significant squeeze on business profits that threatened to bring the process of modernization to a halt. In the absence of labor-market institutions that could produce wage restraint, this heightened the importance of cheap credit and inflation as a means for limiting real wage growth. Yet, as the strike and protest outbreak of 1968 in France suggested, such a strategy had its political limits, resulting more and more in a wage-price spiral. Thus, the rate of real wage growth in France rose from an average of 3.5 percent from 1963 to 1967 to an average of 5.9 percent from 1968 to 1973.

The international leeway for monetary expansion thus declined at the very time that the domestic inflationary consequences of a "cheap-credit" strategy began to increase. The first clear illustration of this came in France, when, following the Grenelle agreement of 1968, the government's attempt to limit real wage increase through a rapid expansion of credit resulted in capital flight and a balance-of-payments crisis, forcing the imposition of credit ceilings and a devaluation of the franc in 1969. These events were mirrored in Spain, where a devaluation in late 1967 led to unprecedented short-term capital outflows, forcing a second devaluation in 1969. In both cases, the devaluations proved insufficient to achieve balance-of-payments stabilization and had to be accompanied by a significant rise in interest rates to match higher international levels.

The upshot was that the cheap-credit growth strategy that had been pursued in these countries during the postwar period was no longer viable. The problem of inflation could no longer be subordinated to other policy-objectives, and this change was sealed by the supply shocks that were to follow in the 1970s. The problem was compounded by the move to flexible exchange rates in 1973, which failed to create the freedom for domestic economic management that economists had predicted. The principal problem with prevailing economic arguments in favor of floating exchange rates was the failure to predict the extent to which capital

---

paternalistic regime for labor (Linz 1981). The upward wage pressure in the 1960s, moreover, was reinforced by the strong wave of labor emigration that followed the stabilization plan of 1959, becoming a fundamental threat to the capital accumulation process (Román). Thus, as in France, the continuation of monetary expansion in Spain by way of cheap investment credit and central bank rediscounting was critical in accommodating the effect of wage increases on corporate profits.

movements would determine exchange rates. In practice, exchange rates became a function of strong capital flows driven by currency speculation, resulting in high levels of volatility that "encouraged a cycle of worldwide inflation and recession" (Gilpin 1987, 146–7).

The constraints produced by such volatility were particularly great in the case of weak-currency countries. In order to avoid speculative capital outflows, weak-currency countries not only had to meet interest-rate levels in other countries (notably Germany and the United States) but were subject to a currency risk-premium over and above the interest-rate differential. This risk premium meant that domestic deflation carried a larger economic cost in terms of the interest rate required to achieve a given reduction in the inflation rate.[35] At the same time, the absence of a patent external constraint reduced the government's leverage in negotiations with labor in countries such as France and Spain, where the wage-bargaining process was characterized by the absence of solidaristic wage restraint. Thus, floating exchange rates decreased the room of maneuver of governments on two fronts—vis-à-vis international currency markets and vis-à-vis domestic producer groups—leading European (and in particular French) policymakers to seek relief in a new exchange rate commitment: the European Monetary System (EMS) created in 1979.

International Change and Domestic Financial Regulation

As discussed above, the altered economic scenario (both international and domestic) of the late 1960s and early 1970s shifted the central policy problem faced by governments from one of managing growth to one of fighting inflationary pressures. This shift was particularly acute for countries such as France and Spain that had followed a "cheap-credit" growth strategy in the postwar period. Lacking the domestic labor market institutions to control inflation through effective wage bargaining, the primary policy problem in these countries came to center on the control of credit growth and monetary magnitudes by monetary authorities. This is turn had important implications for the framework of credit regulation that had been contrived in the postwar period, when the primary policy problem had been managing credit allocation, rather than controlling credit expansion.

As discussed above, the "soft" framework of financial interventionism or selective credit allocation established in France and Spain during the

35. As Loriaux (1991) has argued for the French case, the combined effect of overshooting in currency markets and the ratchet-effect in domestic prices created the threat of a vicious circle of depreciation and inflation, driven by currency speculation.

postwar period was developed in the context of early policy choices not to impose drastic currency reform to stabilize the inflationary overhang from the war, and/or not to make domestic price-stability a cornerstone of postwar strategy. Selective credit allocation had served to rationalize such a monetary policy orientation, and to turn it into a growth strategy. Yet, the expansive tenor of postwar policy also meant that selective credit regulation had been dominated by the element of "rediscounting" rather than by that of "rationing." In other words, interventionism had consisted mainly of selectively expanding rather than selectively withholding credit, so that social conflict was defused "because traditional borrowers [did] not have to be denied directly the funds they sought" (Zysman 1983, 140). Ample rediscounting also provided the implicit "guarantee of liquidity" through which the problem of transformation was resolved under the "soft" interventionist regime. This manner of monetary expansion, however, was rendered nonviable by the onset of stagflation. The new conditions thus altered the effects of the existing regulatory institutions, raising the question of whether these institutions could be harnessed to address the new policy imperatives. The responses to this regulatory challenge in France and Spain differed significantly. In both cases, however, they illustrate the political problems that the old regulatory framework posed for government authorities in the face of new economic conditions.

The French response was marked by a protracted attempt to retain the fundamental character of the regulatory regime, followed by wholesale reform and abandonment of the principles of selective credit regulation in 1984. The first significant adjustment to existing regulatory practices came in 1972 with the institutionalization of credit quotas, or so called *encadrement du crédit*, which previously had been used only as temporary measures. However, it was only with the appointment of Raymond Barre as prime minister in 1976, which followed the second, humiliating withdrawal of the franc from the European currency snake, that this instrument was put to a real test. The Barre Plan of 1977 brought a critical change to the logic of French economic policy, in that it postulated the necessity of monetary stability as a precondition for growth and propounded the maintenance of a strong currency as a matter of policy strategy (Goodman 1992, 119). The most important policy measure resulting from this change in thinking was the French government's decision to follow its European trade partners in targeting monetary aggregates. Yet, in contrast to other countries, where the pursuit of such aggregate control implied the abandonment of control over interest rates, the Barre government resorted to the *encadrement* as a way to gain control over bank liquidity without having to sacrifice control over interest rates.

The *encadrement* mechanism seemed to allow the government to reconcile two seemingly incompatible policy objectives—control of monetary aggregates and of interest rates—by exploiting the existing regulatory structure. Moreover, through the practice of excluding credit going to strategic sectors from the *encadrement*, credit regulation could continue to be geared toward achieving industrial policy objectives. The new emphasis on monetary rigor thus was linked to the announcement of a more parsimoniously spirited industrial-policy orientation, in which "the government sought ... to confine its aid to growth sectors and exporting industries, leaving the others to struggle with the rigors of the marketplace" (René Monory, quoted in Loriaux 1991, 44). This link between the reform of credit rationing and an active industrial-policy stance led one set of observers to argue that the credit ceilings, "so often presented as a clumsy and undesired but necessary implement of monetary control, [were] in fact a subtle, sophisticated, and flexible tool of a selective credit market policy" (Cohen, Galbraith, and Zysman 1982, 58). In this view, the turn to *encadrement* represented an attempt to fine-tune, translate, and adjust the old policy logic of "inflation and selectivity" by strategically reducing the element of "inflation."

Despite such apparent regulatory finesse, however, the Barre government seemed unable to impose real monetary control through *encadrement*, failing to bring about a significant decline in inflation despite a sharp rise in unemployment. The exclusion of rediscountable credits for exports and other purposes encouraged banks to vastly expand these types of credit, so that more than half of all lending fell within exempted categories. The result was a dramatic rise in the proportion of rediscounted export-credit loans in the central bank's assets, which served to fuel rapid growth in other credit categories as well in the late 1970s (See Loriaux 1991, 202–3). Equally significant, however, was the rapid rise in credit extended by the semipublic credit institutes to nonexporting firms that no longer had access to privileged financing from the commercial banks and were being crowded out by *encadrement*. Such continued credit growth, along with complaints that the existing financial system was making it unduly difficult for small- and medium-sized firms to raise financing, led the committees involved in preparing the Eighth Plan and the Banque de France to call for the abolishment of the *encadrement*. Yet, political conditions (including opposition from within the right-wing coalition), the government's falling popularity, and the Left's promise of reflation prevented adoption of the Planning Commission's recommendations (Loriaux 1991, 207).

The story of French regulatory response took a new turn with the Socialist electoral victories of 1981. Defying international constraints, the new government embarked upon a course of aggressive Keynesianism and at the same time carried out a nationalization program that included thirty-two banks, thereby promising to reaffirm the role of the state over investment decisions. Yet by 1983 the experiment with "reflation in one country" had succumbed to relentless downward pressure on the franc. The result was not only a U-turn in macroeconomic policy but also a dramatic reversal in the regulatory sphere. Over the course of the mid-eighties, the French government carried out a wholesale reform of French capital markets, bolstering their role in providing long-term credit to industry, along with banking legislation aimed at making French banks more responsible to both capital markets and their industrial clients. Simultaneously, the government abolished credit controls, including the *encadrement* and privileged lines of rediscounting with the central bank. These decisions entailed the effective abandonment of the postwar framework of state-directed credit regulation and allowed monetary policy to be disconnected from industrial policy imperatives. "The principal locus of monetary control was shifted from the banks to the new reformed money market, [and] this made it possible to control interest rates and monetary growth through intervention by the central bank" (Loriaux 1991, 225–6).

The reversal in the French regulatory course was intimately tied up with the decision faced by the Socialist leadership in 1983 of whether to stay in the EMS and give in to German demands for greater austerity in French domestic policy or to exit the system and avoid deflation through a substantial devaluation of the franc. Until 1983, and despite two forced devaluations in 1982, there remained significant support within the Socialist leadership, including ministers such as Laurent Fabius and Pierre Bérégevoy, for the latter option. According to several accounts, the scale tipped when an early turn to austerity failed to avert a third devaluation in 1983, leading both Mitterrand and the new prime minister, Laurent Fabius, to become convinced that French monetary reserves were not sufficient to avert a free-fall of the franc if it was pulled out of the EMS, and that such a course might not avoid deflation after all (Loriaux 1991, 230–1; Hall 1986, 199–202; Hall 1985, 88; Goodman 1992, 135–6).

The decision to remain in the system by imposing a severe austerity program in 1984 vindicated reformers within the French administration, represented in the government by Jacques Delors, who, impressed by the erosion of French economic power vis-à-vis the German Bundesbank, favored imposition of tighter monetary rigor and creation of an independent central bank. Once the macroeconomic decision had been made, the voice of these reformers within the government increased significantly.

Indeed, the agenda of liberalizing financial reform was now espoused even by those who had formerly backed leaving the EMS, such as Pierre Béréngevoy, who was named minister of finance in 1983. Though the *encadrement* mechanism proved effective in imposing austerity and reducing inflation in the period 1983–84, it clearly highlighted the severity of the government's turnaround by requiring the government to decree explicit credit ceilings. Thus, as the Socialist leadership became convinced that austerity could not be avoided, the attraction of reform proposals rapidly increased. To mitigate the impact of a tighter monetary-policy course on French firms, the French government, before dismantling credit controls and ending privileged rediscounting, instituted a broad reform program to bolster domestic capital markets and encourage banks to provide more long-term lending to industry. While such reform had been advocated by the Planning Commission and the Banque de France for a number of years, its adoption in the mid-1980s was thus closely linked to the decision to tow the German line in macroeconomic policy.

The Spanish case provides coincidences with the French that attest to the centrality of macroeconomic policy considerations in explaining the abandonment of selective credit regulation. The course of financial reform in Spain was strongly conditioned by the emergence of an independently minded elite of central bank reformers who gained considerable influence over Spanish policymaking in the course of the Spanish regime transition. Starting in the late 1960s, these reformers, institutionally anchored in the Research Service of the Banco de España, began formulating a project of financial liberalization that aimed at dismantling selective credit regulation in a manner that would allow monetary management by central bank authorities. Reflecting this early conversion in monetary and financial policy thinking, and the central bankers' new influence after the failure of stabilization through devaluation in 1969, the automatic rediscount lines for credit to privileged sectors were entirely abolished in 1971. They were replaced by a system of compulsory credit ratios that obliged the private banks to allocate given proportions of their resources to certain sectors, without receiving central bank rediscounting in return. At the same time, the Banco de España adopted a policy of targeting monetary aggregates as early as 1974, while beginning a gradual, albeit timid, effort to liberalize interest rates. Prior to the first democratic elections of 1977, however, this reform effort remained constrained by the reformer's inability to pursue any changes that would have significantly altered the private banks' modus operandi as a government-sanctioned cartel. As a consequence, the reform effort was marked by significant inconsistencies. Most important, in this regard, was the liberalization of bank branching in 1974, which, in the context of continued interest-rate regulation and an effective banking cartel, led the banks to carry out a vast expansion of their branch networks, the cost of which was to be passed on to clients with subsequent liberalization measures (Torrero 1982).

If political conditions in the first half of the seventies militated against structural reform, the political transition in 1976 was a watershed for the reformers' project. Critical in this regard was the appointment by Adolfo Suárez of the reformers' leading figure, Enrique Fuentes Quintana, to oversee the economic program of the transition. As a government minister before and after the first democratic elections of 1977, Fuentes passed a major financial liberalization package that included measures aimed at creating a money market along with a time schedule for the dismantlement of the compulsory credit ratios. He also included a commitment to further financial reforms in the social pacts of the Moncloa in 1977.[36] Most important, during his brief tenure Fuentes managed to appoint several members of his network to key positions within the policymaking bureaucracy, thus paving the way for further reform.[37]

The critical event in the course of Spanish financial reform, however, was the clear-cut affirmation of the reformers' position of policy leadership following the sweeping electoral victory of the Socialist Party (PSOE) in 1982. Felipe González appointed a former central-bank economist, Miguel Boyer, as minister of both finance and economics, thereby giving the Banco de España a central voice over policymaking in his administration. The most important factors behind this decision appear to have been, first, the desire to halt capital flight and second, the French fiasco with reflationary policies in 1982. In granting the central bank a position of leadership in economic policy, González chose to lend the PSOE's electoral fiat to the reformers' policy project of dismantling the old structures of privileged financing and placing control over monetary policy squarely in the hands of the central bank. These choices were confirmed by the adoption of an austerity program in 1983–85, which saw unemployment rise to unprecedented levels during the eighties, and they were reasserted by the government's decision to join the EMS one year ahead of schedule in 1989.

36. These pacts, in which the parties of the Left agreed to wage-moderation, are widely regarded as a critical element in the success of the regime transition.

37. The reformers' aim to entirely dismantle the "privileged financing circuits" was undermined during the centrist *Unión de Centro Democrático* (UCD) government's tenure (1977–82) by the collapse in long-term credit that followed the initial liberalization measures. Given the precarious political climate of the last UCD years, this had to be compensated through an expansion of credit extended by the official credit institutions and forced a temporary freeze in the dismantlement of the compulsory investment ratios.

The abandonment of financial interventionism in France and Spain thus involved two important commonalities: (1) the appearance of reformers with an agenda to dismantle the framework of selective credit regulation in favor of a model in which credit growth is controlled through a money market and, (2) the decision on the part of elected governments to espouse the reformers' alternative. In the French case, the most salient feature is the initial resistance by government authorities to accept the reformers' proposals, followed by rapid adoption of reform after 1983. In the Spanish case, the reformers' ascent was notably facilitated by the dramatic deligitimation suffered by the Franco regime's technocratic planning elite in the transition process. This allowed the central bank to gain a position of policy leadership as early as 1977. However, in both cases, the elected authorities' decision to defer to the reformers' arguments was intimately tied to the macroeconomic decision to give priority to the fight against inflation. Elected government leaders accepted the reformers' argument that a system of direct administrative discretion over credit flows represented an obstacle for effective monetary management, and thus for the achievement of disinflation.

Two types of reasons can be adduced as to why selective credit regulation became an obstacle for monetary control in the economic context of the 1970s and 1980s. The first of these are the arguments most commonly offered by reformers, which are largely technical in nature. First among these is the argument that credit rationing is too crude an instrument to control short-term liquidity, which became increasingly important in an economy with strong inflationary tendencies, and that a regulatory framework of administratively controlled credit flows undermined the development of a money market in France and Spain. Early attempts to meet monetary aggregate targets in Spain in the early 1970s, for example, produced dramatic fluctuation in the interbank money market that were ended only once a money market in short-term government securities was created to allow the central bank to control short-term liquidity. On the other hand, the effectiveness of credit ceilings in France is said to have been sharply limited in the eighties "by the amount of unused margins available for new lending" (Raymond 1992, 98). A second technical argument is that credit rationing (as opposed to selective rediscounting, which was expansionary in nature) has tended to give rise to regulation-evading financial innovation. Thus, at different points in time, banks in France and Spain were able to escape the restrictive effect of credit ceilings by sponsoring the creation of a commercial paper market and by issuing debentures. According to one observer, such changes in financial instruments made "accurate control of bank credit an illusion" (Raymond 1992, 98).

While the abandonment of interventionism is typically justified in such technical terms, it is highly unlikely that such arguments provided the main reason for the decision on the part of elected governments to forego discretion over credit flows. Just before its adoption of financial reform in 1983, for example, the Socialist government in France was able to use the *encadrement* mechanism very effectively to impose a sharp reduction in credit growth. Similarly, when inflation was fueled by massive short-term capital inflows in Spain in the late eighties, central bank intervention could do little to halt a credit boom, forcing the government to revert to credit ceilings as the only way to regain monetary control. On the other hand, financial innovation has continued to mar the ability of monetary authorities to gain control over monetary aggregates even in those countries where monetary control is exercised in a highly developed money market. These considerations suggest that technical arguments in favor of central-bank intervention mask the more political dimension of the shift toward a monetary policy directed by the central bank. Selective credit regulation may be a cruder instrument of monetary control than central-bank intervention in a money market. But, as the French experience with the *encadrement* highlights, the principal reason why such a regulatory framework became an obstacle to controlling inflation was political, rather than technical, in nature. In contrast to market-based monetary-policy instruments, credit rationing highlighted the political nature of an anti-inflationary policy stance, because it forced government authorities to selectively allocate the cost of disinflation.

Such political reasoning also lies at the heart of Loriaux's argument that in France interventionism tied the government's hands by creating an "overdraft" economy. According to Loriaux, French authorities were unable to sufficiently restrict the flow of credit through credit rationing because of the vulnerability of French firms to a reduction in liquidity. Yet austerity everywhere implies the failure of a significant number of firms. What set the French or Spanish cases apart was that, in order to reduce credit growth, the existing regulatory framework forced government authorities to decide explicitly which firms would fail and which would be rescued through privileged credit lines. This explains the close connection between the adoption of austerity measures and the adoption of financial reforms. By adopting the reformers' proposals, government officials could extricate state authority, and thereby themselves, from such decisions, reducing the political costs of imposing disinflation.

This political interpretation of the abandonment of interventionism is also supported by the fact that reformers themselves tended to view the issue of reform as a political battle in France and Spain. Loriaux quotes a report by a French government research institute that criticized the framework of selective credit regulation by arguing:

> welfare credit is a financial tranquilizer that becomes addictive if used too much. The symptoms of the crisis are the same as in the case of the welfare state: each sector that benefits becomes a lobby that opposes any withdrawal of financial aid. Aid increases and uses up a growing portion of resources ..., reducing the maneuvering room of the state and economic actors. (238)

An identical view was espoused by reformers in Spain, who saw the framework of selective credit regulation as serving the political use of inflation to quell social conflict, and as undermining any chance for monetary rigor.[38] Political considerations also figured prominently in the Spanish reformers' decision to push through financial liberalization measures in the midst of the regime transition. According to Fuentes (1991), "it was a question of accelerating, visibly, the process of liberalizing change ... [so that] it would be impossible to take a step backward without incurring a very high cost and highly criticizable contradictions (LX–LXII).

Whatever the validity of technical arguments in favor of credit deregulation, such comments suggest that the principal reasons why state discretion over credit regulation was viewed as an obstacle to monetary rigor were political rather than technical in nature. Selective credit regulation had been introduced in the postwar period as part of a decision not to impose radical currency reform. As long as monetary policy could remain expansive, it had been dominated by the element of selective rediscounting, shifting resources to growing sectors while diffusing the costs associated with modernization. Once the tenor of credit regulation shifted from rediscounting to rationing, however, the same regulatory structures forced governments to explicitly decide how the costs of monetary restraint would be borne, thus raising the political costs of achieving disinflation. This explains why the government authorities' decision to adopt the reformers' agenda for regulatory reform was so closely linked to the decision to pursue economic austerity.

This political explanation of the abandonment of selective credit regulation in France and Spain is also compatible with the more stable course exhibited by financial regulation in Germany and Italy. While the German and Italian postwar regimes of financial regulation differed in radical ways, they coincided in that credit regulation did not subsume the central bank's monetary policy instruments in the same manner as it

38. See, for example, the comments on monetary policy of Angle Rojo, who would later head the Banco de España's Research Service and eventually become the central bank's governor, in Rojo (1968) and in Paniker (1969).

came to do in France and Spain. A reduction in central-bank rediscounting did not draw government authority into allocating the costs of disinflation as it did under credit rationing in France and Spain. To be sure, such an argument is more unambiguous in the German case than in the Italian, as the central bank did not have statutory autonomy in Italy and this made it subject to strong governmental interference in the 1970s. In 1975, for example, the Christian Democratic government created a special facility allowing banks to refinance export loans at the central bank (Goodman 1992, 154). However, such experiences remained limited in the Italian case, where state discretion over financial flows was exercised predominantly through the IRI's credit institutes. The battle over monetary policy was settled with the 1981 divorce between the Banca d'Italia and the Treasury without involving an overhaul of the entire model of financial regulation. Similarly, the German private-bank-based model of postwar financial regulation and the central bank's statutory autonomy allowed the Bundesbank to shift to monetary aggregate targeting in 1973 without requiring financial reform (Kloten 1992).

The Abandonment of Interventionism and the Question of Regulatory Convergence

In the forgoing sections, I have sought to explain the abandonment during the last two decades of the type of regulatory regime described by Zysman as the "state-directed, price-administered" financial system. Contrary to other explanations of the recent trend toward financial deregulation that emphasize the competitive pressures of international financial markets and propose a sectoral view in explaining the politics of liberalization, I have argued that the abandonment of interventionism of the French and Spanish variety is to be explained in terms of the political obstacles that this form of interventionism posed for governments in their effort to impose anti-inflationary policies. Such an explanation is compatible with the greater stability exhibited by the German and Italian models of postwar financial regulation, which did not compromise the central bank's policy instruments in the manner that selective credit regulation did in France and Spain. However, the questions remains as to whether the abandonment of this type of regulatory regime reflects a shift toward greater regulatory convergence.

To start, it should be noted that, unlike the market-driven view of financial liberalization that would predict market-conforming convergence in domestic regulation, the explanation of the abandonment of interventionism provided above does not imply the creation of any particular type of new regulatory regime. If governments were driven primarily by the desire to extricate state authority from distributive decisions, this left open the question of the type of financial system that would be created in the aftermath of state-directed credit allocation. Moreover, if the fundamental decision was a negative one on the part of elected authorities rather than a positive one driven by sectoral interests, this left open the door to other domestic political factors in determining the new shape of financial regulation. All of this is confirmed by important differences in the French and Spanish patterns of reform over the last two decades.

As noted above, the French decision to abandon the framework of state-directed credit regulation after 1983 was accompanied by a very determined and comprehensive effort to reform French financial markets in order to provide businesses with alternative sources of long-term financing. In this effort, French officials pursued a two-pronged course. On the one hand, they expanded the available sources of financing for firms by reforming the stock market. On the other hand, they introduced changes in banking legislation meant to encourage the banks to provide long-term financing to their industrial clients based on a direct involvement in their management, rather than on the incentive of cheap central bank rediscounting. To this end, the new banking law of 1984 allowed the commercial banks to become universal banks by acquiring major stakes in nonfinancial firms. This dual course of reform reflected a clear emphasis in the French debate on addressing the financial needs of French businesses. And it corresponded to a vision, coming out of the reform proposals prepared for the Planning Commission, that sought to combine elements of both the Anglo-Saxon and German models of corporate finance. Of the latter two, however, it was the "German model" of bank organized industrial finance, as popularized by Michel Albert's *Capitalisme contre Capitalisme* in 1991, that most captured the imagination of French officials. Thus, the French policy literature suggests that French officials clearly expected reform to lead to the type of tutelary bank-industry partnerships associated with the "German model."[39]

The actual shape that the French financial system has taken in the aftermath of reform has departed substantially from convergence with the "German model." Indeed, as Table 4.3 illustrates, the French pattern of industrial finance in the late eighties moved more in the direction of the Anglo-Saxon countries, with capital markets providing a substantial

39. See, for example, the report of the financial commission of the Ninth Plan, quoted in Loriaux 1991, 238, as well as the report of the commission for the Eleventh Plan, which included an entire section on the German banking system.

share of external financing for French firms.[40] At the same time, the banks demonstrated a marked inability to take on the role that the reformers had envisioned. Not having developed the institutional vocation and capacity to supervise the business of their industrial clients, and accustomed to having the risk of their loans diluted by the provision of cheap central-bank rediscounting, the banks have proven resistant to the task of taking on an entrepreneurial role in providing long-term finance at a time when competition from the equity markets and the higher cost of central-bank rediscounting have heavily squeezed their profit margins. As Jonah Levy (1994) has recently argued, this has put pressure on state authorities to step in where the banks have stepped out—in some cases with rescue operations, in others, as in the case of small and medium-size firms, by offering new, subsidized loans to compensate for the markets' failure to provide adequate financing.

However, despite the discrepancy between the ideological model and the actual results of financial reform, the French reform effort clearly has aimed at addressing the needs of French firms as the state abandoned its traditional role in the financial system. In this, and in other ways, the course of financial reform in France differed markedly from that which followed the decision to end selective credit regulation in Spain. In France, we have seen, the initial response to the new policy dilemmas of stagflation increased reliance on the philosophy of selectivity in credit regulation. This first response was followed by a belated, yet comprehensive, attempt in the eighties to alter the financial structures of the French economy through a broad reform effort. In contrast, the course of financial liberalization in Spain was marked, on the one hand, by a much earlier commitment to credit deregulation, but on the other, by a much more protracted implementation process and a much less balanced approach to reform. Such differences followed from the earlier shift within the Spanish policymaking elite in favor of central-bank reformers, from the almost exclusive control that such reformers exercised over the reform process, and from the relationship of this group to the domestic banking sector.

As in the French case, reform in Spain involved a decision on the part of elected government officials to adopt the proposal put forth by reformers for dismantling interventionism. This decision has been explained above in terms of the political obstacles that selective credit regulation created for government authorities in implementing anti-inflationary policies. Beyond this fundamental similarity, however, the single most important characteristic of the Spanish reform process was the almost

40. The boom of these markets, and their role in providing financing for industry, was slowed by the 1987 stock market crash, but the return to bank financing that this produced among French firms has turned out to be temporary.

complete control that individuals closely tied to the central bank exercised over the design of reforms, and the fact that the specific content of reform was arrived at through negotiations with the private banks.[41] This negotiated character was clearly reflected in Fuentes Quintana's reform package, which represented a compromise worked out through an intensive negotiation process with the Big Seven in the months preceding the first democratic election in July 1977. Despite the extreme financial situation faced by a large number of firms, the 1977 package set in motion the complete liberalization of interest rates and dismantling of compulsory investment ratios, without accompanying measures to alter the highly oligopolistic character of the Spanish financial market. Capital-market reform was not implemented for more than a decade after the initial liberalization package, and the ability of foreign banks to compete in the domestic credit market was sharply curtailed. Proposals by some members of the government to reorganize the official credit institutions to imbue a measure of competition into the domestic credit market were similarly discarded. Thus, in order to gain the private banks' assent, the reform effort in the seventies salvaged those aspects of credit deregulation that were most critical for the Banco de España's monetary management objectives, while it severely compromised structural reforms that would have increased competition in the credit market. In the context of decrepit domestic capital markets, the outcome of this lopsided liberalization effort was a severe aggravation of the financial horizon faced by Spanish businesses.[42]

If the negotiated character of Spanish financial reform led reformers to neglect the financial needs of Spanish firms, it produced deviations from a market-oriented course of reform in other ways as well. In the early 1980s, the central bank's fight against inflation was complicated by the rapid growth of the budget deficit that had taken place during the transition. Given the inadequacy of the Spanish market in government debt, which had been reserved to the private banks and operated through a system of

41. For an extensive development of this argument, and the discussion that follows, see Pérez (forthcoming).

42. As the proportion of long-term credit guaranteed through the credit ratios was reduced, and as interest rates were liberalized, the banks took advantage of their new freedom to increase their interest margins, even as they divested heavily from troubled industrial sectors. While large Spanish enterprise to some extent weathered this situation by borrowing on international capital markets, this option was not available to the majority of Spanish businesses, which lacked the size and conditions required for access. The sharp rise in interest rates on these markets after 1982 also served to limit the benefit of this option for the larger firms. Thus, starting in 1978, Spanish business as a whole became subject to a negative leverage effect that would endure for more than a decade, providing a strong bias against investment in productive capacity (Maroto 1990).

proportional allocation, and given the bankers' opposition to any change in this system, this deficit had to be largely monetized during the last years of the UCD government. Following the appointment of Miguel Boyer in 1983, regulatory reform thus became largely a function of the search for orthodox deficit-financing mechanisms.

Yet, as had been the case in 1977, the Banco de España's leadership in the process of reform increased the weight of concerns about the impact that reform would have on the banking sector. Hence, during the first half of the eighties, the reformers opted not to pursue an aggressive reform of the public-debt market which would have allowed the government to raise deficit financing directly from savers. As an alternative, the government created a new compulsory ratio requiring the banks to allocate a significant share of their deposits to the purchase of Treasury bills, a move that, despite its coercive legal nature, provided the banks with a net gain on their balance sheets.[43] In doing so, the reformers protected the banks' ability to "intermediate the disintermediation process," while foregoing a potentially significant reduction in the government's debt-financing costs. This further exacerbated the conditions under which Spanish businesses could receive financing by aggravating the crowding-out effect of the public debt on credit rates.

Spanish entry into the EC in 1986 brought the reform effort more closely into line with the Anglo-Saxon model that in theory had instructed the central bank's policy-project. A dramatic influx of foreign capital ended the prolonged recession of the Spanish business sector and strongly improved the outlook of the banks. By raising credit demand, it also reduced the banks' willingness to accept the compulsory public-debt ratio, which was abolished in 1987. A secondary market was launched to support the sale of government debt, and this was followed in 1988 by capital-market reform. Driven by the massive influx of foreign investment, the Spanish capital markets experienced a significant boom in the late eighties, leading Madrid to score as the hottest stock market in Europe. Yet, despite this, the market remained heavily dominated by the banks and undercapitalized by international standards, and it continued to play only a limited role in the financing of nonfinancial firms (see Tables 4.3 and 4.4). On the other hand, the advantage afforded to the domestic banks by their massive branch networks limited the extent to which the 1993 integration of the European financial market increased competition in the banking sector. As before, therefore, firms without sufficient size to gain access to international financial markets continued to depend on a domestic financial market that retained much of its old oligopolistic character.

43. This was illustrated by the fact that the banks' public debt holdings consistently exceeded the legal requirement for most of the period that it stayed in effect.

These differences in the French and Spanish reform processes suggest that, while the abandonment of selective credit regulation may have a common explanation in the decision of elected authorities to forego discretion, this commonality has not translated into convergence in the postinterventionist period. Contrary to the market-driven view of regulatory reform, according to which domestic regulatory convergence is enforced through the competitive pressure of international financial markets, both the French and Spanish reform processes have deviated at times from a market-conforming course. One element of postinterventionist divergence has come from the particular ideological visions of national reformers, characterized in the French case by the pursuit of a "German model" and in the Spanish case by a somewhat less explicit embrace of the Anglo-Saxon model. Yet as the brief review of regulatory reform provided here suggests, the actual reform processes deviated substantially even from such visions.

The more important fact seems to have been that the elected authorities' political decision to abandon interventionism implied little in the way of an alternative model of financial regulation or industrial finance. Instead, it opened the way for a reform process that was strongly influenced by the particular dynamics of domestic policy networks. In the French case, the strong identification between public officials and large industrial enterprise, in what Hayward (1986) has described as the French "policy community," introduced into the reform process a strong concern with the "real sectors" of the economy and imposed the imperative of providing alternate sources of long-term financing as the state's role was phased out, whether by altering the behavior of the commercial banks or by expanding the role of the capital markets. In the Spanish case, on the other hand, the reform process came to be controlled by central bank authorities, whose efforts were strongly conditioned by the interests of their main constituency, the private banking sector. In order to gain the consent of the banks, and to shield their position within the financial system in the process of liberalization, these reformers were willing to compromise important aspects of the reform process in order to salvage their central objective: that of deregulating the credit market in such as way as to allow for central-bank control over monetary aggregates.

Conclusion

This essay has argued that the pattern of cross-national regulatory divergence captured in John Zysman's typology was a historical phenomenon, one that was marked by the emergence and subsequent abandonment of a regime of selective credit regulation, in which monetary policy instruments were subjected to industrial policy directives, and that was influenced by the creation and subsequent unravelling of the postwar international economic order. The adoption of such a regulatory regime during the postwar period in France and Spain was closely linked to the political choice in favor of monetary expansion and a "cheap-credit" growth strategy. Selective credit regulation served to rationalize such an expansive macroeconomic policy orientation, and the expansive macroeconomic course rendered selective regulation politically tolerable. Once the overall macroeconomic course was rendered nonviable by change in international and domestic economic conditions, selective credit regulation became an obstacle for the achievement of disinflation. However, the principal reasons for this were not technical, but rather political. Selective credit regulation raised the political cost of austerity because it required state authorities to explicitly decide how the costs of macroeconomic adjustment would be borne. This explains the choice by elected authorities to abandon discretion over financial flows in favor of market-oriented reform proposals. However, because such a choice was driven by political motivations rather than by market forces, the abandonment of interventionism has left room for considerable divergence in the course of domestic regulatory reform.

TABLE 4.1 Claims on Banks and Savings Banks As a Percentage of Total Central-Bank Assets

Year	Italy	FRG	France	Spain
1955	3	10	24	21
1960	1	2	27	12
1965	3	5	19	14

Source: IMF Financial Statistics

TABLE 4.2 Inflation Averages for 1950s and 1960s (percent)

Years	Italy	FRG	France	Spain
1950–1959	2.8	1.2	6.2	5.8
1960–1969	3.4	2.4	3.9	5.8

Source: IMF Financial Statistics

TABLE 4.3 Net Funds Raised by Nonfinancial Enterprises (percentage of total)

France	1977	1982	1989*
Loans	79	72	47
Securities, bonds, and shares	21	28	53
Spain			
Loans	82	82	47
Securities, bonds, and shares	18	18	23

*1989–1990 average for Spain
Source: Based on OECD Financial Accounts, 1990 (France), 1992 (Spain)

TABLE 4.4 Stock Market Capitalization, 1989 (total domestic securities as percentage of GDP)

Frankfurt	Milan	Madrid	New York	Paris	Tokyo	UK (all)
67	67	33	82	68	153	143

Source: OECD Monthly Financial Statistics, April 1992

References

Albert, Michel (1991). *Capitalisme contre Capitalisme*. Paris: Editions du Seuil.

Anderson, Charles W. (1970). *The Political Economy of Modern Spain: Policy-making in an Authoritarian System*. Madison, Wisc.: University of Wisconsin.

Caron, François (1979). *An Economic History of Modern France*. New York: Columbia University.

Cohen, Stephen S., James K. Galbraith, and John Zysman (1982). "Rehabbing the Labyrinth: The financial system and industrial policy in France." In *France in the Troubled World Economy*, edited by Stephen S. Cohen and Peter A. Gourevitch. London: Butterworth.

Dollar, David, and Jeffry Frieden (1990). "The Political Economy of Financial Deregulation in the United States and Japan." In *Structural Change in the American Financial System*, edited by Giacomo Luciani. Rome: Fondazione Olivetti.

Dyson, Kenneth (1984). "The politics of corporate crisis in West Germany." *West European Politics* 7 (1): 24–46.

——— (1986). "The State, Banks, and Industry: The West German Case." In *State, Finance, and Industry: A Comparative Analysis of Post-War Trends in Six Advanced Industrial Economies*, edited by Andrew Cox. Brighton, Sussex: Wheatsheaf.

Espina, Alvaro (1990). *Empleo, democracia y relaciones industriales en España*. Madrid: Ministerio de Trabajo.
Esser, Josef (1990). "Bank Power in West Germany Revisited," *West European Politics* 13 (4).
Feldman, Gerald D. (1991). "Banks and the Problem of Capital Shortage in Germany, 1918–1923." In *The Role of Banks in the Interwar Economy*, edited by Harold James, Hakan Lindgren, and Alice Teichova, pp. 49–79. Cambridge: Cambridge University.
Flanagan, Robert J., David W. Soskice, and Lloyd Ulman (1983). *Unionism, Economic Stabilization, and Incomes Policy*. Washington: Brookings Institution.
Foa, Bruno (1949). *Monetary Reconstruction in Italy*. New York: King's Crown.
Frieden, Jeffry A. (1991). "Invested Interests: the Politics of National Economic Policies in a World of Global Finance." *International Organization* 45 (4).
Fuentes Quintana, Enrique (1991). "Prólogo." In Rafael Termes, *Desde la Banca*. Madrid: Ediciones Rialp.
Gilpin, Robert (1987). *The Political Economy of International Relations*. Princeton: Princeton University.
González, Manuel Jesús (1979). *La Economía Política del Franquismo*. Madrid: Tecnos.
Goodman, John B. (1992). *Monetary Sovereignty: the Politics of Central Banking in Western Europe*. Ithaca, N.Y.: Cornell University.
Hall, Peter A. (1985). "Socialism in One Country: Mitterrand and the Struggle to Define a New Economic Policy for France." In *Socialism, the State, and Public Policy in France*, edited by Philip G. Cerny and Martin A. Schain. New York: Methuen.
——— (1986). *Governing the Economy: The Politics of State Intervention in Britain and France*. New York: Oxford University.
Hardach, Karl (1980). *The Political Economy of Germany in the Twentieth Century*. Berkeley: University of California.
Hayward, Jack (1986). *The State and the Market Economy: Industrial Patriotism and Economic Intervention in France*. Brighton, Sussex: Wheatsheaf.
James, Harold (1986). *The German Slump: Politics and Economics, 1924–1936*. Oxford: Clarendon.
Katzenstein, Peter J. (1987). *Policy and Politics in Germany: A Semi-Sovereign State*. Philadelphia: Temple University.
Kloten, Norbert, Karl-Heinz Ketterer, and Rainer Vollmer (1985). "West Germany's Stabilization Performance." In *The Politics of Inflation and Economic Stagflation*, edited by Leon N. Lindberg and Charles S. Maier. Washington: Brookings Institution.
Kloten, Norbert (1992). "The Control of Monetary Aggregates in the Federal Republic of Germany under Changing Conditions." In *Monetary Policy and Financial Innovations in Five Industrial Countries: The UK, the USA, West Germany, France and Japan*, edited by Stephen F. Frowen and Dietmar Kath. London: Macmillan.
Kreile, Michael (1978). "West Germany: The Dynamics of Expansion." In *Between Power and Plenty: Foreign Economic Policies of Advanced Industrial States*, edited by Peter J. Katzenstein, pp. 191–224. Madison, Wisc.: University of Wisconsin.
Kuisel, Richard F. (1981). *Capitalism and the State in Modern France*. Cambridge: Cambridge University.
Levy, Jonah (1994). *Tocqueville's Revenge: Dilemmas of Institution-Building in Post-Dirigiste France*. Ph.D. Diss., Department of Political Science, MIT, Cambridge, Mass.
Linz, Juan J. (1981). "A Century of Politics and Interests in Spain." In *Organizing Interests in Western Europe*, edited by Suzanne Berger. Cambridge: Cambridge University.
Loriaux, Michael (1991). *France after Hegemony: International Change and Financial Reform*. Ithaca, N.Y.: Cornell University.

Maravall, José María (1978). *Dictadura y disentimiento político: obreros y estudiantes bajo el franquismo*. Madrid: Alfaguara.
Maroto, Juan Antonio (1990). "La situación empresarial española (1982–1989)." *Cuadernos de Información Económica, Papeles de Economía Española* 44/45: 1–17.
Milward, Alan S. (1984). *The Reconstruction of Western Europe*. Los Angeles: University of California.
Muñoz, Juan (1969). *El Poder de la Banca en España*. Vizcaya, Spain: Zero.
Nardozzi, Giangiacomo (1983). *Tre Sistemi Creditizi: Banche ed Economia in Francia, Germania e Italia*. Bologna: Il Mulino.
Olariaga, Luis (1960). *El Dinero*. Madrid: Moneda y Crédito.
Paris Eguilaz, Higinio (1949). *Diez años de política económica*. Madrid: CSIC.
Patat, Jean Pierre, and Michel Lutfalla (1990). *A Monetary History of France in the Twentieth Century*. New York: St. Martin's Press.
Pérez, Sofía (forthcoming). *Banking on Privilege: The Politics of Spanish Financial Liberalization*. Ithaca, N.Y.: Cornell University.
Raymond, Robert (1992). "The effect of Financial Innovation and Deregulation of French Monetary Policy." In *Monetary Policy and Financial Innovation in Five Countries: UK, USA, West Germany, France, and Japan*, edited by Stephen F. Frowen and Dietmar Kath. New York: St. Martin's Press.
Reich, Simon (1990). *The Fruits of Fascism: Postwar Prosperity in Historical Perspective*. Ithaca, N.Y.: Cornell University.
Rioux, Jean-Pierre (1987). *The Fourth Republic, 1944–1958*. Cambridge: Cambridge Univ.
Román, Manuel (1971). *The Limits of Economic Growth in Spain*. New York: Praeger.
Ros Hombravella, J., Joan Clavera, and Joan M. Esteban (1978). *Capitalismo español: de la autarquía a la estabilización 1939–1959*. Madrid: Editorial Cuadernos para el Diálogo.
Salvati, Michele (1985). "The Italian Inflation." In *The Politics of Inflation and Economic Stagflation*, edited by Leon N. Lindberg and Charles S. Maier. Washington: Brookings Institution.
Sassoon, Donald (1986). *Contemporary Italy: Politics, Economy, and Society Since 1945*. London: Longman.
Sayers, R.S. (1962). *Banking in Western Europe*. London: Oxford University.
Schwartz, Pedro, and Manuel Jesús González (1978). *Una Historia del Instituto Nacional de Industria, 1941–1976*. Madrid: Tecnos.
Sheahan, John (1965). *Promotion and Control of Industry in Postwar France*. Cambridge: Harvard University.
Shonfield, Andrew (1965). *Modern Capitalism: The Changing Balance of Public and Private Power*. Oxford: Oxford University.
Spindler, J. Andrew (1984). *The Politics of International Credit: Private Finance and Foreign Policy in Germany and Japan*. Washington: Brookings Institution.
Torrero, Antonio (1982). *Tendencias del Sistema Financiero Español*. Madrid: H. Blume.
Velarde Fuertes, Juan (1967). *Sobre la decadencia económica de España*. Madrid: Tecnos.
Werth, Alexander (1956). *France 1940–1955*. New York: Henry Holt.
Wright, Gordon (1948). *The Reshaping of French Democracy*. New York: Reynal & Hitchcock.
Zysman, John (1983). *Governments, Markets, and Growth: Financial Systems and the Politics of Industrial Change*. Ithaca, N.Y.: Cornell University.

Chapter 5

FINANCIAL SYSTEMS AND INDUSTRIAL POLICY IN GERMANY AND GREAT BRITAIN

The Limits of Convergence

Sigurt Vitols

Introduction

A widely held view is that, since the 1970s, the nation-state has suffered a significant reduction in its capacity to achieve national economic policy goals through regulation of the financial system.[1] According to this view, advances in information technology, the growth of the multinational corporation, and the innovative capacity of financial institutions have resulted in an internationalization of financial markets; these changes have rendered the national systems of regulation erected in the 1930s and 1940s obsolete, and, like a row of falling dominoes, nation-states willingly or unwillingly have dismantled these systems. As a result, according to this argument, national political economies are now characterized by a market-driven convergence toward financial systems dominated by privately owned, internationally active "financial supermarkets" with weak links to both industry and government.

The causes of these regulatory changes are complex and are critically explored in other contributions to this volume. This essay takes as its starting point the reorientation of macroeconomic policy toward price

1. For helpful comments and criticisms, thanks to Richard Deeg, Josef Esser, Paul Lovejoy, Colin Mayer, Christel Lane, John Mawson, David Soskice, and participants in workshops at the Wissenschaftszentrum Berlin and the Center for European Studies.

stability and the associated lifting of capital and exchange controls. It poses the following two questions: (1) what implications do these changes have for the state's capacity to regulate national financial systems, and (2) what implications does this regulatory discretion (if in fact any remains) have for industrial finance and the state's capacity to utilize the financial system to achieve microeconomic industrial policy goals? In response to these questions, I argue that the state retains considerable autonomy in the regulation of financial systems in ways that have significant consequences for industrial finance and industrial policy. I draw upon the German[2] and British financial systems for evidence to back up these claims; these two countries generally are taken to be exemplary cases of two radically different types of financial systems—the bank-based versus credit-market-based—and thus provide suitable test cases for the convergence hypothesis.

After critically reviewing the convergence thesis in the second section, the third section identifies four areas in which the state enjoys significant regulatory discretion and in which there is little or no evidence for convergence between the two countries: (1) regulation of corporate governance, which structures the relationship between financial institutions and industrial companies; (2) regulation of household savings, particularly long-term savings, which has important consequences for the access of companies and financial institutions to long-term funds; (3) regulation of the internal governance of the financial sector, which has important consequences for the preferences and strategies of financial institutions with regard to investment and industrial finance; and (4) regulation of public and parapublic special credit agencies, which influence the behavior of financial institutions by altering the constellation of risks these institutions face in industrial lending. Regulatory differences in these areas have important consequences for defining the universe of institutions providing industrial finance, the spectrum of investments they will seek, and their access to and capacity to provide long-term capital.

The fourth section of the paper argues that this diversity in national systems of regulation results in significant differences in industrial finance and industrial policy capacity in the two countries. An analytical framework for comparing financial systems distinct from the usual bank-based versus market-based typology is developed. This framework focuses on the *capacities* of different systems to provide different types of capital (equity, short-term debt, and long-term debt capital) to different types of companies (small and medium-sized enterprises, or SMEs,

2. Throughout this chapter I use the term "Germany" as an abbreviation for the Federal Republic of Germany with regard to both its "West German" boundaries prior to 1990 and its inclusion of the former German Democratic Republic thereafter.

versus large companies) situated in industries experiencing different types of growth patterns (stable, declining, and new industries). The risk-averse orientation of most financial institutions leads them to prefer investments in larger companies in industries with steady growth paths; however, the successful growth and adjustment of national economies depends on provision of capital for development of new industries and upgrading of "declining" industries. Microeconomic industrial policy is understood as the attempt to influence the flow of capital to declining and growth sectors and the flow of long-term capital to companies in industries with stable growth paths. I draw upon the experience with different sectors in each country to illustrate the argument against convergence.

The final section critically confronts the argument that, while financial systems retain considerable diversity as of the mid-1990s, tendencies toward convergence are long-term and have just started to work themselves out. National regulatory discretion and diversity are rooted in the limits to financial-market internationalization and in the lack of organizational forms and regulatory systems that are clearly "best" across all states and in achieving all goals. The type of productive regime dominant within a national economy, for example, is a key determinant of the demand for various types of external finance. One consequence of this is that the reform of financial systems may have little consequence for the productive sector; a second consequence is that lack of convergence in the productive sphere may be another important factor supporting continued diversity in the financial sphere.

The Convergence Hypothesis

As outlined in other contributions to this volume, during the 1930s and 1940s there was a great increase in the scope of regulation of financial systems in the industrialized countries. In addition to exchange and capital controls designed to insulate domestic financial markets from external pressures, a host of internal regulations were imposed with the intent of increasing the stability of domestic systems. These domestic solutions varied widely and were greatly influenced by internal debates, the domestic balance of power, and domestic economic goals. National regulatory regimes differed according to the degree to which they controlled interest rates and credit creation, the degree to which they restricted the activities of different types of financial institutions, and the extent to which financial institutions were nationalized. Comparative political economists view the 1930s and 1940s as a period in which diversity in the variety of financial systems and their role in national industrial policy greatly increased. At least three distinct types of financial systems can be identified according to their structural characteristics (Gerschenkron 1962; Shonfield 1965; Sayers 1967; Zysman 1983; cf. also Introduction to this volume):

(1) *market-based systems*, in which a large proportion of financial assets are "tradeable" on securities markets. Industrial companies obtain a good deal of their external funds on these markets. Financial institutions in this type of system are specialized in the services they provide, resulting in a segmentation of commercial banking, investment banking and trust-fund functions. The U.K. and the United States typically are cited as the leading examples of this type of system.

(2) *bank-based systems*, in which a high proportion of financial assets are held by banks. Industrial companies obtain much of their external finance from banks. Banks are relatively unrestricted in the types of financial services they may provide, and in the limiting case they are "universal banks" providing the whole palette of financial services. Germany is the leading example of this type of system.

(3) *state-based systems*, in which the state controls or influences allocation of a major portion of capital through the direct ownership of a significant proportion of financial institutions. Securities markets tend to play a small role in these systems. Industrial companies raise a major proportion of their external funds directly from these nationalized financial institutions or indirectly via special refinancing mechanisms. Up to the early 1980s France was the leading example of this system.

At the same time structural characteristics define state capacities for using the financial system for achieving industrial policy goals, with the capacity for state action lowest in the market-based system and highest in the state-based system.[3] In the bank-based system, close links between banks and industrial companies (based in large part on the companies' dependence upon banks for external capital) create the possibility for the state to achieve industrial policy goals by negotiating deals with the banks. Thus in Germany the state has often been able to negotiate with banks in order to influence industrial adjustment; the British state, in contrast, generally has not been able to use the financial system to achieve its industrial policy goals, relying either on the market or on direct nationalization of industrial companies to influence industrial adjustment (Shonfield 1965; Zysman 1983).

According to the convergence view, a number of trends over the past decades have eroded the state's capacity to regulate financial systems. First, the growth of multinationals, which have the capacity to internally reallocate capital raised from different financial markets, has reduced the

3. Zysman (1983) provides the most extended analysis to date of the relationship between the structure of financial systems and national industrial policies.

ability of states to influence the credit creation and allocation process within their national boundaries. Second, the growth of information technology has increased both the capacity of financial institutions to shift capital between different national markets and to innovate more rapidly than the regulatory system can react. Third, the slowdown in economic growth and the rise in unemployment have squeezed state budgets, reducing the resources available to the state to influence the allocation of financial resources. The efficacy of existing controls is reduced by these tendencies, decreasing the incentives to retain them (Rybczynski 1984a, 1984b, 1988; Gardener and Molyneux 1993; Gentle 1993).

These changes, according to the convergence view, have rendered alternatives to the market-based financial system increasingly inviable. The most obvious victim of these changes is the state-based system, as illustrated by the experience with France in the 1980s. Upon coming into office in 1981, the Socialist government attempted to reflate the domestic economy, in part through greater control of the financial system by nationalizing the remaining important private banks. Within a few years, however, the Socialists began dismantling the system of selective credit allocation that they had strengthened. Speculative pressure against the franc as well as the capacity of multinationals to shift funds across borders forced the state to abandon controls on capital movement, to create short-term money markets, to liberalize foreign access to the stock exchange, and to privatize a number of state-owned banks (Goodman and Pauly 1994; Loriaux 1991).[4]

These changes also have led to an undermining of the basis for the bank-based model. One of the sources of the banks' power to "steer" industry was the lack of alternative sources of finance; capital markets, for example, were relatively underdeveloped. Firms' dependence on their primary bank for finance forced them to be responsive to the banks' wishes, thus allowing the state to influence the process of adjustment by negotiating with the banks. The development of German companies into multinationals with access to international financial markets has opened up alternative sources of external finance for German industry, thus weakening the banks' influence–and thus indirectly the state's influence—over industry (Deeg 1992; Sabel et al. 1993).

These changes, furthermore, have driven even the most market-based systems further in the direction of market-orientation. Throughout most of the postwar period, regulatory authorities in both the U.K. and the United States had imposed formal or informal controls limiting the types

4. Note however that Loriaux (1991) advances the thesis that these measures were designed to increase state influence over the financial system in response to the new conditions prevalent under the post-Bretton Woods monetary order.

of financial services that different financial institutions could provide, effectively segmenting the financial system into different categories of specialized institutions; in addition, the United States imposed significant restrictions on the geographical activity of banks, effectively preventing large commercial banks located in "money centers" such as New York from establishing a widespread network of branches for servicing SMEs. This segmentation, however, has been undermined by the ability of financial institutions to innovate and provide new financial services that blur the distinction between market segments (e.g., NOW accounts in the United States). Segmentation has been further undermined by the entrance of a number of nonbank competitors providing a wide variety of financial services refinanced through short-term funds from the money markets. Thus financial institutions are increasingly providing a diversified set of financial services (Reid 1982; Moran 1984; Grady and Weale 1986; Rybczynski 1984a, 1984b, 1988).[5]

To summarize the convergence argument, the bases of state-based and bank-based financial systems have eroded through the decreasing efficacy of financial regulation, forcing regulatory agencies to move sooner or later toward a regulatory regime characterized by the free play of market forces. The type of financial institution emerging within this environment is the internationally active "financial supermarket" offering a wide range of fee-for-service products, taking advantage of economies of scale created through size, and seeking refinancing where it is cheapest. Unlike the traditional universal German Hausbank, with its long-term relationships with customers, however, this financial supermarket competes with other similar institutions, on the basis of short-term price orientation, for a pool of price-discriminating customers.

An alternative view, while acknowledging the sea changes in monetary policy and the removal of exchange and capital controls, nevertheless emphasizes the persistence in regulatory discretion in ways that are significant for industrial finance. The sources of this discretion and the way this has played out in Germany and Britain are reviewed in section 3; the consequences of this discretion for industrial finance are reviewed in section 4.

Persistence of Regulatory Discretion

This section identifies four aspects of financial systems in which the state maintains significant regulatory discretion: the regulation of *corporate governance*, which involves the relationship between financial institutions

5. Rybczynski (1988) for example claims that these developments represent a trend toward a new type of financial system based on the securitization of all financial assets, even

and nonfinancial companies; the regulation of household *savings*, which affects financial institutions' and nonfinancial companies' access to funds; the regulation of *financial sector internal governance*, which affects the goals and capacities of financial institutions; and the regulation of *special-purpose credit agencies*, which influences the risk profiles faced by financial institutions or allows the state to directly allocate resources to the nonfinancial company sector. In each case, Germany and Britain are analyzed to show how this discretion has been exercised, resulting in significant differences between the two countries.[6]

Regulation of Corporate Governance

Of the four aspects of financial system regulation examined in this section, cross-national differences in the role of financial institutions in the governance of nonfinancial corporations have received the greatest attention.[7] The regulation of corporate governance involves the definition of roles that shareholders (including financial institutions) may play in the determination of corporate policy and appointment of key management personnel. In addition to the direct determination of policy through ownership of voting shares and the naming of representatives to company boards, corporate governance also influences corporate strategy through defining the openness of the market for corporate control and thus the ease with which hostile takeovers may be executed.

Germany is characterized by "insider" shareholder dominance of corporate governance and a relatively closed market for corporate control. Financial institutions are key shareholders in the majority of the largest joint-stock corporations and have at their disposal a variety of mechanisms that allow them to "leverage" their influence (Pfeiffer 1993; Neuberger and Neumann 1991; Ziegler et al. 1985). Banks are allowed to proxy vote on shares that typically are left on deposit by small shareholders. When more than one bank holds shares in a larger company, the banks often designate one bank to be the "lead" shareholder, holding the chair of the supervisory board and making policy decisions for the other banks. A provision commonly included in corporate bylaws allows shareholders controlling 25 percent of the voting stock, when they are in

---

mortgages and credit card receivables. This securitized system is a third distinct stage in the development of financial systems after the bank-based system (first stage) and the market-based system (second stage).

6. See Allen (1990) for another strong critique of the convergence argument in the context of a comparison of German and U.S. patterns of financial regulation.

7. Recent comparative work includes Berglöf (1991), Franks and Mayer (1990), De Jong (1991), and Jenkinson and Mayer (1992).

agreement with management, to block outside proposals. Due to the lack of openness of the market for corporate control, there have only been a handful of hostile-takeover attempts in Germany. Long-term stability in ownership supports long-term investment planning, makes companies less prone to fluctuations in markets trends, and eases corporate reorganization (Soskice 1992; Dyson 1986; Esser 1990; Sabel et al. 1993).[8]

Great Britain, in contrast, is characterized by a relatively open market for corporate control and weak relationships between financial institutions and nonfinancial companies (Ingham 1984; Hall 1986; Lisle-Williams 1986; Scott and Griff 1985). Regulations such as those defining a duty to maximize shareholder value strictly limit the defenses available to management to rebuff hostile-takeover attempts. The fragmentation of ownership limits the capacity of shareholders to coordinate, and the trusteeship duty of many institutional investors (e.g., pension funds) to maximize return on investment often obligates them to accept such offers. The increasing importance of shareholdings by institutional investors such as pension funds and insurance companies have meant that even the largest blue-chip companies have become targets for hostile takeovers. The effect of this openness is to undermine long-term investment plans, since companies may have to cut investment when suffering short-term losses in order to avoid a decrease in share price that could trigger a hostile-takeover attempt (Blake 1992).[9] Thus Germany and Britain are at opposite ends of the continuum between "insider" influence over management and corporate policy, on the one hand, and the discipline exerted by the external threat of hostile takeovers, on the other hand.

Regulation of Household Savings

In industrial economies, the household sector generally is the largest net saver, and the nonfinancial company sector generally is a net debtor; the state and financial institutions sectors generally fall somewhere between these two (Dean et al. 1989). One of the key functions of the financial system is to make savings from the household sector available to the

8. These mechanisms have come under periodic attack from a variety of interest groups, including the unions, the Social Democratic Party, and the Liberal Party. Critique of the *Macht der Banken* (power of the banks) ranges from the issue of endangering economic democracy through a concentration of power in a few hands to the issue of economic inefficiency in allocating resources to the "insiders" with close connections, to the banks at the expense of small shareholders and depositors.

9. See, for example, the effect of Hanson's hostile bid for control of Imperial Chemical Industries (ICI), one of Britain's flagship manufacturing companies. ICI long considered itself to be too large for a hostile takeover, but after the bid it reoriented its investment policy toward its share price and shorter-term payoffs (*Financial Times*, 25 March 9, p. 12).

nonfinancial company sector for productive investment. Long-term savings in the form of supplementary pensions and insurance policies have become more important in recent decades, and regulation in the interest of protecting savers has increased; in addition, the level of savings in many countries has become a policy issue, and governments have attempted to create incentives to increase savings. Aspects of regulation of savings include the determination of institutions in which savings may be accumulated, types of investments these institutions may make, and conditions under which these savings may be withdrawn. These regulations affect the form, maturity profile, and quantity of funds available for industrial investment.

In Germany during the postwar period, an increasing proportion of household savings has been channeled into forms that make long-term "patient" capital readily available to the nonfinancial company sector. From 1950 to 1990, the proportion of household financial assets held in the form of cash or short-term bank deposits has decreased from 33 percent to 8 percent.[10] At the same time, savings in the form of company pensions increased from almost nothing to 8 percent of household financial assets. Unlike in the Anglo-American countries, companies are allowed to retain funds set aside for future pension liabilities and reinvest them within the company. This mechanism of pension reserves is used extensively by large companies and now has become a more significant source of capital than long-term bank loans.[11] Direct access to pension commitments increases the predictability of financial planning and helps insulate companies from short-term fluctuations in financial markets (Bundesbank 1984a; Davis 1991).

Another important repository of savings in Germany is the insurance companies, which have increased in importance from 17 percent to 22 percent of household financial assets from 1950 to 1990. Unlike in other countries, German insurance companies invest heavily in long-term bank bonds and certificates of deposit, with these investment vehicles accounting for about 45 percent of insurance company assets (Bundesbank

10. Author's calculations from Deutsche Bundesbank figures; see also Maier (1983).

11. In technical terms, companies create an item on their balance sheets accounting for the reserves they have set aside for future pension payments; companies in effect are allowed to reinvest this money within the company, with future pension payments provided by the revenue stream produced by current productive investments. These companies are members of an insurance fund that assumes noncovered pension liabilities in the case of company insolvency (Hoppenrath 1994). In 1978, the proportion of pension commitments and long-term bank loans was still roughly equal, each accounting for around one-tenth of the value of large companies (Bundesbank 1992). By 1989, pension commitments accounted for 14 percent of the value of large German companies; the comparable figure for bank loans with an outstanding maturity of 5 years or more was 4 percent.

1987). Long-term bank bonds allow insurance companies the advantages of predictable, long-term fixed-interest income, diversification of risk through a broad loan portfolio, and delegation of monitoring of this loan portfolio to the banks; at the same time this is an important source of long-term capital enhancing the banks' capacity to lend long-term to companies. This contrasts with insurance companies in other countries, which invest mainly in the tradeable securities of nonfinancial companies and in real estate. The channeling of insurance company funds through the banks in Germany reinforces the position of banks within the financial system and has important consequences for the access of companies, especially of SMEs, to long-term debt capital.

Finally, by offering a variety of attractive savings vehicles, German banks themselves have become important repositories for long-term household savings. Short-term (sight) deposits have decreased in importance relative to longer-term forms of savings such as savings accounts and certificates of deposits; from 1950 to 1990, short-term deposits decreased from 60 percent to 18 percent of household deposits with banks. Access to these long-term forms of savings enhances the banks' capacity to provide long-term capital to industry.

In Britain, long-term savings have been channeled away from banks toward pension funds, insurance companies, and building societies. The greater portion of household deposits with British banks are short-term in nature.[12] The short-term nature of these deposits and unpredictability in the costs of these deposits (due to fluctuations in the interest rate paid on these deposits) have been cited by the clearing banks in defense of the limited amount of long-term lending they do; since banks generally try to match the maturity and interest-rate structure of liabilities with assets, this restricts the capacity of British banks to lend long-term and with fixed interest rates to industry (CLCB 1977). While restrictions on the type of investments that building societies may make have been partially lifted in the 1980s, their investment activity is still overwhelmingly concentrated in real estate rather than in industrial lending (Callen and Lomax 1990).

In contrast with Germany, the regulation of company pensions in Britain has reduced company access to funds set aside for future pension payments, by requiring companies to turn over these monies to independent pension funds. These funds in turn are required to follow a "prudent man" rule of diversification, restricting the amount that can be invested in any one company. Pension funds thus have widely diversified portfolios, limiting their capacities to monitor investments in individual companies other than through general indicators of short-term performance such as

12. In 1990, sight deposits accounted for 60 percent of U.K. household sterling deposits with banks (author's calculations from CSO 1993).

sales or profitability; another source of pressure for short-term returns is the fact that pension fund managers typically are hired on a short-term basis and evaluated on the basis of the short-term results from their management of funds. The widely held nature of many British publicly traded companies, and thus the difficulty of reaching shareholder agreement on restructuring plans, encourages investors to follow the "exit" option of divestment with early warning signs of financial distress.[13] Most SMEs are cut off from access to pension fund capital, since pension funds concentrate on investments with high liquidity and low costs of evaluation and monitoring (i.e., securities of large publicly traded companies).

Insurance companies, too, are important repositories of long-term savings in Britain.[14] Unlike in Germany, however, the supply of long-term bank bonds is restricted, and British insurance companies have made direct investments in the tradeable securities of nonfinancial companies. With the increase in the level and volatility of inflation in the late 1960s and 1970s, insurance companies have preferred corporate equities to long-term corporate bonds. Insurance companies also are required to follow a diversified investment strategy leading to a similar bias in favor of the "exit" investment strategy. In addition, preference for securities of large publicly traded companies excludes most SMEs from this source of long-term capital (Prodano 1987; Blake 1992).

Thus a major difference between the two countries in the regulation of savings is that in Germany a greater proportion of household savings is channeled into "patient" long-term capital for industrial investment; this occurs either directly, through pension provisions reinvested in the company, or indirectly, through long-term household and insurance company deposits with banks. In Britain, banks have access mainly to short-term deposits and are constrained in the amount of long-term lending they may do; the channeling of long-term household savings through insurance companies and pension funds has the effect of cutting off SMEs from long-term capital and creating pressure on publicly traded industrial companies for short-term financial performance.

Regulation of Financial Sector Governance

A third major aspect of financial system regulation in which the state has significant discretion is the internal governance of the financial sector. Given the strong tendency to concentration in the provision of financial

13. For the logic of these mechanisms in an Anglo-American-style open and fragmented system of ownership of publicly traded companies, see Porter (1992) and Jacobs (1991).

14. In the late 1980s, claims on pension funds and insurance companies accounted for about 45 percent of all household financial assets (author's calculations from OECD data).

services, the regulatory environment greatly influences the survival chances of alternatives to large, private financial services conglomerates. The British regulatory system has constrained such alternatives, and thus the domestic banking sector is dominated by four large clearing banks with a weak capacity to provide many forms of industrial finance. The German system, in contrast, has supported the development of two alternatives to large joint-stock banks; both of these alternative sectors have mechanisms that align their interests closely with the interests of industrial companies, particularly of SMEs.

Analyses of the German financial system have tended to focus on the role of the large joint-stock banks and their relationships with industry; since the 1950s this sector has been dominated by three large private banks (Deutsche Bank, Dresdner Bank, and Commerzbank). This interest stems in part from historical accounts stressing the importance of the large joint-stock banks in the development of heavy industry in Germany, which lagged behind development in countries such as Britain and the U.S. (Riesser 1910; Gerschenkron 1962; Hilferding 1968). However, despite their importance for the large-firm sector, these three banks accounted for just 9 percent of total banking sector assets in 1990.[15] The two main alternatives to the large joint-stock banks for industrial finance, the public savings bank sector and the cooperative bank sector, grew in importance throughout the 1960s and 1970s, in large part by concentrating on the SME's growing need for financial services.[16]

The most important banking sector, in terms of total assets, is the savings bank (Sparkassen) sector, accounting for 35 percent of banking assets in 1990. This sector has a three-tier structure; the bottom tier consists of about 750 public savings banks owned by cities or counties. These public savings banks have focused on lending to SMEs and on investment in municipal infrastructure; they also have become increasingly involved in local economic development, for example, through the financing of technology parks. The relatively small size of many of these banks limits their access to national capital markets and their capacity to independently develop specialized services such as management consulting or brokerage services. The savings banks nevertheless have been able to provide these services to their customers by drawing on the regional and national tiers of the savings bank organization; these upper tiers, due to their size, are able to take advantage of economies of scale

15. Author's calculations from Deutsche Bundesbank data.

16. For an excellent English-language account of these developments, see Deeg (1992). The proportion of employment provided by SMEs in Germany is large in comparison with the proportion in other industrialized countries; the importance of SMEs in Germany can in part be accounted for by the support given to modernization through the high quality of service provided by the public savings banks and cooperative banks (Vitols 1995).

and extend these services to the lower-tier banks (Guthardt 1988). The Landesbanken at the regional level, which are owned by the states and regional public savings bank associations, also have become increasingly involved in lending to large firms as well as in restructuring regionally significant employers, often stepping in where the joint-stock banks have reduced their commitments (Poullain 1979; Girke and Kopplin 1977). The charters of local and regional banks in this sector require them to take into account the economic development needs of their jurisdiction and reinvest a significant proportion of their funds there, resulting in a greater commitment to supporting restructuring of distressed firms.[17]

The cooperative banking sector developed as part of the response of agriculture and small-scale craft production to industrialization in the nineteenth century and provided the capital needed for these sectors to modernize (Kluge 1991). This sector grew rapidly in the 1960s and 1970s, and by 1990 it accounted for 15 percent of all banking assets. Like the savings bank sector, the cooperative bank sector also has a three-tier structure; the lowest tier is composed of some 3,400 banks owned and governed predominantly by small firms. The regional and national levels provide the lower levels with specialized financial services, refinancing, and training services. Cooperative banking associations have the responsibility of auditing cooperative banks and controlling membership (e.g., through the authorization of entry). The fact that these cooperative banks are owned by their customers have led them to be especially supportive of modernization efforts in the SME sector (Deeg 1992).

In the 1970s and 1980s the large joint-stock banks, which historically have concentrated on servicing large firms, became increasingly interested in small business lending. The volume of business coming from large firms has declined due to the growth of reinvested pension reserves and the provision of in-house financial services through the development of corporate treasury departments. However, in order to acquire small firm business, the large banks have to compete with the high level of service provided by the public savings bank and cooperative banking sectors.

Britain, in contrast, is characterized by a paucity of alternatives to large joint-stock banks. Banking was dominated by small "country" banks at the beginning of the nineteenth century (Pressnell 1956), but the authorization of joint-stock banking, with the Banking Act of 1826, led to a proliferation of joint-stock banks at the expense of the country banks. A series of banking crises, along with legislation allowing the joint-stock banks to operate in London, in competition with the Bank of England,

17. See, for example, Edwards and Fisher (1994), who generally argue that differences in bank behavior between the two countries are minimal; nevertheless, they show that German banks are more willing than British banks to support restructuring plans for distressed

created tremendous pressure for concentration; joint-stock banks bought up each other and the country banks or forced them out of business. Alternative forms of ownership were prohibited or severely restricted, and since World War I the domestic commercial banking sector has been dominated by a handful of London-based clearing banks (Sykes 1926; Sayers 1967; Sheppard 1971).[18]

The weakness of the clearing banks' industrial finance capacity has been the subject of a number of official inquiries[19] and extensive academic analysis (Ingham 1984; Lisle-Williams 1986; Carrington and Edwards 1979, 1981). Finance for SMEs has been a particular cause for concern, since their size limits their access to many forms of external finance, such as the stock exchange; SMEs thus are dependent upon the four large London clearing banks for the bulk of their external finance. Partially due to their great dependence on short-term deposits, however, banks prefer to give SMEs short-term finance in the form of overdrafts with limits that are renegotiated periodically (Deakins and Philpott 1993; EOSME 1991). While overdrafts often are "rolled over" to finance long-term investments in equipment, the fluctuation of overdraft interest rates according to market conditions renders the costs of financing uncertain over the medium- and long-term. Additionally, shifts in the internal credit-allocation policies of banks mean that small businesses often gain easy access to credit during expansions but are one of the main types of customers to be "credit rationed" during recessions. The clearing banks currently are considering expanding their activity in the SME sector but are uncertain about how to do this and uncertain about the potential costs and benefits (Bank of England 1991, 1994; DTI 1991; Hutchinson and McKillop 1992; *Economist*, 13 November 1993, pp. 75–6).

Banks provide more medium-term finance to large companies, often in the form of syndicated credits, but have played a relatively modest role in the restructuring of distressed industrial companies relative to their German counterparts; nonrenewal of short-term bank loans to companies

---

companies. Regional governments, out of a belief that the savings banks have a greater commitment than private banks to local and regional economies, have resisted suggestions that the savings banks be privatized (*Financial Times*, 28 September 1993, p. 2; 23 March 1994, p. 18).

18. At least some of the foundations for alternative banking sectors were present in the nineteenth and early twentieth centuries. See, for example, the extended debate about the establishment and powers of a municipal savings bank in Birmingham. In principle, the country banks could have formed the core of a cooperative banking sector. The joint-stock banks, however, were able to hinder Parliamentary authorization of permanent status for the Birmingham savings banks; and the Bank of England encouraged country bank dependence on the London-based banks rather than the formation of their own clearing and refinancing system.

19. These include the Macmillan Committee on Finance and Industry, in the early 1930s, the Radcliffe Committee on the Workings of the Monetary System, in the late 1950s, and the Wilson Committee to Review the Functioning of Financial Institutions, in the late 1970s.

is often the final step before receivership and/or government intervention. Indicators of dissatisfaction with British bank performance include the rapid growth of leasing and the expansion of foreign banks' market share in lending to industry.[20]

Regulation of Special-Purpose Credit Agencies

A fourth area where the state has considerable discretion is the regulation of special-purpose public or quasi-public credit agencies. These credit agencies typically are perceived as *correctives for financial market deficiencies* in providing credit to specific types of clients. In some countries special credit agencies have been mechanisms for deliberately channeling capital toward "national champions." However, these agencies also may dramatically affect the pattern of capital allocation with relatively little public cost, either through a redistribution of the risks of industrial investment or through creating access to long-term capital where institutional mechanisms for channeling long-term capital do not already exist. Special credit agencies also may play a role in supporting industrial restructuring, for example in supporting capacity reduction or in overcoming fragmented ownership structure. Special credit agencies exist in both Germany and Britain but play a much greater role in the former (Hu 1975, 1984).

The most important of the German special credit agencies is the Kreditanstalt für Wiederaufbau (Bank for Reconstruction), which was established to supervise the reconstruction of the West German economy after World War II (Pohl 1973; Hahn 1984). The large private banks traditionally provided short-term loans, and the German government felt it was necessary to create an agency that could bypass normal credit-evaluation policies and "jump start" investment in the capital-intensive energy and raw-materials sectors with long-term loans. With the successful completion of this assignment, the Bank for Reconstruction shifted its concentration to providing long-term finance for SMEs through issuing long-term bonds on national capital markets; these long-term funds would then be channeled to SMEs through their Hausbank, with the Hausbank taking over responsibility for default risk and monitoring the loan (Menzel 1960). This source of long-term finance is especially important for smaller banks and smaller companies, which have

20. Interestingly, the expansion of foreign business has been among companies with better-than-average credit quality rather than among marginal firms (*Financial Times*, 25 July 1994, p. 6). While finance companies provide a medium-term financing alternative to short-term bank overdrafts through installment plans, this finance is generally limited to easily resealable assets such as standardized office equipment and autos (*Financial Times*, special section on leasing, 6 March 1993).

little or no direct access to long-term capital markets. The Kreditanstalt für Wiederaufbau provides approximately one quarter of long-term loans to manufacturing in West Germany, with relatively little public subsidy. It also has been used as a tool for reorganizing sectors, for example, the steel and shipbuilding industries in the late 1970s and early 1980s; the rapid reduction of capacity and modernization investments in these sectors enabled them to regain profitability relatively rapidly in international terms (Vitols 1993).

The other major special credit institute for industrial finance is the Deutsche Ausgleichsbank (German Bank for Settlements). This was established after World War II to compensate refugees from the eastern provinces and help them start businesses in West Germany. Subsequently the Deutsche Ausgleichsbank has become the major source of public funds for business start-ups. The Deutsche Ausgleichsbank is funded mainly through the issue of its own long-term bonds, with a small public subsidy to reduce financing costs; loans typically are provided for ten years with no amortization in the first years. As is the case with the Kreditanstalt für Wiederaufbau, loans are not made directly but rather through the company's Hausbank. The Deutsche Ausgleichsbank has become particularly active in the development of a small business sector in East Germany after unification (Deeg 1994). Almost two thirds of industry start-ups receive financial assistance from either the Deutsche Ausgleichsbank or regional financing programs; due to the great selectivity in support for start-ups, however, relatively few of these ventures go bankrupt (when compared with start-ups in other countries), so the cost to the public is relatively low (Braun 1989; Vitols 1994).

A number of special credit agencies also were established in Britain in the postwar period with the intent to correct for shortcomings of private financial institutions. One of the major problems identified in the 1931 final report of the Macmillan Committee was the lack of long-term capital, particularly for SMEs. At the initiative of the British government, two special credit agencies were formed in 1945: the Industrial and Commercial Finance Corporation Limited (ICFC) for equity and long-term debt capital for SMEs, and the Finance Corporation for Industry Limited (FCI) for long-term loans for large industry. FCI, however, was rarely used and was merged with ICFC, in 1973, creating Finance for Industry Limited (FFI); in 1983 FFI was once again renamed Investors in Industry or 3i; 3i currently accounts for about 2 percent of lending to manufacturing.[21] Unlike the German special credit agencies, 3i lends directly to companies; the clearing banks, which are its primary owners (the Bank of England has a minority share), have seen 3i as a competitor and

21. Estimate based on 3i annual reports and Bank of England (1993).

generally have been reluctant to see it well-funded; only in 1959 was this institute allowed to raise funds independently through the issue of listed bonds and stock (Hu 1984).

In addition to special agencies for the provision of long-term capital, a number of other special agencies have been created at the national and regional level, mainly at the initiative of the Labour Party. In 1966 the Wilson administration established the Industrial Reorganisation Corporation (IRC), which was given broad powers to acquire, hold, and dispose of shares; to form new companies; to make loans and loan guarantees; and, on behalf of companies, to acquire land, plant, and equipment. The IRC quickly became involved in reorganizing companies in crisis, in sectors such as autos, shipbuilding, and machine tools. However, the IRC was abolished by the 1970–74 Conservative government in favor of a market-driven approach to reorganization (Hague and Wilkinson 1983). In 1975 the new Labour government established the National Enterprise Board (NEB), with an even broader mandate of selective nationalization of larger companies and the negotiation of planning agreements with companies; through these agreements, long-term finance would be provided, in exchange for promises to invest in training, R&D, and new plant and equipment. Like the IRC, however, the NEB became involved primarily in the reorganization or nationalization of a number of large companies in crisis, such as British Leyland (autos), Rolls Royce (airplane engines), and Herbert (machine tools); it was abolished by the new Conservative administration in 1979 before it had a chance to implement its mandate to influence a broad segment of British manufacturing (Paar 1979). In addition to these national initiatives, in the late 1970s and early 1980s a number of Labour-dominated municipal and county councils set up Enterprise Boards to channel pension and tax funds to SMEs; however, the abolition of the municipal county councils and a variety of restrictions on municipalities imposed in the mid-1980s by the Thatcher government greatly constrained subnational activities in this area (Spencer et al. 1986).

Capacities of the German and British Financial Systems Compared

This section analyzes the impact of the differences in financial regulation identified in the last section on industrial finance and microeconomic industrial policies in Germany and Britain. The comparative framework used here focuses on the capacity of financial systems to provide different types of financing to a variety of companies in industries with different growth trajectories. Specifically, the analysis differentiates between the provision of short-term debt, long-term debt, and equity capital. Furthermore, the strategic goals and risk preferences of financial institutions are analyzed in terms of the propensity to invest in different types of companies, namely SMEs versus large firms, and companies in industries with "stable" growth paths versus those in new industries and those in declining industries. Each country's financial system can thus be analyzed in terms of a *matrix of capacities* (see Table 5.1 on page 250).

The "classic" preference of risk-averse financial institutions is the provision of short-term credit to companies in stable industries; the earliest financial institutions started out providing trade credit to such companies. Since economic growth can be better supported by a financial system with a broad variety of capacities, industrial policy with regard to industrial finance can be conceived of as the attempt to enhance financial system capacities beyond the traditional competence in short-term lending to stable companies. These can be summarized as three general industrial policy tasks: (1) the provision of long-term finance to companies in stable industries; (2) the provision of all types of finance to companies in declining industries; and (3) the provision of all types of finance to companies in growing industries. These can be achieved by the state *directly*, through the conscious use of state power to allocate financing to specific companies, or *indirectly*, through influencing the framework within which financial institutions operate, and thus their goals and risk preferences.

This capacity-based framework for analyzing financial systems thus differs from comparative models focusing on the structural characteristics of financial systems (e.g., bank-based versus market-based versus state-based); this alternative framework recognizes that financial systems with the same structural characteristics (e.g., different bank-based systems) may in fact have varying capacities to provide different types of finance (e.g., long-term finance to SMEs). Similarly, it differs from most principal-agent financial models in analyzing the refinancing constraints under which financial institutions invest, rather than just the characteristics of the microeconomic relationship between investor and entrepreneur. It thus has more in common with competency and evolutionary perspectives on organizations (Nelson and Winter 1982; Foss 1993).[22]

This framework emphasizes that financial institutions seek to achieve a variety of goals through managing investment risk under a variety of constraints. The major types of risk involved in domestic lending include default risk, liquidity risk, interest-rate risk, and inflation risk:

22. Classic analyses using the structural framework are Gerschenkron (1962) and Zysman (1983); an important example of work using principal-agent models is Berglöf (1991).

Default risk is the risk that the company to which a financial institution has provided capital will not meet its obligations to repay interest and/or principle on an agreed-upon time schedule. This danger arises through the possibility of financial weakness, fraud, or other reasons. Part of the interest-rate margin or capital gains that financial institutions receive from their investment activities goes towards covering this risk.[23]

Liquidity risk is the risk that liabilities become due or are withdrawn without adequate liquid asset coverage. The financial institution thus may be required either to recall its loans early, possibly facing a loss or forcing customers into bankruptcy, or to raise funds from other, more costly sources. One of the traditional "golden rules" of financial management is to try to match the maturity structure of liabilities with assets; the implication is that financial institutions are constrained by their liability-maturity structure in the amount of long-term lending that they may do.

Interest-rate risk is the risk that the interest rate a financial institution must pay on its liabilities will rise more rapidly than the interest rate received on loans made. Increasing volatility of interest rates in the last two decades has caused financial institutions to pay more attention to matching the interest sensitivities of their assets and liabilities. Financial institutions depending heavily on interest-sensitive sources of funds for financing thus will be limited in the extent to which they can make fixed-interest-rate loans. Increasing interest rate volatility since the 1970s has constrained the extent to which financial institutions can offer fixed interest rates on long-term lending.

Inflation risk is the risk that inflation will substantially increase, eroding the real value of long-term financial assets. The rapid increase in the level and volatility of inflation in the late 1960s and 1970s in Britain, and thus the reluctance to invest in long-term financial assets, is cited as a major reason for decline in the use of long-term bonds to fund industrial companies (Benzie 1988).

These risks are to some extent interdependent; for example a bank that lends long-term but is refinanced primarily by short-term deposits with variable interest rates faces both liquidity, interest rate, and inflation risk.[24]

In the attempt to manage these risks, financial institutions follow a variety of general procedures and rules of thumb in the search for profitable

23. Most principal-agent investment models focus on the problem of reducing this type of risk, e.g., by improving information about the viability of investment projects or the effort level of the entrepreneur, or by altering the incentive structure faced by the entrepreneur (Stiglitz and Weiss 1981; Williamson 1988; Berglöf 1991).

24. Financial institutions that deal with two or more currencies must, in addition, deal with *exchange rate risk*, i.e., risk that the exchange rate between these currencies will change in a direction that increases the real value of the liabilities the financial intermediary faces relative to its assets.

investment opportunities. Two types of "market failure" result: first, financial institutions generally will not search extensively for profitable investment opportunities or follow extended project-review procedures.[25] One implication is the tendency for financial institutions to seek "safe" projects according to general criteria. Thus many projects that could be profitable but do not meet these criteria do not receive financing during periods of credit shortage (*credit rationing*); on the other hand, projects of dubious merit will receive finance during credit booms, when financial institutions are trying to "push funds out of the door." The second major type of "market failure" is the effective segmentation of different types of capital; for example, though demand for long-term capital may exist in industry, the institutional structure of long-term savings may not channel these funds to industrial companies.[26] Most problematic for financial systems is the supply of long-term capital to SMEs and finance in general to new and declining industries.

Industrial Finance in Stable Industries

Financial systems generally have the greatest capacity to provide external capital to companies in stable industries. Financial institutions depend heavily on a company's credit history as an indicator of the probability of repayment in the future; credit history gives insight into the "character" of the company (i.e., whether it is a reliable repayer of loans) as well as into the financial strength of the company. Furthermore, the growth characteristics of the industry provide an indicator of the difficulty of the environment the company faces.

Both British and German financial institutions have a strong capacity to provide short-term credit to both large companies and SMEs in industries with stable growth paths (see Table 5.1). This is the banks' traditional area of strength; the core competence of the financial system historically has been and continues to be the provision of short-term credit to companies in stable industries. The oldest function of banking, which originally was a side business of merchants, was to provide short-term credit for trade (Cameron 1967; Pressnell 1956). Short-term lending involves a low degree of maturity risk (since the financial institution's assets are not locked into an investment for long periods of time) as well

25. Financial institutions' capacity to gather better "insider" information is limited, and these institutions seek to minimize risk through the examination of credit histories as an indicator of the reliability of management; through preference for companies in industries with stable, less-risky growth paths; and through requiring collateral to reduce losses in the case of bankruptcy.

26. For a discussion of the financial market segmentation hypothesis see Culbertson (1957).

as of interest rate and default risk (since there is less time for economic conditions to change than is the case for long-term capital). Credit evaluation is relatively easy for this type of financing, relying heavily on the financial history of the borrower, comparison of the borrower's balance sheets with other companies in the same industry, and the use of rules-of-thumb for the extent of credit granted. SMEs in both countries raise the bulk of external short-term capital from banks; in addition to short-term bank credits, larger companies in both countries also rely on money markets for short-term funds (Bundesbank 1992; Benzie 1988).[27]

Since the nineteenth century, most financial systems have expanded their capacities beyond the provision of short-term credit. Both the British and German financial systems have developed a strong capacity to provide equity capital to large companies in stable industries. The development of both the joint-stock company, which allows for a large number of stockholders with changing identities, and of stock exchanges on which the shares of these companies may be traded, made it possible to raise the large sums of equity capital needed for the development of large companies in both countries (Chandler 1990; Pohl 1992).

Both systems, however, have a weak capacity to provide equity capital to SMEs. Few SMEs in either country have outside participation by financial institutions, and the creation of means to channel equity capital to SMEs is a public policy issue. In Germany the larger banks have set up investment companies (Beteiligungsgesellschaften) for SME participations, though the number of participations remains small (Kokalj 1989). Relatively few medium-sized companies are publicly traded, and small steps have been taken to make it easier for these companies to become listed; the Landesbanken, for example, are moving into market-making for medium-size companies listed on the regional exchanges (Bundesbank 1984b; WestLB 1992).

In Britain the main financial institutions active in this area are venture capital firms; during the 1980s a large part of the increase in venture capital actually went to support the expansion of established companies or management buy-outs of branch plants rather than companies in new industries (Pratt 1990; Murray 1991; Mason 1987). Britain, which throughout the twentieth century has had a considerably greater number of publicly traded companies than Germany, has taken considerably greater steps to allow medium-sized companies to be publicly listed; the biggest step in this direction was the creation in 1980 of the Unlisted

27. Trade credit (i.e., short-term obligations between suppliers and their customers) is also an important short-term credit item; generally, however, a company's credit from suppliers is largely balanced out by obligations on the part of its purchasers; thus trade credit has relatively little net significance.

Securities Market (USM) with less regulation and fewer reporting requirements than the regular stock exchange. The experience with the USM has been unsatisfactory for many companies, however, particularly during the last recession; many investment-banking firms have reduced services such as market-making to the USM, and rating agencies have cut back their ratings of USM firms, hurting liquidity and making it difficult to get access to new investment. The London Stock Exchange is currently considering closing the USM (*Financial Times*, 1 December 1992, p. 16; 8 March 1994, p. 16).

The German financial system has developed a comparative advantage in the capacity to provide long-term debt capital to both SMEs and large companies. German banks throughout the first half of the 1900s were reluctant to provide long-term debt capital, and a debate ensued in the 1930s and postwar period about the need and possible sources for long-term debt capital. The Kreditanstalt für Wiederaufbau and the Industriekreditbank (Industrial Credit Bank) were set up in order to directly provide these loans to companies, and a division of labor was established, these banks providing long-term credit and the universal banks providing short-term credit (Weber 1954; Pohl 1973; Cassier 1977). The universal banks, however, overcame their reluctance to do this type of lending, and by the late 1960s approximately one-third of bank credits to industry were long-term.[28] Industrial companies made little use of long-term bond markets; long-term household savings were instead channeled to industry through the banks in the form of deposits from households or the purchase of bank bonds by institutional investors such as insurance companies. The demand from large companies for long-term bank loans has decreased since the 1970s with the growth of pension reserves. The demand from SMEs for medium and long-term loans, however, has increased greatly, from 14 percent of net worth in 1978 to 19 percent in 1989. Through the savings banks and cooperative banks, long-term bank loans are available even for the smallest companies. By 1990 slightly over half of bank credits to industry were long-term in nature.

The British system, in contrast, has a low capacity to provide long-term debt capital to both large and small companies. The clearing banks depend mainly on short-term retail deposits and wholesale money markets for their funding; given the short-term maturity of these funds and the fluctuation of interest rates that must be paid on these funds, the banks have been reluctant to lend to industry long-term and at fixed interest rates

28. Author's calculations from Deutsche Bundesbank statistics. According to the Bundesbank definition, long-term loans have maturities of four or more years, medium-term loans have maturities of between one and four years, and short-term loans have maturities of one year or less.

(Wilson Committee 1980). An alternative for large companies is the issuance of long-term bonds, but since the inflation of the late 1960s and 1970s British investors have avoided these bonds; pension funds and insurance companies, which in many countries provide the bulk of long-term corporate debt, have instead sought to invest in equity, with the expectation that the value of these securities would appreciate with inflation (Benzie 1988). For external financing, SMEs rely mainly on short-term overdrafts on their bank accounts (Deakins and Philpott 1993; EOSME 1993). Finance companies have become an increasingly important source of external financing but have focused on medium-term leasing of standardized equipment (e.g., data-processing equipment) and vehicles.[29]

Industrial Finance in Declining Industries

Long-term reductions in demand create a number of problems for industrial finance in declining industries. These industries are typically characterized by overcapacity, leading to increased price competition, and reduced profits as producers fight over a shrinking market. Low profitability reduces the capacity of companies in these industries to internally finance investment; at the same time, the companies' reduced capacity to make dividend and interest payments reduces financial institutions' willingness to provide external capital. Companies in declining industries thus may be caught in a vicious cycle of low profitability, low investment, and low innovation (Harrigan 1980).[30]

Two strategies may be available to mitigate industrial finance problems in declining industries. One way is through the rapid reduction of excess capacity, thus helping boost prices, profit margins, and the capacity to finance investment. Since each company will be tempted to "free ride" on the capacity reductions of others, however, this may require coordination between different producers. Secondly, through product innovations it may be possible to slow down or reverse declines in

29. In the postwar period there were debates in both countries about the extent to which financial institutions could act as *maturity transformers*, using short-term deposits to finance longer-term loans; deposit activity has a random component to it; thus withdrawals by one customer are often balanced out by increases in deposits from other customers. In practice banks act as maturity transformers to a certain extent, but the increasing volatility of depositor behavior and the financial environment has forced these financial institutions to limit the extent to which they violate the "golden rule"; thus the much greater reliance by British banks than by German banks on short-term deposits limits the capacity of the former, relative to the latter, to make long-term investments (Weber 1954; Carrington and Edwards 1979, 1981).

30. Similar effects may be created by industries with stagnant growth paths but in which overcapacity has been created, e.g., due to overinvestment during previous growth periods or through new entrants such as the NICs.

demand, for example, by developing demand for customized products or by increasing the attractiveness of the product relative to substitute products. The solution of the excess capacity problem may be a prerequisite for this second strategy, since extensive investments are often required for product innovation; the provision of other resources, such as increased training, may also be required in order to implement higher-quality production strategies.[31] Financial institutions, however, may not have the ability to help coordinate elimination of excess capacity needed to reduce investment risk; they also may be uncertain about the probability of success of the product innovations undertaken. The contribution of industrial policy toward overcoming this situation thus can be to coordinate the reduction of capacity or to shift risk to other actors (such as the state), increasing the willingness of financial institutions to provide capital.

The capacity of the German financial system to provide finance to both large firms and SMEs in declining sectors is greater than that of the British financial system. Many industries affected by decline are dominated by a few large companies that enjoy close connections with the large universal banks, and the large banks may use this system of extensive shareholdings and representation on the supervisory boards to help coordinate reduction of excess capacity. In Germany, however, the banks face limits in the capacity to autonomously coordinate restructuring and thus are typically reluctant to intervene beyond a certain point without the intervention of the state. The state has done this in a number of crisis sectors, acting as a mediator bringing together the various parties needed to develop and support restructuring plans and at the same time taking over some of the risks of further investment in these industries. Both the Kreditanstalt für Wiederaufbau and the regional public savings banks (Landesbanken) have been important providers of capital or of loan guarantees that have allowed successful restructuring under the auspices of private ownership.[32]

In the British system, the fragmentation of ownership and limited equity holdings by banks renders it more difficult for financial institutions to coordinate to influence the decisions of industrial companies. In contrast with Germany, the more common pattern of state intervention

31. On the possibility of restructuring traditional industries through innovation, see the extensive literature on post-Fordist production models such as diversified quality production (Sorge and Streeck 1988) and flexible specialization (Piore 1984).

32. Along with protection from hostile takeovers, this capacity to coordinate restructuring in declining industries may be the main contribution to corporate governance of the close links between the Hausbank and its industrial customers; the weight of evidence is that by the end of World War I, with the possible exception of the immediate post-World War II period, German banks had ceased playing the active role in "steering" the German economy often attributed to them (Feldman 1977; Esser 1990; Edwards and Fisher 1994).

has been to directly assume responsibility for restructuring through nationalizing large companies in declining industries rather than to indirectly provide financial incentives for restructuring.[33]

In Britain as in Germany, the decline of industries dominated by SMEs poses a particular problem for financial institutions, given the difficulties of developing a coherent and implementable restructuring plan for a large number of companies. Nevertheless, the German public savings bank and cooperative bank sectors have been more willing to continue lending to SMEs in declining industries than private German banks or the British clearing banks; the public savings banks are obligated to take into account the economic development interests of their locality, while the cooperative banks are owned by SMEs and see their primary goal as the assistance of their membership. Nevertheless, this willingness to lend also has its limits and is typically dependent upon the formulation of a credible restructuring plan by the company (Edwards and Fisher 1994).[34]

Industrial Finance in New Industries

The development of new industries is important for the long-term growth of national economies. For a number of reasons, however, financial institutions generally are reluctant to provide finance to companies in these industries. First, companies in new industries are often new themselves and thus lack the financial history that financial institutions use as an indicator of the financial strength of the company and the reliability of management. Second, companies in these industries tend to be research-intensive or invest in specialized equipment, thus there is often an absence of easily resalable assets which can serve as loan collateral. Third, the potential of a new product may be difficult to judge since financial institutions generally lack this expertise themselves; even given the use of outside technical experts, it may be extremely difficult to judge the potential of a new product. Finally,

33. Industries in decline or with major overcapacity problems since the mid-1970s and dominated by large firms include coal, shipbuilding, autos, steel, and aerospace. In each of these cases, the British government nationalized (if not already in public ownership) and directly took responsibility for restructuring one or more major firms in these industries; in Germany, in the majority of these cases "private" solutions, with the state playing a supportive role, were found (Schaaf 1978; Esser et al. 1983; Hague and Wilkinson 1983; Streeck 1984).

34. In Germany, declining industries dominated by SMEs that have been successful in restructuring toward higher-quality production include machine tools, textiles, and foundries; in Britain these industries have been less successful in restructuring. Interestingly, in Britain the average firm size in some of these industries is significantly higher than in Germany (Weißbach 1989; Whitston 1989; Herrigel 1990).

even if the firm is successful in developing its new product, new industries often undergo rapid product and process innovation, making it difficult to estimate the probability of the firm being able to keep up with new innovations.

Finance to companies in new industries therefore is generally provided by financial institutions with an explicit orientation toward high-risk projects in the hope that large payoffs from a few projects will cover the losses from other failed projects. These institutions generally develop a specialized capacity to judge these risks; this typically requires a staff with technical knowledge or the use of outside experts as consultants. Furthermore, the management skills of the company are often underdeveloped, and the ability of the financial institution to supplement these management skills can be important for the survival chances of the firm. These institutions take equity shares or options in order to share the gains of the projects with big successes. In the literature, these types of institutions traditionally have been referred to as industrial banks, although in the last few decades the term venture capital has become more predominant (Hu 1984).

The British financial system has a moderate comparative advantage in providing industrial finance to companies in new industries. Britain has developed the second-largest venture capital market in the world after the United States. In the 1980s, institutional investors greatly increased their investments in venture capital funds, to a total of over £1 thousand million in the late 1980s. Much of the increase in the 1980s did not in fact take the "classic" form of patient venture capital, but instead was invested in expansions of established companies and management buyouts. Nevertheless about one-fifth of projects supported in important new industries such as electronics, computers, biotechnology, and medical technology were in the start-up phase. Thus, the British financial system can be said to have a moderate capacity to support companies in new industries (Pratt 1990; Murray 1991; Mason 1987).

The problem of providing finance to companies in new industries has been one of the dominant themes in German discussions of industrial finance in the last decade (Albach 1983; Kokalj 1989). Although the German joint-stock banks historically have been admired for their entrepreneurial abilities in identifying promising new growth fields, gathering the capital needed for product development and production facilities, and providing management skills, banks apparently had ceased playing this role by the interwar period. Both the reluctance of German banks to lend to companies lacking credit histories and their emphasis on equipment and property as collateral for long-term loans excludes companies in new industries from normal credit channels.

Thus the lack of venture capital generally is acknowledged to be one of the factors explaining the weakness of the German economy in new high-technology areas. Both the banks and the state have taken actions designed to counter this weakness, but to date these efforts remain modest. The major banks have set up their own venture capital firms, but the capital at their disposal, as well as specialized staff, remains small. Federal, state, and local levels of government have all taken actions to foster industrial lending to companies in new "technology oriented" areas (Legler 1982; Legler et al. 1992).

Comparative Capacities Summarized

This section has developed and applied an alternative framework for analyzing the differences between financial systems in terms of their impact on industrial finance (see Table 5.1 for a summary). Significant differences between the British and German systems have been identified as stemming from the differences in regulation discussed in the previous section, with neither system being equal or superior to the other in all respects. Accounts which have claimed that one system is superior have tended to emphasize one subset of problems: those claiming the superiority of the German system, with its close bank-industry relations, tend to focus on the problem of restructuring in declining industries, while those praising the Anglo-American venture capital funds tend to focus on the problem of developing new industries. The creation of appropriate institutions and incentives in both countries, however, could well improve the availability of finance in areas in which they currently have difficulties.

Conclusion: Possibilities for Future Convergence

The previous sections have established that nation-states retain considerable discretion in financial regulation (as reflected in continued divergence between the German and British financial systems) and that these differences have important consequences for industrial finance. In defense of the convergence view, one might argue that convergence is a long-run tendency that has just started to emerge, perhaps with an accelerating dynamic. This section reflects critically on the convergence thesis by emphasizing the "social nature" of industrial finance, its embeddedness within a national institutional framework including the production regime, and the lack of an unambiguous, objective definition of efficiency by which industrial policy can be judged.

The Social Nature of Industrial Finance and the Limits on Internationalization

The provision of industrial finance by the financial system is a labor-intensive process dependent upon the evaluation of risk, the monitoring of company financial performance, and the reorganization of financial claims in cases of financial distress. Greater competition among financial institutions and an increase in almost all types of risk are pushing financial institutions to isolate and manage the different sources of risk through more conscious matching of liabilities, more vigorous attempts at diversification, and so forth. Greater use is being made of statistics to manage overall portfolio risk, to evaluate individual loan applications, and to provide an "early warning" of company financial distress. Institutional investors rely largely on rating agencies for judgement about the riskiness of investment in specific companies.

Practitioners, however, stress the limits of the usefulness of these techniques, particularly in the case of industrial finance. Unlike other types of finance (e.g., residential mortgages), industrial finance is very difficult to standardize. The judgement of risk is dependent upon a fine sense of the character of a company's management and the environment within which the company operates and thus is difficult to reliably quantify; lending officers stress the degree to which many years of experience often are needed to build up sufficient judgement capacity. Financial institutions are recognizing that the provision of labor-intensive advisory services covering areas such as cash-flow management and accounting systems can both be an additional source of income and reduce default risk by improving customer performance. Furthermore, many companies have specific needs and are willing to pay a premium for customization of financial services. As evidenced by the discovery of "relationship banking," the social nature of industrial finance puts limits on the extent to which financial products can be standardized and centrally produced. Large financial institutions thus have been struggling with the problem of decentralization in order to have customer contact at the local level and to delegate decision-making authority to this level.

These characteristics of industrial finance constrain the extent to which economies of scale can be exploited and thus the extent to which smaller, nationally based financial institutions can be driven out of business by large, internationally active financial institutions. Internationalization of finance has been confined largely to interbank lending and to finance for the largest blue-chip industrial companies and public authorities. Banks' extensive efforts, in the 1970s and early 1980s, to develop their international business by establishing foreign offices have been cut back; of the large U.S. banks, only Citibank has not given up attempts to set up an international retail network. Banks have turned instead to a strategy of expanding by buying up banks in other countries, which, however, are subject to regulation by national authorities and must follow national procedures. These limits on internationalization mean that national factors will continue to play a significant role in determining the characteristics of financial systems and industrial finance.

Interdependence with the Productive Sphere

A growing body of evidence shows that, in the 1970s, after a period of hegemony of the mass-production system, advanced industrialized countries began to diverge in characteristics such as the organization of work and the level of investment in equipment, training, and research and development. A contrast is often drawn between the Anglo-American countries, on the one hand, and Germany and Japan, on the other. In the former, companies have reacted to increasing instability in world markets by increasing their flexibility to lay off noncore workers and to quickly shut down unprofitable plants during downturns. In the latter, long-term attachments have developed between workers and (at least large) industrial companies, and workers are kept on during downturns, allowing for the maintenance of human capital. These differences support the movement of companies in the latter countries into higher-quality, nonprice-competitive production; in the former, companies focus more on the reduction of costs for standardized goods.

A relatively unexplored area is the interdependence between the structure of the productive and the financial systems. It may well be that different types of production regimes have varying demands for different types of capital; companies relying on cheaper labor and less new equipment and placing great value on short-term flexibility are likely to have less demand for long-term debt capital than companies relying on greater quantities of new equipment and long-term planning. Thus, an increase in the supply of long-term debt capital in Britain might not be matched by unfilled demand for such finance from the productive sphere. Conversely, stability in industrial organization due to constraints on laying off labor may produce stability in industrial finance; the long-term stability of company workforce in Germany and Japan reduce the moral hazard of allowing company management to retain pension reserves within the company. Thus significant differences in productive systems and their

35. For a comparison of industrial finance and the modernization of the SME sector, see Vitols (1994). One implication of this analysis is that financial systems may influence the

TABLE 5.1 Comparative Capacities of the British and German Financial Systems

Type of Capital	Type of Industry Stable	 Declining	 New
Short-term debt	GB: SME + Lf +	GB: SME - Lf -	GB: SME 0
	DE: SME + Lf +	DE: SME 0 Lf 0/+	DE: SME -
Long-term debt	GB: SME - Lf -	GB: SME - Lf -	GB: SME 0
	DE: SME + Lf +	DE: SME 0 Lf 0/+	DE: SME -
Equity	GB: SME - Lf +	GB: SME - Lf -	GB: SME 0
	DE: SME - Lf +	DE: SME - Lf 0/+	DE: SME -

Legend: GB = Great Britain; DE = Germany; + = positive capacity; 0 = moderate capacity; - = low/no capacity; Lf = large firm; SME = small and medium-size enterprise. More than two ratings means that capacity is further differentiated by type of company.

relations with financial systems may be an important factor constraining financial system convergence over the long-term.[35]

Lack of "One-Best" Solutions in Industrial Policy

Finally, a number of factors are likely to constrain convergence in industrial policy styles between countries toward a "one-best" solution. Industrial policy intervention may be relatively low-cost or even more efficient than market-driven restructuring. From the special credit agencies in Germany, we see that institutional access to long-term finance for SMEs may be created at relatively little cost. The start-up costs of innovative new companies may be quite low; thus, given a risk-friendly orientation among investors, the gains from the support of new industries may be

---

development of industrial structure, e.g., in increasing the difficulties for survival of SMEs by providing financing at much more favorable terms for large companies. In the long run, this may result in an institutional equilibrium (Soskice 1992), e.g., where there are few SMEs and thus limited demand for the type of financial services that are provided by the cooperative and savings banks in Germany to the large population of SMEs.

quite substantial. Finally, the provision of financing for the restructuring of "old" industries may be quite successful given the solution of coordination problems. Thus efficiency grounds themselves do not lead to the provision of certain kinds of finance and not others.

The second point is that efficiency itself is an ambiguous concept and is in part politically defined. National goals may place greater emphasis on employment stability than on the profitability of industrial companies, for example; electorates may measure the success of governments on different grounds and be willing to support the allocation of resources toward different goals. The huge amount of resources allocated to the restructuring of the new German Länder through the special credit agencies and the continued importance of the French state in the restructuring of "national champions" to be competitive on international markets are significant examples of the continued importance of domestic factors in the determination of industrial policy.

References

Albach, Horst (1983). *Zur Versorgung der deutschen Wirtschaft mit Risikokapital*. IfM-Materialien, Nr. 9. Bonn: Institut für Mittelstandsforschung.

Allen, Christopher S. (1990). *Democratic Politics and Private Investment: Financial Regulation in the Federal Republic of Germany and the United States*. Research Report #2. Washington: American Institute for Contemporary German Studies.

Bank of England (1994). *Finance for Small Firms: Note by the Bank of England*. Unpublished manuscript.

———. (1991). "Is there a 'credit crunch?'" *Bank of England Quarterly Bulletin* 31 (May):256–59.

Benzie, R. S. (1988). "The financial behavior of industrial and commercial companies, 1970–86." *Bank of England Quarterly Bulletin* 28 (February):75–82.

Berglöf, Erik (1991). *Corporate Control and Capital Structure: Essays on Property Rights and Financial Contracts*. Stockholm: Institute of International Business.

Blake, David (1992). *Issues in Pension Funding*. London: Routledge.

Braun, Dirk (1989). *Die öffentliche Förderung von Existenzgründungen in Baden-Württemberg*. Konstanz: Hartung-Gorre.

Callen, T.S., and J.W. Lomax (1990). "The development of the building societies sector in the 1980s." *Bank of England Quarterly Bulletin* 30 (November):503–13.

Cameron, Rondo (1967). *Banking in the Early Stages of Industrialization: A Study in Comparative Economic History*. London: Oxford University.

Carrington, John, and George Edwards (1981). *Reversing Economic Decline*. London: Macmillan.

———. (1979). *Financing Industrial Investment*. London: Macmillan.

Central Statistical Office (CSO) (1993). *United Kingdom National Accounts*. London: HMSO.

Chandler, Alfred (1990). *Scale and Scope: The Dynamics of Industrial Capitalism*. Cambridge, Mass.: Belknap.
Committee of London Clearing Banks (CLCB) (1980). "Written Evidence." Committee to Review the Functioning of Financial Institutions (Wilson Committee). *Final Report*. Cmnd. 7937. London: HMSO.
Culbertson, J. (1957). "The term structure of interest rates." *International Economic Review* 17 (November):485–517.
Davis, E.P. (1991). "The development of pension funds—An international comparison." *Bank of England Quarterly Bulletin* 31 (August):380–90.
De Jong, Henry (1991). "The takeover market in Europe: Control structures and the performance of large companies compared." *Review of Industrial Organization* 6 (1):1–18.
Deakins, David, and Toby Philpott (1993). *Comparative European Practices in the Finance of Small Firms: UK, Germany and Holland*. Research Report and Occasional Paper. Birmingham: University of Central England Business School.
Dean, Andrew, Martine Durand, John Fallon, and Peter Hoeller (1989). "Saving Trends and Behavior in OECD Countries." OECD Dept. of Economics and Statistics Working Paper No. 67.
Deeg, Richard (1992). "Banks and the State in Germany: The Critical Role of Subnational Institutions in Economic Governance." Ph.D. Diss. in Political Science, at MIT, Cambridge, Mass.
Department of Trade and Industry (DTI) (1991). *Constraints on the Growth of Small Firms*. London: HMSO.
Deutsche Bundesbank (1992). "Longer-term trends in the financing patterns of West German enterprises." *Monthly Report* 44 (10):25–39.
———. (1987). "Kapitalbildung und Anlagepolitik der Versicherungsunternehmen seit 1979." *Monatsberichte* 39 (January):17–26.
———. (1984a). "Company pension schemes in the Federal Republic of Germany." *Monthly Report* 36 (August):30–37.
———. (1984b). "Der Aktienmarkt in der Bundesrepublik Deutschland und seine Entwicklungsmöglichkeiten." *Monatsberichte* 36 (April):12–21.
Dyson, Kenneth (1986). "The State, Banks and Industry: The West German Case." In *State, Finance and Industry: A Comparative Analysis of Post-War Trends in Six Advanced Industrial Economies,* edited by A. Cox. Brighton: Wheatsheaf.
Edwards, Jeremy, and Klaus Fischer (1994). *Banks, Finance, and Investment in Germany*. Cambridge: Cambridge University.
Esser, Josef (1990). "Bank power in Germany revisited." *West European Politics* 13 (1):17–32.
Esser, Josef, Wolfgang Fach, and Werner Väth (1983). *Krisenregulierung. Zur politischen Durchsetzung ökonomischer Zwänge*. Frankfurt: Suhrkamp.
European Observatory for SMEs (EOSME) (1991). "First Annual Report."
Feldman, Gerald (1977). *Iron and Steel in the German Inflation 1916–1923*. Princeton: Princeton University.
Foss, Nicolai (1993). "Theories of the firm: Contractual and competence perspectives." *Journal of Evolutionary Economics* 3 (2):127–44.
Franks, Julian, and Colin Mayer (1990). "Capital markets and corporate control: A study of France, Germany and the U.K." *Economic Policy* 5 (1): 191–231.
Gardener, Edward, and Philip Molyneux (1993). *Changes in Western European Banking*. London: Routledge.
Gentle, Christopher (1993). *The Financial Services Industry. The Impact of Corporate Reorganisation on Regional Economic Development*. Aldershot: Averbury.

Gerschenkron, Alexander (1962). *Economic Backwardness in Historical Perspective. A Book of Essays*. Cambridge, Mass.: Belknap.

Girke, Werner, and Bernd Kopplin (1977). *Beteiligungspolitik deutscher Kreditinstitute*. Münster: Erich Schmidt.

Goodman, John, and Louis Pauly (1994). "The obsolescence of capital controls? Economic management in an age of global markets." *World Politics* 46 (1):50–82.

Grady, John, and Martin Weale (1986). *British Banking, 1960–85*. London: Macmillan.

Guthardt, Helmut (1988). "Kann ein Bankenverbund die Vorteile der Größe ersetzen?" In *Bankensymposium*, edited by W. Engels. Frankfurt: Fritz Knapp.

Hague, D., and G. Wilkinson (1983). *The IRC—An Experiment in Industrial Intervention: A History of the Industrial Reorganisation Corporation*. London: George Allen & Unwin.

Hahn, Oswald (1984). *Struktur der Bankwirtschaft. Band II. Spezialbanken und Internationale Banken*. Frankfurt: Fritz Knapp.

Hall, Peter (1986). *Governing the Economy: The Politics of State Intervention in Britain and France*. Cambridge, Mass.: Polity.

Harrigan, Kathryn (1980). *Strategies for Declining Industries*. Lexington, Mass.: Lexington.

Herrigel, Gary (1990). "Industrial organization and the politics of industry: Centralization and decentralization." Ph.D. diss., Political Science, MIT, Cambridge, Mass.

Hilferding, R. (1968). *Das Finanzkapital*. Frankfurt: Europäische Verlagsanstalt.

Hoppenrath, Martin (1994). "Hohe Effizienz bei Sicherung der Betriebsrenten." *Der Arbeitgeber* 46 (9):325–28.

Hu, Yao-Su (1984). *Industrial Banking and Special Credit Institutions. A Comparative Study*. London: Policy Studies Institute.

———. (1975). *National Attitudes and the Financing of Industry*. London: Political and Economic Planning Agency.

Hutchinson, R., and D. McKillop (1992). "Banks and small to medium sized business financing in the United Kingdom: Some general issues." *National Westminster Bank Quarterly Review* (February):84–95.

Ingham, G. (1984). *Capitalism Divided? The City and Industry in British Social Development*. Basingstoke, Hampshire: Macmillan.

Jacobs, Michael (1991). *Short-Term America: The Causes and Cures of our Business Myopia*. Boston: Harvard Business School.

Jenkinson, T., and C. Mayer (1992). "The assessement: Corporate governance and corporate control." *Oxford Review of Economic Policy* 8 (1):1–10.

Kluge, Arnd (1991). *Geschichte der deutschen Bankgenossenschaften. Zur Entwicklung mitgliederorientierter Unternehmen*. Frankfurt: Fritz Knapp.

Kokalj, Ljuba (1989). "Der deutsche Venture Capital-Markt. Bestandaufnahme und Entwicklungsperspektiven." *IfM Materialien* 69. Bonn: Institut für Mittelstandsforschung.

Legler, Harald (1982). *Zur Position der Bundesrepublik Deutschland im internationalen Wettbewerb*. Hannover: Niedersächsisches Institut für Wirtschaftsforschung.

Legler, Harald, Hariof Grupp, Birgit Gehrke, and Ulrich Schasse (1992). *Innovationspotential und Hochtechnologie. Technologische Position Deutschlands im internationalen Wettbewerb*. Heidelberg: Physica.

Lisle-Williams, M. (1986). "The State, Finance and Industry in Britain," In *State, Finance, and Industry: A Comparative Analysis of Post-War Trends in Six Advanced Industrial Economies*, edited by A. Cox. Brighton: Wheatsheaf.

Loriaux, Michael (1991). *France After Hegemony. International Change and Financial Reform*. Ithaca, N.Y.: Cornell University.

Maier, Kurt (1983). *Der Sparprozeß in der Bundesrepublik Deutschland.* Frankfurt: Peter Lang.
Mason, Colin (1987). "Venture capital in the United Kingdom: A geographical perspective." *National Westminster Quarterly Review* (May):47–59.
Menzel, H. (1960). *Die Mitwirkung der Hausbanken bei der Vergebung und Verwaltung öffentlicher Kredite.* Berlin: Dunker & Humblot.
Moran, Michael (1984). *The Politics of Banking. The Strange Case of Competition and Credit Control.* London: Macmillan.
Murray, G (1991). "The changing nature of competition in the UK Venture Capital Industry." *National Westminster Bank Quarterly Review* (November):65–80.
Nelson, Richard, and Sidney Winter (1982). *An Evolutionary Theory of Economic Change.* Cambridge, Mass.: Bellknap.
Neuberger, Doris, and Manfred Neumann (1991). "Banking and antitrust: Limiting industrial ownership by banks?" *Journal of Institutional and Theoretical Economics* 147 (March):188–99.
Paar, Michael (1979). "The National Enterprise Board." *National Westminster Quarterly Review* (February):51–62.
Pfeiffer, Hermanus (1993). *Die Macht der Banken. Die personellen Verflechtungen der Commerzbank, der Deutschen Bank und der Dresdner Bank mit Unternehmen.* Frankfurt: Campus.
Piore, Michael and Charles Sabel (1984). *The Second Industrial Divide: Possibilities for Prosperity.* New York: Basic.
Pohl, Hans (1992). *Deutsche Börsengeschichte.* Frankfurt: Fritz Knapp.
Pohl, Manfred (1973). *Wiederaufbau: Kunst und Technik der Finanzierung 1947–1953. Die ersten Jahre der Kreditanstalt für Wiederaufbau.* Frankfurt: Fritz Knapp.
Porter, Michael (1992). *Capital Choices.* Washington: Council on Competitiveness.
Poullain, Ludwig (1979). *Tätigkeitsbericht.* Stuttgart: Seewald.
Pratt, Gillian (1990). "Venture Capital in the United Kingdom." *Bank of England Quarterly Bulletin* 30 (February):78–83.
Pressnell, L.S. (1956). *Country Banking in the Industrial Revolution.* Oxford: Clarendon.
Reid, M. (1982). *The Secondary Banking Crisis, 1973–75.* London: Macmillan.
Riesser, J. (1910). *Die deutschen Großbanken und ihre Konzentration.* Jena: Gustav Fischer.
Rybczynski, T. (1988). "Financial systems and industrial restructuring." *National Westminster Bank Quarterly Review* (November):3–13.
———. (1984a). "Industrial finance systems in Europe, U.S. and Japan." *Journal of Economic Behavior and Organization* 5 (4):275–86.
———. (1984b). "The U.K. financial system in transition." *National Westminster Bank Quarterly Review* (November):26–42.
Sabel, Charles, John Griffin, and Richard Deeg (1993). "Making Money Talk: Towards a New Debtor-Creditor Relation in German Banking." Paper presented at the Conference on Relational Investing, Center for Law and Economic Studies, Columbia University School of Law, New York, 6–7 May.
Sayers, R.S. (1967). *Modern Banking.* Seventh ed. Oxford: Clarendon.
Schaaf, Peter. (1978). *Ruhrbergbau und Sozialdemokratie: Die Energiepolitik der Großen Koalition 1966–69.* Marburg: Verlag Arbeiterbewegung und Gesellschaftswissenschaft.
Scott, John, and Catherine Griff (1985). "Bank spheres of influence in the British corporate network." In *Networks of Corporate Power: A Comparative Analysis of Ten Countries,* edited by F. Stokman, R. Ziegler, and J. Scott. Cambridge, Mass.: Polity.

Sheppard, David (1971). *The Growth and Role of UK Financial Institutions 1880–1962*. London: Methuen.
Shonfield, Andrew (1965). *Modern Capitalism*. London: Oxford.
Sorge, A., and W. Streeck (1988). "Industrial relations and technical change: The case for an extended perspective." In *New Technology and Industrial Relations,* edited by R. Hyman and W. Streeck. Oxford: Basil Blackwell.
Soskice, David (1992). "The institutional infrastructure for international competitiveness: A comparative analysis of the UK and Germany." In *The Economics of the New Europe*, edited by A. B. Atkinson and R.Brunettac. International Economic Association conference volume. London: Macmillan.
Spencer, Ken, Andy Taylor, et al. (1986). *Crisis in the Industrial Heartland*. Oxford: Clarendon.
Stiglitz, Joseph E., and Andrew Weiss (1981). "Credit rationing in markets with imperfect information." *American Economic Review* 71 (3):393–410.
Streeck, Wolfgang (1984). *Industrial Relations in West Germany: A Case Study of the Car Industry*. London: Heinemann.
Sykes, Joseph (1926). *The Amalgamation Movement in English Banking, 1825–1924*. London: P.S. King & Son.
Vitols, Sigurt (1995). "German Banks and the Modernization of the Small Firm Sector: Long-term Finance in Comparative Perspective." Wissenschaftszentrum Berlin Discussion Paper FS I 95–309.
———. (1993). "Industrial Relations and Restructuring in the German Steel Industry." Wissenschaftszentrum Berlin Discussion Paper FS I 93–302.
Weber, Adolf (1954). *Bankkredit und langfristige Investitionen. Bericht über eine Aussprache führender Sachkundiger*. Berlin: Duncker & Humblot.
Weißbach, Hans-Jürgen (1989). "Textilindustrie." In *Trends betrieblicher Produktionsmodernisierung*, edited by L. Pries, R. Schmidt, and R. Trinczek. Opladen: Westdeutscher.
Westdeutsche Landesbank (WestLB) (1992). "Jahresbericht."
Whitston, Colin (1989). "Rationalizing Foundries." In *Manufacturing Change: Industrial Relations and Restructuring*, edited by S. Tailby and C. Whitston. Oxford: Basil Blackwell.
Williamson, Oliver (1988). "Corporate finance and corporate governance." *Journal of Finance* 43 (3):567–91.
Ziegler, Rolf, Donald Bender, and Hermann Biehler (1985). "Industry and Banking in the German Corporate Network." In *Networks of Corporate Power: A Comparative Analysis of Ten Countries*, edited by F. Stockman, R. Ziegler, and J. Scott. Cambridge, Mass.: Polity.
Zysman, John (1983). *Governments, Markets and Growth: Financial Systems and the Politics of Industrial Change*. Ithaca: Cornell University.

Chapter 6

THE ROLE OF 1930S REGULATIONS IN THE DEVELOPMENT OF FINANCIAL MARKETS IN POSTWAR UNITED STATES, GERMANY, AND GREAT BRITAIN

Jan A. Kregel

Introduction

The change in macroeconomic policy regime that is the subject of this volume may be represented by the shift from the concern for price deflation during the 1930s to the battle to eliminate inflation in the 1970s. The new financial system regulations introduced in the 1930s were designed primarily to prevent recurrence of the sharp collapse in asset prices and financial instability which had contributed to the depth of the Great Depression, while monetary policy in the 1970s targeted growth of the money supply to control inflation. This shift meant abandoning policies to control interest rates and to direct lending to defined uses through rationing or rate subsidies that had emerged from the 1930s regulatory framework. It also meant that the determination of asset prices was left to market forces. Part of the shift in policy thus involved steps to strengthen competition in financial markets through elimination of the regulations introduced in most countries in the aftermath of the Great Depression. The shift in policy regime thus represented a reversal of the concerns addressed by the financial regulations introduced in the 1930s.

Although most countries experienced sharp and sustained declines in income and employment, the financial crises that are thought to have been the major determinants of the Great Depression appear to have differed substantially across countries. For example, the 1929 stock market Crash was followed by the collapse of the U.S. banking system symbolized in the March 1933 Bank Holiday almost three years later, while in Europe collapse of the gold standard and problems of war debt and reparations were important factors leading to the collapse of the Creditanstalt and the crisis in the German financial system during 1931. While bank failure characterized the German crisis, the U.K. experienced virtually no financial instability.

Thus, although virtually all countries experienced a generalized fall in asset prices that eventually spread to product and labor markets and produced a decline in industrial prices and profits, along with losses in production and employment, the degree of instability in financial markets differed across countries. This meant that the response to financial instability was more varied than the response to the general decline in economic activity that produced the postwar macroeconomic policy regime in support of employment and economic activity.

Despite the various forms taken by government intervention, the actions undertaken can be classified according to two separate goals. The first was to introduce measures to deal with the impact of declining asset prices on economic activity, the second to integrate monetary policy with other government policies to stimulate product prices and wages and support economic activity.

The first set of measures involved structural changes to limit the impact of asset price deflation on the payments system and the financing of production. In the U.S. this led to the separation of banks providing means of payment from other types of financial institution. What are generally known as "commercial" banks were forbidden from engaging in investment banking activities. In other countries, such as Germany, banks were allowed to continue to undertake all types of activity. This diverse regulatory response created the distinction between "segmented" and "mixed" bank systems. As will be seen below, liberalization affects these two systems differently.

A second set of measures aimed at making financial markets more effective instruments in the application of macrostabilization policies designed to counter the Depression. With the collapse of the Gold standard, monetary policy had by necessity become government responsibility, and it was in the interwar period that the concept of "managed money" set the stage for active monetary policy.

However, it was only after the outbreak of World War II that "Keynesian"-inspired policies of low interest rates and demand management were introduced to facilitate financing of the war effort and to avoid the inflation and profiteering that had occurred in the first war. This successful experience encouraged governments to play a more active policy role to counter the resumption of the depressed conditions most economists and politicians expected once the war was over. The necessity for reconversion of the war economy and the reconstruction of the European economies, plus the threat of economic hardship producing political instability, were enough to create general acceptance of a regime of active policy intervention in which financial markets would serve as the handmaiden of active government demand management to stabilize the economy.

In many countries the introduction of active stabilization policies for income and employment was accompanied by government decisions to prevent the return of the personal suffering experienced during the Depression by guaranteeing minimum standards of living to their citizens. These "welfare state" policies called for the provision of health care, subsidized housing or loans to finance house ownership, minimum pension benefits, and so forth. Keynes' recommendation concerning active control of government expenditure to prevent depression and provide economic stability was often used as justification for policies to provide political stability and social equity.

The increasing importance of these social expenditure policies had two unexpected effects. On one hand, it tended to reduce the importance of capital spending in the government budget and shifted the overall composition of national output toward consumption of services. On the other, decisions concerning the provision of funded public and private pensions generated a change in public savings patterns and provision for retirement that influenced the structure of demand for financial assets. Social security funds provided a demand for government securities, and private pension legislation provided demand for private sector financial assets. This concentration of private savings in "contractual" schemes such as social security, life insurance, and private pensions meant that decisions over the allocations of private savings were shifted to the hands of professional portfolio managers hired by the institutions and out of the direct control of the private individuals they represented.

This concentration of control over the allocation of financial resources in the hands of "institutional investors" produced pressure for structural changes in the organization of financial markets that eventually came into conflict with the securities market regulations introduced in the aftermath of the Great Crash in order to produce stability in asset prices. These changes joined with the sustained inflationary conditions which emerged in the late sixties, and which became entrenched in the 1970s after the oil crisis, to produce a shift in the operation of monetary policy. The decision to use monetary policy to influence aggregate expenditures through control of monetary aggregates meant abandoning control over the behavior of interest rates and asset prices. These measures were thus in direct conflict with the New Deal regulations that had been set up to produce stability in asset prices (and thus interest rates) in order to support income and expenditure.

The combination of these two factors eventually produced a return to the liberal financial policies of the pre-Depression period via a piecemeal process of "deregulation" of financial markets. Although some of these changes in financial markets can be traced to peculiar historical events, such as the breakdown of Bretton Woods and the extended crisis in the Middle East, many can be traced to the inherent contradictions between the growth of institutional investors and, on one hand the changes in the operation of monetary policy to fight inflation and, on the other, the financial regulations which emerged from the Great Depression that aimed to prevent deflation of asset prices and support incomes through policies of reflation.

It is against the background of diverse governmental and prudential regulations in response to the 1930s crisis that the impact of liberalization and deregulation in producing convergence of national financial systems has to be assessed. This chapter will concentrate on the different ways in which the United States, Germany, and the United Kingdom responded to the threat of economic collapse due to falling prices in the 1930s and the differences which this response produced in their postwar evolution and the policies they adopted to combat rising prices in the 1970s. The next three sections will present a sketch of the pre-Depression financial structure of each economy and its response to the financial crises experienced in the 1930s. Against this background, the legislative responses and their impact on the financial structure will be considered. Finally, each section will evaluate how these structures performed in the inflationary environment of the 1970s, along with the changes introduced as a result of the shift in policy regime.

Financial Market Developments in the U.S.: Separation and Segmentation

The legislative response of the United States to the conditions of the Great Depression was the most extensive of those in the three countries compared in this essay. The changes that were introduced into the U.S. financial system were thus the most far-reaching. This makes it necessary to provide a summary of the pre-Crash financial system as well as its role in the financial crises.

The U.S. system often is presented as one in which corporations' financing depends on the sale of equity to the general public via free and open capital markets. However, few facts support this interpretation, either before or after New Deal regulatory reforms of financial markets. At the beginning of the 1920s the majority of corporate equity was still in the possession of the founders of family firms and a small number of wealthy inside investors. Banks were not directly involved either as owners or as managers of business, while investment banks operated mainly as marriage brokers for consolidation, and their primary activity was the provision of banking services for companies. They competed with commercial banks that provided for the short-term financing needs of business, such as the payment of wages, which were primarily in cash. It was not common for commercial banks to offer their services to any other clients except wealthy private individuals, usually the owners of the firms served by the banks.

As a result of the policy of low interest rates introduced in the U.S. in order to facilitate Britain's return to the Gold standard, foreign borrowing of funds in the U.S. was extensive and New York became an international and national underwriting center. Much of this lending went to Germany and served indirectly to finance German reparation payments. International lending was facilitated by the Federal Reserve Act, which allowed banks to operate internationally, and by the 1927 McFadden Act,[1] which permitted banks with national charters to compete with state-chartered banks in offering investment banking services, usually through affiliated subsidiaries.[2]

1. National banks were forbidden to branch unless specific authorization was granted by the Comptroller of the Currency, and then only for offices in the same city. Between 1922 and 1929 around 4,000 mergers of all types occurred (Shannon, 667). Since mergers between national banks and state banks usually were accomplished by converting the acquired banks (and their branches) into branches, national banks would have been excluded from merger activity unless they converted to state charters, which would have meant a drain on Fed membership. The act thus allowed the merged banks, including existing branches, to retain national charters and their Fed membership, as long as the branches were permitted under state law. It is for this reason that McFadden is known as the act that restricted branching, a far from exact description of either the intentions or the results of the Act.

To evade state branching restrictions, banks created chains of "banking associations," and affiliates organized as holding companies, which escaped all regulation: "Since such companies are not directly engaged in the business of banking as defined in Federal and state statutes, they have not been subject to supervision or regular examination by banking authorities." (*Annual Report* of the Federal Reserve System for 1927, quoted in Day, 25). The Bank of the United States, whose failure in 1930 is often cited as the real cause of the Depression and the subsequent bank holiday, had 60 such unsupervised affiliates.

2. After 1908 national banks were limited to commercial banking activities and the comptroller challenged the large New York banks' ability to operate in securities. The Pepper-McFadden Act gave national banks the power to "buy and sell without recourse marketable

TABLE 6.1 Banks Engaged in Securities Business

	1922	1925	1929	1930	1933
National	62	112	151	126	102
National affiliates	10	33	84	105	76
State	197	254	308	260	169
State affiliates	8	14	48	75	32

Source: Valentine, 401.

TABLE 6.2 Origination of Bond Issues of U.S. Banks (percentage)

	1927	1928	1929	1930
Commercial banks and affiliates	22.0	29.5	45.5	44.6
by national affiliates	10.1	15.6	24.6	27.6
by other affiliates	2.7	7.7	16.9	11.6
Investment banks	78.0	70.5	54.5	55.4

Source: Valentine, 401.

TABLE 6.3 Assets of U.S. Banks by Type
($ million) [Number of banks in parenthesis]

Bank Type	1925	1930	1932
National charter	24,351 (8,072)	29,116 (7,252)	22,367 (6,150)
State charter	15,979 (16,963)	16,270 (13,582)	9,478 (10,455)
Private	11,565 (1,680)	17,702 (1,564)	13,118 (1,235)
Mutual savings	10,006 (1,583)	11,816 (1,320)	12,224 (1,096)
Total	62,057 (28,841)	74,020 (24,079)	57,245 (19,163)

Source: Bogart, 816.

The stock market boom of the late 1920s already had started to attract the attention of foreign investors, and when the Federal Reserve finally moved to break the boom by increasing interest rates this action reinforced the reversal of the flows of international finance from Europe toward U.S. capital markets. The resulting pressure on European exchange rates eventually forced sterling off gold and prepared the way for what became an international financial crisis.

---

obligations in the form of bonds, notes or debentures, commonly known as investment securities.... This did not include the power to buy and sell stocks" (Valentine, 400); these activities remained in separate securities affiliates organized by state charter, and "certain banks and bank affiliates were active distributors of stock issues as well.... Generally speaking it may be said that by 1929 in the field of long-term financing the commercial banks and their affiliates occupied a position comparable to that of private investment bankers from the standpoint of physical facilities, capital employed, and the volume of securities underwritten and distributed" (ibid., 401).

Urgent Measures to Save the Banks

The collapse of the Florida real estate boom in 1927 produced a series of bank failures even before the 1929 stock market Crash. The collapse of the Bank of the United States in 1930,[3] just as the stock market appeared to be recovering, produced another market break in early 1931 and generated another round of bank failures. Together with the spreading failure of European banks in the summer, mounting unemployment, increasing bankruptcies, and pressure on U.S. gold reserves as investors withdrew funds in the belief that the U.S. would follow the U.K. off gold created increased uncertainty about the stability of the financial system.

As conditions in Britain improved on the strength of easy money and more competitive exports, signs of recovery started to become visible during 1932. Yet the worst of the U.S. bank crisis, in the form of a string of state bank holidays, was yet to come and convinced the newly inaugurated president, Roosevelt, to declare a national bank holiday on 6 March 1933.[4]

During his campaign Roosevelt not only had criticized Hoover for excessive government interference in the economy,[5] but pledged to put government finances in order by balancing the budget and to defend the gold value of the dollar. Roosevelt charged that the Republican administration had engineered the speculative stock market boom and defended members of the stock exchange after the Crash. He promised an official investigation of abuse and a full reform of securities law, including the

3. It is interesting to note that this bank, which attempted to grow rapidly by attracting deposits from immigrants who presumed it was the U.S. central bank, was heavily involved in (second and third) mortgage lending and in addition had set up the Bankus Corporation to manipulate its stock. On the other hand, most mutual savings banks, which lent predominantly on first mortgage (usually at 60 percent of appraised value), suffered little difficulty (most did not even have to impose the required notice on deposit withdrawals), and deposits in savings banks actually increased in this period.

4. The bank holiday is usually explained by the fraud and fall in prices during the Crash, but it occurred some three years later in conditions of incipient recovery. One important element was that 1932 was an election year, and another was that this was the last of the lame duck congresses that met before the March inauguration. Garner's illegal decision to order publication of the list of banks that had received RFC funds in order to claim that the Republicans were looking after their own led to a large number of failures at the end of 1932 and in the first quarter of 1933. There was also great uncertainty over Roosevelt's position on inter-allied debts, on which payment was due to be resumed in December after the Hoover moratorium. Finally, the inability of Congress to pass a credible budget led to widespread expectation that Roosevelt would not honor his campaign promise to defend the gold dollar, producing a large increase in gold hoarding by domestic residents and foreign holders of the dollar at the beginning of 1933. Cf. Sullivan (1936), who makes a case that the bank failures were a purely internal political phenomenon.

5. Indeed, it was the Hoover administration that first experimented with government spending on public works programs financed by borrowing in capital markets. As part of its

regulation of securities exchanges and prohibition of dealings in the stock exchange by commercial banks (Seligman, 19).

But on inauguration day there was no time for debate; the crisis required immediate action, and Roosevelt employed a government entity created by the Hoover Administration, the Reconstruction Finance Corporation (RFC), to deal with the banking crisis via the Emergency Banking Relief/Bank Conservation Act introduced just three days after the declaration of the bank holiday. The act provided for the recapitalization of banks through RFC purchase of preferred stock issued by the banks.[6] By mid-April nearly 13,000 recapitalized banks were again operating. The U.S. government, through the RFC, had equity interest in more than half of them. Two-thirds of the banks aided by the RFC were state-chartered banks.

Broader Legislative Reform

The administration then moved quickly to fulfill its pledge to provide reform legislation, in particular through amendment of the Federal Reserve Act. The Federal Reserve, which had been created primarily to provide an elastic currency, was neither prepared nor equipped to deal with a collapse of investment values of the magnitude experienced in the 1930s.[7] The difficulties facing banks after the stock market Crash can be divided roughly

antideflationary policy, it had sponsored the creation of the privately funded National Credit Corporation to support asset prices by providing rediscounting of bank assets not eligible for discount by the Federal Reserve. When this industry "self-help" organization proved insufficient because private banks were unwilling to provide sufficient funding, a similar government-funded organization, the Reconstruction Finance Corporation, was created to replace it. It had been supporting banks since February 1932, when it rescued the Bank of America.

6. During the bank holiday the RFC classified banks in three categories: those which had sufficient capital to be considered healthy and able to operate after recapitalization, those which had insufficient capital but enough assets to meet deposit liabilities, and those with both insufficient assets and no capital. Banks in the first category were opened immediately after the end of the Bank holiday on 10 March, those in the second were opened as soon as they were recapitalized, while those in the third were placed in conservatorship and either reorganized or closed. By 16 March only 1,400 national banks were unable to open. According to Jones "This program of putting capital into banks prevented the failure of our whole credit system" (Jones, 26).

7. The Federal Reserve Banks could issue Federal Reserve Notes only by discounting good commercial bills, which banks did not have; lending against stock was excluded. The possibility of lending against government securities, introduced in the Glass-Steagall Banking Act of 1932 amending Fed discounting rules, along with Hoover's National Credit Corporation, which was meant to provide for discounting of assets not eligible under the Federal Reserve Act, and was eventually transformed into the Reconstruction Finance Corporation, all produced additional leeway to offset the monetary contraction that was then occurring due to the outflow of gold caused by the fear that the U.S. would follow the U.K. off the gold standard.

into two types. The small, state-chartered country banks with land and farm equipment loans were hit the hardest, and the most bank failures were in the Midwestern states. Their position was aggravated, however, by the fact that, in addition to providing banking and lending services to farmers, they also took savings deposits and invested them in long-term bonds and securities. When bank runs occurred, the withdrawals were primarily of savings deposits, and the banks were forced to liquidate their securities portfolios to repay them, putting additional downward pressure on security prices. Since the sales proceeds were generally insufficient to meet repayments, these banks also had to start calling in commercial loans and to stop lending, forcing their commercial farm clients into bankruptcy and causing the appropriation and forced liquidation of farm lands. This had the effect of depressing land prices below the value of the mortgages that they secured and produced additional losses for the banks.[8]

On the other hand, a small number of state-chartered banks, along with national banks operating in the large financial centers who had availed themselves of the possibility of trading securities provided by Pepper-McFadden, were responsible for most of the clearly fraudulent practices.[9] The operations of the Bank of the United States were typical. Their influence on the system is reflected in a June 1929 American Bankers Association report announcing the first recorded decline in savings deposits as a result of a shift of funds into more speculative investments organized by bank securities affiliates.

In addition, the evidence of widespread fraud that emerged after the Crash confirmed deficiencies in the supervisory function of the federal agencies (in particular, the lack of control of bank "chains" and securities affiliates) and an inability of Fed monetary policy to prevent the failure of even well-run banks in conditions of general panic.

8. In a study of failed Wisconsin banks, Garlock notes that: "Despite the inherent weakness of unit banking it appears that Wisconsin banks could have met their commercial banking liabilities, protected their solvency, and rendered an adequate short-term credit service in their communities had they not been deeply engaged in savings banking. … [W]ithdrawals by time and savings depositors accounted for about two-thirds of the total shrinkage of deposits and required a much greater liquidation of assets than could be accomplished with the kinds of assets which had been acquired.… The breakdown of Wisconsin banking facilities appears to have resulted chiefly from the banks' savings and investment operations" (Garlock, 61–2). He goes on to note that one of the main difficulties was that banks did not impose the contractual restrictions on time and savings deposits, but allowed clients to "withdraw funds virtually at will" (ibid., 63).

9. Among the abuses were "the formation and operation of pools, the giving of preferential treatment to certain individuals in the distribution of securities, manipulation of markets for the benefit of special groups, the furnishing of inadequate information regarding new securities issues, handling reorganization in a manner to control the future financing of the reorganized company, and the use by commercial banks of their investment affiliates for the disposal of slow or poor loans" (Valentine, 403).

Proposals for the reform of securities markets were introduced immediately after the Crash and dealt with presentation of corporate financial statements, margin loans, and short sales of stock. However, the seeming recovery of the stock market in 1930–31 diverted attention, and it was only the publicity given the role of short sales in the collapse of the market after Sterling went off gold in September 1931 that created pressure for investigation and regulation of the market. A government committee originally set up by the Hoover administration after the Crash was resurrected in 1933 and produced the now famous Pecora hearings publicizing the extent of misdealings in the financial markets during the early months of the Roosevelt administration.

The public outrage generated by these hearings provided propitious conditions for Roosevelt's campaign promise to introduce legislation to separate deposit-taking banks from those financing and underwriting corporate investments. The June 1933 Banking Act also provided for the introduction of government-guaranteed deposit insurance through a federal agency.[10] The legislation also included provisions to prevent the type of fraudulent activity that had occurred during the boom of the 1920s by imposing controls on both bank assets and liabilities. By prohibiting payment of interest on demand deposits and granting the Federal Reserve power to set maximum rates on time and savings deposits in member banks (this power was activated through Federal Reserve Board Regulation Q), it limited the ability of commercial banks to attract deposits via price competition.[11] It also placed limits on the types of asset that could be held by forbidding underwriting, ownership, secondary trading, and brokerage of corporate securities by commercial banks or their affiliates. The Securities Act of 1933 and the Securities and Exchange Act of 1934 strictly regulated the affairs of banks that continued to act as underwriters and brokers, as well as placing regulations on the companies issuing liabilities; it also provided for government control and surveillance of the markets in which these securities were traded. The primary goal was to prevent a repetition of the full-scale destruction of asset values by making

10. It is widely believed that deposit insurance saved the banking system, but the deposit insurance provisions of the act did not come into operation until the beginning of 1934. It was the role of the RFC to put the banks in a position to become Class A stockholders of the Federal Deposit Insurance Corporation, the minimum condition for national banks to operate and for state banks to become Fed members.

11. It has been suggested that the preclusion of payment of interest on deposits was to offset the 0.5 percent insurance premium on the banks' deposit liabilities. The magnitudes do not seem comparable. However, the large money-center banks considered deposit insurance a subsidy to small unit banks, and they stood to lose substantial earnings from correspondent deposits as a result of the imposition of the 10 percent liquidity requirement on asset concentration. Thus, there were costs to the large banks other than the insurance premiums, and eliminating deposit interest was a way of reducing the presumed advantage derived by small banks.

fraudulent dealing impossible, while the Banking Act meant to seal off the bank payments system from the impact of changes in asset prices in organized financial markets.

Additional legislative measures went beyond the campaign promises to introduce "separation" of commercial and investment banking and regulation of securities markets. These measures were aimed primarily at the broader goal of income and employment stabilization and had the impact of producing what is now called the "segmentation" of the U.S. financial market. Many were simple extensions of existing legislation. The Federal Home Loan Bank Act of 1932 created the equivalent of a Federal Reserve System for savings and loan banks. The Home Owners' Loan Act[12] of 1933 provided savings deposits with insurance similar to that in the Banking Act, and made provision for federally chartered savings and loan banks. Controls over savings and time-deposit interest rates introduced in the Banking Act were not extended to the savings and loan system (this was only done in the Interest Rate Control Act of 1966).

In 1916 the Federal Farm Loan Act had created a system of Federal Land Banks, patterned on the Federal Reserve System. In 1923 a system of Federal Intermediate Credit Banks was also created. These systems had to be integrated into the new legislation, which was done in the Farm Credit Act of 1933 by placing all agricultural credit agencies under the control of the Farm Credit Administration. However, subsequent agricultural agencies, such as the Commodity Credit Corporation, the Rural Electrification Association, and the Farmers' Home Administration were given independent agency status. The legislation provided for both controls and subsidies on agricultural lending as well as government guarantees for the liabilities of the agencies. The National Housing Act of 1934 established the Federal Housing Administration (FHA), which provided federal insurance to private mortgage lenders. In 1938 the Federal National Mortgage Association was created to provide a secondary market for mortgages insured through the FHA.

The result of New Deal legislation thus was not only the separation of deposit-taking and commercial lending from capital market instability but the creation of a series of specialized federal institutions to oversee particular segments of the financial markets, such as rural electrification, lending against farm land, farm equipment, residential housing, etc., all with federal guarantees that often included insured deposits, and controls or even subsidies on lending rates.

12. Part of the responsibility of the Home Owners' Loan Corporation was to take over direct lending to savings and loan banks by the RFC as well as the assumption of bank lending to thrifts during the recapitalization of the banks.

Although it seems not to have been fully recognized at the time, this system of subsidies and controls was erected on the basis of the prohibition of interest on commercial bank demand deposits, on the powers granted to the Federal Reserve to set maximum rates on all other commercial bank deposits, and on the presumption that the economic environment would permanently resemble the 1930s, with low and stable interest rates in conditions of stable or falling prices.

The financial system that emerged from this flurry of legislation was similar to that which had existed before the 1920s boom and crisis, but it was different in one crucial respect. In the pre-1920s financial structure the bulk of private individuals' savings had been held in mutual savings banks, in credit unions, and as savings deposits in commercial banks on a long-term basis to finance long-term assets such as residential housing. Banking was split into state and national charter commercial banks, i.e., banks offering commercial services to companies, such as deposits, discounting and foreign exchange, and large, private, nonchartered and largely unregulated investment banks offering underwriting, merger and acquisition services and advice. Most state-chartered banks and national banks were forbidden from offering "nonbanking" services.[13] National trust banks were required to operate as separate units to manage fiduciary business.[14] This natural separation of banking activities broke down only during the 1920s as the expansion of foreign lending and the stock market boom attracted commercial banks into investment banking activities, primarily through creation of securities affiliates that fell outside of the then-existing regulatory structure.

The major problems of the banking system during the 1930s crisis might then be simplified as: (a) concentration of lending in agriculture by the state-chartered country banks; (b) the combination of commercial banking and saving deposits in country banks; (c) the combination of commercial and investment banking in the large city commercial banks. The various farm credit laws acted to relieve the first of these problems; the Federal Home Loan and associated acts the second; and the Glass-Steagall

13. First National Bank of New York formed the First Securities Company in 1908, and National City Bank created the National City Company in 1911 as "independent" securities investment firms in order to circumvent these regulations. By 1922 sixty-two commercial banks were involved in securities investment.

14. State-chartered trusts usually could offer both commercial and investment banking services and could act as trustees. National charter trust banks were equivalent to national banks, except that they could not issue notes. They had lower reserve requirements and fewer restrictions on their investments; they generally paid higher interest rates and thus could compete with commercial banks, which were obliged to refer trust business to them. The leeway allowed on investment portfolio could lead to fraud, as in the case of the Knickerbocker Trust, the cause of the 1907 Panic.

Banking Reform Act, along with the Securities Act, the Securities and Exchange Act, followed by extension of regulation to Bank Holding companies, the third.[15]

Thus, the New Deal legislation can be considered an attempt to return to the *status quo ante* by repealing the liberty granted to national banks in 1927 and by making state banks subject to the same provisions. But, the Banking Act and the Home Owners' Loan Act would have been sufficient to achieve this goal. The problems listed under (a) and (b) could have been resolved by relaxing branching restrictions to allow increased portfolio diversification for banks operating in agricultural areas. Instead they were solved by isolating agriculture credit and household lending in segmented markets under government guidance and protection.

Thus, the legislative program extended the use of federal agencies and institutions and the subsidies and insurance guarantees for particular segments of the population to provide the income supports that were thought necessary for the policy of reflation. It is these aspects of the New Deal financial market regulations that came under most specific pressure when economic conditions changed and sustained economic expansion made the control of inflation, rather than falling prices, the major economic problem.

Although the 1933 Banking Act provided for the Federal Reserve Open Market Committee, it was left to the Banking Act of 1935 to redirect the operation of the Federal Reserve toward a policy of general economic stabilization. Along with the creation of agencies such as the National Recovery Administration, Civilian Conservation Corps, and the Agricultural Adjustment Administration (which also had responsibility for the gold parity) to provide direct price and income maintenance, these measures were meant to provide the basis for the reflation of prices to pre-Crash levels.

Thus, while New Deal financial legislation dealt with all the main problems, it left two crucial areas of difficulty untouched. The first, as already mentioned, was the predominance of unit banking. The new banking legislation only partially extended branching privileges (to anywhere in a state where state banks already had the right to branch) granted by Pepper-McFadden. Second, while specific legislation defined the role of the various segments of the system, little attention appears to have been given to the role of investment banks in particular, and to the question of the long-term financing of industry in general. Indeed, it

15. With the exception of fraud, all of these problems result from liabilities too liquid relative to assets. The intent of the legislation may also have been to segment the system into sections that matched the maturities of assets and liabilities, and where this was not possible to use side-payments, such as deposit insurance, to make liquid liabilities less volatile.

seems that the provisions of the 1933 act were extended to private, unincorporated and thus unchartered investment banks at the last minute before the floor vote.

As a result, the U.S. found itself with a system in which there were few alternatives to financing industry save via retentions or securities issues in the capital market. The investment banks that survived the slump did not have sufficient fundraising power to replace the unregulated commercial banks. The major burden of lending to industry thus passed to the RFC which acted much like a government-owned investment bank, engaging in activities ranging from refinancing the railroads and the real estate markets to the creation of the export-import bank and the operations in the gold market to set the new gold value of the dollar. During the preparation for war, these investment banking activities increased markedly (cf. Jones 1951).

The Postwar Slump That Never Came

This separated and segmented New Deal financial system, which had been designed to operate in conditions of stable or falling asset and goods prices and low and stable interest rates, had to deal with far different conditions in the 1950s. Throughout the war the Federal Reserve and the Treasury had followed Keynesian policies and kept interest rates, as well as wages and prices, under strict control. Long-term interest rates were pegged at 2.5 percent, and short rates were around 0.375 percent, so that the proscription of interest rates on demand deposits was about what market forces would have determined. However, after the Fed-Treasury Accord of 1951, the experience of Korean war expansion, and the fear of inflation replaced the expectation that the depression would resume, the Fed once again started to use monetary policy to restrain the economy. As banks' large business clients found that their borrowing costs were rising, while their deposits were restricted to zero interest, they soon found it advantageous to hold excess funds in short-term treasury bills. Since savings and loans were exempt from interest rate limitations, they started to drain smaller retail clients from the banks as market rates rose towards those Regulation Q limits. Commercial banks thus found themselves losing their large business depositors; restricted by branching constraints, they found it difficult to enlarge their retail client base. The banks responded by introducing the negotiable certificate of deposit (CD) in the early 1960s.[16] This was the first break in the system of interest rate controls and subsidies upon which

16. These certificates, originated by the (then) First National City Bank of New York, became such an important source of bank funding that they were eventually exempted from Regulation Q during the Penn Central crisis in 1970.

market segmentation and control had been based. As commercial banks continued to produce products that circumvented interest rate regulations, they began to attract funds that had been held in protected segments of the financial market. Some, such as savings and loan banks, defended themselves by raising rates above those offered by banks.

A turning point was reached in 1965 when the Fed decided to use restrictive monetary policy to stop the inflation associated with the budget deficit created by the build-up in the Vietnam conflict. Market interest rates were pushed above the Regulation Q limits, and banks suffered a massive outflow of funds as business clients failed to renew their CDs and a "credit crunch" developed in which many banks faced a liquidity crisis, if not insolvency. It was during this period that many U.S. banks first entered the Euromarkets to obtain funds they could not raise at home by borrowing dollar deposits held outside the U.S. It was in the aftermath of the "credit crunch" that interest rate controls were extended to thrifts (with an additional competitive advantage of a quarter-point margin above the rates set for commercial banks).

This meant that in 1969–70, when the Fed next used tight monetary policy, the savings and loans, as well as the commercial banks, lost deposits. Since the thrifts could no longer respond by increasing interest rates, they tried to make their deposits more competitive by making them more liquid. Since they could not offer demand deposits, they countered the drain of funds by introducing the "negotiable order of withdrawal" (1972), which provided for payment on demand via the automatic transfer of funds held in a savings deposit account. Soon other nonbank financial institutions joined the competition for deposit funds via money market deposit accounts (1973), and finally brokerage house cash management accounts (1980), all of which effectively bypassed the interest rate controls on deposit accounts. As the frequency of tight monetary policy to combat inflation increased, so did the risk of deposit loss by banks and thrifts. This increased use of tight money simply served to increase pressure on the interest rate regulations that had created protected segments of the market and the possibility of subsidizing interest rates for particular sectors, such as housing and agriculture.

As savings and loan banks, brokerages, and investment banks started to encroach on the provision of payments activities normally reserved to commercial banks, large corporations were being offered the possibility of raising the short-term funds they had traditionally borrowed from commercial banks through short-term commercial paper underwritten by large brokers and investment banks. The commercial banks' loss of traditional short-term commercial borrowers to investment banks pushed them to seek elimination of "separation" between commercial and investment banking, which prevented commercial banks from expanding the services they could offer to their commercial and industrial borrowers.

These innovations in transactions accounts and other liabilities, all of which were used by the banks and other nonbank financial institutions to increase competition for funds via interest rates, were the basis for calls for a "level playing field" for all financial institutions—commercial banks, saving and loans, brokerage houses, investment banks, and insurance companies—since nearly all of them were subject to different regulators and regulations with respect to their ability to compete for funds and supply financial services.

The Elimination of the Savings and Loan Protected Segment

The initial response to the new conditions in U.S. financial markets resulting from increased competition and financial innovation was the passage of the Depository Institutions Deregulation and Monetary Control Act of 1980, which eliminated Federal Reserve Regulation Q interest rate controls on time and savings deposits[17] for both banks and thrifts by 1986; provided for more uniform regulations to apply to all financial institutions acting as deposit takers; preempted state usury laws on certain types of lending, such as mortgages (removing a major obstacle to the introduction of adjustable interest rate lending); and raised Federal Deposit Insurance Corporation coverage from deposits of $40,000 to deposits up to *and including* $100,000 for all deposit-taking institutions.

This latter change was particularly important since, at that time, interest rate controls applied to deposits up to, *but not including* $100,000 (the exemption from Regulation Q applied to CDs in excess of that figure), so that deposits of this amount were now exempt from interest rate controls yet guaranteed by federal deposit insurance. This is one of the major causes of the "so-called" moral hazard problem of the deposit insurance system (but which has nothing to do with the insurance aspects *per se*) and of the high interest rates offered by troubled savings and loan banks which thus could invest in high-risk, high-return assets and still offer a guarantee on investors' funds as long as each deposit was no greater than $100,000. As a result, a brokered market grew up in which investment banks distributed these deposits to the highest bidder without any reference to the financial conditions of the S&L's that purchased them. The same investment banks could then sell the same S&Ls high-yield, high-risk junk bonds or derivative products funded with the brokered deposits, producing another set of commissions and fees (cf. Mayer 1990).

17. However, it left intact however the first paragraph of Section 11(b) of the 1933 Banking Act prohibiting the payment of interest on demand deposits.

Most importantly, these regulatory changes occurred at precisely the time the Fed had decided to institute permanent changes in its operating procedures in order to target monetary aggregates to eliminate inflation. In 1979 the Fed stopped using monetary policy to influence interest rates and started to control monetary aggregates via an unborrowed reserves target. This change in policy, together with the decision to abolish Regulation Q for commercial banks, marked the end of the protected market segment the New Deal legislation had provided for thrift institutions.

The change in policy led to sharp increases in both the level and the volatility of interest rates. But the new freedom to compete for demand liabilities offered by the "level playing field" did little to resolve the difficulties faced by savings and loans banks which were saddled with long-term mortgage loans at low interest rates, but forced to compete for funds with commercial banks and money market funds at competitive market rates. Even if they succeeded in defending their deposit base, the difference between the competitive short-term rates they paid to depositors and the far lower rates they were earning on outstanding mortgages meant that most savings and loan banks were soon technically insolvent.

To meet the continuing difficulties of savings and loan banks, the 1982 Depository Institutions Act eased the acquisition of failing banking units by banks located in other states. The effect was a *de facto* abrogation of state laws prohibiting interstate branching. In addition, the new legislation provided emergency government financing for failing savings and loan banks in the form of "net worth certificates" that effectively made bad loans "good" by giving them guaranteed discounting. It also allowed savings banks to engage in certain types of commercial lending and acquire securities which had previously been prohibited. This allowed them access to investment opportunities with higher interest rates to compensate the low rates on their outstanding mortgage lending. It was this provision that led to investments in commercial real estate and "junk" bonds that has been the cause of most of the fraud and continued losses of these banks. Thus, although most savings banks were already insolvent as a result of the introduction of the "level playing field" for deposits in the early 1980s, savings and loan banks were allowed to continue to operate, raising funds through the use of $100,000 deposits that were exempt from interest rate control, but government insured, and investing in assets with the highest, and thus riskiest, returns available in order to keep themselves from declaring insolvency. The result was the eventual bankruptcy of the Federal Savings and Loan insurance fund and the entire apparatus that had been erected after the Depression to create a segmented market for subsidized long-term mortgage lending for house purchase.

By the late 1980s the U.S. banking system was moving toward a system in which virtually all financial institutions were competing for the same deposit funds, in which restrictions between commercial and investment banks were slowly disappearing, and in which the need to bail out failed savings banks had led to free regional, if not national, branching. But the process of deregulation has had a varied impact on the different financial institutions that comprise the U.S. money and capital markets. The savings and loans banks, as a specific market segment created to match long-term mortgage lending to long-term saving, no longer exist. The commercial banks have fared little better, for in their attempt to expand externally and internally they have accumulated assets of increasingly high risk, by first lending to developing countries in the 1970s and then financing domestic corporate restructuring through merger and acquisition loans (HLTs: highly leveraged transactions), and by extending loans to commercial real estate speculators (remember the Bank of the United States in 1930).[18] On the other hand, the investment banks, which escaped detailed regulation in the New Deal legislation but have been subject of continuous surveillance by the SEC, have been more successful in adapting to the changing conditions.

The Rise of the Institutional Investor

Only during the 1960s did U.S. capital markets start to recover from the disruption caused by the New Deal regulations, the Depression, and war. The memory of the Crash and the associated fraud meant that household savings were directed primarily to savings deposits and insurance premiums. Direct purchase of shares by individuals increased 75 percent between 1959 and 1965 and another 50 percent by 1970. This demand for equities was reinforced by the stimulus provided by the Social Security Act of 1935 on private company pension plans, which continued to increase throughout the Depression years to provide a supplement to the minimum public benefits for the higher-paid workers. These private plans were further advantaged during the war, because benefits were exempt from controls on wages. Growth in nonwage benefits accelerated with postwar prosperity, and total assets held in all pension funds nearly trebled between 1960 and 1970, while the percentage of pension fund assets held in equities nearly doubled. In addition, ERISA (Employee Retirement Income Security Act) legislation, introduced in 1974 to protect pension rights, led to an increase in equity investment by pension

18. Further, commercial banks the Federal Reserve considers to be sufficiently capitalized have been granted permission to operate "securities" affiliates (again, recall Bank of the United States) through which they may do limited underwriting.

funds. Since that time the indirect ownership of equities via "institutions," broadly defined as pension funds, investment companies (open- and closed-end mutual funds and investment trusts), insurance companies, and trusts and endowments, has continued to displace direct ownership of equity by individuals. As a result investment decisions have come to be dominated by professional portfolio managers who manage and trade much larger blocks of stock than a single individual investor.

TABLE 6.4 Annual Flows of Funds into U.S. Equities, 1950–91 ($ billion)

	1950–59	1960–69	1970–79	1980–89	1990	1991*
Private pension funds	8.3	32.2	76.5	2.3	-6.9	6.9
State and local pensions	0.3	5.7	30.9	173.4	16.8	10.3
Life insurance companies	1.4	6.6	21.2	23.6	2.8	4.3
Other insurance companies	1.6	3.7	15.0	8.0	-2.4	-0.6
Mutual funds	5.1	13.0	-14.2	63.3	15.3	35.9
Foreign sector	1.6	4.2	21.5	60.4	-14.5	11.5
Households	4.4	-42.3	-72.8	-793.8	-54.1	-24.4
Net issues	22.9	16.5	80.5	-462.3	-50.0	44.1

*Annual rate based on first 3 quarters
Source: *New York Stock Exchange Fact Book*, 1992, 31.

TABLE 6.5 Institutional Investors—Total Assets and Percentage of Equity Markets, 1981 and 1986 ($ billion)

	1981 Assets	% Equity	$ Equity	% Market Value of Equities	1986 Assets	% Equity	$ Equity	% Market Value of Equities
Pension funds	891.2	32.0	285.2	18.5	1,814.5	35.0	635.1	20.4
Private trustee	486.7	45.9	223.4	14.5	938.5	48.6	456.1	14.i
Private insured	180.3	8.7	15.7	1.0	406.5	9.1	37.0	1.2
State/local gov.	224.2	21.0	47.1	3.1	469.5	32.0	150.2	4.8
Investment coms.	248.3				727.0			
Open-end mutual	241.3	16.0	38.6	2.5	716.5	28.0	200.6	6.5
Closed trusts	6.9	na			10.7	na		
Insurance coms.	559.0	15.6	87.6	5.7	992.0	14.2	141.0	4.5
Life	347.0	9.1	47.7	3.1	618.0	9.7	60.0	1.9
Prop./casualty	212.0	18.7	39.6	2.6	374.0	21.7	81.0	2.6
Banks trusts								
Nonpension	344.9	45.0	155.2	10.1	614.6	47.7	293	9.4
Foundations/ endowments	56.0	50.0	28.0	1.8	114.9	50.0	57.5	1.8
All institutions	2,099.4	–	594.3	38.5	4,263.0	–	1,327.2	42.7

Source: Brancato in Sametz, 1991, 20.

The first expression of the changes in securities markets brought about by the increasing importance of institutional investors was an increase in the use of "private placements" of securities involving the direct sale of corporate liabilities to an institutional investor. From 1946 to 1961 the proportion of all publicly offered corporate securities sold privately ranged from a low of 27 percent to a high of 44 percent. For fixed interest debt issues, the figures are 38 percent and 58 percent. More important than the fact that they were sold outside the organized securities markets, private placements effectively eliminated the need for the services of investment banks. If investment bankers are not required for the public sale of shares via initial distribution in the market, why should they be required for secondary market purchases for institutions' portfolio readjustments? Institutions thus started to bypass brokers, moving their business outside the market.

Since there is a steady flow of funds to the institutions in the form of premiums and contributions, the size of the portfolio under management tends to increase as a function of time. As a result the average size of trades that the portfolio managers have to execute also increases. The increasing proportion of institutional funds managed professionally in the market created a structural change in the way stocks were traded. The impact started to be felt as early as the 1950s, and in 1956 the New York Stock Exchange expanded the exemptions for trading large blocks of stock. The trading in large blocks had two effects on investment banks and brokerage houses. First, it often required brokers to "position" stock, that is, to hold it temporarily on their books until final buyers were located, which required the firm to commit its own capital. Second, it increased earnings dramatically, since the brokerage commission charged per share was the same on a 100,000–share trade as on a 100–share trade.

The Recovery of Investment Banking

At this time both commercial banks, under Regulation Q, and brokers, under fixed commissions, were operating in regulated markets that prevented price competition for clients. The same types of controls on competition that led banks to offer toasters and televisions led brokers to offer "soft dollar" commissions and "give ups" in lieu of commission discounts to the managers of large institutional portfolios. In the 1960s this was primarily free research services and the transfer of commissions to other broker-dealers who provided services to the institution.

The advent of large blocks also had an impact on the "specialist" firms operating on the New York Stock Exchange, because it made it more difficult for them to provide stability and depth without large capital. Thus, just as the corporate clients were becoming too large for commercial bankers, portfolio managers representing pension funds and insurance companies were becoming too large for the investment banks and brokerage houses and specialist firms which comprised the long-term capital markets. While there were regulations limiting the growth of banks, there were none limiting the growth of Wall Street brokerage firms.[19] When the big institutional traders, with the aid of pressure from the SEC,[20] eventually succeeded in substituting competitive commissions for fixed commission soft-dollar kickbacks in May 1976, change became inevitable. Thus, the rise of large-scale institutional trading made larger capital bases necessary for traders to be able to deal in larger blocks by taking position, and the loss of fixed commissions made it necessary to seek business and capital from sources other than partners' capital, initiating a process of concentration and expansion into new fields of activity.

Until the mid-1970s investment banking employed what may be called the "one bank model," with a single bank acting exclusively for a corporation, without any active attempt by other banks to compete for the business. As the required capitalization of the investment banks increased, the need to generate income to remunerate that capital increased. This process was further accelerated in March 1982 when the SEC introduced Rule 415, allowing "self-registration" for securities issues, and producing outright bidding among investment banks for "bought deals," in which the winning bank is required to complete the issue of securities in a period of time too short to allow syndication, thus requiring the winning bidder to position the entire deal, and run the risk of market volatility, until it is sold into the market.[21] Merger and acquisition (M&A) activity, which appeared first in the 1960s, was thus an attractive alternative line of business because it required little capital and provided higher returns than straightforward underwriting. It was only in the 1980s that

19. Except the partnership form imposed by the NYSE. This was broken in 1969 when Donaldson, Lufkin Jenrette announced its intention to incorporate and the regulation was lifted in 1970. Until that time publicly held corporations had been banned, primarily to prevent institutional investors from becoming exchange members and trading for themselves. Although the London Exchange allowed limited liability beginning in June 1969, the restrictions were much stricter: directors were held personally liable for the debts of the company and nonexchange members were prohibited from holding more than 10 percent of the share capital.

20. The SEC's case against fixed commissions was based on the use of give-ups creating potential conflicts of interest between fund managers and brokers, rather than an absence of competitive pricing. Cf. Seligman.

21. The first deal under Rule 415 was an ATT shelf registration of ten million shares won in competitive bid by ATT's former main bank, Morgan Stanley, who offered to underwrite two million shares without a syndicate at a guaranteed price of $55.40, 15 cents above market, which meant taking a position of over $100 million in ATT stock (cf. Brooks, 114ff).

an important part of arranging an M&A deal became the ability of the investment bank to finance it with its own capital.

Thus change in the structure of share ownership and the size of corporations led to changes in capital market financial institutions that produced concentration and increased capitalization and an increased need for earnings, shifting emphasis to proprietary trading and deal-making. While this trend may have decreased the competitive efficiency of the markets themselves, it increased competition among investment banks and brokers and led to the decline of the traditional "main bank" model of financing, which relies on unique "relationships." It also meant that all Wall Street firms had to become highly capitalized "investment bankers" in order to survive.

Furthermore, it led these institutions to seek to encroach on the domain of the commercial banks. The securities industry, which had always resisted repeal of the separation of commercial and investment banking, recognized that with its newly capitalized structures it was better placed to offer many of the services that legislation reserved to commercial banks and thrifts. This competition extended not only to deposit-taking via the cash management account but also to providing short-term finance to corporations by, for example, underwriting commercial paper offerings. It is this process that has introduced market competition into the U.S. system and also gone a long way toward recreating investment banks, operating on an international level, similar to those which populated Wall Street in the 1920s. There is little to distinguish commercial banks such as Morgan Guaranty, Bankers Trust, or Nations Bank from investment banker-brokers such as Merrill Lynch or the newly formed Primerica group—both of which resemble the large investment banks and national commercial banks operating in securities trading that were legislated out of existence by the Glass Banking Act—except that they are much more highly capitalized and the majority of their revenues now come not from underwriting but from proprietary trading supported by their own capital.

On the other hand, it is the commercial banks—which attempted to compensate for their losses in commercial and industrial lending by increasing investments in alternative types of assets, such as commercial real estate (e.g., Donald Trump, Olympia and York), highly leveraged transactions, and bridge loans for M&A and management buyouts—that now have difficulty meeting capital requirements and have had to initiate a process of concentration similar to that in the investment banking sphere in the 1970s.

Conclusions

The decisions made by the Federal Reserve, first in the Fed-Treasury Accord of 1951 and then to change operating procedures to control of monetary aggregates, represent the elevation of inflation fighting to its number one policy goal. This decision created conflicts with the existing financial structure, which had been designed by New Deal legislation to fight falling prices and support government policies to stabilize incomes and employment. The first victim of this conflict was the system of protected, segmented financial markets in which interest rate controls and subsidies were used to direct financial flows and support incomes, in particular in finance for agriculture and residential housing. Misguided legislative attempts in the early 1980s to preserve the position of the saving and loan banks in this system simply made their downfall more costly and risked producing a financial crisis similar to that of the 1930s.

The shift in the goal of monetary policy also increased pressure on commercial banks to support repeal of the separation of commercial and investment banking. However, the commercial banks' attempts to grow within the existing regulations have substantially weakened their capital positions; and, paradoxically, after extreme weakness from the 1930s to the 1960s, it was the investment banks that emerged as the dominant institutions. Their growth was accompanied by the accumulation of capital and investment decision-making in a small group of portfolio managers operating on behalf of the large institutions who produced a change in the structure of share ownership as well as substantial changes in the organization of capital markets.

This leads to the conclusion that, even if the provisions of the 1933 Banking Act separating commercial and investment banking were to be repealed today, it is unlikely that more than a very few of the large money center commercial banks and larger regional bank groups would be either willing or able to enter the underwriting or brokerage businesses. Most commercial banks are too small and not sufficiently capitalized to benefit from repeal. Neither would this move the U.S. system nearer to a German system of universal banking that allows investment in corporate equity for control purposes. Again, this is because current capital positions are not sufficient to allow most commercial banks to take strategic investment positions.[22] Rather, it is the large institutional investors who have taken on this role, even though their ownership of firm equity is insufficient to give them a control position. In contrast to the 1920s, most of the activities that would be opened to commercial banks by abolishing segmented markets now require substantial capital resources, which is precisely what most banks currently lack because of limits on their expansion due to unit banking restrictions and dual regulation.

22. The lack of ownership of corporations has not, however, prevented control by means of interlocking directorships, as Munkirs documents.

Evolution of the Financial System in Germany: The Importance of Bank Supervision

The German experience of the 1930s bears a number of striking similarities to that of the U.S. In both countries bank holidays were declared in order to prevent collapse of the financial system, and both governments created official committees to investigate the operations of "mixed" banks. However, in contrast to the U.S. government, the German government decided not to introduce legislation to impose separation of banking and finance. The German system thus is often presented as the opposite of the U.S. system. The German government did, however, introduce new controls over banks' balance sheets that produced the same general results as formal separation of financial institutions operating in banking and finance. This different approach provides a large part of the explanation of the different response of the German system after the change of policy regime in the 1970s.

The German banking system often is called a "mixed" or "universal" banking system. It is generally characterized as being dominated by a small number of very large banks that are major direct owners, and indirect managers, of German industrial firms. Yet German banks today own for their own account only about 15 percent of the outstanding equity of German companies with shares quoted on a public stock exchange. Nonetheless, German banks were more directly involved in the financing of industry than in the U.S. in the period before the Great Crash.

Originally involved in financing the building of the railways, the forerunners of today's "universal" banks, the Kreditbanken, were forced to branch out into industrial financing when Bismarck started his projected nationalization of the railway system in the 1870s. While U.S. investment banks were small, unlimited partnerships, the Kreditbanken were joint-stock banks that pooled investor funds for investment. Because these banks looked upon their investment in industrial companies as short- or medium-term development financing that would be recovered when the companies were sold to the public in the stock market, they were actively involved in the operation of the stock market, unlike British merchant bankers or U.S. private investment bankers. The banks did, however, offer deposit and underwriting services to the firms they had launched, and this *Kontokorrentverbindung* became the basis of their influence over industrial companies; it was quite normal for a bank to fund a firm's capital investment through short-term lending via their *Kontokorrent*, and then to provide the long-term funding via a new issue of shares. By the beginning of the century, large Kreditbanken were operating in all areas of finance.

However, these large, multipurpose banks were not the only financial institutions. The system included note-issuing banks; joint-stock Hypothek banks that issued *Pfandbriefe* against mortgages on real property; Landesbanken, operated by the provincial governments to provide local authority finances and provided giro services; Sparkassen, created by municipal authorities to encourage savings; and cooperative credit societies grouped together in the Zentralgenossenschafteskasse. Both the Notenbanken and the Hypothekenbanken were subject to special regulations because they issued special credit instruments, which the Kreditbanken theoretically did not.

The Weakness of German Banks in the 1920s

Despite difficulties similar to those in the U.S., this multiform structure was to emerge virtually untouched from the experience of the 1930s. The hyperinflation of the 1920s had sharply reduced bank capital.[23] Banks extended additional credits to support firms they had launched and whose shares they were holding. Thus, they were doubly exposed as business conditions worsened in the Depression, and the value of the shares they held started to decline. Although the banks' shares had resisted the general market trend, they too fell after the election of September 1930, which brought the Nazi party to national prominence. Many banks attempted to stabilize prices by repurchasing their own shares, further reducing their capital and making them more vulnerable to debt deflation. Throughout this period the collapse of the banks was delayed only by flows of foreign lending to German banks.

Thus, despite the inherent weakness of the large German banks, the financial crisis did not start with a bank default, or a run on the banks, but rather with a run by foreign investors caused by uncertainty over Germany's ability to meet its foreign commitments. As in the U.K., the situation was aggravated by the fact that U.S. funds had ceased to flow to Germany with the run-up in the U.S. stock market in 1928; the subsequent increase in U.S. interest rates started to draw foreign funds back to the U.S. The election results, speculation surrounding the condition of the Austrian Creditanstalt, which most foreign investors thought was a German bank, and the financial difficulties of Nordstern, an insurance company, and Karstadt, a department store chain, all increased foreign nervousness. Foreign investors started to seek refuge with the announcement of the

23. The ratio of equity to liabilities fell from 1:3.5 to 1:13 between 1913 and 1929. In 1929 foreign funds accounted for about 75 percent of borrowed funds, 97 percent of which were short-term funds, up from 86 percent in 1913. 40 percent of short-term funds were foreign. Foreign liabilities were almost nine times capital. Cf. Born, 245.

Creditanstalt collapse[24] and the failure of one of the largest clients of the Danat bank in June.

In addition to the large Kreditbanken, by July the savings banks and their central Giro-institutions were also reporting difficulty as a result of their lending to local and state governments, of which they were formally a part, and which had also borrowed heavily abroad. At this point the Reichsbank's gold and foreign reserves had fallen to less than a third of the large banks' outstanding foreign short-term indebtedness. It was clear that rapid intervention was necessary, and the government sought to reduce pressure on reserves by seeking delays and reductions in foreign interest and debt payments. This was the origin of the Hoover reparations moratorium and international loan negotiations, which eventually failed, leading to the imposition of foreign exchange controls at the beginning of August.

Bank Nationalization

The withdrawal of foreign funds finally exposed the insolvency of the banks. As in the U.S., the first reaction was a "bankers" rescue, which failed because of Deutsche Bank's refusal to participate. As a result the Danat bank folded on 13 July. This produced a full-scale domestic run on deposits held in the large banks, and the German government was forced to intervene to restore order, declaring two bank holidays during July 1931. Payments of deposits were restored only in August 1931.

The first formal regulatory change, introduced in October, was to make the savings banks legally independent of local authorities by making them public law institutions and forbidding them to lend to local governments (a restriction lifted in 1939).

As in the U.S., existing institutions were initially used to provide government recapitalization of the banks. The government was already represented in the financial sector by the Reichskreditgesellschaft, an institution originally founded to dispose of the government-owned "war companies" remaining after World War I; instead it grouped them into a holding company and joined them as a government-owned bank in 1924. In the same year the Reichsbank formed the Golddiskontobank as a vehicle to undertake the trade, money market, and foreign exchange business, which was forbidden under the Dawes Plan. In addition to the

24. Born, chapter IX, suggests that French hesitancy to approve the Hoover moratorium on reparation payments in June and the political conditions (including no renegotiation of the Dawes reparations settlement) that France placed on providing a loan to Germany in July were crucial factors in undermining international confidence in Germany's ability to meet its foreign commitments.

government-owned Prussian *Landschaften*, a number of special purpose banks had been formed in the 1920s. The government also created the Akzept- und Garantiebank with a joint-stock capital of 200 million marks to provide the third signatures for bank acceptances required in order for them to be discounted by the Reichsbank. This provided temporary liquidity to the system, but a more fundamental solution was achieved only by using the Golddiskontobank to reorganize the private banks by taking direct equity ownership and extending emergency credit by methods that foreshadowed those of the Reconstruction Finance Corporation under Jesse Jones, as well, by using other rescue operations.[25] The result was that the German government subsequently came to own, directly or indirectly (through government-owned financial institutions), 91 percent of Dresdner Bank, 70 percent of Commerzbank, and 35 percent of Deutsche Bank. The government takeover and refinancing of the banking system was achieved by the end of 1932.

As in the U.S., a government investigation of the crisis was organized; its declared intention was the abolition of universal banking. Since the German system faced similar problems caused by banks operating in both commercial and investment banking, it seemed that the separation of banking and finance was the logical solution. But the report of the Banking Enquiry, produced under the new National Socialist government in 1933, concluded that there were no structural defects in the banking system and that its precise organizational form was best left to private initiative, subject only to general overall supervision by the government.

The German Banking Law (Kreditwesengesetz) of 1934 thus left the structure of the financial system unchanged. However it attempted to produce the equivalent of separation of banking and finance by making what were considered to be safe banking practices legally binding. It also introduced closer bank surveillance through the creation of a single supervisory agency with jurisdiction over every type of financial institution, except insurance companies.

The 1934 act, which provides the basis for current bank legislation, included the creation of the Bank Supervisory Board, which was to license banks and which required monthly reporting, already made provisions for broad maturity matching of bank assets and liabilities and reporting of large loans. In effect, the law proposed the separation of

25. Part of which were the famous large public works programs that were initiated in 1932 as pump-priming for private sector investments. When the latter failed to appear, military spending provided a ready substitute. The financing of these expenditures was undertaken by some thirty-one public "central credit institutes," which may be classified as providing financing for: public works and utilities, personal credit, agricultural credit, manufacturing credit, rural settlement and cultivation of the soil, and urban credit and building (cf. Poole). They very much resemble a decentralized RFC.

banking and finance within a single large organization by making it match its short-term obligations with liquid assets.[26]

The nationalization of the banks was quickly reversed with the initiation of a plan by a group of private banks to repurchase the shares in the big Berlin "universal" banks, a process that was completed in 1936. Thus, despite similar direct intervention to stem the crisis, in contrast with the U.S. system, the German financial system emerged from the 1930s crisis without any major legislation to produce structural changes but with the potential for substantial indirect governmental controls, which were exercised by the National Socialist government.

While the basic structure of the German financial system emerged from the financial crises of the 1930s virtually intact, its modern development has been conditioned by the application of the 1934 Banking Law and by a series of decisions made during postwar reconstruction that have been of crucial importance in changing its overall structure. As the result of the close relationship between banks and manufacturing industry during the prewar period, there were proposals to recast the German system along American lines (e.g., the Dodge Plan of 1945) in order to reduce the potential for abuse of power by the large banks and industrial cartels, which were thought to have brought the National Socialists to power and provided support for German military pretension. The large Kreditbanken were thus broken up as independent regional institutions in April 1948. The liberalization of controls on branch organizations introduced in the Large Banks laws of 1952 and 1956, and finally the elimination of any controls on bank location in 1958, allowed Deutsche, Dresdner, and Commerz banks to regroup their regional units into national institutions within a decade. The intended introduction of "unit" banking with regional branching was thus scrapped as soon as Germany was free from direct Allied control.

The 1934 Banking Law was replaced in 1962 and amended in 1976, 1985, 1990, and most recently in 1993 to incorporate the financial directives of the European Community's Single Market Act. The new law preserved the basic regulation of German banks via a Federal Banking Supervisory Office; it also reconfirmed the position of the 1933 Banking Enquiry that direct control over the structure of financial institutions and restriction of entry into markets was unnecessary, although it did reconfirm the power of the central bank to set maximum interest rates. This power was relinquished in the 1960s.

The Banking Law attempts to deal with the inherent instability associated with the universal banks' practice of taking long-term investments

26. With its weak centralization of bank supervision, and the defense of unit banking by state interests, this path was not open to the U.S., even if it had been considered.

financed by liquid deposits which had been exposed in the 1931 crisis, via an indirect approach set out in the "Principles Concerning the Capital Resources and Liquidity of Credit Institutions".[27] These "Principles" exemplify the differences in the basic philosophies behind German and U.S. prudential bank regulation and investor protection.

In contrast with New Deal banking and securities market legislation, the German system does not restrict financial institutions' field of activity in any way, nor attempt to regulate specific financial product markets; rather it imposes limits on the mismatching of the maturity structure of balance sheets and sets minimum capital ratios and maximum risk exposures. Within this structure, financial institutions are free to enter any activity and to act in any market without restriction or other direct government regulation.

The Postwar Reconstruction

Other factors have been of more lasting importance in determining the postwar structure of the system. The 1948 currency reform had the effect of wiping financial balance sheets clean, in both the public and private sectors. As a result, until 1974 the German government remained a net creditor to the private sector, while families were slowly rebuilding their wealth positions through small savings deposits.[28] In 1950–51 the savings ratio of private households was barely over 2 percent. Most firms had been able to write down or eliminate their liabilities and build "hidden reserves" by overvaluing assets (which could be translated into large depreciation allowances against taxable earnings) when they drew up their new balance sheets in marks after the currency reform. Banks resumed operations with liabilities composed of DM deposits held by the public (originally to be converted from Reichsmarks at a rate of 10:1, but the ultimate rate of conversion was in fact at 106.5:1). To replace their worthless loans to firms, special compensation credits, *Ausgleichsforderungen*, paying 3 percent annual interest were issued to the banks by the government to allow the banks to establish balance sheets with income earning assets.

New capital investments by firms were financed primarily from retained earnings and secondarily by bank financing as the banks' deposits

27. *Bundesbank Annual Report*, 1962, pp. 97ff. These principles simply made formal the "Guiding Ratios for Credits" that had been applied previously by the Bank Deutscher Länder and then the Bundesbank.

28. This helps to explain why open market operations have never played a very important part in monetary policy—the Bundesbank had to be given powers to force the government to create financial assets it could trade in the markets.

increased, rather than through borrowing in capital markets.[29] Thus the war had the effect of virtually wiping out the existing supply of both government and private securities, eliminating both the primary and secondary capital markets, and centralizing the financing of new investment through retained earnings and short-term bank borrowing.

This situation required a sharp change in the operation of the banks. First, it meant that the banks could not finance and underwrite the issue of share capital in the formation of new firms because there was no market in which to float shares once the companies were launched. It also meant that the *Kontokorrent* mechanism in which the banks lent short-term to finance fixed investments that would then be floated in the securities markets, could no longer be utilized, since there was no active capital market to absorb the new issues.

Banks thus continued to build up demand and time deposits, and short-term loans to firms were rolled over into medium and long-term loans (the ratio of short to medium-long lending was split about evenly in 1954), since they could not be repaid by floating securities in capital markets. Only 5 percent of bank assets were securities. The banks thus were faced with an ever-increasing maturity mismatch. The financing of reconstruction by the large banks in the absence of capital markets thus created potential instability, because short-term deposits could be withdrawn at any time, creating a liquidity crisis, and any change in the yield differential, as might be caused by inflation, could cause insolvency if short rates had to be increased rapidly to retain deposits. The former was a threat for the smaller banks, but for the larger banks with extensive branches the threat of a deposit drain was small. The inflation threat applied to all banks. There was an additional threat due to a drain of deposits abroad, but this possibility was eliminated by the existence of controls on both trade and financial flows. This may also explain the government's concern to maintain balance of payments surpluses, which were achieved very rapidly during reconstruction and have been defended tenaciously in the face of international criticism long after.[30]

29. In addition, the tax credits used to encourage investment provided an interesting impact on financial markets. Tax rebates were given on the entire value of interest-free loans made by individuals or corporations for the financing of housing, shipbuilding, and reconstruction investment by third parties. The loans were taxable when called. See Wallich, 160ff. Wallich estimates that up to 20 percent of investment in the housing sector was financed in this way. Accelerated depreciation allowed the firms to keep most of their profits, as assets were overvalued in the preparation of the new DM balance sheets.

30. The modern criticism of the universal bank system as being inherently unstable stems primarily from its operation in the postwar period without the benefit of an active capital market. It must be presumed that the detailed attention to balance sheet ratios in the supervisory system, as well as the attention to inflation, were largely determined by this anomalous

TABLE 6.6 **Securities Issues in Germany, 1951–1953 (percentage of total value of issues)**

	Mortgage Bonds	Muni Bonds	Special Credit Institutions	Industrial Bonds	Govt Bonds	Shares
1951	51.3	17.4	0.2	6.8	6.2	18.0
1952	38.8	9.9	1.2	8.1	25.9	16.0
1953	32.7	13.5	8.1	12.3	15.3	8.4

Elaboration of Wallich, 186.

There were a number of policy initiatives to revive the capital market. These included a tax deduction for savings invested (by direct purchase from the issuer and held for at least three years) in federal, state, and some municipal bonds and for low-cost housing mortgage bonds. The deduction did not, however, apply to private sector issues. The first Capital Market Law of 1952 applied a flat 30 percent withholding tax on interest paid on private bonds, confirmed the tax-exempt status of mortgage bonds and freed them from all interest controls. After the law was passed these bonds sold in the market at 5 percent, implying that the rates paid on taxable, private issues would have had to be in the range of 7.5 to 8 percent to be competitive. With interest expensed from corporate tax, which averaged around 70 percent (except for income paid as dividends, which was subject to a special 30 percent rate), equity finance was, by comparison, extremely expensive, especially since it did not enjoy the tax deduction on income saved and since dividends were taxed fully at the personal tax rate. It does not take much more than this to explain why equity issues played such a minor role in the reconstruction of the German financial system. As can be seen in Table 6.6, in the immediate postwar period the use of equity actually declined as a proportion of capital market issues.

The Capital Market Law did, however, give a boost to the issue of fixed interest securities, although the buyers were initially predominantly in the public sector; the banks eventually became the principal purchasers and issuers.

Note that while the government provided 15 percent of the issues, it bought approximately twice that amount. Much of this difference was represented by the purchase of mortgage bonds for low-cost housing, a large proportion of which financed contracts with private sector construction companies, an indirect form of government support. The purchases

structure of bank balance sheets during the reconstruction period. This link between bank balance sheets, financial stability, and the importance of the control of inflation is stressed in Nardozzi.

TABLE 6.7 Buyers of Securities in Germany, 1953 (percentage of value of securities issued in 1953)

Banks	34.6
Nonfinancial business	10.2
Individuals	10.2
Insurance companies	8.6
Government and other	36.3

Elaboration of Wallich, 187.

TABLE 6.8 Household Asset Portfolios in Germany, 1950–1980—Proportions of Households' Total Monetary Assets (percent)

	Deposits	Thrifts	Insurance	Bonds	Shares	Other
1950	50.00	2.27	16.82	1.36	25.00	4.09
1960	61.56	7.34	17.70	4.94	7.89	7.18
1970	59.07	8.66	16.69	10.24	4.99	6.37
1980	52.99	6.91	17.03	13.21	2.13	9.33

Source: Tables accompanying the article "The capital finance account of the Federal Republic of Germany for (various years)," published annually in the May issue of the *Monthly Report of the Deutsche Bundesbank.*

by the banks can be explained by the tax advantages, for their profits were taxed at the same rates as industry. Thus the most profitable strategy for a bank in this period would have been to lend to the point at which net interest margins covered operating and funding costs and then to place the rest of its funds in tax-free securities earning 5 percent, which would constitute tax-free profits. Firms also borrowed extensively at market rates of 8 percent in order to purchase tax-free securities paying 5 percent. The insurance companies, which paid only minimal tax, placed hardly any of their funds in securities. Thus the tax structure discriminated against equity and did little to satisfy its goal of increasing the sales of bonds to households.

The postwar reconstruction of the economy thus was intermediated by the banking system as households' savings were held in savings deposits; firms financed their expansion in excess of the growth of internal funds by increasing their medium and long-term borrowing from the banks. Table 6.8 shows the relative stability of bank deposits in household portfolios, along with the slow increase in fixed interest assets and the decline in their holdings of equity.

On the side of the firms' balance sheets (cf. Table 6.9) there is a slow decline in the ratio of self-financing to gross investment, offset by the rise in borrowing from domestic banks, along with a slow shift in the composition of deposits from domestic to foreign banks.

TABLE 6.9 Share of Selected Assets and Liabilities in German Firms' Portfolios, 1950–1990 (percent)

	Self-Financing Ratio	Share of Financial Assets: Domestic Deposits	Share of Financial Assets: Foreign Deposits	Share of Liabilities: Domestic Borrowing	Share of Liabilities: Foreign Borrowing
1950	71.14	61.88	17.33	48.37	11.16
1960	63.86	50.45	21.68	57.74	7.64
1970	65.79	49.34	25.28	59.74	11.13
1980	67.37	48.71	28.36	60.46	10.18
1989	64.50	40.26	35.85	60.11	9.62
1990	65.00				

Source: Tables accompanying the article "The capital finance account of the Federal Republic of Germany for (various years)," published annually in the May issue of the *Monthly Report of the Deutsche Bundesbank.*

TABLE 6.10 Pattern of Share Ownership in Germany, 1960–1990 (percentages of total)

Sector:	1960	1970	1980	1990
Households	27	28	19	17
Enterprises	44	41	45	42
Public Authorities	14	11	10	5
Banks	6	7	9	10
Nonresidents	6	8	11	14
Insurance Companies	3	4	6	12

Source: "The significance of shares as financing instruments," *Monthly Report of the Deutsche Bundesbank*, October 1991.

Thus, in the 1980s share financing took on a more important role in providing finance for the small proportion of German firms listed on public exchanges. At the same time, internal funds also increased and the "own funds ratio" calculated as the ratio of equity capital and reserves to the balance sheet total for public limited companies recovered to 30 percent, 4 percentage points above the low reached in 1981. The decline of the importance of internal funds stabilized in the 1980s, as corporate earnings improved dramatically. This increase in earnings also was accompanied by a three-fold increase in share prices and an increase in the issue of corporate equity. Yet this did not represent a sharp increase in the role of capital markets in allocating financial resources.[31] At the end of 1990

31. This increase, however, is not directly visible in company accounts. The average issue prices for new shares in the 1980s was four times par value. In company accounts the increase in equity is given in terms of par value, while the excess of issue over par is entered as reserves.

TABLE 6.11 German Families' Capital Market Assets, 1980–1989 (shares of annual flows)

	1980	1985	1986	1987	1988	1989
Bonds	20.9	17.7	7.3	18.9	11.0	37.0
Shares	-0.7	2.8	1.1	3.5	3.0	-4.1
Insurance	21.2	31.1	30.8	29.6	30.8	29.6
Pensions	11.3	9.0	9.6	8.1	6.8	7.8

Source: Tables accompanying the article "The capital finance account of the Federal Republic of Germany for (various years)," published annually in the May issue of the *Monthly Report of the Deutsche Bundesbank.*

the number of listed companies was only 42 higher than in 1980, reaching 501, or only one-fifth of the total of public limited companies (in 1912 there were 5,400 AG).[32] There are more than 400,000 private limited companies and 100,000 partnerships in the German economy.[33]

New issues were particularly high in 1990 in the boom that preceded unification. This increase in new issues in the 1980s does not seem to have changed the distribution of share ownership dramatically (see Table 6.10), although the banks became more active in the process of underwriting the new issues.

In the face of the almost complete failure of recovery of the equity market (and the failure of the recovery of the underwriting activities of the big universal banks) in the postwar period, the dilemma caused for the banks by the absence of an active equity market was resolved by increasing long-term bank funding via the bond market, primarily by selling to other banks and institutions (see Tables 6.12 and 6.13), with households remaining largely absent from securities markets, as may be seen from Table 6.11.

32. Clapham, 399. The German system is not directly comparable due to the wider range of legal organizations available to companies. In 1896, German Stock Exchange Law tightened registration requirements for new listings and information requirements for new issues. To prevent foreigners from profiting from the information and to limit the possibility for speculation, a new "company with limited liability" (Gesellschaft mit beschränkter Haftung–GmbH) was created to allow limited liability to a small group of "private" shareholders without the information requirements of exchange listing. In the ten years following their introduction the number of GmbH firms increased 970 percent. The continued predominance of this form of organization in the reconstruction period helps explain the small number of official exchange listings of unrestricted joint stock companies (Aktiengesellschaft–AG) as well as the resistance to complying with U.S. Securities Exchange Commission requirements to obtain NYSE listing.

33. In 1987 a secondary market (the *geregelter Markt*) was instituted with less stringent listing requirements for smaller firms. At the end of 1990 more than 150 enterprises were listed. Also in 1987 "Risk Capital Investment Companies," limited liability public companies that raised capital in the stock market to lend to small- and medium-size companies unable to meet listing requirements were introduced. In 1993 fewer than twenty such companies were listed.

TABLE 6.12 German Bank Investments in Selected Financial Assets (percent of total value outstanding)

	1980	1985	1986	1987	1988	1989
Shares	9.03	10.17	10.72	9.87	11.82	14.42
Bonds	38.89	38.20	38.77	39.85	37.68	36.49
Bank	42.75	44.20	46.03	47.86	45.01	43.53
Industrial	11.26	12.07	11.71	12.52	12.95	14.21
Public	29.86	25.92	25.71	27.16	25.95	25.18

Source: *Monthly Report of the Deutsche Bundesbank*, various years.

TABLE 6.13 German Bank Investments in Selected Financial Assets (percent of annual flows)

	1980	1985	1986	1987	1988	1989
Bank loans						
Short-term	29.60	9.00	-3.70	-12.30	-17.90	17.76
Long-term	24.50	37.10	59.40	45.50	36.70	43.33
Institutions	4.50	5.90	-0.60	3.60	1.40	0.10
Bonds	0.90	6.20	11.00	14.30	3.50	-0.00
Shares	6.10	7.70	20.00	11.70	5.60	7.22
Money market						
Liabilities	1.00	–	–	-0.60	-0.50	-0.21
Other*	33.40	34.10	13.90	37.80	35.60	30.55

*Includes households claims under company pension commitments.
Source: See Table 6.11.

German Institutional Investors

It is for this reason that the role played by "institutional" investors in the German financial system differs from the U.S. system. The composition of institutional investors is also different, limited primiarily to banks, insurance companies, and the government. These "institutions" tend to hold a much lower proportion of their portfolios in equity investments than their U.S. counterparts, unless nonfinancial firms are included in the definition of institutions; firms own roughly the same proportion of outstanding equity issues as institutional investors in the U.S. (cf. Table 6.10 and Table 6.15), while the dominance of medium and long-term bank finance has led to a dominant position for bond financing in the total system.

In addition to the influence of postwar developments and tax factors (almost all of which were eliminated in the 1977 tax reform, which abolished double taxation of dividends), the difference in the role of institutional investors is due to the fact that Germany has had a full and comprehensive statutory pension scheme since the time of Bismarck. In contrast with the U.S., there was less pressure to provide supplementary schemes, and private and company pension schemes have only recently been instituted as the benefits of the government scheme have been scaled back. As yet they have had little influence on capital markets. Since these private and company pension schemes are administered either through insurance companies, which have a high preference for liquid assets and bond investments, or by the companies themselves, they do little to offset the low proportion of equity in household portfolios. The company-administered funds are usually managed "in house" by the company and may be used to provide internal financing either directly or indirectly via lending to the firm,[34] so that they are, in a sense, a substitute for the issue of equity in capital markets.

In the 1970s and 1980s the increase in importance of *publikum* and *spezial* investment funds has provided a new institutional investor in the German financial system. The public funds are open to the general public, while special funds are created specially for particular customers or tailored to customers needs (e.g., a company pension fund). Originally set up to encourage private household investment in equity by reducing the transactions costs of diversification and providing easier access to securities markets, the funds have invested primarily in bonds. They have served as the primary vehicle for households' diversification of their portfolios into foreign assets, but still primarily in bonds rather than shares. They also have come to be used by insurance companies and private and company pension funds, which explains the large proportion of domestic securities in the special fund portfolios. The Act on Investment Companies (KAGG) permitted investments of up to 30 percent in unlisted securities and created open-end funds, which have invested primarily in real estate. A number of German banks offer funds through their Luxembourg subsidiaries in order to avoid national regulations, which are much stricter than the minimum EEC legislation that applies there.

The anomalous nature of the share of equity in German investment portfolios may be seen from a comparison of share ownership patterns with the U.S., U.K., and Japan in Table 6.15

Conclusions

Unlike the U.S. system, the German financial system was exposed to hyperinflation at the beginning of the 1920s. This was a major factor in the deterioration of the capital base of German banks, producing their reliance on short-term borrowing from foreign sources. The underlying

34. Deutsche Bundesbank (1984a, 36) estimates that in 1982 15.5 percent of own and borrowed long-term capital available to companies came from companies' pension funds.

TABLE 6.14 Composition of *Publikum* and *Spezial* Investment Fund Portfolios in Germany, 1970–88 (percent of total)

	Domestic Bonds	Foreign Bonds	Domestic Shares	Foreign Shares	Cash reserves and Other
Publikum					
1970	33.7	6.4	39.6	11.9	8.3
1980	56.1	7.4	25.0	3.4	8.2
1985	35.5	35.8	18.4	4.6	5.7
1988	31.0	48.3	9.6	3.7	7.4
Spezial					
1970	39.8	9.2	23.4	14.9	12.6
1980	57.1	3.4	24.8	6.3	8.4
1985	48.2	7.2	31.9	8.5	4.2
1988	54.2	7.3	23.5	6.3	8.8

Source: *Monthly Report of the Deutsche Bundesbank*, October 1988.

TABLE 6.15 Common Stock Ownership—U.S., U.K., Japan, and Germany, 1970 and 1988 (percent of total outstanding shares)

1970	**U.S.**	**U.K.**	**Japan**	**Germany**
Financial institutions	15.8	40.9	34.9	12
Commercial banks	0	0	11.6	8
Insurance companies	2.9	12.2	15.4	
Pension funds	8.2	9	7.8	4
Other financial	4.7	19.7		
Nonfinancial business	9.1	5.4	23.1	35
Individuals	72.2	47.4	39.9	29
Foreigners	2.9	6.6	3.2	15
Other	0	2.6	0.2	10
1988				
Financial institutions	30.4	52.5	51.2	15
Commercial banks	0	4.3	18.9	9
Insurance companies	4.6	19.6		
Pension funds	20.1	48.5	12.7	6
Other financial	5.7			
Nonfinancial business	14.1	10.1	24.9	40
Individuals	50.2	28	22.4	16
Foreigners	5.4	6.5	4.0	21
Other	0	2.5	0.7	8

Source: Prowse, in Sametz 1991, 50.

weakness of the banks was finally exposed by the end of the 1920s as international capital flows ceased and global depression and domestic deflation put downward pressure on bank asset prices. It was aggravated by the banks' attempt to support share prices, further weakening the banks' capital base and creating further imbalance in their balance sheets. The banking crisis that developed in the summer of 1931 as a result of the fall in asset prices thus took place against the background of a rather different historical experience than that in the U.S. The response of the regulatory authorities and the central bank to the 1930s crisis was also different from that in the U.S.

The outstanding characteristic of the German financial structure is not that the banks, being exempt from U.S.-style separation and segmentation, are free to hold shares (the holdings are small, indeed smaller than in Japan, where there are restrictions similar to those in the U.S.) but the large proportion of shares held by businesses themselves. The other side of this coin is the predominance of bonds in bank portfolios and the portfolios of other institutions, such as pension funds and insurance companies, compared with holdings in other countries.

Thus, both the dominance of banks in the stock market and their dominance in bond trading have not produced the same push for changes that institutional investors exercised in both the U.S. and the U.K. Nor has the use of monetary policy, when necessary to control inflation, produced conflicts with existing financial regulations. Nor has it produced a disappearance of credit supports to particular borrowing segments, as the various special purpose banks have continued to operate alongside the universal banks, whose relative position has not changed radically in the postwar period.

Given the stability in the structure of the financial system, it is likely to be the foreign banks that apply pressure for change. The real problem thus remains the issue and sale of equity by firms and the purchase of equity by households and institutions. This is the real "innovation" and "deregulation" that is still to occur in the German market. It is clear that there will no "Mayday," as in the U.S., or "Big Bang," as in the U.K., providing rapid deregulation of financial markets in Germany. This is because many of the financial innovations in other markets have been due to attempts to escape interest rate control, market segmentation, or separation of banking and finance, none of which is present in the German financial system. Yet, while the innovations may not be actively sought by German banks or institutional investors, foreign banks still may seek the possibility of offering them to German investors, forcing German banks to respond. This process may be seen in the opening of the DTB (Germany's futures market, Deutsche Terminbörse) to trade futures and options. It has also brought an expansion of German banks, through takeovers of foreign nonbank financial institutions, into foreign financial markets. Further changes may be expected if Germany is to compete successfully with Paris and London for the role of Finanzplatz Europa.

The United Kingdom: Natural Separation and Segmentation

The U.K. presents a very different experience from both the U.S. and Germany in that the Stock Market Crash and the Slump of the 1930s had little impact on financial markets. This is primarily because the U.K. experienced neither the roaring 1920s and the stock market boom which occurred in the U.S., nor the German hyperinflation. There was no financial crisis or bank holiday.

Although the depression in the U.K. started earlier, due largely to the policies surrounding the return to gold, and hit some sections of the economy, such as the Lancashire textile industry, extremely hard, there were no widespread bank failures. Only one of the clearing house member banks, William Deacon's, experienced difficulty, and this was resolved by the Bank of England secretly arranging its sale (with a guarantee of bad assets) to the Royal Bank of Scotland, forming the basis for what, with the addition of Glyn Mills, became the "sixth" big clearing bank in the form of the "Three Banks Group" (cf. Sayers 1976, I: 253–9). As in Germany and the U.S., a government institution was formed to aid in bank rescues. The Bankers Industrial Development Company, partially capitalized by the Bank of England, administered securities the Bank had acquired through support actions such as the Deacon's rescue. Unlike similar institutions in the U.S. and Germany, it never became a vehicle for public ownership of failed banks.

The British financial system had conserved a natural separation similar to that of the U.S. system in the pre-1920s period. The clearing banks undertook deposit business and made short-term business loans; merchant banks engaged in financing of internal and international trade and finance, including underwriting; discount houses dealt in the wholesale short-term money market; and savings banks and building societies took small savers' deposits to finance house purchase. As in Germany, there was little change in structure as a result of the Depression.

The "big five" clearing banks, who through a process of concentration dominated the deposit business, did not make long-term industrial loans, nor did merchant banks or discount houses do so. The clearing banks did accept "debt for equity" swaps in the case of borrowers in difficulty during the Depression, and investments held by the five clearing banks more than doubled between 1930 and 1933 (cf. Dacey, 99, diagram 8). Yet their cash ratios remained above 10 percent (11 percent in 1930, reaching levels of 12 percent in 1934), and their solvency was never in doubt. It was, rather, the merchant banks that experienced difficulty, particularly when England was forced off gold in 1931, as most of their business was financed by foreign borrowing. When the German crisis broke in the summer of 1931, foreign lenders to German sought to build liquidity by drawing down their sterling balances, and the merchant bankers were the first to be caught up in the outflow. Thus they were already weakened when the sterling crisis hit in September.

In Britain there was no equivalent to the German Kreditbanken and the U.S. private investment banks; long-term investment capital, in addition to retained earnings, was supplied primarily by investment trust companies that sold participation to small savers for diversified investment in industrial ventures. The first investment trusts, which date from the 1860s, were involved primarily in foreign investment. They became very popular in the 1920s, and more than 700 were founded between 1924 and 1929. They were particularly active in the U.S. market (cf. Born, 233). By the 1930s roughly half of their investments were in domestic issues.

The fact that these trusts started primarily in foreign investments raises another distinctive characteristic of British financial markets. British companies tended to remain within the control of family owners; neither the business "trusts," followed by the holding companies, in the U.S., or formal cartels and state enterprises that characterized the concentration of Germany industry and produced large joint-stock companies with dispersed ownership under the control of professional managers, occurred in Britain. The stock market thus was not required for expansion, either internal or through concentration; and short-term bank lending, along with retained earnings and closely held local share issues, were sufficient.

Thus the impact of the stock exchange collapse was diffused over the holders of shares in investment trusts, and the impact of the Depression on the value of bank assets remained within the limits of bank reserves. Without any major threat to the payments system, there was little pressure for financial market reform similar to that which emerged in the U.S.

On the other hand, the depression of output and employment was of much longer duration in the U.K. and it is perhaps not surprising that Britain took the lead in the use of financial markets to support government stabilization and welfare policies. Such measures had, of course, been blocked by the decision to return to gold, but after 1931 cheap money became the official policy to produce recovery.

As in the U.S., the major fear in the postwar period was the resumption of depression and falling prices, and low interest rates were part of postwar policy. The Labour Party document "Full Employment and Financial Policy," published in April 1944, proposed budgetary policy "to maintain purchasing power in the context of continued wartime controls, a nationalization of the Bank of England and a National Investment Board. Price controls would prevent inflation in the immediate postwar period, exchange control would prevent capital outflows and, along with large-scale government borrowing from the banks as in wartime, would prevent interest rates from rising and thus allow the government cheaply to finance its expenditure, both in the transitional period and in the longer term when unemployment was feared" (Howson, 46).

The most visible result of the policy was Dalton's decision to reduce rates to 0.5 percent for short rates and on gilts to 2.5 percent from 3 percent, below the rates experienced during the war. This could only be achieved at the cost of a massive expansion in clearing bank deposits and an increase in the ratio of deposits to national income from around 45 percent in the 1940s to an historical peak of 60–65 percent in 1947 (cf. Paish, 27–8) in a period when goods were still being rationed. Part of this increase was due to government borrowing, which continued at near wartime levels (cf. Dow, 226), and the ratio dropped when Exchequer borrowing was reduced. In any event, the convertibility crisis of August 1947, which broke out when the funds from the American loan ran out, effectively put an end to the policy as the government bond market collapsed and long rates went above 3 percent.

Postwar Developments in Financial Structure

As the primary postwar problem turned out to be inflation and the foreign balance, rather than deflation, the needs were more for credit restriction; and although the 1946 Act nationalizing the Bank of England gave the Treasury power to instruct the Bank to control bank lending, this power was never exercised. Instead, the government relied on "requests" to the clearing banks to restrict lending. In 1958 this was replaced by a scheme of "special deposits" that would not qualify as liquid assets in the calculation of the normal ratios between liquid assets and total deposits. The scheme was not very effective, since the banks could always fund lending by selling other assets.

Throughout this period, controls on borrowing in capital markets that had been initiated during the war were maintained in order to facilitate government funding of the outstanding debt and manage the debt. Although this system could have been used as part of a policy of sectoral credit control, it was not, and was only mildly effective. More important was a Treasury decision in 1955 requiring local authorities to fund in the open market, rather than through government loans. This created an outlet for short-term investments by businesses at interest rates higher than those available from the clearing banks, and brokers soon developed in what became the "parallel" money market.[35] Hire purchase companies soon also joined the market as borrowers, drawing deposits from the banks. At this time bank deposit and lending rates were set by the clearing banks' cartel, and they considered competing by raising deposit rates but decided against it. Since their lending was restricted, they had no use for additional funds, and they preferred avoiding having to pay higher rates for their existing funding. It was the creation of this wholesale market that opened the way for rapid expansion of the "secondary" banks that funded their property, stock exchange, and mergers and acquisition business with private deposits, but primarily with wholesale deposits.[36] Restraints on lending introduced with the 1967 devaluation further benefitted the wholesale or secondary banks and led to a decline in the proportion of deposits of the large clearing banks.

In 1967 a report of the Prices and Incomes Board challenged bank charges and the role of the clearing banks cartel in setting interest rates. It recommended abandoning credit ceilings and introducing reserve ratios and competition to determine interest rates. Many of these proposals eventually were introduced in the Competition and Credit Control Act in 1971. The removal of credit restraints and the emphasis on the use of prices to allocate credit freed the banks to compete for funds and increase lending in areas that had been monopolized by the secondary banks. This also created difficulty for another segment of the market that had indirectly benefitted from controls on bank lending: the building societies.

Building societies were traditionally separate from the financial system; as mutual societies operated for the benefit of their members, they were not regulated as companies or as banks. Neither have they benefitted from any special government treatment or protection. They had been able to compete for funding by offering higher deposit rates than banks. They were able to do this because, in contrast with U.S. thrifts, their lending has always been at adjustable rates. Although dominant in retail housing finance, their deposits represented only around 10 percent of retail savings

35. Parallel with respect to the discount market traditionally used by the banks. The distinction of the parallel market was that the deposits were unsecured. Certificates of deposit make their appearance in the U.K. market at this time.

36. This formed the basis for the secondary banking crisis, which in many respects resembles the problems of the securities affiliates in the U.S. These nonbank banks, were unregulated and unsupervised, but counted many traditional financial institutions as investors. Cf. Reid.

until the 1960s. However, they expanded rapidly, reaching 50 percent of savings and 75 percent of the mortgage market by 1980. Thus, rather than any direct regulatory advantage, building societies were at first protected by the neglect of natural competitors in the commercial and savings banks as well as by the use of balance sheet restrictions to regulate monetary policy, which meant that clearing banks had no interest in competing for building society deposits since they could not expand their lending. Although the secondary banks were active in property lending, this was usually commercial property development or second and third mortgage lending.

However, these conditions changed when lending restrictions were lifted and the interest rate cartel abolished with the introduction of the Competition and Credit Control Act. Banks moved rapidly into mortgage lending in 1973, using higher rates to attract funds. This drove the building societies to increase rates; the government had to intervene to subsidize building society rates, and the Bank of England placed a 9.5 percent maximum on the interest rates banks could pay on deposits below £10,000 in order to keep mortgage rates from rising above 10 percent. At the same time restraints, in the form of supplementary deposits, were reintroduced, which made it unattractive to compete with building society deposits in order to expand any kind of lending, much less mortgage lending.

The removal of exchange controls in 1979 made lending restraints in the form of the supplementary deposit "corset" on bank lending untenable, as domestic British banks now had recourse to borrowing in the "local" Eurodollar markets. When the corset was removed in 1980 this indirect defense of the mortgage market disappeared, and in 1981 the banks again expanded into mortgage lending, causing building societies to consider more seriously the possibility of providing traditional banking services. In 1986 the Building Societies Act broadened the types of services that could be offered, by setting limits of 90 percent on mortgage loans to owner-occupiers of residential property, with 5 percent of the remaining 10 percent in unsecured loans. This created the possibility of offering a full range of transactions accounts.[37] The act thus opened the way for what will probably be the eventual transformation of most building societies into regular commercial banks; a number have already done so.

The Role of Institutional Investors

As a result of the early development of building and friendly societies for holding small private savings, as a result of highly favorable tax treatment

37. For example, it became possible to offer overdraft lending on deposit accounts, and thus to offer cheque-guarantee cards, which had been impossible while restricted 100 percent to mortgage lending.

for savings through insurance policies, and as a result of investment trusts to pool small investors' securities holdings, individual investors have played an even smaller direct role in British securities markets than in U.S. markets. By the early 1980s individuals held only some 28 percent and institutions about 55 percent of British equity. Contractual savings for life premiums and pension funds have accounted for about half of total savings from the 1960s, and in 1987 reached 97 percent (Thomas, 159–60). Institutional business thus has come to dominate the market, as may be seen from Table 6.15.

Although the organization of the London Stock Exchange is far different from that of the New York Stock Exchange, institutional investors have had a similar effect. The London Stock Exchange was organized around brokers, who acted as agents for the general public, and around jobbers, who bought and sold shares as principals for their own account by quoting bid and ask prices for trades with other jobbers and with brokers. The practice was for brokers to complete their clients' orders through jobbers on the exchange, although, until the turn of the century when the growth of trading on the provincial exchanges led jobbers to do business directly with provincial brokers, there were no exchange regulations restricting jobbers from dealing with nonmembers. London brokers retaliated by quoting prices on London stocks to provincial correspondents. By 1904 ten London broking and jobbing firms, working with dedicated telephone lines, had come to dominate market making in London and stock trading on the provincial exchanges. It was clear that there was little need for any of this trading to take place through other brokers or through jobbers on the London Stock Exchange itself.

This threat led to calls from the other members for regulation to forbid brokers from making prices and trading with nonmembers and to prevent jobbers from dealing with nonmembers. Thus single capacity trading, in which brokers could act only as agents for their public orders through exchange member jobbers, and in which jobbers were prevented from dealing with anyone outside the exchange, was introduced in February 1909 in order to protect the London Stock Exchange from the potential threat of a national market system organized off the exchange floor.

In response, jobbers started to do their arbitrage trading on the provincial exchanges through cooperative London brokers who passed their orders without charging commission to the provincial brokers. This attempt to circumvent the intention of restricting trading to London soon produced a response from the exchange in the form of a regulation imposing minimum commission rates on exchange trading (cf. Michie).

In the end, institutional trading provided a more potent threat to the dominance of the London exchange. Brokers acting on behalf of institutional investors found that they frequently were receiving buy and sell orders for the same stocks that they could match or "marry" without the necessity of making two separate trades with a jobber, thereby avoiding the "jobbers turn" (the bid-ask spread of the jobber's quoted price). They soon found it worth their while to try to solicit institutional clients in the hope of finding a counter-party for a large order without having to go through a jobber, passing part of the cost saving on to the client. In principle, the exchange regulations discussed above required such business to be "put through" a jobber, a process by which the broker presents both sides of the transaction to the jobber, who makes a "closer" (i.e., a smaller spread between) buying and selling price than his normal "turn," since it is a simultaneous transaction carrying no price risk. Already in 1939 the increase in "put through" business was attracting complaints from jobbers, and in 1959 a formal rule [90(1)] required brokers to expose all business to a jobber to be priced before seeking counter-parties and to allow him to take as much of the order as he desired at that price.

The consequences for the earnings of jobbers is visible in the decline in the number of firms and jobbers operating in the market. In 1918 jobbers outnumbered brokers, while in 1920 there were 475 broker firms with 1,513 partners and 411 jobbing firms with 1,465 partners; by 1938 brokers had risen to 2,491, against only 1,433 jobbers. In 1971 the number of partners in broker firms was 1,773, while there were only 268 jobbers in 27 firms; by 1981 there were 17 jobbers and 234 brokers firms.

Finally, the increase in the size of bargains of large institutional investors made it increasingly difficult for jobbers to keep sufficient inventories of shares on their books, because they were limited to partnership form, which virtually prevented the accumulation of equity. Instead of buying and selling from their own book, jobbers increasingly were acting as brokers among themselves in order to minimize inventory. This, along with the decline in the number of jobbers making markets in particular stocks, often to just a single firm, meant that competitive bidding among jobbers was compromised. As a result large bargains could be arranged more cheaply outside the market by brokers and then "put through," because the spreads required by jobbers for unmatched trades were too high. It was only in 1969 that the exchange permitted limited liability companies, and even then there were restrictions, such as a limit of 10 percent on the ownership of shares by outside owners.

While the growth of institutional trading first seemed to benefit brokers at the expense of jobbers, brokers also were threatened as institutions discovered that they could trade securities directly among themselves. This was encouraged by the creation of Ariel, a computer system that was set up by the merchant banks to disseminate information on prices and trades but that the institutional fund managers soon discovered could also be used to exchange shares among themselves without going through the exchange. Initially brokers were able to supplement their lost trading commissions by selling research to institutional investors, but most institutions soon developed their own research departments as they increased their own trading.

Despite the fact that the same pressures that were present in the U.S. were present in the U.K., the British "Big Bang" was not the result of direct pressure from the large institutions or from the securities market regulator (the U.K. had no equivalent to the SEC), but rather from the largest borrower in the securities markets, the British government. The Thatcher government had been elected on a policy of cutting government involvement in the economy, reducing government expenditure, and eliminating restrictive practices. One of the first targets was the trade unions; then came solicitors and conveyancing. As a result of the experience with the program of privatization, it had become clear that the government was paying large commissions and fees to brokers of government securities for what appeared to be a rather simple process of placing securities with large institutional investors. The London Stock Market not only fixed prices and commissions, it also restricted entry. Increasing competition in the securities market would serve two government objectives by eliminating restrictive practices and reducing the costs of floating and servicing its own debt.

As a result of the removal of capital account restrictions on foreign exchange transactions in 1979, there was a good deal of international rebalancing of portfolios. When the Bank of England discovered that hardly any of this business had been done through members of the London Stock Exchange or through U.K. estate agents, it became concerned that the policy of financial liberalization then occurring in U.S. markets would eliminate what had been the one star performer of the British economy, the financial services sector. Thus the Bank joined the government in arguing in favor of changes in the market, but the Bank also was motivated primarily by the need to assure markets for the sale of government debt. Internationalization of the London Stock Exchange would prevent the loss of a major export earner and provide better access for foreign buyers (cf. Hamilton, 130).

The government thus instructed the Office of Fair Trading to challenge the regulations of the London Stock Exchange in the courts under the Restrictive Practices Act. Once before, in 1894, the threat of public scrutiny had produced a rapid closing of ranks between the exchange's owner-managers and the member-users committee. On that occasion a group of members and proprietors had proposed a change in the Constitution to abolish the dual members-proprietors system of control, but the plan was dropped when it was realized that incorporation would open the exchange to public inspection and control by the Board of Trade (Morgan, 145). In 1983 the same feelings prevailed, and the president of the exchange, under pressure from the Secretary of State for Trade and Industry, agreed both to implement free entry to membership and to abolish commissions by 1986 in exchange for suspension of the legal proceedings and the associated public scrutiny.

The Stock Exchange Council was also motivated by its fear that if some change was not implemented, the majority of trading would move off the exchange floor and the exchange would become redundant. This had already started to occur with institutional "put through" trading, and two U.S. investment banks had begun making markets off the exchange in selected shares. However, the removal of fixed commissions meant a substantial decline in brokers' incomes. In order to offset this possibility, brokers requested the ability to complement their earnings by dealing for their own account, to which the few remaining jobber firms, without the compensation of being able to deal as agents with the general public, objected. As a result, single capacity trading was eliminated. This also meant no net advantage for either group, as competition was simply increased so that both groups, which had very low capitalization, by international standards, would require increased capital to undertake proprietary trading and act as market makers. Thus, the reform of the exchange included the creation of two distinct classes, registered dealers and brokers,[38] with no restriction on trading. The registered dealers were required to quote two-way prices in minimum size, but brokers were free to make agency trades directly among themselves.

The opening of the market to outsiders, in particular to corporations, also meant that much more highly capitalized firms would be entering the market. The result was a series of mergers and acquisitions that saw merchant and investment banks buy brokers and jobbers to produce integrated financial units. In 1983 jobbers in gilts were dominated by two of six firms that held 80 percent of the business. After the Big Bang there were no less than 29 registered market makers, 14 of them British, so that the Bank's worry about the collapse of the market for want of jobbers had been met. And this at precisely the time when government policy was raising fears that its continued surpluses would soon reduce the supply of government securities to zero.

38. At the insistence of the Bank of England, which patterned the market for gilts after the U.S. government securities market which was comprised of primary dealers and interdealer brokers, interdealer brokers were also introduced in the gilts market.

Conclusions

In contrast with both the U.S. and Germany, the U.K. did not impose either separation and segmentation or new balance sheet regulations on financial institutions as a result of the 1930s crisis. This was, first, because the British clearing banks already had concentrated the deposit market, avoiding the difficulties that unit banking produced in the U.S.; and second, because British banks refrained from operating in securities markets via investment affiliates and from direct long-term industrial lending, which had produced losses due to fraud and industrial recession in the U.S. and German financial systems. On the other hand, the U.K. was more incisive in its use of the financial system in support of overall stabilization policy, and the fear of a continuation of the Depression was soon replaced by the threat of wage inflation. Direct controls were the preferred form of policy, and the use of monetary policy for inflation control occurred only in 1971, with the Competition and Credit Control Act. This change in policy direction was completed by the end of the decade with the abolition of exchange controls and the supplementary lending controls that had accompanied the move to market-based monetary policy. As in the U.S., this produced higher interest rates and increased competition among financial institutions. However, largely as a result of government controls on lending and the clearing bank cartel on interest rates, the crisis occurred in the secondary banks that had grown up outside formal bank supervision and control, rather than in the thrift industry; building societies are now making a transition in which they will eventually lose their distinctive character as mortgage lenders. Thus the U.K. system, aside from the changes introduced by the Big Bang, has remained stable.

General Conclusions

Initially, all three financial systems considered here exhibited a broad division of labor between commercial banking, investment banking servicing industry, and savings banks providing assets for the general public. Because these divisions started to erode in both Germany and the U.S. at the beginning of the century, the decline in financial asset prices after the stock market crash had a more destabilizing impact in these countries than in the U.K. In the U.S. it was commercial banks that moved into investment banking, through the creation of securities affiliates to provide underwriting and investment in industry. In Germany, on the other hand, it was the Kreditbanken, through expansion of their activities to include the taking of deposits to finance their investment banking activities. Only the British clearing banks respected the natural separation of deposit taking and investment finance. Thus, in the period before the financial crises of the 1930s the financial institutions of all three countries were capable of undertaking activity in both banking and finance, providing transactions deposits as well as engaging in both long-term investments in industry and short-term commercial lending.

The major difference was the joint-stock corporate form of British and German banks. While German banks exploited this organizational form to launch industrial enterprises and finance investment activity, banks in the U.K. limited such activity to minority portfolio investments in company shares. Investment banks in America and Britain were private partnerships providing underwriting and trade financing to business. The long-term capital requirements of firms in these countries were met by their owners and their friends and through the reinvestment of earnings.

Since the German Kreditbanken often were quoted on the stock market and recovered capital invested in the formation of new firms by floating the shares of these firms' in the stock market, the financing of German industry, before World War II, was more dependent on the stock market than in either the U.S. or the U.K. These conditions changed radically after World War II.

The instability experienced in the U.S. was aggravated by branching restrictions that limited the growth of banks and produced the banking chains and securities affiliates outside the supervision of the Federal Reserve. This led to substantial mismatching of balance sheets and created opportunities for fraudulent activities.

Similar difficulties were present in Germany, where the large Kreditbanken, whose equity capital had been eroded by hyperinflation, continued to lend to support their failing industrial clients, reducing the liquidity of their balance sheets. Difficulties also were experienced in the local savings banks, which were captive long-term lenders to municipal and regional governments.

Thus both the U.S. and Germany experienced the classic instability associated with the combination of banking and finance, caused by the long-term lending of funds raised by the issue of short-term liabilities. This maturity mismatching was conspicuously absent in the U.K. This was because of the prevalence of retained earnings finance in family-owned British companies as compared to the large trusts and combines of the U.S. and Germany, as well as the British use of investment trust companies and insurance companies as sources for long-term investment finance.

The regulatory response to the crisis thus was different in all three countries. In the U.K. there was virtually no threat to the payments system, nor was there any destruction of wealth due to bank failures. There thus was very little political or economic pressure for change in the regulatory regime for financial institutions. In the U.S. a complete breakdown of the payments mechanism took place, and depositors lost substantial amounts through the decline in stock prices and through bank failure. Regulation therefore took the form of guarantees to the payments mechanism through a legal separation between banks offering transactions deposits and those providing for the long-term finance of industry. These regulations involved restrictions on investment activity, control over interest rates on deposits, and government deposit insurance.

Germany took a rather different approach to a similar experience of bank failures. Instead of restricting the markets and products open to financial institutions providing means of payment to the public, it instead imposed broad balance sheet restrictions to ensure a general matching of the maturities of assets and liabilities. It thus retained the freedom of financial institutions to operate in any banking activity but produced a *de facto* separation within each bank's balance sheet. This produced results very similar to the separation of banking and finance introduced in the U.S. but without creating segregation of different types of financial institutions.

This difference in regulatory response has been crucial in the reaction of financial systems to the liberalization and deregulation introduced in the postwar period, when the major problem facing policymakers shifted from the prevention of asset price deflation to the prevention of goods price inflation. In both the U.S. and the U.K., the shift in the use of monetary policy to combat inflation forced the elimination of regulations meant to provide controlled or subsidized financing to particular sectors, for example, the finance of residential housing through savings institutions. However, unlike the U.S., where protection was based on interest rate controls, in the U.K. mortgage lending was traditionally at adjustable rates. Thus, the introduction of tight monetary policy and controls of monetary aggregates, producing increased variability in short-term market interest rates, did not put the same pressure on building societies as it did on U.S. savings and loan banks. In the U.K. what protection existed was a byproduct of the clearing banks interest rate cartel and the quantitative controls on bank lending which made mortgage lending unattractive to banks. However, when monetary controls led to the elimination of exchange controls and the removal of quantitative bank lending constraints, building societies suffered in much the same way from competition from commercial banks, and legislation was introduced to allow building societies to offer a fuller range of services to allow them to compete with clearing banks. As a result of the difficulties created for the unregulated operation of the secondary banks, however, the removal of these restrictions did produce a nearly full-scale crisis similar to that in the U.S.

In Germany legislation governing savings banks was changed after the crisis of the 1930s to free them from control and direction by local authorities. Since savings banks, through their regional and national *giro* systems, traditionally had been the major source of payments services for the general public, they soon came to operate in a manner similar to large universal banks, and no special legislation was required to allow them to provide these services. Other mortgage institutions had, and today retain, special status within the German system.

In general it was not necessary for Germany to eliminate regulations and reduce barriers between different types of financial institutions, because they did not exist. On the other hand, Germany did maintain separation for institutions engaged in particular types of lending, such as residential mortgage lending, which has now all but disappeared in the U.S. Any possible convergence of the U.S. system and the German universal bank structure due to deregulation and liberalization is thus blocked, on the one hand, by the persistence of regulations restricting branching, and, on the other, despite Glass Steagall, by the less restrictive segregation on different types of banking in the U.S.

Institutional investors also have played a diverse role in the process of financial market deregulation in the three countries. The early development of institutional investors in the U.K. provides part of the explanation of why the clearing banks did not enter long-term industrial lending and were better able to withstand the decline in asset prices. In Germany, the presence of comprehensive government provision of retirement pensions has left little need for private pension funds and minimal impact on capital markets. In the U.S., on the other hand, private pension schemes provided the initial impulse for the growth of institutional investors, who have taken on a dominant role in influencing capital markets. Their pressure to create more competitive pricing of brokerage services produced changes in financial market organization that have allowed investment banks to become the dominant institutions in the U.S. as the separation between banking and finance has slowly broken down. Although institutional investors in the U.K. have faced similar problems, the major impetus for liberalization in the U.K. market was primarily government policy.

A further factor reducing the role of institutional investors in Germany is the relatively minor role played by the equity market in financing industry. This is in part due to the radical changes that occurred in Germany after the war and to the extended use of closely held, private limited liability companies, which implies a minimal presence on public stock markets for all but the largest firms. The reliance on banks for industrial financing has meant a disproportionate reliance on bond finance, and the investment activities of institutional investors tend to reflect this bias.

The financial innovations and deregulation that occurred in the U.S. market were the result of the introduction of interest rate controls and the failure to abolish the unit, dual banking system in the 1930s; without the possibility of expansion within their restricted market activities, banks naturally have sought expansion by moving into new activities linked to investment banking. Since this is blocked by Glass-Steagall, a byproduct of the existence of branching restrictions has been pressure to reduce the restriction on commercial bank activities legislated in Glass-Steagall. The competition allowed under deregulation and liberalization in the 1970s and 1980s so weakened the commercial and saving banks that it is unlikely any but the strongest, most highly capitalized banks, which are already exempt from most of the restrictions of Glass-Steagall through the operations of wholly owned subsidiaries, would be able to benefit from its elimination except by merging into much larger consolidated nationwide banking units. The basic constraint thus remains the dual state-federal regulatory regime and the restrictions on nationwide branching.

Thus, while in the U.S. regulations introduced in support of economic stabilization generally have been reversed by the shift in policy to combat inflation in the 1970s, in Germany they have survived more or less intact. The basic reason for this may be that in Germany these changes were merely a codification of prudent banking practice and the lessons learned in the interwar period of hyperinflation, which dominated German concerns, in contrast to the experience of debt deflation that dominated regulatory reform in the U.S. Paradoxically, in the U.K.—where these prudential principles were practiced by the clearing banks during the 1930s without the necessity of even minimum legal reserve requirements—liberalization of the banking system in the 1970s and 1980s first produced difficulty in the secondary banks, and then even the clearing banks found themselves in difficulty because of the expansion of their long-term lending on financial assets and commercial property.

Thus, despite the existence of liberalization in most financial markets, and despite moves toward eliminating separation of banking and finance, important differences remain. In Germany, the stock market and institutional investors remain relatively unimportant. Paradoxically, despite the relative absence of regulations on bank activities, the German system now appears more tightly controlled than the U.S. or U.K. systems. There is thus little evidence to suggest that the liberalization of financial markets that has accompanied the shift in macropolicy also has produced a tendency of convergence in financial systems in support of this shift.

References

Anderson, B.M. (1979) *Economics and the Public Welfare*, 2nd ed. Indianapolis: Liberty.

Balogh, Thomas. (1947) *Financial Organization*. Cambridge: Cambridge University.

Bogart, Ernest Ludlow. (1935) *Economic History of the American People*. London: Longmans, Green.

Boleat, Mark. (1987) "Building societies: The new supervisory framework." *National Westminister Bank Quarterly Review* (August): 26–34.

Born, Karl. (1983) *International Banking in the 19th and 20th Centuries*. New York: St. Martin's.

Briston, R.J. (1970) *The Stock Exchange and Investment Analysis*. London: Allen and Unwin.

Brooks, John. (1988) *The Takeover Game*. New York: E.P. Dutton.

Dacey, W. Manning. (1951) *The British Banking Mechanism*. London: Hutchinson University Library.

Day, John P. (1930) *An Introduction to the Money and Banking System of the United States*. London: Macmillan.

Deutsche Bundesbank. (1962) "The New Banking Law and the Deutsche Bundesbank's Cooperation in Bank Supervision." *Annual Report* 94–110.

———. (1984a) "Company Pension Schemes in the Federal Republic of Germany." *Monthly Report*. (August): 30–37.

———. (1984b) "Business Finance in the United Kingdom and Germany." *Monthly Report* (November): 33–42.

———. (1985) "Amendment of the Banking Act." *Monthly Report* (March): 35–41.

———. (1987) "Longer-term Trends in the Banks' Investments in Securities." *Monthly Report* (May): 24–33.

———. (1988) "Saving Through Investment Companies on the Ascent." *Monthly Report* (October): 30–37.

———. (1989) "Securities Ownership in the Federal Republic of Germany in the Light of the Domestic Securities Deposit Statistics." *Monthly Report* (May): 20–26.

———. (1990) "The New Principles I and Ia Concerning the Capital of Banks." *Monthly Report* (August): 36–43.

———. (1991) "The Significance of Shares as Financing Instruments." *Monthly Report* (October): 21–28.

———. (1992) "Financial Center Germany: Underlying Conditions and Recent Developments." *Monthly Report* (March): 23–31.

Dow, J.C.R. (1964) *The Management of the British Economy, 1945–60*. Cambridge: Cambridge University.

Francke, Hans-Hermann, and Michael Hudson. (1984) *Banking and Finance in West Germany*. New York: St. Martins.

Garlock, Fred L. (1952) *Country Banking in Wisconsin during the Depression*. Partially reprinted in Charles Whittlesey, ed. *Readings in Money and Banking*. New York: Norton.

Hamilton, Adrian. (1986) *The Financial Revolution*. London: Penguin.

Howson, Susan. (1988) "Monetary Policy and the Labor Government in the 1940s." In *Keynes and Public Policy After Fifty Years*, edited by O.F. Hamouda and J.N. Smithin. Aldershot: E. Elgar.

Jones, Jesse (with Edward Angly). (1951) *Fifty Billion Dollars: My Thirteen Years with the RFC*. New York: Macmillan.

Leffler, George L. (1951) *The Stock Market*. New York: The Ronald Press.

Mayer, Martin. (1988) *Markets*. New York: Norton.

———. (1992) *The Greatest-Ever Bank Robbery*. New York: Collier Books (1990), 2nd ed.
Michie, R.C. (1987) *The London and New York Stock Exchanges: 1850–1914*. London: Allen & Unwin.
Morgan, E. Victor, and W. A. Thomas. (1962) *The Stock Exchange: Its History and Functions*. London: Elek Books.
Munkirs, John R. (1985) *The Transformation of American Capitalism*. Armonk, N.Y.: M.E. Sharpe.
Nardozzi, Giangiacomo. (1983) *Tre sistemi creditizi*. Bologna: Il mulino.
———. (1990) "The Structural Evolution of Financial Systems in the '80s: From Its Determinants to its Possible Outcomes." *Banca Nazionale del Lavoro, Quarterly Review* 172 (March): 71–90.
Paish, Frank W. (1950) *The Postwar Financial Problem*. London:Macmillan.
Pawley, Michael, David Winstone, and Patrick Bentley. (1991) *U.K. Financial Institutions and Markets*. London: Macmillan.
Poole, Kenyon E. (1969) *German Financial Policies, 1932–39*. New York: Russell & Russell.
Reid, Margaret. (1982) *The Secondary Banking Crisis, 1973–75*. London: Macmillan.
Revell, Jack. (1973) *The British Financial System*. London: Macmillan.
Sametz, Arnold W., ed. (1991) *Institutional Investing*. Homewood, Ill.: Business One Irwin.
Sayers, Richard S. (1976) *The Bank of England: 1891–1944*. Cambridge University Press.
Schwartz, Robert A. (1991) *Reshaping the Equity Markets*. New York: Harper Business.
Seligman, Joel. (1982) *The Transformation of Wall Street*. New York: Houghton Mifflin.
Shannon, Fred Albert. (1951) *America's Economic Growth*. New York: Macmillan.
Stephan, Audley H. F. (1951) "Stockbrokers and Dealers." In *American Financial Institutions,* edited by Herbert V. Prochnow. New York: Prentice Hall.
Stolper, Gustav, K. Hauser, and K. Borchardt. (1967) *The German Economy–1870 to the Present*. Translated by Toni Stolper. New York: Harcourt, Brace & World.
Sullivan, Lawrence. (1936) *Prelude to Panic*. Washington, D.C.: Statesman.
Thomas, W.A. (1989) *Securities Markets*. Hemel Hempstead: Philip Allan.
Valentine, Roger W. (1951) "Investment Banking—History and Regulation." In *American Financial Institutions*, edited by Herbert V. Prochnow. New York: Prentice Hall.
Wallich, Henry C. (1955) *Mainsprings of the German Revival*. New Haven: Yale University.
Whale, P. Barrett. (1930) *Joint Stock Banking in Germany*. London: Macmillan.

INDEX

www.ingramcontent.com/pod-product-compliance
Ingram Content Group UK Ltd.
Pitfield, Milton Keynes, MK11 3LW, UK
UKHW021834100926
8556IPUK00004B/334

9 781571 810434